75 Years of the Constitution of Ireland:
An Irish-Italian Dialogue

75 YEARS OF THE CONSTITUTION OF IRELAND: AN IRISH-ITALIAN DIALOGUE

Edited by

Giuseppe Franco Ferrari

and

John O'Dowd

CLARUS PRESS

Published by
Clarus Press Ltd,
Griffith Campus,
South Circular Road,
Dublin 8.
www.claruspress.ie

Typeset by
Gough Typesetting Services, Dublin

Printed by
Sprint Print Ltd,
Dublin,
Ireland

ISBN
978-1-905536-66-5

Foreword

This book gives an important view on Irish Constitutionalism through the essays presented at the Seminar held in Dublin the 3-4 November 2011. The essays depict the Irish legal system in a European context, giving particular relevance to the Italian viewpoint. Professor Ferrari of the Bocconi University of Milano and Professor Scott of the University College of Dublin (UCD) were the driving force of the project and were able to collect an important number of academics who gave an exhaustive view of the issues on the agenda.

The Seminar is therefore a precious tool for those, and I am among them, who are fascinated by the strong relations which bind Ireland with Italy, despite the distance, the history, the environment, the traditions. On the other hand the Irish cultural life is indeed influenced by the Italian experience. Needless to remind that the Georgian architecture draws its roots from Palladio, as the very successful exhibition which I organised in Dublin, Galway and Limerick illustrated.

Which is why I strongly and immediately welcomed under the auspices of The Embassy of Italy the Seminar and gave a relevant support to its organisation. The Italian Ministry of Foreign Affairs approved my decision. The Seminar also pointed out the superb quality of the cooperation among the academicians who took part in it and who were the standard bearers of common a work aimed at showing the important contribution given to the European rule of law by the Irish legal system.

Had I had some doubts, and I had not, one of the most relevant results of the Seminar was actually to point out the Irish contribution, as seen from an Italian viewpoint, to the cultural heritage of an united Europe. The publication of this book just after the Irish Presidency of the Council of European Union marks the importance of the action of Dublin for the development of the Treaty of Rome. And I would like to stress the collaboration between Italy and Ireland aimed at repairing and leading the Presidency towards common goals. The continuous contacts among our Prime Ministers, just remind the two visits of Enda Kenny to Rome in 2012, of former Prime Minister Enrico Letta and the meetings between other Ministers of the countries, prove how in the very hard current economic and financial situation Italy and Ireland are not a part of the problems but an active part of their solution.

I shall confine myself to these short remarks, leaving to the academicians the substance of the issues.

My thanks to professors Ferrari and Scott for their outstanding efforts and to all the participants in the Seminar for their inspiring contributions which are also a credit for their universities and a honour for the Embassy of Italy. My thanks go also to UniCredit Bank Ireland p.l.c. and Mediolanum International Funds for their sponsorship and to Miss Althea Brandonisio, my personal assistant as Head of Mission, for her relentless help.

Valerio Augusto Astraldi
Ambassador of Italy to Ireland (2009-2011)

About the Editors

Giuseppe Franco Ferrari has been professor of comparative public law at Bocconi University Milan since 1999. Previously professor at Teramo (1986-1989) and Pavia (1989-1999) and associate professor in the Catholic University of Milan (1983-1986). Member of the editorial boards of *Giurisprudenza Costituzionale* and *Diritto Costituzionale*. Editor of the journal *Diritto Pubblico Comparato ed Europeo* since 1999 and president of the Association of Comparative and European Public Law since 1998.

John O'Dowd has been a lecturer in the Faculty (and subsequently the School) of Law at UCD since 1991, where he has taught courses in constitutional law, administrative law, media law and the law of the European Convention on Human Rights. He has published extensively on constitutional issues, including several book chapters and articles in journals including the *European Review of Public Law*, the *Journal of Media Law* and *The Irish Jurist*.

Table of Contents

PART II: ELEMENTS OF THE CONSTITUTIONAL DESIGN

Part I

The Mechanism of Judicial Review

CHAPTER 1

Constitutional Rights in Ireland between Domestic and Supranational Courts

Giuseppe Franco Ferrari[1]

1. Citizens' and Human Rights in the Irish Context

In the Irish context, several rights belong to citizens (Art 40) that elsewhere either belong to persons or human beings or, as in Italy, are declared inviolable in order to be attributed to every person subject to the jurisdiction of the State where they are physically located or to be considered fundamental (e.g. Art 10 of the Spanish Constitution). In contrast, the Constitution of Ireland declares as human rights some rights, such as property rights, that other systems of constitutional law no longer describe as human rights or have simply reduced to their core and submitted to stricter limitations than before. This choice may reflect the epoch of adoption of the present Constitution, which precedes the post-World War II constitutional phase and its renewed sensitivity towards international law and the internationalisation of rights, as well as the need to emphasise the legal condition of citizens after the recent achievement of independence from the United Kingdom through the experience of the Irish Free State. This last hypothesis seems to be confirmed by the use of basic terms such as "State", "nation" and "people" in parts of the constitutional text not directly concerning rights.

The "State", as in Arts 4, 5 and 6, apparently defines a legal person, cumulating most of the powers formerly belonging to the King or the Crown, although not all of them. The Irish Supreme Court has actually repeatedly denied that the royal prerogatives had been carried over into the Irish Free State in 1922 and by Art 49 in 1937[2]: that should mean they have been repealed as a category, although some of them revived under different names and on different foundations. For instance, the immunity of the State from suit has disappeared, while the executive's inherent power to control immigration[3] and the treasure trove as at common law can stem from the sovereignty of the State according to Art 5 and (in the latter case) Art 11 of the Constitution.[4]

"Nation" is often used as a synonym of "people". In Art 1, the "Irish nation" affirms its inalienable right to choose its form of government. In Art 3, amended along with

1 Full Professor of Comparative Public Law at the Bocconi University, Milan.

2 *Byrne v Ireland* [1972] IR 241; *Webb v Ireland* [1988] IR 353; *Howard v Commissioners of Public Works* [1994] 1 IR 101.

3 *Laurenţiu v Minister for Justice, Equality and Law Reform* [1999] 4 IR 26 (SC).

4 *Webb v Ireland* [1988] IR 353.

Art 2 in 1998 after the Belfast agreement,[5] the original territorial claim has been superseded and replaced by a statement of the will of the nation to unite all the people who share the territory of the island through peaceful means and with the consent of a majority of the people, democratically expressed in both jurisdictions. Finally, in Art 2, the definition of the Irish nation as the unity of all persons born in the islands and seas of Ireland presupposes a preference for the *ius soli* entitlement as the ordinary way of access to citizenship, following the former text of the Irish Nationality and Citizenship Act 1956. If the nation—regardless whether it is conceived as a group of persons kept together by objective facts only or by subjective ties as well, such as a common culture and willingness to live together in a republican context—is a sum of citizens, then it is hard to draw a clear line between the nation of Art 1 and People of Art 6, having the right to designate the rulers of the State.

This interpretation is supported by the constitutional revision of 2004, which, lest foreigners could be tempted to move to Ireland in order to get the citizenship for their children, amended Art 9(2) in order to prevent, at least for the future, persons born in Ireland but having no parents being, or entitled to be, Irish citizens from getting the citizenship. Shortly after, the Irish Nationality and Citizenship Act 2004 introduced the possibility for the baby born in Ireland to a parent not being Irish citizen but having lived in Ireland three of the last four years to get the citizenship. The emphasis on citizenship as the founding condition of the nation equates the nation with the people. The choice of the Irish language as official national language in Art 8 supports this interpretation. The special care historically dedicated to citizenship as a precondition of nation and people justifies the concentration on the citizen of the most part of civil rights and of all political rights.

The same approach is distinguishable in Art 40.1. Opening the title dedicated to fundamental rights with the principle of equality, the article states that "all citizens shall, as human persons, be held equal before the law", without prejudice to individual differences of capacity and social function. The Irish Supreme Court, like all European constitutional and supreme courts, has elaborated the classical categories of equality, such as the distinction between formal and non-formal equality and the standards of scrutiny in relation to direct or indirect discriminations based on various parameters, such as gender, religion, race, age.[6] But the peculiar formulation of the equality principle in the Irish context has raised the doubt that a challenge to a statutory provision under Art 40.1 could be mounted only when some characteristics of the human personality are at stake, although it remains unclear which might be the essential attributes of human personality.

Kenny J was very active in developing this interpretation of the clause: for instance, in excluding its application to trading activities and conditions of employment as essential attributes of personality, as well as to the ability to work, an individual's fiscal capacity and the qualification for receiving social benefits.[7] Yet, this approach makes it very hard to distinguish between the parameter or basis of the discrimination and the context where the discrimination takes place, which is of great importance

5 Nineteenth Amendment of the Constitution Act 1998.

6 As in *Re Article 26 of the Constitution and the Employment Equality Bill 1996* [1997] 2 IR 321.

7 *Quinn's Supermarket Ltd v Attorney General* [1972] IR 1 (SC); *Murtagh Properties Ltd v Cleary* [1972] IR 330 (HC).

in evaluating the reasonableness of the discrimination from the factual viewpoint of its effects. Following this method, the Supreme Court has not been disposed to recognise the violation of the essential attributes of human personality in the treatment of parcels of land respecting the application of the property tax.[8] The distinction between relevant and insignificant characteristics of human personality ends up either in an analysis about the more or less serious impairment of human dignity or in a search of the more or less deferential standard of review towards the legislative classification at stake. In other words, the "citizen" versus "human person" alternative in the equality case law seems to be nothing else than the Irish way of interpreting the equality principle: the onus of justification, the narrow or wide character of the suspect classification, the ends/means verification, the compelling versus merely legitimate purpose, the tiers of scrutiny—all of them are techniques converging or included in the equality analysis under the "citizens as human persons" label.

2. Unenumerated Rights

Several constitutional systems in the last 50 years or so have elaborated theories implying the introduction into their respective constitutional contexts of unenumerated rights.

The US Supreme Court since the time of Chief Justice Warren has used alternatively the penumbra doctrine and the Ninth Amendment in order to recognise rights not codified in the constitutional catalogue. Only Justice Harlan, in *Poe v Ullman*,[9] has suggested the use of natural law as a storeroom of ideas and values from which to extract claims worth being recognised and eventually declared fundamental. Justice Hugo Black strongly opposed such an approach; value-oriented theories followed by some scholars, such as Bruce Ackerman, Michael Perry and Lawrence Tribe, incline to the recognition of new rights through moral and political philosophy.

In other contexts, either it is for the constitution itself to contemplate rights of nature similar to the listed rights (e.g. the Constitution of Portugal in Art 17) or the courts have elaborated new claims stemming from constitutional principles or international treaties, as in Norway, or from rights already recognised or being indispensable elements of the democratic order, as in Switzerland.

The Irish system is foremost in the techniques of recognition of unenumerated rights construing them on natural law doctrines. The constitutional instrument opening such a way has been Art 40.3, binding the State "by its laws to defend and vindicate the personal rights of the citizen" and specifying, in the following proposition, that protection and vindication shall concern "in particular … the life, person, good name, and property rights". The words "in particular" have been construed as to imply the existence of some implicitly guaranteed rights above and beyond the written text of the Constitution and the catalogue of rights listed in it.

This method somehow resembles the approach of the Belgian Cour d'arbitrage,

---

8 [1984] ILRM 355 at 364. This contrasts with Barrington J's more flexible attitude in *Brennan v Attorney General* [1983] ILRM 449 (HC).

9 367 US 497 (1961).

whose interpretation of the word "*notamment*" in Art 23, opening the list of rights in the Charter, also implies the recognition of the fundamental character of claims not formally included in it.

It is well known that the Irish case law started to incorporate the unenumerated rights doctrine in 1965, in the opinion by Kenny J in *Ryan v Attorney General.*[10] The interpreter can now wonder whether the protection of an individual from the fluoridation of public water (as a measure to reduce dental caries) could not be included in the defence of "the person" required by Art 40.3.1° and whether it really needed such an ambitious foundation in a non-textual right to "bodily integrity", above all because Kenny J and the Supreme Court went on to conclude that such a right had not been illegitimately restricted. Yet, that has been the initial move of a long chain of precedents, elaborating the sources of the personal rights of the citizen. Since then, Irish scholars have dedicated the best of their intellectual efforts to rationalising the case law and classifying the various types of unenumerated rights, their methods of identification and their compatibility with the constitutional text, in a never-ending search of equilibrium in constitutional interpretation and judicial review between (at least initially) natural law and positive constitutional mandates. Curiously, while the originalist position in American scholarship opposes the introduction of new rights and favours a strict interpretation of the Bill of Rights, in Ireland, those who support the recognition or creation of new non-textual rights have often looked for their foundation in Christian values or in the natural law as a theological concept, assuming that they are formally recognised in the Constitution (e.g. in the Preamble and in Art 6) and should therefore provide a sort of "higher law" guidance to judges and scholars.

One of the best descriptions of the diachronic evolution of the unenumerated rights doctrine[11] suggests that since *Ryan* at least four different paths have been followed to protect rights not explicitly enumerated, such as the rights to bodily integrity, to travel, to privacy and to marital privacy. It has been assumed that (i) they stem from the Christian and democratic nature of the State, (ii) they are inherent in the human personality, (iii) they are protected by natural law and (iv) that their protection is implicit in some constitutional provisions.

During the almost fifty years after *Ryan* some or even all of these arguments have been used together in support of the same conclusion.

The Christian and democratic nature of the State appears in Kenny J's judgment in *Ryan*, integrated with citations of the Encyclical Letter "Peace on Earth" and other Catholic social teachings, and is expanded in 1979 with reference to the right to travel[12] and in 1987[13] and 1999[14] to the right to privacy. The human personality

---

[10] [1965] IR 294. An examination of Ryan 25 years later in a comparative law perspective was undertaken by GW Hogan, "Unenumerated Personal Rights: Ryan's Case Re-evaluated" (1990–1992) 25–27 Irish Jurist 95.

[11] O Doyle, *Constitutional Law: Text, Cases and Materials* (Clarus Press, Dublin, 2009), p 85.

[12] *State (M) v Attorney General* [1979] IR 73 (HC) Finlay P.

[13] *Kennedy v Ireland* [1987] IR 587 (HC) Hamilton P.

[14] *Haughey v Moriarty* [1999] 3 IR 1 (HC) Hamilton CJ.

argument is first used by Henchy J in 1974, in *McGee v Attorney General*,[15] in order to give constitutional protection to marital privacy and later, in the dissenting opinion in *Norris*,[16] where, however, textual arguments were applied as well, such as the secret ballot guarantee of Art 16 or the Preamble, which refers to the common good, the observance of Prudence, Justice and Charity, and the dignity and freedom of the individual.

The same propositions of the Preamble are used to demonstrate the rooting of Christian values in the constitutional text. The natural law argument came to the fore in *McGee v Attorney General* in the words of Walsh J and was developed in later years, as it was in 1980 by O'Higgins CJ[17]: the idea that there are individual and family rights not created by law and guaranteed to be beyond of the control of the State as superior or antecedent to positive law and simply recognised by the Constitution is completed through the suggestion that the Constitution itself provides guidelines for the discretion of judges in identifying the principles of natural law to be followed. Finally, the theory that some rights are implicit in other constitutional provisions and can be protected through Art 40.3.1° has brought about the right to access to courts via Art 34.1,[18] which provides that justice is to be administered in courts established by law, and the right to marry via Art 41, concerning the status of family.

Scholarly discussion about natural law and the Constitution is kept lively by some accentuation of the opposing positions. Those authors, such as Desmond Clarke and Gerald Hogan,[19] who criticise the recurrent use of natural law or of its proxies to carve out new rights also complain about the apparently unprincipled expansion of the judicial review. Those who support the judicial reliance on natural law sometimes resort to exaggeration in their disapproval of positivism, such as Richard Humphreys.[20] The reasoning becomes circular and paradoxical when some judges and scholars try to create a link between natural law and the Constitution by assuming that the Constitution derives its authority and validity from natural law, which continues to be superior to positive law, although the discovery of its content is committed to the agents of positive law themselves, in the words of Oran Doyle.[21] If there is scope for such an approach, it is possible, for instance, to pave the way for a declaration and vindication of socio-economic rights through the clause of Art 40.3.1°, which apparently relates only to rights not included in the directive principles of social policy, set out in Art 45. To avoid this, Keane CJ called for a careful self-restraint.[22] It is even possible—and this has happened, although unsuccessfully, at least a couple of times[23]—to invoke natural law to strike down not only ordinary

---

15 [1974] IR 284 (SC).

16 *Norris v Attorney General* [1984] IR 36 (SC).

17 *G v An Bord Uchtála* [1980] IR 32 at 55 (SC).

18 *Macauley v Minister for Posts and Telegraphs* [1966] IR 345 (HC) Kenny J.

19 D Clarke "The role of natural law in Irish constitutional law" (1982) 17 Irish Jurist 187; G Hogan, "Unenumerated personal rights: Ryan's case re-evaluated" (1990–1992) 25–27 Irish Jurist 95.

20 "Interpreting natural rights" (1993–1995) 28–30 Irish Jurist 221.

21 "Legal validity: reflections on the Irish Constitution" (2003) 25 DULJ 56.

22 *O'T v B* [2001] 2 IR 259 (SC).

23 In 1935, it arose with reference to legislation introduced to regulate police arrest powers and to create a tribunal staffed with military personnel, according to Amendment 2A to the 1922 Irish Free State Constitution: *State (Ryan) v Lennon* [1935] IR 170, Kennedy, CJ,

legislation, but also to question the legitimacy of a constitutional amendment, on the assumption that the Constitution recognises natural law as a source of its own validity situated outside its sphere.

It is hard for a foreign observer to reach final conclusions on a debate that has passionately divided the legal culture of a country. Apparently, the inheritance of a deeply rooted Catholic culture has had overwhelming weight in favouring interpretative solutions that privilege some forms of natural law in a context where citizens' rights have been positivised and constitutionalised. The most evident consequence is that through Art 40.3.1° several rights formally defined in Constitution as citizens' rights have a chance of becoming or being described and protected as human rights. On the one hand, natural law can do and sometimes does transformative work, giving a right defined as citizen's a status that would elsewhere be qualified fundamental, which comes very close to that of a right belonging to the person as such. On the other hand, however, the same constitutional clause can generate an inflation of rights rooted in the natural law and can widen the discretion of the judiciary, notwithstanding possible guidelines included in Constitution as to the use of the values assumed to be implied in the natural law itself.

3. Overview of Irish Approach to Rights: Some Peculiarities of this Constitutional System

"Personal rights", in the language of the title of Art 40, include property and in addition life, person and good name (listed in Art 40.3.2°), personal liberty (Art 40.4.1°), the dwelling (Art 40.5) and—subject to public order and morality—freedom of expression, right to assemble peacefully and without arms, and right to form associations and unions (all three guaranteed under Art 40.6.1°). The inclusion of property in this group instead among the principles of social policy aimed at improving the welfare of the whole people, set out in Art 45, is a matter of the era of enactment: all the charters of the period immediately following World War II include property among the socio-economic rights, limited on account of compelling public interests; Ireland in 1937 was still inclined either to Lockean or to Catholic concepts.

The right to life has generated no controversies with regard to the death penalty, both due to the suspension of capital execution in 1954 and the amendments to Arts 15.5 and 28.3 introducing the prohibition of death penalty even in time of war. It has helped, however, in construing the right to die a natural death.[24] And, above all, it has been pivotal in what started with the "sale of contraceptives"

dissenting. In 1995, the Supreme Court (*Re Article 26 and the Regulation of Information (Services Outside the State for Termination of Pregnancies) Bill 1995* [1995] 1 IR 1 at 43) took pains to reach the conclusion that courts "at no stage recognized the provisions of natural law as superior to the Constitution". It had been argued by the counsel for the unborn child that the Regulation of Information (Services Outside the State for Termination of Pregnancies) Bill 1995 might be unconstitutional together with the 1992 Amendment due to violation of Art 46 together with its limits in terms of natural law. This followed the 1983 Amendment, which had to give formal protection to the life of the unborn child, and the 1992 Amendment to protect the right to obtain or make available information relating to abortion services available in other States.

[24] *Re a Ward of Court* (withholding medical treatment) (No 2) [1996] 2 IR 79. See GF Whyte, "The Right to Die and the Irish Constitution" (1997) 3 Eur Pub L 235.

saga, the story of the right to life of the unborn. The introduction in 1983 of Art 40.3.3° into the text of the Constitution starts that story, with the introduction of a formal constitutional right of the unborn, to be balanced with the right to life of the mother. Then the Supreme Court in 1988 granted an injunction restraining clinics from assisting pregnant women to travel abroad to obtain abortions, making travel arrangements or informing them about locations and methods.[25] This decision was found to be in violation of Art 10 of the European Convention on Human Rights by the Strasbourg Court in 1992.[26] That same year the Supreme Court discharged an injunction that had restrained a 14-year-old girl pregnant due to an alleged rape from travelling abroad.[27] After the *X* case, the people were twice requested to give their opinion concerning the issue of abortion, in 1992 and 2002, and twice rejected a constitutional amendment that would have restricted the grounds on which an abortion could lawfully be performed in Ireland. Also in 1992, two other amendments succeeded in introducing provisions concerning the freedom to travel and the freedom to obtain and make available information, bringing the second and third sentences of Art 40.3.3° to the present text. Finally, in 2006,[28] the High Court excluded the application of Art 40.3.3° to embryos created in vitro and Supreme Court confirmed this in 2009.[29]

The right to a good name has been construed around a cluster of procedural safeguards in case of investigation.[30]

The protection and vindication of "the personal rights of the citizen" has generated a right to bodily integrity[31] as an unspecified right. The interpretation of this right treats it in negative terms, considered to be the exclusion or limitation of physical intrusions on one's body, the courts having declined to attach to it the positive meaning of a socio-economic claim, carrying resource implications.[32] At the same time, the protection and vindication of the person should be root of the right to earn a livelihood, although not a particular livelihood, first construed by the High Court in a case concerning a picketing of commercial premises[33]: in this case, although it is still conceived in merely negative terms, the claim takes some colour of labour law.

The Irish courts relied on the same root to build up the right to privacy, defined by Henchy J as "a complex of rights, varying in nature, purpose and range, each necessarily a facet of the citizen's core of individuality within the constitutional order".[34] The outlines of this right have been drawn more precisely in the 1980s and 1990s, coming to include, although not in an absolute form, protection against telephone tapping,[35] a right to refuse to receive medical treatment,[36] the prevention of

---

25 *Attorney General (Society for the Protection of Unborn Children (Ireland) Ltd) v Open Door Counselling Ltd* [1988] IR 593.
26 *Open Door Counselling Ltd v Ireland* (1992) 14 EHRR 131.
27 *Attorney General v X* [1992] 1 IR 1.
28 *Roche v Roche* [2006] IEHC 359; [2010] 2 IR 321.
29 *ibid*; [2009] IESC 82.
30 Since *Re Haughey* [1971] IR 217. See the chapter by Dr Ailbhe O'Neill in this volume.
31 *Ryan v Attorney General* [1965] IR 294 (SC).
32 At least after *TD v Minister for Education* [2001] 4 IR 249 (SC).
33 *Murtagh Properties Ltd v Cleary* [1972] IR 330 (HC).
34 *Norris v Attorney General* [1984] IR 36 (SC) 71.
35 *Kennedy v Ireland* [1987] IR 587 (HC).
36 *Re a Ward of Court (Withholding Medical Treatment) (No 2)* [1996] 2 IR 79 (SC).

information about a medical practitioner's misconduct from being publicised,[37] and freedom from being watched by journalists.[38] Many of the cases after 1974 obviously concern the marital sphere of autonomy, possibly due to the earlier identification of a distinct right to marital privacy.

Finally, the rights of access to courts and to litigate have been also construed on the same basis, i.e. initially around the idea of personal liberty,[39] a sort of leafy tree whose penumbra may disclose several claims not otherwise attributable to specific constitutional provisions.

As far as private property rights are concerned, their protection and vindication usually relies on Art 40.3.2°, but also on the more detailed guarantee of Art 43. The natural law roots of the right property according to its constitutional formulation have already been pointed out: judicial dicta underline both the centrality of property to the humanity of each individual in a free and democratic society and the importance of economic rights in the social doctrine of the Catholic Church.[40] In more strictly legal terms, O'Higgins CJ in 1982[41] explained the difference between the two constitutional protections afforded to property. Art 43 is directed to the State and protects property as an institution, together with the right to transfer, bequeath and inherit, against its abolition, although requiring its regulation, while Art 40.3.2° is aimed at safeguarding the items belonging to an individual as a personal right. The Irish courts have developed a cluster of judicial tests in order to review the admissibility of restrictions of property rights by Oireachtas, tests that closely resemble the scrutiny applied by the US Supreme Court and the European Court in Luxembourg: they require that the aim of the piece of legislation be legitimate, that the means be compatible with the aim and not be overbroad, that the right be impaired as little as possible, usually that compensation be provided, and that the statute be not retrospective.

Summing up, Irish courts have elaborated something as a proportionality test, according to the European legal language.

In the sphere of social policy, the directive principles set out in Art 45 were initially interpreted, emphasising its initial words, as implying only "general guidance" for the Oireachtas and excluding any power of the courts to enforce positive obligations, although *a contrario* it could also be inferred that the duties prescribed in Arts 40 to 44 are real duties.[42] Later on, some decisions recognised a right to work as a personal right within the meaning of Art 40.3, founding this also upon the right to work and earn a livelihood mentioned in Art 45.2.1°.[43] The same provisions have

37 *Barry v Medical Council* [1998] 3 IR 387 (SC).

38 *X v Flynn* 19 May 1994 (HC).

39 As in *State (Quinn) v Ryan* [1965] IR 70 (SC). Later cases, such as *Tuohy v Courtney* [1994] 3 IR 1 (SC) and *White v Dublin City Council* [2004] 1 IR 545 (SC), have considered the right of access to the courts and the right to litigate in circumstances where the right to property, rather than personal liberty, is more closely implicated.

40 As in *Re Article 26 and the Health (Amendment) (No 2) Bill 2004* [2005] IESC 7; [2005] 1 IR 105 at 201–202.

41 *Blake v Attorney General* [1982] IR 117 (SC).

42 See GW Hogan and GF Whyte (eds) *JM Kelly, The Irish Constitution* (Butterworth, Dublin, 2003), p 2077 ff.

43 *Tierney v Amalgamated Society of Woodworkers* [1959] IR 254 (SC); *Murtagh Properties*

been relied upon (unsuccessfully) in order to protect private enterprise against state monopolies[44] and to define the limits of the restraint of trade in the traditional construction of the common law.[45]

4. Ireland and the Strasbourg Court

The relationship between the ECHR and the Irish State in some ways parallels that between the Convention and the United Kingdom, both from the viewpoint of history and in terms of constitutional solutions.[46] This is reflected in the fact that the ECHR, which entered into force for Ireland in September 1953 after the ratification of its text, and all of the Protocols with the exception of the Twelfth, have been incorporated, through a special indirect or "interpretive" form of incorporation, at the end of 2003, i.e. five years after the U.K. Human Rights Act 1998, which has incorporated the Convention in a very similar way. The Belfast agreement for the settlement of the Northern Ireland peace process is not unrelated to this choice.

Before 2003, the Irish approach to international law could not avoid observing the constitutional principles formulated in 1937, which were very dualistic, due to the period to which they belonged. Art 29 actually opened the Irish system to "the generally recognized principles of international law" (s 3), but in s 6 it prescribed that "No international agreement shall be part of the domestic law of the State save as may be determined by the Oireachtas". Therefore, the situation before 2003 was such as to make the Convention binding on Ireland, but not in it[47]: in other words, the Government was obliged to accept the decisions of the Strasbourg Court when the State was sued and convicted before it, but legislative provisions, judicial decisions and even administrative acts could not be challenged in Irish courts on the basis that they violated Convention obligations or principles, because these were not part of Irish law and could be vindicated at Strasbourg only after exhausting the remedies offered in the domestic system.

In the half century between 1953 and 2003, Ireland was one of the States most observant of the ECHR, being sued as respondent only 12 times and losing nine such cases,[48] and a significant proportion of them concerned problems relating the family sphere and various aspects of sexual behaviour.[49]

Ltd v Cleary [1972] IR 330 (HC); *Rogers v ITGWU* [1978] ILRM 5 (HC).

[44] *Attorney General v Paperlink Ltd* [1984] ILRM 373 (HC).

[45] As in *Kerry Co-operative Creameries Ltd v An Bord Bainne* [1991] ILRM 851 (SC).

[46] The consequences of the Belfast agreement of 1998 are analytically described in G Hogan, "Ireland. The British-Irish agreement and the Irish Constitution" (2000) 6 Eur Pub L 1.

[47] In the words of the introduction to U Kilkelly, *ECHR and Irish Law* (Jordans, Bristol, 2004), p vi.

[48] For a chronicle by D O'Connell "Ireland" in *Fundamental Rights in Europe – The ECHR and its Member States, 1950–2000* (R Blackburn and J Polakiewicz eds, OUP, Oxford, 2001), p 423 and "The ECHR Act 2003: A critical perspective" in U Kilkelly, *op. cit*, p 1; G Hogan "Incorporation of the ECHR: Some Issues of Methodology and Process" in U Kilkelly, *op. cit*, p 13. For a description, sector by sector, see, B Moriarty and E Massa eds, *Human Rights Law*, Law Society of Ireland (3rd ed, OUP, Oxford, 2011).

[49] Such as *Airey v Ireland* (1979) 2 EHRR 305 (absence of legal aid to married woman seeking separation from violent husband); *Johnston v Ireland* (1987) 9 EHRR 203 (inheritance rights of child born out of wedlock); *Norris v Ireland* (1991) 13 EHRR 186 (criminal prohibition of male homosexual acts); *Open Door Counselling Ltd v Ireland* (1993) 15 EHRR 244 (ban on abortion information); *Keegan v Ireland* (1994) 18 EHRR 342

The European Convention on Human Rights Act 2003 finally incorporated the Convention, although in a very prudent manner, trying to apply a filter to the possible production of drastic effects on domestic law and to maintain the equilibrium of the system of legal sources as presently structured in Irish constitutional law.

First of all, according to s 2(1) of the 2003 Act, Irish courts are required to interpret and apply national statutes and rules of law, insofar as possible, "subject to the rules of law relating to such interpretation and application" in a manner compatible with the Convention: this conformity obligation has been present in several European Constitutions since the 1970s and does not represent a serious alteration to the functioning of the judicial power, although it renders it necessary to get accustomed to a sort of double standard of interpretation.[50]

Secondly, if such interpretation is impossible and no other adequate legal remedy is available, the High Court or the Supreme Court must make a declaration of incompatibility of the relevant provision, which has no impact on the enduring operation of it, but starts a procedure in each House of the Oireachtas and entitles the injured party to apply the Attorney General for *ex gratia* compensation for any loss caused by the incompatibility.

Thirdly, all the organs of the State must, according to s 3(1), perform their functions in a Convention-compliant manner, but the President, Oireachtas and the courts are excluded; persons suffering damage or loss as a result of contraventions of subs (1) can, within one year from the contravention occurring, institute proceedings in a circuit court or the High Court in order to recover appropriate damages.

Fourth, s 4 prescribes that judicial notice shall be taken of the decisions of the Strasbourg Court and that Irish courts in interpreting Convention provisions shall take due account of the principles laid down in such judgements.

It is too early to evaluate how the ECHR Act 2003 has been applied. Yet, it is apparent that the Irish solution in the incorporation or, as it is sometimes said, the "patriation" of international human rights norms is a compromise formula. As such, it has been criticised by some authors and NGOs for its weakness and its possible drawbacks.[51] Actually, Ireland being the last of the then 45 member States of the Council of Europe to incorporate the Convention, the method chosen is cautious and prudent. Above all, it closely resembles the British approach, which probably the Irish did not want to go beyond, although the constitutional context is quite different: the UK still needs to preserve parliamentary supremacy, at least until Diceyan features of the British legal system are not swept away for the sake of a new constitutional order capable of making domestic government, devolution, Europe and the ECHR compatible. Ireland has long passed this phase, adopting a written constitution and introducing judicial review of legislation capable of producing a declaration of invalidity with *erga omnes* effect. In comparison, the declaration of incompatibility is devoid of direct and immediate effects, valid only *inter partes*

(rights of natural fathers). The other cases concerned planning law, the criminal process or religious matters.

50 However, some scholars maintain that this "double construction" test is to some extent traditional in Irish constitutional law: see Hogan and Whyte, *op. cit*, p 798.

51 See the debate in D O'Connell, "The ECHR Act 2003", *op. cit*, pp 2–3.

and able only to provoke an intervention of Parliament and possibly a pecuniary reparation, but not of an obligatory kind.

Timid as it may seem, this solution has several advantages.

First, it opens the way to a gradual domestication of the ECHR, although the first fifty years of application should have already allowed Irish jurists to envisage all possible systemic changes that would be made necessary as a result of a full, direct incorporation.

Secondly, it mitigates and slows down the impact on the domestic system of legal sources: declarations of invalidity due to reasons of unconstitutionality, declarations of incompatibility with conventional human rights norms and the supremacy of European law all need to be accommodated, harmonised and made mutually compatible. Such a result requires time, flexibility and moderation on the part of the judicial power, which has suddenly been entrusted with an "overdose of discretion". A constitutional amendment, similar to those adopted with regard to Art 29.4 or otherwise, might help to achieve such a demanding aim. From this point of view, the compromise formula chosen by the Irish legislature could prove to be wiser than other more enthusiastic approaches to incorporation. In fact, as a result of this compromise, the dialogue between domestic law and international human rights obligations can take place in a more relaxed and gradual way; the dualistic separation can be softened rather than abandoned completely; the penetration of conventional obligations in the system of legal sources based on domestic constitutional law can be put off to some future date when that system has been adequately prepared to comply with these obligations. Meanwhile, the recognition of a merely sub-constitutional status for the ECHR, rather than that of a "higher law of the land", has prevented a sudden and substantial rationalisation of the hierarchy of domestic legal sources.

5. Ireland and the European Union Court

Ireland joined the European Economic Community in 1973 and, perceiving the profound implications of the relationship between the two legal orders, the people amended the Constitution in order to achieve full compatibility. Art 29.4 was therefore revised initially through the addition of a subs 4.3°; later, several other amendments authorised Ireland to sign the Treaties of Maastricht, Amsterdam and Nice (the former Arts 29.4.4°, 29.4.5° and 29.4.7°). The Twenty-eighth Amendment of the Constitution (Treaty of Lisbon) Act 2009 modernised and rationalised this portion of Art 29.4, leaving it in the form that it currently takes.[52]

It should be noted that this procedure was required—politically if not in strictly legal terms in all cases—following the 1987 decision of the Irish Supreme Court in *Crotty v An Taoiseach*[53] concerning the Single European Act (SEA). In this important case, which delayed the coming into force of the SEA, the Supreme Court concluded (albeit in a fragmented decision) that the original authorisation (contained in the

[52] The Thirtieth Amendment of the Constitution (Treaty on Stability, Co-ordination and Governance in the Economic and Monetary Union) Act 2012 added a new Art 29.10, authorising ratification and implementation of that treaty.

[53] [1987] IR 713.

original amendment to Art 29.4 made in 1972) to join the Communities included the acceptance of all amendments to the Treaties that did not alter their essential scope and objectives; however, Title III of the SEA introduced a European foreign policy and therefore, according to a majority of three out of five members of the Court, went significantly beyond the range of functions of any of the Communities that the people had in 1972 authorised Ireland to join. As a consequence, in order to avoid a "clear disregard" of the Constitution, the concrete diminution of State sovereignty implied in the treaty required an amendment to the Constitution, including a referendum.[54]

Later, in 1994,[55] the Supreme Court was also confronted with the problem of the kind of domestic legal source necessary or sufficient to fulfil the adaptation of Irish law to European norms: on that occasion, the constitutionality of s 3(2) of the European Communities Act 1972 was upheld. Section 2 of that Act prescribes that treaties and other acts adopted by the institutions of the Communities are binding on the State and shall be part of the domestic law. Section 3(1) provides that any minister may make regulations to give full effect to such provision and s 3(2) that such regulations "may contain ... provisions repealing, amending or applying, with or without modification, other law". Any Act containing a similar authorisation would have been clearly unconstitutional without the constitutional support of what was then Art 29.4.3° (corresponding to the present Art 29.4.6°), which was a protection against possible constitutional challenges.[56] The Court did not establish, however, that it was always appropriate to implement Community legislation by way of secondary legislation. Therefore, it had further occasion to explain when the Government could use statutory instruments or other forms of secondary legislation in order to implement Community law and when it acts *ultra vires*.[57] Finally, the 1972 Act was amended by the European Communities (Amendment) Act 2007 in order to allow Ministers to make statutory instruments on matters related to, if not directly concerning, obligations deriving from Community law, including the creation of indictable offences in relation to such matters. The High Court and the Supreme Court have interpreted the provision of Art 29.4.6°, which immunises domestic laws "necessitated" by EU law from constitutional challenges: at first they considered such immunity as sweepingly inclusive of any measure consequent to EEC law[58]; later cases have brought more nuance to this issue.[59]

In the historical perspective, Ireland joined the then EEC shortly before the 1973–1977 economic recession, in a moment when the community's regulatory charge was growing faster and faster and its territory was also growing with the addition of Britain and Denmark. Initially, the Irish judiciary accepted primacy and supremacy of EC law wholeheartedly.[60] Similarly, the Irish people approved the Maastricht Treaty

54 As is also well-known, an initial popular vote in 2008 rejected the amendment necessary to ratify the Lisbon Treaty, although a second proposal was successful the following year.

55 *Meagher v Minister for Agriculture* [1994] 1 IR 329 (SC).

56 See M Cahill "Constitutional Exclusion Clauses, Article 29.4.6, and the Constitutional Reception of European Law" (2011) 33 DULJ 74.

57 *Maher v Minister of Agriculture* [2001] 2 IR 139; *Browne v Ireland* [2003] 3 IR 205; *Kennedy v Attorney General* [2007] 2 IR 45.

58 *Lawlor v Minister for Agriculture* [1990] 1 IR 356 (HC).

59 *Greene v Minister for Agriculture* [1990] 2 IR 17 (HC); *Condon v Minister for Agriculture* [1993] IJEL 151 (HC).

60 See G Hogan and A Whelan, *Ireland and the European Union: Constitutional and Statutory*

by a vote of almost 69 percent and Amsterdam by 61.7 percent, joined the Eurozone from the beginning and admitted citizens of the accession states as workers in 2004. On the other side, the Irish people rejected Nice on the first round[61] and Lisbon by 53.4 percent of the popular vote with a turnout of 53 percent, changing their minds on the second occasion by a 67 percent majority[62]; it opted out of the Schengen package and obtained its abortion protocol to the Maastricht Treaty. Ireland has been probably the best beneficiary of EU funds and of EU fiscal policies, experiencing a long period of brilliant economic growth; but it also required the first and strongest financial assistance in times of economic crisis, at least until now. Ireland has a low record of litigation in the Court of Justice, up to the controversy about the Data Retention Directive 2006/24[63] and a low rate of preliminary references from domestic courts, at least till the nomination to the Supreme Court of Murray CJ and of Fennelly and Macken JJ, all former members of the Luxembourg Court,[64] nor does it intervene frequently in the Luxembourg pending litigation.

The problems concerning the protection of fundamental rights in the EU system, the interaction with the work of the Strasbourg Court and of the national courts, the different approaches and standards of protection have been frequently studied in recent years,[65] even with reference to the Irish context. The main difficulty that Ireland's legal system might have to address in the near future is the issue of the different position that is assigned to the ECHR and to EU law within the context of domestic constitutional law. As underlined above, the ECHR has been incorporated at a sub-constitutional position, while EU law has entered the Irish legal system through several constitutional amendments. The ECHR operates in Ireland in an indirect and filtered way, while EU law is capable of having direct effect, thus ensuring its primacy and supremacy.

In conclusion, it will need great care on the part of the Irish courts in handling this complex situation, but it is just as clear that this complexity promotes flexibility and capacity of blending techniques and methods. Comparative analysis is thus very helpful from this point of view.

Texts and Commentary (Butterworths, Dublin, 1995); B Laffan and J O'Mahony, *Ireland and the European Union* (Palgrave Macmillan, Basingstoke, 2008).

61 See G Hogan, "Ireland 2002–2003" (2003) 9 Eur Pub L 461.

62 See M Cahill, "Ireland's Constitutional Amendability and Europe's Constitutional Ambition: the Lisbon Referendum in Context" (2008) 9 German LJ 1191.

63 *Ireland v Council and European Parliament*, Case C-301/06, [2009] ECR I-0593.

64 See E Fahey, *EU Law in Ireland* (Clarus, Dublin, 2010) pp 8 and 71 ff.

65 See for instance GF Ferrari, *Le libertà, profili comparatistici* (Giappichelli, Torino, 2011), chs 20–22; C Costello and E Browne "ECHR and the European Union" in U Kilkelly, *ECHR and Irish Law*, p 35.

CHAPTER 2

Irish Judicial Review of Legislation: A Comparative Perspective

Paolo Passaglia[1]

1. Introduction

The Irish procedure for judicial review of legislation attracts the attention of foreign scholars due to the numerous peculiarities that it presents. Indeed, the origins of the system and its configuration cannot be easily classified according to the traditional canons that developed in Western history and theory of constitutional justice, although it may appear that a choice of an American-based model was rather clear.

In this paper, I have tried to highlight some of the features of the Irish system that strike foreign observers as peculiar, distinguishing those that have characterised the system since its origins (and, sometimes, even before) from those that have resulted from the evolution of one of the oldest systems of constitutional justice in Europe.

2. The Origins of Judicial Review of Legislation

2.1 Judicial Review and (the End of) Colonialism

In the history of judicial review of legislation, Ireland certainly assumes a peculiar position. The key element to recall when analysing the Irish system consists, in my opinion, of the efforts made to reject the United Kingdom's grasp. This overarching aim led to two main arguments in favour of judicial review of legislation.

First, judicial review was intended to reject parliamentary sovereignty and thus to signal a departure from English constitutional tradition.[2] The severing of colonial links, then, ought to have opened a new national tradition, the autonomy of which required at least some distinguishing features.[3] After all, even before independence, the Constitution of the Irish Free State, adopted in 1922, provided for judicial review:

---

1 Professor of Constitutional Law, University of Pisa. Pro tempore Scientific Coordinator of the Comparative Law Area, Research Service, Constitutional Court of the Italian Republic. The author wishes to thank Sarah Pasetto for her comments and suggestions.

2 "When framing the new constitution Éamon de Valera may have been influenced more by a wish to break the colonial link than in giving reign to the judiciary, steeped as he was in a conservative tradition"; S O'Tuama, "Judicial Review under the Irish Constitution: More American than Commonwealth" (2008) 12.2 *Electronic Journal of Comparative Law* 1 (www.ejcl.org/122/art122-2.pdf; accessed 20 January 2014).

3 See C Murray, "Human Rights in Irish Legal History: Cahillane on Judicial Review (Guest Contribution)" (26 May 2010) *Human Rights in Ireland* (http://humanrights.ie/constitution-of-ireland/human-rights-in-irish-legal-history-cahillane-on-judicial-review/; accessed 20 January

> "The judicial power of the High Court shall extend to the question of the validity of any law having regard to the provisions of the Constitution."[4]

Yet, the will (and the need) to "be different" alone cannot explain the choices that were made in both 1922 and 1937. It is worth noting that in the period between the two constitutions, heated controversy arose in relation to the Colonial Laws Validity Act 1865, which gave the Judicial Committee of the Privy Council the power to strike down colonial laws that were repugnant to the provisions of any Act of Parliament enacted by Westminster. As far as the time of the Irish Free State is concerned, the main problems resulted from the Canadian case of *Nadar v King,*[5] in which the Privy Council confirmed (after an extended period of dormancy) the applicability of the repugnancy clause to legislation enacted by dominions. The power of constitutional adjudication that the Constitution of 1922 sought to concentrate in the hands of the High Court became a potential subject of dispute between the Irish and the English courts, until s 2(1) of the Statute of Westminster 1931 abolished the supremacy of imperial statutes.[6] The reform of 1933 thus made the Supreme Court (established nine years previously) the final court of appeal from the High Court. The Constitution of 1937 could only confirm this system.

In other words, the establishment of the Irish Supreme Court can be interpreted as an expression of the will to end all colonial ties and to create, instead, a completely independent court system. This is a further illustration of the different attitude towards the United Kingdom that prevailed in Ireland, as opposed to the stance assumed by other dominions. For instance, the institution of the Canadian Supreme Court, in 1876, did not entail an abolition of the power to appeal to the Privy Council, which endured—in civil cases, at least—until 1949. It is not by chance that while Irish independence was achieved in a single stage, Canadian independence (not only as far as the judiciary is concerned) was the result of a lengthy process due to a long-standing amicable and privileged relationship. After all, unlike Canada, Ireland had hardly accepted that she was one of the "daughters of mother Britannia".[7]

2.2 The Irish System and Foreign Models (A Double Hybrid System)

The particularity of the Irish system for judicial review of legislation derives not only from the aim pursued by the framers of the Constitution, but also from the historical period when judicial review was introduced.

In the aftermath of the First World War, an initial significant development of

2014): "In Britain, judges would not interfere in legislative decisions because of the fact that Parliament was supreme. So if the Irish were to introduce a clause whereby the judiciary would actually be supervising the actions of the Oireachtas this would constitute a huge leap from the previous system".

4 Article 65 of The Constitution of the Irish Free State (Saorstát Éireann) Act 1922. The same Article also provided that "[i]n all cases in which such matters shall come into question, the High Court alone shall exercise original jurisdiction".

5 [1926] AC 482.

6 On the impact of the Colonial Laws Validity Act 1865 upon Irish Free State laws, see T Mohr, "The Colonial Laws Validity Act and the Irish Free State", in University College Dublin Working Papers in Law, Criminology & Socio-Legal Studies, Research Paper No. 18/2009 (http://papers.ssrn.com/sol3/papers.cfm?abstract_id =1481738 ; accessed 20 January 2014).

7 Mohr, "The Colonial Laws Validity Act", *op. cit*, p 8 *et seq*.

constitutional justice unfolded in Europe on the theoretical basis provided by Hans Kelsen.[8] Most of the countries where judicial review was introduced followed to some extent the model of the Austrian Constitution, at least insofar as instituting a special court entrusted with the task of reviewing legislation.[9]

In Ireland, a different system was chosen to protect the Constitution, based on an alternative model that did not emerge from theory alone, but, on the contrary, was solidly rooted in practice.

Chief Justice Marshall's words perfectly matched the need to define the Constitution as a turning point in Irish history, in both legal and political terms:

> "Certainly all those who have framed written Constitutions contemplate them as forming the fundamental and paramount law of the nation, and consequently the theory of every such government must be that an act of the Legislature repugnant to the Constitution is void".[10]

Thus, the US model could certainly not be neglected, also because it provided a means of reviewing legislation with which Irish lawyers had some acquaintance, due to the existence during 1922–1933 of an external court that exercised appellate jurisdiction and also reviewed the validity of laws made in the Irish Free State.

However, the reference to the US did not simply lead to a direct transplant.[11] Rather, the American model was followed to configure ways and methods for judicial review. In particular, it is worth highlighting that in Ireland, like in the US, the decision on the validity of the enactment in question constitutes one of the stages of legal reasoning (whereas in the Kelsenian model, it is identified with the case to be decided), and the enforcement of the decision on validity relies on the doctrine of precedent (rather than on the nullification of the unconstitutional enactment by means of a formal court declaration that completely removes the enactment from the legal order).

As far as courts having the power to review legislation are concerned, a major difference emerges between the US and Ireland. In the passage of the *Marbury v Madison* opinion cited above, the Constitution is above all a supreme law; thus, all courts are supposed to implement this supremacy, by simple reason of the fact that

---

8 See H Kelsen, "La garantie juridictionnelle de la Constitution (La justice constitutionnelle)" (1928) XXXV *Revue du droit public et de la science politique* 197 *et seq.*

9 Probably the main exception, in Continental Europe, was that of the Romanian Constitution of 1923, which endowed the Court of Cassation with the power to strike down legislation.

10 *Marbury v Madison* (1803) 5 US (1 Cranch) 137 at 177.

11 Even if "[t]he Irish Constitution operated entirely within the compass of the modern genre in the United States, mediated by the younger judges who pushed out the frontiers of judicial review, drawing on their own knowledge and experience of the American model" (S O'Tuama, "Judicial Review under the Irish Constitution", *op. cit.*, p 2), there are some differences between the two systems, such that if the American model and the weak judicial review of the "New Commonwealth Model of Constitutionalism" are taken as opposite ends of a spectrum (S Gardbaum, "The New Commonwealth Model of Constitutionalism" (2001) 49 (Fall) *American Journal of Comparative Law* 707 *et seq.*), Ireland can be considered as occupying an intermediate position, albeit much closer to the American model (O'Tuama, "Judicial Review under the Irish Constitution", *op. cit*, p 21).

the courts' duty is to enforce the law. In Ireland, the position of the Constitution is not in question, but its protection is entrusted only to selected courts, namely, the superior courts:

> "the jurisdiction of the High Court shall extend to the question of the validity of any law having regard to the provisions of th[e] Constitution, and no such question shall be raised (whether by pleading, argument or otherwise) in any Court established under … th[e] Constitution other than the High Court or the Supreme Court".[12]

When review of legislation is at issue, the High Court is invested with full original jurisdiction; the other courts of first instance have no jurisdiction at all in relation to such a question.

The reduction of the number of courts empowered to review legislation makes Ireland's a hybrid system, in the context of the opposition between diffuse and concentrated models of judicial review.[13] The system cannot indeed be defined as "diffuse", as judicial review is not widespread; but neither can it be defined as "concentrated", since there is no single special court holding monopoly over the review of legislation.

However, the Irish system is a hybrid not only because of the limited number of courts that are allowed to strike down legislation. Its mixed nature also derives from the coexistence of concrete and abstract forms of review. A Bill

> "other than a Money Bill, or a Bill expressed to be a Bill containing a proposal to amend the Constitution, or a Bill the time for the consideration of which by Seanad Éireann shall have been abridged under Article 24 of th[e] Constitution"[14]

can be the object of a reference to the Supreme Court made by the President "after consultation with the Council of State"[15] for

> "a decision on the question as to whether such a Bill or any specified provision

[12] Article 34.3.2° of the Constitution. Once it is established, the new Court of Appeal, envisaged by the Thirty-third Amendment of the Constitution (Court of Appeal) Act 2013 will also exercise this constitutional review jurisdiction; this was one of the key reasons why a constitutional amendment was considered necessary to establish this new intermediate court of appeal. On the establishment of the new court, Art 34.3.2° will be amended so as to include the Court of Appeal as one of the courts in which the question of the validity of any law having regard to the provisions of the Constitution may be raised and decided: Thirty-third Amendment of the Constitution (Court of Appeal) Act 2013 Sch 6, Pt 2 (Ref 4). A guarantee that such questions cannot be excluded by law from the appellate jurisdiction of the Court of Appeal will also be incorporated in the Constitution, from the establishment of the new court: new Art 34.4.2° (to be inserted by Sch 3 Pt 2 of the Thirty-third Amendment of the Constitution (Court of Appeal) Act 2013).

[13] The definition of these concepts is provided by, e.g. M Cappelletti, *The Judicial Process in Comparative Perspective* (Oxford University Press, New York, 1989), p 133 *et seq*.

[14] Article 26 of the Constitution.

[15] Article 26.1.1° of the Constitution.

> or provisions of such a Bill is or are repugnant to th[e] Constitution or to any provision thereof".[16]

The reference procedure must take place prior to the President's signature, since

> "[e]very such reference shall be made not later that the seventh day after the date on which such Bill shall have been presented by the Taoiseach to the President for his signature"[17]

and

> "[t]he President shall not sign any Bill the subject of a reference to the Supreme Court … pending the pronouncement of the decision of the Court".[18]

The aim of this mechanism for references is clearly that of preventing the entry into force of a statute that is inconsistent with the Constitution.[19] Such an objective and the procedure established by Art 26 of the Irish Constitution are completely alien to the US model (at the federal level, at least). Thus, models must be sought elsewhere —assuming that any appropriate ones exist.

The name and the procedure (especially in relation to the President's power to submit requests) recall the reference jurisdiction established in Canada by s 53 of the Supreme Court Act of 1875, by which

> "[t]he Governor in Council may refer to the Court for hearing and consideration important questions of law or fact concerning (*a*) the interpretation of the Constitution Acts; (*b*) the constitutionality or interpretation of any federal or provincial legislation; (*c*) the appellate jurisdiction respecting educational matters, by the Constitution Act, 1867, or by any other Act or law vested in the Governor in Council; or (*d*) the powers of the Parliament of Canada, or of the legislatures of the provinces, or of the respective governments thereof, whether or not the particular power in question has been or is proposed to be exercised."[20]

Despite the presence of some similarities, the Canadian reference procedure is, on the whole, fairly different from that followed in Ireland. On the one hand, the former may be invoked more widely, since the Governor may refer any "important question" of constitutional law, while the Irish President may refer only Bills, and is, furthermore, constrained by strict time limits. On the other hand, decisions of the Irish Supreme Court in this respect have much greater binding power, as the declaration of unconstitutionality puts an end to the legislative process; decisions of the Canadian Supreme Court are, instead, nothing more than advisory opinions, which naturally hold great authority but are ultimately not binding.

---

16 *ibid.*

17 Article 26.1.2° of the Constitution.

18 Article 26.1.3° of the Constitution.

19 Article 26.3.1° of the Constitution: "In every case in which the Supreme Court decides that any provision of a Bill the subject of a reference to the Supreme Court […] is repugnant to th[e] Constitution or to any provision thereof, the President shall decline to sign such Bill".

20 Supreme Court Act (RSC, 1985, c S-26), s 53(1).

Thus, the Irish reference procedure does not appear to result from a simple legal transplant of its Canadian counterpart; rather, the Irish Constitution established a *sui generis* procedure. Nevertheless, this does not exclude the possibility that other models may have had some influence when the Constitution was drafted, although it is difficult to suggest a precise source of transplant or even imitation.

In the introduction of judicial review, one of the main aims (perhaps, *the* main aim) was to escape the parliamentary sovereignty once held by Westminster. The possibility for *a priori* references to the Supreme Court was therefore a key aspect of this purpose, as it constituted the most immediate means of preventing parliamentary infringements of individual rights and the principle of separation of powers.

In this connection, one could highlight that the concern for limiting legislative authority to the benefit of the Constitution was, prior to 1937, the basis for "political" review of legislation in some French (namely Bonapartist) regimes and, formerly, in Sieyès's theory of the *jury constitutionnaire*.[21] In the French constitutional tradition, this purpose had to be pursued without neglecting Rousseau's conception of the law as the expression of the general will,[22] a conception acknowledged in the Declaration of the Rights of Man and of the Citizen of 1789.[23] The solution was to allow reviews for constitutionality, but only of Bills adopted by Parliament, and thus of texts which were, in technical terms, not yet laws. In other words, review of legislation did not undermine the principle of law being the expression of the general will.

Once the theoretical aim of the review is clear, the foregoing considerations could be taken to suggest the usefulness of a comparison between the Irish reference procedure and the past procedures in France. In any case, the main difference fundamentally remains in the nature of the body endowed with the power to review legislation. In France, a political body was chosen (both in Sieyès's theory and in the Bonapartist regimes which established a *Sénat conservateur*), due to the fear of a "government of judges" that was (and, to some extent, still is) a significant feature of the French post-revolution tradition.[24] On the contrary, the framers of the Irish Constitution abandoned the British tradition of parliamentary sovereignty in favour of the American theory of separation of powers. As a result, the main beneficiaries of the new direction taken by Irish constitutionalism were judges.

The Irish reference procedure was therefore a truly *sui generis* solution. Although it is emphasised that there is no firm evidence to this effect, perhaps this very solution may have had some influence in the framing of France's Constitution of the Fifth

21 E-J Sieyès, "Convention nationale. Opinion de Sieyès sur les attributions et l'organisation du Jury constitutionnaire proposé le 2 thermidor, prononcée à la Convention nationale le 18 du même mois, l'an III de la République; imprimée par ordre de la Convention nationale" (1795), in *Essai sur les privilèges et autres textes* (E-J Sieyès, Dalloz, Paris, 2007), p 129 *et seq.*

22 See J-J Rousseau, *Du contrat social, ou Principes du droit politique* (Rey, Amsterdam, 1762), Book I, Ch VI.

23 Article 6: "Law is the expression of the general will". One might contrast this with Article 6.1 of the Constitution of Ireland: "All powers of government, legislative, executive and judicial, derive, under God, from the people, whose right it is to designate the rulers of the State and, *in final appeal*, to decide all questions of national policy, according to the requirements of the common good." (Emphasis supplied.)

24 See É Lambert, *Le gouvernement des juges et la lutte contre la législation sociale aux États-Unis* (Giard, Paris, 1921).

Republic of 1958, and in the establishment of the French Constitutional Council, which had the function of holding Parliament in check by means of an *a priori* review, which could be requested by a limited number of bodies, including the President of the Republic. The Constitutional Council was not originally a judicial body, but its evolution led to a change in its nature. Indeed, today, French scholars tend to perceive the Council as a (constitutional) court. In other words, the French *a priori* review is a means to refer Bills to a judicial body: a comparison with the Irish reference procedure, therefore, no longer appears to be so inappropriate.

3. Some Peculiar Features of the Irish System

3.1 The Delayed Implementation of Constitutional Provisions on Judicial Review of Legislation

The Constitution of 1937 had established a form of judicial review of legislation that was intended to be more effective than the system previously in place. As a matter of fact, the entry into force of the Constitution did not instantly lead to the development of a strictly "Irish-style" form of judicial review.[25]

Several reasons may be considered to explain why implementation of the provisions on judicial review of legislation was delayed.

The most important reason appears to be the conservative attitude displayed by the judges in office in the 1930s and in the following decade. Their legal culture was rooted in the British tradition and they were used to a system in which judges deferred to Westminster. The written Constitution, conceived as the supreme law of the land, had obviously changed their approach to legislation, but nevertheless they naturally tended, as much as possible, to follow precedents and, in any case, to limit the impact of the new constitutional provisions.

A good example of this attitude is the decision *Re Article 26 of the Constitution and the Offences against the State (Amendment) Bill 1940*,[26] in which a Bill for a law providing for internment without trial on the basis of an order made by a government minister was upheld because it did not—in the Court's opinion—take away the right of habeas corpus or infringe the general guarantee (in Art 40.4.1°) that no citizen should be deprived of his liberty "save in accordance with law". In this decision, Sullivan CJ stated that

> "[n]otwithstanding the provisions of the Bill, a person who is detained is entitled under Article 40, clause 4, par. 2, to have the legality of his detention enquired into and to obtain an order for his release, unless the Court or Judge, enquiring into the matter, is satisfied that all the provisions of the Bill has been complied with and that the detention is legal."[27]

In other words, it seemed that detention would be legal if it was carried out in compliance with the Bill, apparently regardless of its conformity to the Constitution:

---

[25] This subject was first analysed in detail by LP Beth, *The Development of Judicial Review in Ireland 1937–1966* (Institute of Public Administration, Dublin, 1967).

[26] [1940] IR 470.

[27] ibid, p 482.

the latter was then conceived of as a "broken reed",[28] since its provisions were not (expressly, at least) considered in determining whether the detention was lawful or unlawful.

The development of judicial review of legislation required a couple of decades or perhaps more: indeed, it is since the 1960s that Irish courts have reshaped the relations between the Constitution and Parliament, thus creating the conditions necessary for strong judicial review of legislation.

In theory, one could assume that such a gestation period and its length constitute distinctive features of Irish judicial review. However, from a comparative perspective, neither the gestation period in itself nor its duration can support this view.

In several countries, the establishment of judicial review of legislation required a lengthy period of implementation, especially when it came to the consolidation of a strong form of judicial review. The Canadian experience can be cited in this respect, although the development of judicial review did not depend on the implementation of constitutional provisions through statutes or on the evolution of case law: the turning point was rather the constitutional reform of 1982, which introduced a Charter of Rights that allowed courts to eventually perform effective review. The most revealing experience, however, is that of the United States of America, where the introduction of review in 1803 with the *Marbury v Madison* case was followed by a long gestation period that ended only after the Civil War, and during which judicial review of legislation rarely led to a declaration of unconstitutionality.

As far as Continental Europe is concerned, there is no general norm. In some cases, the constitutional provisions establishing (strong) judicial review of legislation were implemented immediately (e.g. in Germany or Spain), while in other cases implementation was delayed (e.g. in Italy) or the body dedicated to administering constitutional justice gained real power only after some time (e.g. in France or Belgium).

In this connection, it is perhaps worth examining the French and Italian experiences.

In France, it is only since the 1971 decision on freedom of association[29] (and the constitutional reform of 1974 that established the parliamentary opposition's right to appeal) that the Constitutional Council has been regarded as an effective guardian of the Constitution. French constitutional justice, in the form that then developed into actual judicial review, thus began almost 13 years after the institution of the body that held the power to review legislation. This gestation period was marked by a progressive gain of authority (and legitimacy) on part of the Constitutional Council, but also by the emergence of the prerequisites of constitutional justice, namely the acknowledgment of the force and effects of the Constitution in relation to the law.

From an Irish perspective, the Italian case is even more interesting. Italian judicial review of legislation, which was established by the Constitution of 1947 (in

[28] See D Barrington, "The Constitution in the Courts" in *The Constitution of Ireland 1937–1987* (F Litton ed, IPA, Dublin, 1987) 110 *et seq*.

[29] Constitutional Council, Decision No. 71-44 DC, 7-16-1971.

force since 1 January 1948), was effectively implemented only in 1956, when the Constitutional Court commenced its activity. Therefore, the gestation period was due to Parliament's inaction, since the statutes required by the Constitution for the Court's effectual operation were enacted only in 1953, and the first judges of the Court were appointed only in 1955. However, the establishment of an efficient system of judicial review took even longer, although the Constitution provided for its own protection ever since its entry into force. Pending the complete establishment of the Constitutional Court, transitional provisions empowered existing courts to review legislation, thus temporarily adopting the American model. Nevertheless, the conservative attitude displayed by judges—whose culture was rooted in the past and whose legal education, in many cases, dated back to the years of the Fascist dictatorship—hampered the thorough implementation of constitutional provisions, especially as far as individual rights were concerned. This attitude towards the new Constitution was still followed by most courts (and, especially, the superior courts) when the Constitutional Court was fully established; this factor strongly obstructed the latter's activity in its early years, as judicial review in the Italian system basically requires ordinary courts to refer alleged unconstitutionalities to the Constitutional Court. In the beginning, there were few references (most of them originating only from the lower courts), and the Court therefore took some years to assert itself and to affirm constitutional principles within the legal order.

In light of these examples, the presence of a gestation period does not seem to constitute a trait peculiar to the Irish system. On the contrary, the delay appears to be quite "ordinary", all the more if it is borne in mind that judicial review was established before the end of the Second World War, namely before the tragedy of totalitarianism led to the need for strong protection of the Constitution and of the values that it enshrines.

3.2 Judicial Appointments

The effectiveness of judicial review of legislation naturally depends on the individuals entrusted with this power. A key feature of any system of constitutional justice is, therefore, the independence of judges in relation to political bodies, since only courts that are capable of functioning freely from external influences are able to give the Constitution a central role in its decisions. This subject is too wide to address in this paper; the different factors affecting the independence of courts also cannot be analysed here, as the subject would stray too far from the main topic.

Some remarks shall, however, be made on one of the most controversial issues, that of judicial appointments. The Constitution gives the President, "on the advice of the Government",[30] the power to appoint "[t]he judges of the Supreme Court, the High Court and all other Courts established in pursuance of Article 34".[31]

On the basis of these provisions, the Irish system falls within the common law tradition—and is thus rather different from that of civil law countries, as regards both courts in general and constitutional courts. As in most common law countries, the system of judicial appointments has been criticised for being excessively

30 Article 13.9 of the Constitution.
31 Article 35.1 of the Constitution.

susceptible to influence from political claims. Also, and again as in most common law countries, reforms were introduced to ensure fuller consideration of the legal qualifications held by candidates and high-profile appointments.[32] Ireland preceded the United Kingdom or Canada in showing its concerns in this respect, since the Judicial Appointments Advisory Board commenced operation in 1996: a rather long time before the Commission for Judicial Appointments for England and Wales began reviewing appointment processes (in 2001), before the Constitutional Reform Act 2005 created the Judicial Appointments Commission and the Supreme Court Selection Commission or, in relation to Canada, before an ad hoc committee of the Canadian House of Commons was tasked (in 2004) with interviewing nominees, in an imitation of the US model.

It is perhaps due to anticipating this that the Irish system conferred fewer powers on the Judicial Appointments Advisory Board than those held by its foreign counterparts (a comparison with the English Commissions could be especially revealing), such that the alleged excess of political (i.e. governmental) influence on judicial appointments remains a controversial subject to this day.[33]

As much as the Irish system differs from other (more or less) similar systems, it clearly belongs to the common law tradition and its distinctive features do not appear sufficiently material to set it apart.

3.3 The Single Opinion

A specific feature of Irish judicial review has certainly been that of the "single opinion" requirement. An amendment made in 1941 provided that, in the contexts of both the reference procedure[34] and the appellate jurisdiction,[35]

> "[t]he decision of the Supreme Court on a question as to the validity of a law having regard to the provisions of th[e] Constitution shall be pronounced by such one of the judges of that Court as that Court shall direct, and no other opinion on such question, whether assenting or dissenting, shall be pronounced, nor shall the existence of any such other opinion be disclosed".[36]

It is only as a result of the most recent amendment of the Constitution that the single opinion rule will be removed (in relation to the Supreme Court's appellate jurisdiction, but not in relation to references under Art 26).[37]

This provision leads to an exception, as is clearly demonstrated by its introduction by means of constitutional amendment. Furthermore, it appears to constitute an exception not only as far as the Irish system and the common law tradition are concerned, but also, to some extent, in relation to many of the courts empowered to strike down unconstitutional legislation.

32 See D Feenan, "Judicial Appointments in Ireland in Comparative Perspective" (2008) 1 *Judicial Studies Institute Journal* 37 *et seq.*

33 See the comparative analysis by Feenan, *op. cit*, 56 *et seq.*

34 Article 26.2.2° of the Constitution.

35 Article 34.4.5° of the Constitution.

36 *ibid.*

37 Thirty-third Amendment of the Constitution (Court of Appeal) Act 2013, s 5(2)(g).

As a matter of fact, the structure of the judgments given by Irish courts follows that established by the common law tradition, and, in particular, the principle that requires a judgment to be the sum of the opinions of each individual judge. In contrast, in the civil law tradition, judgments must present a single opinion, probably due to the conception of the judge as the mouthpiece of the law, inherited from the times of the French Revolution. However, when it comes to constitutional courts, the single opinion is no longer axiomatic, as in many systems (e.g. in Germany or Spain) constitutional court judges are entitled to draft their own opinions, which may dissent or concur with that given by the majority.

The practice followed by the Judicial Committee of the Privy Council, according to which dissenting opinions were banned until 1966, may have played a role, perhaps due to the Privy Council's power to strike down (colonial) laws. In any case, the will to break away from the colonial experience makes it difficult to identify one of the main symbols of English supremacy as a model for Irish Supreme Court judgments.

Despite the obvious differences, Irish constitutional provisions may, rather, have been associated with the practice followed by the US Supreme Court and established by Chief Justice Marshall. Even though concurring and dissenting opinions are allowed in the US or, rather, *per curiam* opinions appear to be the exception, Marshall's main aim in adopting the practice of issuing single opinions was to make the Court speak in a more definitive voice.[38]

Similarly, the prohibition of *seriatim* opinions in Irish constitutional litigation was probably established to strengthen Supreme Court decisions:

> "From the point of view of the public interest, it is better to have a single judgment pronounced and no indication given that other judges held a different view".[39]

This is an unquestionable concern, as clearly proved by the debates on the introduction of dissenting or concurring opinions in European constitutional courts. Indeed, the main argument advanced against the introduction of individual judges' opinions highlights the possible risk of weakening the authority of courts' judgments. Nevertheless, arguments in favour of this introduction cannot be neglected, especially as far as the evolution of case law is concerned: public debate between judges could lead to different results in the future, as implementation of the judgment, changes in society, etc may prove that the views held by the minority were (or have become) stronger than those of the majority. The subject generates controversy in several countries. The arguments in favour of removing the single opinion rule have now prevailed in Ireland, with the Thirty-third Amendment of the Constitution Act 2013, which has scheduled its repeal in conjunction with the forthcoming establishment of a Court of Appeal.

To briefly sum up, the certainty that the single opinion has been supposed to guarantee must be balanced with the rigidity and the lack of disclosed arguments

38 That of the Chief Justice, since Marshall CJ wrote most of the opinions during his tenure.

39 J. Casey, "Changing the Constitution: Amendment and Judicial Review" in *De Valera's Constitution and Ours* (B Farrell ed, Gill & Macmillan, Dublin, 1988), p 161.

that the same institution naturally entails, and that are factors that could undermine a dynamic approach to constitutional interpretation. For the Irish Supreme Court, certainty was until recently favoured; the same decision was made for many other constitutional courts (Italy) or councils (France).

These remarks lead to the conclusion that, from a general point of view, single opinions have not been a specific feature of the Irish system. The Irish exception can be identified from two particular points of view: on the one hand, in relation to the principle governing common law countries according to which judges are entitled to express their views either by means of *seriatim* opinions or by means of dissenting or concurring opinions; on the other, in relation to the particularity of constitutional litigation, which is, in general, the only type of litigation where (some) civil law systems allow for opinions by individual judges. Thus, Ireland until recently adopted an opposite approach in all these respects (and will still do so in relation to references under Art 26).

3.4. Natural Law and Judicial Activism

A legal order in which the separation of powers is a founding principle must naturally be concerned with the mutual respect that the branches must pay to each other's boundaries. In this perspective, a subject often recalled is that of judicial activism, as opposed to the self-restraint that may be displayed by the courts.

The subject is not typical of the Irish system alone, since the abovementioned concern can be found to some extent in every Western legal order: the tendency for the judiciary to intervene in areas reserved to the executive or legislative branches is often reported, rightly or wrongly, in most countries.

A comparative study proceeding from Ireland may benefit from a narrower definition of "judicial activism", in particular, one that refers to

> "a willingness on the part of the judges to go behind the written text of a constitution and find interpretations and meanings which may not at first sight always be obvious".[40]

The reason why Ireland displays some peculiarities in this respect is associated with the references to natural law that the Constitution itself appears to evoke, although in a specific perspective.

The references to religion (made in the Preamble but also in several Articles of the Constitution) and to the "Christian and democratic nature of the State" proved, in the 1960s, to be key elements for the development of a new jurisprudence, aimed at recognising unenumerated rights.[41] The leading case within this trend is one of

[40] See J Hamilton, "Judicial Activism in Irish Constitutional Law" in *Judicial Activism and Restraint. Theory and Practice of Constitutional Rights*, proceedings of the European Commission for Democracy through Law Conference, Batumi (Georgia), 13–14 July 2010, p 2 (http://www.venice.coe.int/webforms/documents/?pdf=CDL-JU(2010)013-e; accessed 20 January 2014).

[41] See V Bradley Lewis, "Natural Law in Irish Constitutional Jurisprudence" (1997) II *Catholic Social Science Review* 171 *et seq.*

the most important cases of Irish history: in *Ryan v Attorney General*,[42] Kenny J, for the High Court, stated that

> "the personal rights which may be involved to invalidate legislation are not confined to those specified in Article 40 but include all those rights which result from the Christian and democratic nature of the State".[43]

The Supreme Court upheld this judgment, although O'Dálaigh CJ's opinion omitted any reference to Christianity or democracy.

Natural law as a basis for judicial activism (in the sense defined above) is expressly mentioned in a case of the 1970s, *McGee v Attorney General.*[44] Walsh J, in his concurring judgment, accepted the notion of natural law and its corollaries in terms of constitutional interpretation, and acknowledged the link between the Christian religion and natural law. However, he contested the need to deduce the contents of natural law from this link alone:

> "...[N]atural or human rights ... are part of what is generally called the natural law. There are many to argue that natural law may be regarded only as an ethical concept and as such is a re-affirmation of the ethical content of law in its ideal of justice. The natural law as a theological concept is the law of God promulgated by reason and is the ultimate governor of all the laws of men. In view of the acknowledgment of Christianity in the preamble and in view of the reference to God in Article 6 of the Constitution, it must be accepted that the Constitution intended the natural human rights I have mentioned as being in the latter category rather than simply an acknowledgment of the ethical content of law in its ideal of justice. What exactly natural law is and what precisely it imports is a question which has exercised the minds of theologians for many centuries and on which they are not yet fully agreed."[45]

Therefore, he concluded:

> "It is sufficient for the court to examine and to search for the rights which may be discoverable in the particular case before the court in which these rights are invoked. In a pluralist society such as ours, the Courts cannot as a matter of constitutional law be asked to choose between the differing views, where they exist, of experts on the interpretation by the different religious denominations of either the nature or extent of these natural rights as they are to be found in the natural law".[46]

Even if respect for Christian morality was a key issue in the famous case on sodomy *Norris v Attorney General*[47] and in other judgments, the path for a secular notion of natural law was traced, one that could even lead to rejection of reliance upon natural law itself.

---

42 [1965] IR 294.
43 *ibid* at 312.
44 [1974] IR 284.
45 *ibid* at 317 *et seq*.
46 *ibid*.
47 [1984] IR 36.

In *Attorney General v X*, in 1992, the Supreme Court recognised the right, in particular circumstances, to travel abroad for an abortion.[48] A constitutional amendment was then enacted guaranteeing a freedom to obtain and make available, subject to such conditions as may be laid down by law, information about services for the termination of pregnancy that are lawfully available outside the State.[49] A Bill was passed, setting out what those conditions were to be and was referred under Art 26.[50] Hamilton CJ, delivered the decision of the Supreme Court, which expressly rejected the argument against the validity of the constitutional amendment (and therefore the Bill) based on natural law, demonstrating that constitutional law no longer required a reference to natural law to ensure the protection of rights that were not explicitly enshrined in the Constitution. The court held as follows:

> "From a consideration of all the cases which recognised the existence of a personal right which was not specifically enumerated in the Constitution, it is manifest that the Court in each such case had satisfied itself that such personal right was one which could be reasonably implied from and was guaranteed by the provisions of the Constitution, interpreted in accordance with its ideas of prudence, justice and charity.
>
> The Courts, as they were and are bound to, recognised the Constitution as the fundamental law of the State to which the organs of the State were subject and at no stage recognised the provisions of the natural law as superior to the Constitution.
>
> The people were entitled to amend the Constitution in accordance with the provisions of Article 46 of the Constitution and the Constitution as so amended by the Fourteenth Amendment is the fundamental and supreme law of the State representing as it does the will of the people."[51]

Since these statements, the judicial activism (such as is alleged to exist) in Ireland appears to be similar to that in foreign courts. It is the Constitution itself and the way in which it applies to evolving society to require interpretation. But interpretation does not always lead to self-evident results, thus suggesting to some observers that courts may have gone too far. This issue is debated in Ireland as in all other Western countries. Any peculiarity in this respect appears to have vanished with the rejection of natural law arguments.

3.5 Non-Justiciable Matters: Amendments to the Constitution

In almost every legal order, there are matters on which courts are not allowed to decide. The Irish system is not an exception, since the jurisdiction of superior courts may be hampered in areas that are—and must remain—immune from scrutiny.[52]

Yet, some clarifications are necessary. Stating that jurisdiction is hampered does

---

48 [1992] 1 IR 1.

49 Article 40.3.3° (third sentence) as inserted by the Fourteenth Amendment of the Constitution Act 1992.

50 *Re Article 26 of the Constitution and the Regulation of Information (Services outside the State for Termination of Pregnancies) Bill, 1995* [1995] IR 1.

51 *ibid* at 43.

52 Such a concern was generally expressed in the US with the "political question doctrine". See *Baker v Carr* (1962) 369 US 186.

not mean, in general, that courts cannot decide: in many cases, their jurisdiction is simply limited, because the scrutiny performed must only not be too strict. In other words, when deciding on certain matters, courts must take into account other bodies' prerogatives, to avoid taking their place and thus exercising a function beyond those entrusted to the judiciary. In these cases, justiciability is not an issue, since courts are capable of considering the merits of the cases that come before them: therefore, the issue is about how far courts can go in reviewing a decision.

Irish case law is relatively rich in disputes on the boundaries of the judicial function with respect to political decisions.[53] But the same could be said for any country and in relation to any system of judicial review (of legislation).

When it comes to non-justiciability, the number of cases decreases dramatically, since once cases came before them, Irish superior courts generally did not decline jurisdiction; however, when they did not consider the merits, they assumed that their judgment was hampered by particular circumstances, the absence or removal of which would have enabled a decision on the merits. A clear example of this type of limitation on the judiciary is discussed in the next paragraph.

However, at least one non-justiciable matter does exist: the use of referenda as an instrument for constitutional change. In 1983, Justice Barrington, in the High Court, stated that he was "satisfied that by Article 46.1 the people intended to give themselves full power to amend any provision of the Constitution".[54] Later, Hederman J, for the Supreme Court, confirmed this doctrine by underlining that

> "with the exception of a Bill referred by the President to the Supreme Court under Article 26 of the Constitution, the courts have no jurisdiction to construe or review any Bill which has as its purpose the amendment of the Constitution, whatever its nature, [since a] proposal to amend the Constitution cannot *per se* be unconstitutional and the procedure adopted for so doing cannot be unconstitutional if it complies with the requirements of the Constitution".[55]

As a result,

> "the only possible grounds of challenge would relate to procedure, as where, in defiance of Article 46.3, the Bill was not expressed to be an Act to amend the Constitution, or where, contrary to Article 46.4, the Bill contained some other proposal".[56]

With these exceptions,

> "[t]o ask the Supreme Court to enquire whether the Bill was or was not

---

53 See, e.g. P Daly, "'Political Questions' and Judicial Review in Ireland" (2008) 2 *Judicial Studies Institute Journal* 116 *et seq.*

54 *Finn v Minister for the Environment* [1983] IR 154 at 164.

55 *Slattery v An Taoiseach* [1993] IR 286 at 300.

56 See J Casey, "Constitutional Justice and Democracy by Referendum in Ireland" in *Constitutional Justice and Democracy by Referendum: Seminar Proceedings*, European Commission for Democracy through Law, Strasbourg, 23–24 June 1995 (Council of Europe Publishing, Strasbourg, 1996), p 118.

> 'repugnant' to the existing provisions of the Constitution would be a futile exercise".[57]

The decision in *Re Article 26 and the Regulation of Information (Services outside the State for Termination of Pregnancies) Bill, 1995* confirms the futility of such an inquiry in relation to a constitutional amendment, except on the ground that it has not been enacted in accordance with the procedure required by the Constitution.

The doctrine of non-justiciability, as applied to referenda and to constitutional reform, is far from being a peculiar feature of the Irish system. In this respect, one could cite the US Supreme Court, which in 1915 declined jurisdiction and whose case law since then has made very little changes on the subject.[58] But it is in Continental Europe that the issue is widely debated, as in some countries the power of constitutional courts to review even constitutional laws, when their repugnancy with fundamental principles is alleged, is granted by the Constitution (e.g. in Germany)[59] or was asserted by the Courts themselves by means of their judgments (e.g. in Italy).[60]

Other legal orders reject the existence of supra-constitutional law. Among these, the most interesting is the case of France, where the Constitutional Council stated, in 1962, that it did not have jurisdiction over a constitutional reform adopted by means of a referendum, since laws "adopted by the People [...] are the direct expression of national sovereignty".[61] More recently, the Council clarified its doctrine by extending non-justiciability to constitutional laws passed by the Parliament.[62] The similarities with the Irish doctrine, also due to the reference to the People's power to freely change the Constitution, cannot be ignored, even though in France referenda are only one of the ways in which the Constitution can be amended. The Irish system makes it clearer than in France that the People is the ultimate authority when the supreme law of the land requires changing. This principle too can be seen as further evidence of the will to escape the British tradition of parliamentary sovereignty.

3.6 Single Review: The Relationship between the Reference Procedure and Constitutional Litigation

The Second Amendment of the Constitution Act 1941 added a provision according to which

> "[n]o Court whatever shall have jurisdiction to question the validity of a law, or any provision of a law, the Bill of which shall have been referred to the Supreme Court by the President under Article 26 of th[e] Constitution, or to question the validity of a provision of a law where the corresponding provision

---

[57] *Finn v Minister for the Environment* [1983] IR 154 at 161.

[58] See *Myers v Anderson* (1915) 238 US 368. In later judgments, the Supreme Court did not explicitly confirm the doctrine of non-justiciability, but real judicial review of constitutional amendments has not taken place in any case.

[59] Article 79.3 of the Basic Law for the Federal Republic of Germany: "Amendments to this Basic Law affecting the division of the Federation into Länder, their participation on principle in the legislative process, or the principles laid down in Articles 1 and 20 shall be inadmissible".

[60] Constitutional Court, Judgment No. 1146, 29 December 1988.

[61] Constitutional Council, Decision No. 62-20 DC, 6 November 1962.

[62] Constitutional Council, Decision No. 2003-469 DC, 26 March 2003.

> in the Bill for such law shall have been referred to the Supreme Court by the President under the said Article 26".[63]

The same rule does not apply when a provision has been upheld following a challenge made after its enactment into law; in that situation, the Supreme Court is free to reverse its earlier finding that the provision was valid.[64]

This provision must be analysed from two different points of view.

In theory, what has been called the "Single Opinion Crux"[65] sought to bring certainty: once the constitutionality of a Bill was upheld by the Supreme Court, no court could question the validity of the resulting Act anymore; as a result, the People could rely upon it as a lasting regulation. Moreover, the single review performed by the Supreme Court made the national parliament the only body entitled to change the law, in case its provisions needed updating due to social, economic or political changes.

This limitation imposed on judicial review does not imply a prohibition on any judicial activity regarding the law: statutory interpretation remains possible and can have major effects on the meaning of a provision (and on its implementation).[66] The constitutional courts of Continental Europe have experimented for quite some time with the potential of rules of interpretation for constructing statutory law in conformity with the Constitution.[67]

Although the role of statutory interpretation in updating legislative enactments cannot be underestimated, the impact of the single review provision on judicial review of legislation is undeniable. Whether this provision nourishes the particularity of the Irish system is, depends on the point of view adopted. In comparison with other common law systems, the Irish prohibition on second reviews of legislation that has been subject to *ex ante* review constitutes an exception to the general principle according to which courts may review a provision as many times as is necessary. If the Irish system is compared with the European model of constitutional courts,

63 Article 34.3.3° of the Constitution.

64 This occurred, albeit in relation to a pre-Constitution statute, as between *State (Shanahan) v AG* [1964] IR 239 (in which the Courts of Justice Act 1936 s 62 was held to be consistent with the Constitution) and *Costello v DPP* [1984] IR 436 (in which the Supreme Court departed from that earlier decision and held s 62 to be inconsistent with the Constitution).

65 O'Tuama, "Judicial Review under the Irish Constitution", *op. cit*, p 17.

66 It is worth noting that the Supreme Court itself highlighted that the Constitution imposes interpretation rules which differ from those traditionally found in common law. In *McDonald v Bord na gCom (No 2)* [1965] IR 217, reference was made to the "double construction rule": "where an enactment is capable of bearing two interpretations one of which is compatible with the Constitution and the other incompatible, the Court must adopt the former rather than declare the enactment unconstitutional". See P Brady, "Constitutional Interpretation and the Irish Supreme Court: Some Reflections on a Neighbouring Common Law Court's Approaches to Interpretation" in *Legislation and the Supreme Court: Statute Law Society Conference 2010*, London, 9 October 2010, p 1 (www.statutelawsociety.org/__data/assets/pdf_file/0004/93586/Paul_Brady.pdf; accessed 20 January 2014). For further information on the subject, the main reference is D Dodd, *Statutory Interpretation in Ireland* (Tottel, Dublin, 2008).

67 The Italian Constitutional Court, for instance, established the principle that "a law can be struck down not because its interpretation may lead to a breach of the Constitution [...], but because it is impossible to adapt it to constitutional provisions by way of interpretation" (see Constitutional Court, Judgment No. 356 of 22 October 1996).

the answer changes significantly: indeed, in many jurisdictions (e.g. Germany and France), the constitutional court has the final word, either because the law is struck down or because it acquires that which French scholars call a "certificate of constitutionality" (*brevet de constitutionnalité*), meaning that the validity of the enactment can no longer be questioned.[68]

Notwithstanding the similarities with other renowned systems, the single review provision does not appear to be unobjectionable, as it grants a "certificate of constitutionality" on the basis of an abstract review of laws only, which may, however, turn out to be inconsistent with the Constitution only upon their implementation.[69] But, in this case, given that concrete review is forbidden, the only solution is to defer to the will of Parliament, hoping that the author of the law shall accept to change it.

In theory, these remarks can be endorsed. In practice, however, this assessment must be changed, as the reference procedure has been invoked only 15 times since 1937, and the negative effects alleged to result from an Art 26 judgment are thus restrained by the reluctant attitude displayed by presidents towards this type of jurisdiction. It is also possible to infer that one of the (main) reasons for this reluctance is precisely the need to "handle with care" a procedure that leads to a final decision, establishing a doctrine that is supposed to last indefinitely.

3.7 The Use of Comparative Law Arguments

High Court and Supreme Court judgments are often enriched with references to foreign law and, in particular, foreign courts' decisions. This practice is not a special feature of the Irish courts, although in many jurisdictions—of either common or civil law—the appropriateness of references to foreign law is still under debate.

A comparative analysis shows that common law courts are keener on foreign references than civil law courts. There are notable exceptions, such as the US or the United Kingdom; but, generally, it is easier to find foreign law quoted in a common law rather than a civil law judgment. The reasons for this can involve the different styles in which judgments are written (especially when the object of comparison is the sober French style), but in my opinion the strongest reason is that common law courts benefit from two combined elements: English-speaking courts can communicate with each other directly, while other courts often require translation, which can give rise to risks of misunderstandings; and English-speaking courts share a common root, on which national legal systems were then built. The common law style associates different jurisdictions with one another and allows each jurisdiction

68 This principle does not exist in other systems (e.g. the Spanish and the Italian ones), which thus allow the Constitutional Court to return upon the issue when a law has not been struck down.

69 Not to mention the fact that the Supreme Court judgment is delivered only a few weeks (or days, sometimes) after the political debate has come to an end. The Supreme Court, deciding in the heat of the moment, may not be safe from political influence and, above all, its decision may be read in the light of the political controversy rather than subjected to analysis for its legal reasoning. Such concerns were expressed, for instance, by many Italian scholars to criticise a constitutional reform which sought to give Members of Parliament the power to appeal Bills before the Constitutional Court. The constitutional reform, drafted in 1997, did not pass, but the arguments that were then expounded still appear to be valid.

to understand deeply the legal reasoning adopted by others; in civil law countries, the medieval *jus commune* was overcome at various turning points, related to law reforms that separated individual legal systems, eventually making it difficult for anything but general principles to be shared.

Rather than constituting an exception, foreign references that enrich Irish judgments are a sign of a shared tradition that associates common law countries. What can be said of the Irish Supreme Court could be confirmed in relation to the Canadian Supreme Court, the Indian courts, the South African Constitutional Court,[70] etc. Even the types of references made appear to unite those different jurisdictions. For example, American case law has gained supremacy at England's expense. The Irish Supreme Court reflects this evolution: in older judgments, references to English Courts prevail over US ones; however, recent practice provides opposite results,[71] as well as an increasing number of references to Canadian judgments. The rejection of the colonial experience appears to have nothing to do with this evolution, which is rather ascribable to the general trend of the US becoming the leading legal model for common law countries (and beyond). The adoption of a written Constitution and the similarities between the Bills of Rights make it natural for Ireland to look increasingly westwards, to the other side of the Atlantic Sea, rather than eastwards, to the other shore of the Irish Sea.

4. Conclusion

Irish judicial review of legislation is not easy to classify on the basis of the most common models of constitutional justice. This may explain the reason why it has not always attracted the attention of (Italian) comparative scholars.

Nevertheless, some of its features, as peculiar as they may be, outline an original way to ensure protection of the constitution: by neither creating a brand new model nor simply imitating foreign systems, Ireland succeeded in the tricky task of strengthening the rule of law without endangering democracy and freedom of political choices. Difficulties and inadequacies can, of course, be found, but every system has to manage its own deficiencies. From this point of view, the Irish system is far from being peculiar. Furthermore, it also can suggest some productive solutions. That is to say, Ireland should certainly be studied in a comparative perspective. The present paper is, therefore, only a sketch of a broader research that would be well worth undertaking.

70 As far as South Africa is concerned, a real particularity arises from Article 39.1.c of the Constitution, which provides that "[w]hen interpreting the Bill of Rights, a court, tribunal or forum […] may consider foreign law": the Constitution itself thus gives foreign law a special status as a mean of interpretation.

71 On the references to US Supreme Court judgments on part of the Irish Supreme Court, see B Carolan, "The Search for Coherence in the Use of Foreign Court Judgments by the Supreme Court of Ireland" (2004–2005) 12 *Tulsa Journal of Comparative & International Law* 123.

Chapter 3

Constitutional Interpretation in Ireland

Elisabetta Pulice[1]

1. Preliminary Remarks on Judicial Review in Ireland

Constitutional interpretation in Ireland inevitably raises intricate issues and multi-faceted problems, due both to the very nature of the constitutional source of law involved (a written and judicially enforceable Constitution) and to the intellectual activity inherent in any legal interpretation. In particular, problems involved in the interpretation of the Irish Constitution are even more complex to deal with when the analysis is carried out by a lawyer mainly trained in a civil law system, a circumstance that requires an implicit comparative approach.

This article aims to outline the main characteristics of the different approaches to constitutional interpretation adopted by Irish judges. The purpose is to highlight both the complexity of this issue and the vital role of constitutional interpretation.[2]

Therefore, before focusing on the complex theme of constitutional interpretation as such, we should make some preliminary remarks on the context we have to deal with, in particular on the common law tradition of the Irish legal system, its framework for judicial review and its distinctive features as a common law country.

As to the first point, we should consider that, on the one hand, Ireland has a written and rigid[3] Constitution and, on the other hand, its legal system is rooted in the common law tradition.

In this respect, the clear, although often implicit, manner in which constitutional provisions incline towards judicial application, together with a detailed wording of provisions, disclose and are symptomatic of the common law tradition of the Irish legal system.[4]

---

[1] PhD candidate in Public Law at the Doctoral School in Comparative and European Legal Studies, University of Trento. The author is grateful to Professor Roberto Toniatti, Professor Rory O'Connell, Professor Carlo Casonato and Dr Cinzia Piciocchi for their comments.

[2] In this respect, reference needs to be made to literature: see JM Kelly, *The Irish Constitution* (4th ed, Gerard W Hogan and Gerry Whyte ed, Lexis Nexis Butterworths, 2003) 3, where the editors decide to begin the examination of the Irish Constitution with a consideration of the different interpretative approaches "since the theme of constitutional interpretation is probably best described as 'adjectival' rather than 'substantive' in character (in the sense that it informs every provision in the Constitution)".

[3] Constitution of Ireland, Art 46.

[4] See R Toniatti, "Irlanda (Repubblica d')" in *Digesto delle discipline privatistiche* (UTET, 1993) 178–189, 181.

Moreover, the Irish Constitution itself, although meant to be a radical break with the past, provided for continuity with Ireland's previous legal system as part of the United Kingdom, by declaring all laws in force immediately prior to the coming into operation of the Constitution to be fully in force and of effect "to the extent to which they are not inconsistent" with the Constitution.[5] Under the same conditions, continuity is therefore ensured also for rules of common law.

With reference to judicial review, we should first point out that the date of coming into force of the Constitution (29 December 1937) is decisive: its enactment marked the beginning of a new legal system, also as regards the validity of laws in relation to constitutional provisions.

According to this circumstance, one should distinguish the review of pre-Constitution law, i.e. pre-1937 statute law and rules of common law, from the review of post-1937 Acts.

As to the first category, Ireland might appear to operate a decentralised system since judicial review seems potentially within the jurisdiction of any court.[6] However, the Supreme Court has held that this form of judicial review is centralised in the High Court and Supreme Court.[7] Under Art 50, as mentioned above, there have been constitutional cases involving the question whether certain supposed rules of common law have remained valid after the enactment of the Constitution.[8]

With reference to post-1937 laws' review, despite the absence of an *ad hoc* court, Ireland still operates as a centralised system, although jurisdiction is distributed over two judicial levels: the High Court (first instance) and the Supreme Court (on appeal), which have exclusive jurisdiction on judicial review of post-Constitution Acts.[9] There is indeed an express exclusion of courts other than the High Court and the Supreme Court, from judicial review of post-1937 laws: Art 34.3.2° prohibits other courts from judging the validity of laws and even from allowing any such question to be raised "whether by pleading, argument or otherwise".[10]

In addition to this method by which the constitutionality of a post-1937 Act may be tested, there is the pre-legislative and abstract review under Art 26. According to this provision, the Supreme Court has the duty to consider Bills referred to it by

5 Art 50.1: "Subject to this Constitution and to the extent to which they are not inconsistent therewith, the laws in force in Saorstát Éireann immediately prior to the date of the coming into operation of this Constitution shall continue to be of full force and effect until the same or any of them shall have been repealed or amended by enactment of the Oireachtas". See also B Chubb, *The Constitution and Constitutional Change in Ireland* (Institute of Public Administration, 1985) 38.

6 At least from a technical point of view, although it seems to be largely theoretical.

7 *People (DPP) v MS* [2003] 1 IR 606.

8 See JP Casey, *Constitutional Law in Ireland* (3rd ed, Sweet & Maxwell, 2000) 340.

9 For a general classification of systems of judicial review by Italian scholarship, see, among others, L Pegoraro, *Giustizia Costituzionale comparata* (Giappichelli, 2007); L Mezzetti ed, *Sistemi e modelli di giustizia costituzionale* (Cedam, 2009); L Mezzetti, M Belletti, E D'Orlando and E Ferioli, *La Giustizia Costituzionale* (Cedam, 2007).

10 Art 34.3.2°: "… the jurisdiction of the High Court shall extend to the question of the validity of any law having regard to the provisions of this Constitution, and no such question shall be raised (whether by pleading, argument or otherwise) in any Court established under this or any other Article of this Constitution other than the High Court or the Supreme Court.".

the President of Ireland, after consultation with the Council of State, "for a decision on the question as to whether such Bill or any specified provision or provisions of such Bill is or are repugnant to this Constitution or to any provision thereof".

Article 34.3.3° of the Constitution states that a law, the Bill for which has been upheld by the Supreme Court under Art 26, cannot be challenged again. This provision might be seen as one of the main disadvantages of the pre-legislative and abstract review in Ireland, which is actually rarely used.[11] The Irish system seems rather to prefer the concrete judicial review, i.e. considering in a real legal controversy how the challenged law works in practice. This is actually the procedure in which the need and usefulness of different interpretative approaches arise in the most significant way.

The power to review the constitutionality of legislation is expressly contained in the Irish Constitution since 1937: that was "a novel aspect of the Constitution in 1937. No such power existed expressly elsewhere in Common Law jurisdictions".[12] Indeed, it is not left to be inferred, as in other common law legal systems, such as in the United States or Australia.[13]

The Irish Constitution also forbids the Oireachtas from passing laws repugnant to any of its provisions and expressly states that every law that is in any respect repugnant to the Constitution shall be invalid.[14]

A presumption of constitutionality therefore characterises the Acts enacted by the Irish national parliament, implying that in constitutional cases the burden of proof rests on the plaintiff.[15]

This presumption applies also to Bills referred to the Supreme Court on the President's initiative under Art 26, whereas pre-Constitutional laws do not obviously benefit from it.

It may be interesting to note that constitutional judicial review in Ireland is to some extent still influenced by the common law tradition. First, courts are bound by previous precedents in constitutional cases too. Secondly, one should probably mention the vital and leading role of the judiciary in the development of Irish constitutional law.[16]

Moreover, the fact that the parliament is obliged not to enact any law that is repugnant

---

11 See JP Casey, *Constitutional Law in Ireland* (3rd ed, Sweet & Maxwell, 2000) 338.

12 See Denham J in the case *A v Governor of Arbour Hill Prison* [2006] 4 IR 88 (SC) 146.

13 See JP Casey, *Constitutional Law in Ireland* (3rd ed, Sweet & Maxwell, 2000) 339; P Gallagher, "The Irish Constitution: Its Unique Nature and the Relevance of International Jurisprudence" (2010) 45 *Irish Jurist* 22, 30.

14 Art 15: "1° The Oireachtas shall not enact any law which is in any respect repugnant to this Constitution or any provision thereof. 2° Every law enacted by the Oireachtas which is in any respect repugnant to this Constitution or to any provision thereof, shall, but to the extent only of such repugnancy, be invalid."

15 See, among others, JP Casey, *Constitutional Law in Ireland* (3rd ed, Sweet & Maxwell, 2000) 364; JM Kelly, *The Irish Constitution* (4th ed, Gerard W Hogan and Gerry Whyte ed, Lexis Nexis Butterworths, 2003) 448.

16 See, for instance, the unenumerated constitutional rights doctrine and the role of courts in their identification (below sections 2 and 4)

to the Constitution and that the invalidity of unconstitutional laws is expressly stated by the Constitution itself means that judges simply declare the Act invalid. In particular, as regards the effects of this declaration of invalidity, it has been argued that although a law held invalid ceases to have any effect, it does not mean that it is automatically repealed.[17]

This might be important considering that the Supreme Court introduced certain elements of flexibility into the doctrine of *stare decisis*. Thus, since the Supreme Court is "the creation of the Constitution", it held itself in *State (Quinn) v Ryan* in 1965 to be free from its own precedents in constitutional cases, even if only for "the most compelling cases".[18]

In any case, unlike in the common law tradition, in cases of constitutional review the "one-judgement rule" should apply, though actually restricted by courts. This rule is embodied in Art 34.4.5°:

> "The decision of the Supreme Court on a question as to the validity of a law having regard to the provisions of this Constitution shall be pronounced by such one of the judges of that Court … and no other opinion on such question, whether assenting or dissenting, shall be pronounced, nor shall the existence of any such other opinion be disclosed".

The "one-judgement rule" was introduced by the Second Amendment to the Constitution in 1941 and has actually been interpreted by the Supreme Court as applicable only to post-Constitution laws.[19]

Lastly, we should point out that in Ireland judicial review is not unlimited. Art 28.3 of the Constitution expressly excludes from judicial review all Acts passed in time of war or armed rebellion or armed conflict. EU law also benefits from the exception provided for by Art 29.4.6°:

> "[n]o provision of this Constitution invalidates laws enacted, acts done or measures adopted by the State, before, on or after the entry into force of the Treaty of Lisbon, that are necessitated by the obligations of membership of the European Union … or of the European Atomic Energy Community …".

Furthermore, probably the most interesting limit to courts' jurisdiction, at least in a comparative perspective, is embodied in Art 45, i.e. in the field of the so-called directive principles of social policy. The latter are intended only "for the general

---

17 See R Toniatti, "Irlanda (Repubblica d')" in *Digesto delle discipline privatistiche* (UTET, 1993) 188; RH Grimes and T Horgan, *Introduction to Law in the Republic of Ireland* (Merlin Publishing, 1988) 171; JP Casey, *Constitutional Law in Ireland* (3rd ed, Sweet & Maxwell, 2000) 373; B Doolan *Constitutional Law and Constitutional Rights in Ireland* (Gill & Macmillan, 1988) 114. As regards the operative time and effect of the finding of invalidity or inconsistency, the Supreme Court had to take into account some important consequences and, as we will see below (section 3) it used foreign law in deciding these issues.

18 *State (Quinn) v Ryan* [1965] IR 294.

19 See, for instance, RH Grimes and PT Horgan, *Introduction to Law in the Republic of Ireland* (Merlin Publishing, 1988) 172, and—with reference also to further limits to the "one-judgement rule"—see JM Kelly, *The Irish Constitution* (4th ed, Gerard W Hogan and Gerry Whyte ed, Lexis Nexis Butterworths, 2003) 527–530.

guidance of the Oireachtas" and their application in the making of laws "shall be the care of the Oireachtas exclusively, and shall not be cognisable by any Court under any of the provisions of this Constitution".[20]

2. Five Principal Interpretative Approaches: Literal, Historical, Purposive (or Broad), Harmonious and Natural Law

Judicial review in Ireland began to thrive only in the early 1960s, thanks to a deeper awareness of fundamental rights and of the role of the Constitution itself.[21] From that moment on, constitutional interpretation became increasingly important, especially in the field of fundamental rights.[22]

In the course of time, Irish courts adopted five different interpretative approaches: literal, historical, purposive (or broad), harmonious and natural law.[23] Although it has been argued that there is often little consistency among them and although they sometimes do overlap,[24] it is worth trying to describe each approach, in order to have a general overview of the most important issues related to them.

2.1 Literal Approach

According to the literal interpretation, the Constitution essentially means what its plain words mean.

This approach has been significantly applied in two cases involving Art 34.4.3° of the Constitution. Under this provision, the Supreme Court "shall have appellate jurisdiction from all decisions of the High Court".[25] According to the literal interpretation "all decisions" means exactly *all decisions* and therefore an appeal is admissible also against an acquittal in a criminal case.[26]

---

[20] Art 45: "The principles of social policy set forth in this Article are intended for the general guidance of the Oireachtas. The application of those principles in the making of laws shall be the care of the Oireachtas exclusively, and shall not be cognisable by any Court under any of the provisions of this Constitution". From a comparative point of view, it is interesting to note that in the Spanish Constitution of 1978 there is a similar limit to the review cognition of the *Tribunal Constitucional*. According to Art 53.3 principles recognised in Ch 3 of the Constitution on "Governing Principles of Economic and Social Policy" "may only be invoked in the ordinary courts in the context of the legal provisions by which they are developed". See *Comentarios a la Constitución Española de 1978,* Edersa, 2006.

[21] JP Casey, *Constitutional Law in Ireland* (3rd ed, Sweet & Maxwell, 2000) 25.

[22] See below section 4.

[23] See, among others, JM Kelly, *The Irish Constitution* (4th ed, Gerard W Hogan and Gerry Whyte ed, Lexis Nexis Butterworths, 2003) xcviii-cxxii; R O'Connell, "75 Years of Irish Constitutionalism" paper at *Constitutional Interpretation* conference, 3 November 2011, organised by UCD and the Italian Embassy in Dublin (paper on file with author); JP Casey, *Constitutional Law in Ireland* (3rd ed, Sweet & Maxwell, 2000) 376.

[24] JM Kelly, *The Irish Constitution* (4th ed, Gerard W Hogan and Gerry Whyte ed, Lexis Nexis Butterworths, 2003) xcviii.

[25] Art 34.4.3°: "The Supreme Court shall, with such exceptions and subject to such regulations as may be prescribed by law, have appellate jurisdiction from *all decisions* of the High Court, and shall also have appellate jurisdiction from such decisions of other courts as may be prescribed by law." Emphasis added.

[26] See *State (Browne) v Feran* [1967] IR 147 and *People (DPP) v O'Shea* [1982] IR 384.

In *O'Shea*, in particular, the court stated that "the Constitution, as the fundamental law of the State, must be accepted, interpreted and construed according to the words which are used; and these words must be given their literal meaning".[27]

One advantage of this approach is that courts can follow closely the actual language of the text of the Constitution, in contrast to judicial subjectivity, which might instead be typical of other approaches.[28]

However, there are disadvantages too. Among them, one should notice that the literal approach applies only when the text is unambiguous.[29] Besides, this approach obliges courts to fall back upon standard common law principles of statutory interpretation, but these principles seem not to be appropriate in the case of the Constitution, as it inevitably lays down general principles. Indeed, the Constitution is not a detailed and easily changeable statute, whereas legislation, following the common law tradition, has been drafted having these standard common law principles of interpretation in mind.[30]

It seems, then, to be wrong to subject the Constitution, which is concerned with the statement of broad principles in general language, to a process of line-by-line parsing as if "it were a Finance Act".[31] By doing so, this approach may actually lead to unworkable and unacceptable results, which courts try to avoid by construing the text of the Constitution in a broad and purposive manner or by using a harmonious interpretation.[32]

It is moreover clear that the framers never intended the Constitution to be so construed; otherwise, they would probably have harmonised the drafting of Arts 40 to 44 in order to provide for uniformity as regards the State's duty to vindicate and protect fundamental rights.[33]

2.2 Historical Approach

By using the historical approach, regard may be had to the background in which the Constitution was passed.

27 "The Constitution, as the fundamental law of the State, must be accepted, interpreted and construed according to the words which are used; and these words must be given their literal meaning. Of course, the Constitution must be construed as a whole and not merely in parts and, where doubts or ambiguity exists, regard may be had to other provisions of the Constitution and to the situation that obtained and the laws which were in force when it was enacted. Plain words must, however, be given their plain meaning unless qualified or restricted by the Constitution itself" (*People (DPP) v O'Shea* [1982] IR 384)

28 See JM Kelly *The Irish Constitution* (4th ed, Gerard W Hogan and Gerry Whyte ed, Lexis Nexis Butterworths, 2003) xcix

29 R O' Connell, "Constitutional Interpretation" (2011).

30 See JM Kelly *The Irish Constitution* (4th ed, Gerard W Hogan and Gerry Whyte ed, Lexis Nexis Butterworths, 2003) xcix.

31 *ibid.* See also Gavan Duffy P in *NUR v Sullivan* [1947] IR 77; Dixon J in *O'Byrne v Minister for Finance* [1959] IR1; Costello J in *AG v Paperlink Ltd* [1984] ILRM 348.

32 See JM Kelly *The Irish Constitution* (4th ed, Gerard W Hogan and Gerry Whyte ed, Lexis Nexis Butterworths, 2003) xcix; R O'Connell, "Constitutional Interpretation" (2011).

33 See again JM Kelly, *The Irish Constitution* (4th ed, Gerard W Hogan and Gerry Whyte ed, Lexis Nexis Butterworths, 2003) xcix.

Accordingly, in the case *Crowley v Ireland*, the Supreme Court stated that "the Constitution must not be interpreted without reference to our history and to the conditions and intellectual climate of 1937".[34]

There are three versions of this approach. The first one, which is actually based, at least in part, on a long-established canon of ordinary interpretation of statute law,[35] focuses on the state of law in 1937: in order to gather the scope and intent of a constitutional provision, judges ought to consider the state of law when the Constitution was enacted.

As a case in point, in *Re Offences Against the State (Amendment) Bill*, concerning internment without trial, considerable weight should be attached, in the opinion of the Supreme Court, to the fact that several Acts authorising the detention of persons had been passed by the Irish Parliament prior to the enactment of the Constitution. Therefore,

> "the existence and effect of these Acts must have been within the knowledge of the framers of the Constitution and, nevertheless, there is no express prohibition in the Constitution against such legislation".[36]

In other words, if internment were to be regarded as prohibited at all, since it was a measure widely used before 1937, one would have expected an explicit prohibition of it in the text of Constitution.[37] Hence, the Supreme Court upheld the Bill.

The second version in based on the state of public opinion: the meaning of the Constitution should be determined by using the opinions and morals of the people at the time of the adoption of the Constitution.

Accordingly, in *McGee v Ireland*, a case concerning s 17 of the Criminal Law (Amendment) Act 1935 prohibiting the importation of contraceptives, the High Court considered that the section was enacted in 1935, only two years before the new Constitution. Furthermore, the provision was founded in the views expressed and public opinion when it was being passed into law and, in point of time, this was close to the moment at which the Constitution has been approved by the Parliament. Therefore, the latter must have believed that s 17 was valid under the new Constitution.

As one can easily guess, this interpretative method also is open to criticism.[38]

The Supreme Court has indeed rejected this approach in many cases, including the

---

34 *Crowley v Ireland* [1980] IR 102, 126 Kenny J.

35 JM Kelly, *The Irish Constitution* (4th ed, Gerard W Hogan and Gerry Whyte ed, Lexis Nexis Butterworths, 2003), cxi.

36 *In re Art 26 of the Constitution and the Offences Against the State (Amendment) Bill 1940* [1940] I.R. 470, at 478

37 R O'Connell, "Constitutional Interpretation" (2011).

38 In a comparative perspective, it is worth mentioning that the debate between originalism and living constitutionalism has been particular lively in the United States. For a critical analysis of this issue in the field of abortion, a field we will focus on below, see JM Balkin, "Abortion and Original Meaning" in *Constitutional Commentary* (University of Minnesota Law School), Vol 24, No 101, 2007.

McGee case, where the Supreme Court reversed the High Court decision, disclosing the idea that "it is the public opinion or mores of today, not of 1937, which ought to be looked at" in measuring a law against the Constitution.[39] Moreover, with particular reference to the values of prudence, justice and charity declared in the Preamble, Walsh J stated that "it is natural that from time to time the prevailing ideas may be conditioned by the passage of time; no interpretation of the Constitution is intended to be final for all time".[40]

Thus, in *TF v Ireland*, it was stated "regard must be had to the extent to which ideas and values prevailing at one period have been conditioned by the passage of time".[41] Similarly in *State (Healy) v O'Donoghue*, it was held that interpretation must accord with respect for the concepts of prudence, justice and charity.[42]

In other words, the Constitution has to be seen as a living and dynamic document.

For instance, in *A v Governor of Arbour Hill*, the Supreme Court, also citing the case *Sinnott v Minister for Education*, stressed that "the Constitution may be viewed as a living document 'which falls to be interpreted in accordance with contemporary circumstances including prevailing ideas and mores'".[43] In particular, the court explicitly highlights the "dynamic quality" of certain constitutional provisions, which "refer to concepts involving standards and values such as 'personal rights', 'the common good' and 'social justice'".[44] The issue of general clauses, while being shared with other branches of law, is of particular relevance in constitutional law, due to the statement of rather broad principles which deeply characterise the text of the Constitution and which are likely to change in the light of contemporary evolving ideas.

In any case, judicial practice with regard to the historical approach is uneven and shows some discontinuities.

For instance, in *State (Rollinson) v Kelly*, Henchy J stated: "I do not consider that the state of the law when the Constitution was enacted in 1937, or public opinion at the time of that enactment, are crucial consideration".[45] Scepticism about the historical approach emerges also in *Brennan v AG*, where Barrington J stated that historical interpretation might be influential or persuasive but will rarely be decisive.[46]

In two other cases, *Attorney General v Hamilton (No.1)* and *Attorney General v Hamilton (No.2)*, reference to historical circumstances, in order to demonstrate

---

39 *McGee v Ireland* [1974] IR 284.

40 *ibid*, 319.

41 [1995] 1 IR 321 (HC) 335.

42 See below section 2.

43 *A v Governor of Arbour Hill Prison* [2006] 4 IR 88 at 129.

44 *A v Governor of Arbour Hill Prison* [2006] 4 IR 88, 129 Murray CJ. See, among others, P Gallagher, "The Irish Constitution: Its Unique Nature and the Relevance of International Jurisprudence" (2010) 45 *Irish Jurist* 22, 31. In a comparative perspective, the idea of the Constitution as a living document is actually widespread, and, as a case in point, particularly interesting is the Canadian living-tree doctrine, which ensures interpretative dynamism in Canadian constitutional case law.

45 [1984] ILRM (SC) 636.

46 *Brennan v AG* [1983] ILRM 449 (HC) 478.

the manner by which a constitutional rule came to be drafted and reference to the historical background and historic case law, was considered to be highly relevant to the matters at issue and helpful to the interpretation of constitutional provisions.[47]

Such discrepancies in case law probably demonstrates how scarcely reliable the historical approach may be as a subjective application of it seems likely to prevail.[48]

Nevertheless, it has been argued that this approach can be of some usefulness with respect to certain legal institutions defined by the constitutional text, such as parliamentary privileges, the guarantee of jury trial, the concept of minor offences, etc.[49]

On the one hand, when the Constitution carefully defines certain powers, rights, privileges and procedures, it may be said that judges must follow the text carefully and that, if necessary, they should be aided by a historical understanding of what the framers sought to achieve. On the other hand, many fundamental concepts, such as equality before the law, personal liberty, property rights, etc, seem to have been deliberately left vague and imprecise by the drafters in order to let their scope become clearer in the light of experience, changing facts and circumstances.[50]

In any event, in many cases historical institutions existing when the Constitution was enacted, and sometimes even mentioned in the text, have been removed from the constitutional order by using other interpretative approaches.[51]

Moreover, it is impossible to exactly define the standards and mores of the Irish people in 1937, or even today.[52] It is also difficult to know what the precise state of affairs was in 1937, since parliamentary debates do not help ascertain the objective intention of the framers, and records of the drafting of the Constitution were made available only in 1987. In any case, it seems to be odd to use the state of law in 1937 to construe the Constitution, since it is itself the benchmark of legality.[53]

Another version of the historical interpretation that should be mentioned is the original understanding approach. It is important to point out that, despite occasional judicial references to it, this approach in unlikely to have widespread application in Irish courts for various reasons.[54] Indeed, in contrast to the US original intent doctrine, in Ireland documentary materials that might support the reasoning are not generally available. The drafting of the 1937 Constitution took place in secret and parliamentary debates, as already indicated, cannot assist with an objective assessment of the drafters' intention. Moreover, the mere fact that the Constitution

---

47 *Attorney General v Hamilton (No.1)* [1993] 2 IR 250 (SC); *Attorney General v Hamilton (No.2)* [1993] 3 IR 227 (SC).See J M Kelly, *The Irish Constitution* (4th ed, Gerard W Hogan and Gerry Whyte ed, Lexis Nexis Butterworths, 2003) cxii.

48 *ibid*, cxiii.

49 *ibid.*

50 *ibid.*

51 R O'Connell, "Constitutional Interpretation" (2011).

52 See *Norris v AG* [1984] IR 36.

53 R O'Connell, "Constitutional Interpretation" (2011).

54 See JM Kelly, *The Irish Constitution* (4th ed, Gerard W Hogan and Gerry Whyte ed, Lexis Nexis Butterworths, 2003) cxvi.

has been enacted by plebiscite and quite often amended through referenda[55] suggests that the objective meaning of the text, rather than the supposed intention of the framers, should carry the most weight in constitutional interpretation.[56]

2.3 Purposive (or Broad) Approach

By using the purposive approach judges reject the excessive literalism of some instances and choose rather to construe the text of the Constitution in a broad way so as to carry into effect its purposes and objectives, thus making the Constitution an effective tool to achieve them. This way judges are less likely to fall back on standard common law methods of interpretation.[57]

In *Attorney General v Paperlink Ltd*, the court stressed the fact that "(t)he Constitution is a political instrument as well as a legal document … A purposive, rather than a strictly literal approach to the interpretation … is appropriate".[58]

By using this approach, in *Murray*, the Supreme Court rejected the claim by a married couple, who were serving a life sentence for the murder of a policeman, to be allowed to conceive children. The court gave a purposive reading to the family rights provisions: despite the reference to "inalienable and imprescriptible rights, antecedent and superior to all positive law",[59] the exercise of these rights can be reasonably limited by the State like the exercise of other constitutional rights.[60] The High Court held that the correct approach to interpretation was the one "which would look at the whole text of the Constitution and identify its purpose and objective in protecting human rights".[61] The Supreme Court upheld this decision on appeal.[62]

According to this approach, it is inappropriate to rely only on a literal or historical interpretation, especially as regards the fundamental rights protected by the Constitution, which cannot be confined by a literal interpretation of its text.

---

55 Amendments to the Irish Constitution since 1937 up to now are 29, but some of them, although listed in the Constitution, have not been actually enacted. Except for the first two amendments enacted under transitory provisions, according to Art 46, any proposal for an amendment to the Constitution shall "be submitted by Referendum to the decision of the people".

56 See JM Kelly *The Irish Constitution* (4th ed, Gerard W Hogan and Gerry Whyte ed, Lexis Nexis Butterworths, 2003) cxvii.

57 *ibid*, xcix.

58 [1984] ILRM 373 (HC) 385.

59 Art 41.1.1°: "The State recognises the Family as the natural primary and fundamental unit group of Society, and as a moral institution possessing inalienable and imprescriptible rights, antecedent and superior to all positive law".

60 As Costello J observed in the High Court "the power of the State to delimit the exercise of constitutionally protected rights is expressly given in some Articles and not referred to at all in others, but this cannot mean that, where absent, the power does not exist. For example, no reference is made in Article 41, to any restrictive power, but it is clear that the exercise by the Family of its imprescriptible and inalienable rights to integrity as a unit group can be severely and validly restricted by the State when, for example, its laws permit a father to be banned from a family home or allow for the imprisonment of both parents of young children". *Murray v Ireland* [1985] IR 532, 538.

61 *ibid*, 539.

62 [1991] ILRM 465.

Thus, in *State (Quinn) v Ryan*, the Supreme Court held that the intention of the Constitution

> "was that rights of substance were being assured to the individual and that the courts were the custodians of these rights. As a necessary corollary, it follows that no one can with impunity set these rights at naught or circumvent them, and that the court's powers in this regard are as ample as the defence of the Constitution requires".[63]

As we shall see below, a similar idea led to the acknowledgement of unenumerated constitutional rights.

2.4 Harmonious Approach

The harmonious approach, although it "should, in logic, be the first canon of interpretation of the Constitution", was articulated at a later stage,[64] when the wide and deep normative impact of the Constitution had started to be experienced.

This approach requires the Constitution to be read as a whole by construing each provision in order to harmonise it with the other parts of the Fundamental Law, thus smoothing out any apparent contradictions.[65]

It was first expressed in *Dillane v Ireland*, where the Supreme Court ruled

> "[u]nder the doctrine of harmonious interpretation, which requires, where possible, the relevant constitutional provisions to be construed and applied so that each will be given due weight in the circumstances of the case".[66]

Also, in *O'Shea*, one of the dissenters based his opinion on the idea of harmonious interpretation saying that:

> "[a]ny single constitutional right or power is but a component in an ensemble of interconnected and interacting provisions which must be brought into play as part of a larger composition, and which must be given such an integrated interpretation as will fit it harmoniously into the general constitutional order and modulation".[67]

Again, in *Tormey v Ireland*, the Supreme Court, adopting a harmonious interpretation, stated that constitutional provisions "must not be looked at in isolation, but be treated as interlocking parts of the general constitutional scheme". Consequently,

> "where two constructions of a provision are open in the light of the Constitution

---

63 [1965] IR 70, 133.

64 See J M Kelly, *The Irish Constitution* (4th ed, Gerard W Hogan and Gerry Whyte ed, Lexis Nexis Butterworths, 2003) ci.

65 *ibid*; see also, among others, O'Connell, "Constitutional Interpretation" (2011); JP Casey, *Constitutional Law in Ireland* (3rd ed, Sweet & Maxwell, 2000) 378; R Byrne and P McCutcheon *The Irish Legal System: Cases and Materials* (5th ed, Bloomsbury Professional, 2009) 629.

66 *Dillane v Ireland* [1980] ILRM 167.

67 *People (DPP) v O'Shea* [1982] IR 384 (SC) 436 Henchy J.

as a whole …, the court should adopt the construction which will achieve the smooth and harmonious operation of the Constitution".[68]

It might be interesting to note that as regards this interpretative method, it has been argued that there might be a problem when the reference is not to further articles of the Constitution but rather to some tacitly understood principle or even to the "spirit" of the Constitution. Accordingly, the harmonious approach, if not related to other parts of the expressed text of the Constitution, seems, to some extent, likely to open the door to judicial policy-making.[69]

This interpretative approach is invoked[70] or mentioned as important, or at least used though not directly mentioned, in many cases, such as in *Attorney General v X* concerning abortion and in *A v Governor of Arbour Hill Prison*.[71] As we shall further see below, harmonious interpretation has a significant role in the field of fundamental rights. Moreover, according to the harmonious interpretation doctrine, Irish judges acknowledged the idea of a hierarchy of constitutional rights.[72]

2.5 "Natural Law" Approach

This method of interpretation is characterised by the reference to prevailing ideas, extra-textual values, seen as "evolving moral standards".

A good example of this approach may be found in *State (Healy) v Donoghue*, in which O'Higgins CJ expressly stated:

> "the Preamble makes it clear that the rights given by the Constitution must be considered in accordance with the concepts of prudence, justice and charity which may gradually change or develop as society changes and develops, and which fall to be interpreted from time to time in accordance with prevailing ideas. … The Constitution did not seek to impose for all time the ideas prevalent or accepted with regard to those virtues at the time of its enactment."[73]

We have already seen what Walsh J said in *McGee* with reference to the values of prudence, justice and charity declared in the Preamble, in whose light judges ought to interpret the Constitution and which may be conditioned by the passage of time.

A "natural law" approach may also be used to avoid an excessively literalist interpretation of particular constitutional provisions, especially when this method can lead to an interpretation inconsistent with generally accepted principles of justice.[74]

---

68 *Tormey v Ireland* [1985] IR 289, 296 Henchy J.

69 See JM Kelly, *The Irish Constitution* (4th ed, Gerard W Hogan and Gerry Whyte ed, Lexis Nexis Butterworths, 2003) civ.

70 See, among others, *State v Walsh* [1981] IR 412 or, more recently, *MS case* [2003] 1 IR 606. See also O'Connell, "Constitutional Interpretation" (2011).

71 See below section 4 and section §3.

72 See below section 4.

73 [1976] IR 325, 347.

74 See JM Kelly *The Irish Constitution* (4th ed, Gerard W Hogan and Gerry Whyte ed, Lexis Nexis Butterworths, 2003) cxviii.

Above all, this natural law reasoning had an important influence on the development of the unenumerated personal rights doctrine. The leading case in this area is *Ryan v Attorney General*, where the courts held that personal rights are not confined to those rights expressly specified in Art 40.3 of the Constitution, but should be extended to other rights implicit in it or which can be inferred from it. In particular, this case recognised the "right of bodily integrity" even if it is not specifically mentioned in the Constitution.

The emergence and identification of these unenumerated constitutional rights by the judiciary is highly linked to the use of natural law, i.e. to the prevailing moral standards and extra-textual values, which are often tied to the Christian nature of the State, emerging from the wording of the Preamble.[75]

Thus, in *Ryan*, Kenny J in the High Court held that

> "the personal rights which may be involved to invalidate legislation are not confined to those specified in Article 40, but include all those rights which result from Christian and democratic nature of the State … There are many personal rights of the citizen which follow from the Christian and democratic nature of the State which are not mentioned in Article 40 at all".[76]

The Supreme Court confirmed the existence of such rights, but expressed no opinion about Kenny J's derivation of them.[77]

As a further example, although in the opposite direction, in *State (Nicolaou) v An Bord Uchtála*, the Supreme Court refused to acknowledge what the applicant considered to be the "natural right" of the father of an illegitimate child to be involved in its upbringing, arguing that "the Court has not been satisfied that any such right has ever been recognized as part of the natural law". Indeed "[i]f an illegitimate child has a natural right to look to his father for support that would impose a duty on the father but would not of itself confer any right upon the father".[78]

Once again, in *McGee*, the Supreme Court clearly stated:

> "natural rights or human rights are not created by law but the Constitution … confirms their existence and gives them protection. The individual has natural and human rights over which the State has no authority".[79]

---

75 See below section 4.

76 [1965] IR 294 (HC) 313.

77 *ibid*, 344–345. This reticence has been noted as a reason for treating the unenumerated rights doctrine with some reserve: *TD v Minister for Education* [2001] 4 IR 259 (SC) 281 Keane CJ.

78 *State (Nicolaou) v An Bord Uchtála* [1966] IR 567, 643.

79 [1974] IR 284 (SC) 310. From a comparative point of view, it might be interesting to mention the Italian debate on the open or closed nature of the provision on inviolable rights under Art 2 of the Italian Constitution, which, similarly to the idea enshrined in the Irish Constitution that personal rights are antecedent to the Constitution itself, declares: "The Republic recognises and guarantees inviolable rights of man". A similar idea might be also gathered from the Ninth Amendment to the US Constitution, according to which: "The enumeration in the Constitution, of certain rights, shall not be construed to deny or disparage others retained by the people". Unwritten rights have been also widely recognised by the Supreme Court in India, as well as in Switzerland, where the *Tribunal Fédéral*—interpreting the former Constitution—recognised

It means that not only ought constitutional rights, insofar as they are rooted in natural law, to be regarded as superior to positive law and may invalidate it, but that there are many natural rights that are antecedent to the Constitution and are not expressly mentioned therein and that can be rather found in extra-textual sources and values.[80] Natural law is therefore seen as a source of fundamental rights.

It has even been argued that certain natural rights are so fundamental as to represent a natural law limit on the constitutional amendment by referendum. However, it is important to stress that this idea is repugnant to the very text of Art 46 of the Constitution, according to which "[a]ny provision of this Constitution may be amended" and "[e]very proposal for an amendment of this Constitution shall ... be submitted by Referendum to the decision of the people". It follows that it might be at odds with the principles of democratic government and popular sovereignty.[81] Above all, as we shall see below, the Supreme Court itself, in the abortion information case, clearly rejected the notion of limits on the Constitution based on natural law.[82]

Moreover, we may here briefly note that the "natural law" approach is also open to criticism because it might be difficult to determine exactly in each case which idea of natural law courts are referring to. In addition, this approach might too easily lead to a greater amount of judicial discretion and judicial policy-making.[83]

However, although "natural law" as an interpretative method has actually only a limited application,[84] the Supreme Court continues to recognise the applicability of evolving moral standards as a legitimate tool in interpreting the Constitution.[85]

The reference to these prevailing standards and to the values declared in the Preamble, in the specific field of fundamental rights, will be further analysed below. Prior to it, we should now briefly mention other important sources to which Irish courts often refer in interpreting the Constitution, particularly foreign and international materials.

3. The Relevance of Foreign and International Case Law and Legal Provisions

The relevance of extra-textual values and principles in constitutional interpretation, discussed above, implies that values considered as relevant moral standards by judges might be found outside the Constitution and even outside other Irish legal

---

the existence of "libertés non écrites". See, for instance, M Rossinelli, *Les libertés non écrites. Contribution à l'étude du pouvoir créateur du juge constitutionnel* (Payot, 1987).

80 See also B Doolan, *Constitutional Law and Constitutional Rights in Ireland* (Gill & Macmillan, 1988) 133.

81 See, among others, JM Kelly, *The Irish Constitution* (4th ed, Gerard W Hogan and Gerry Whyte ed, Lexis Nexis Butterworths, 2003) cxviii.

82 The Supreme Court thus recognised the Constitution to be superior to natural law, see below section 4.

83 See JM Kelly, *The Irish Constitution* (4th ed, Gerard W Hogan and Gerry Whyte ed, Lexis Nexis Butterworths, 2003) cxviii.

84 *ibid.*

85 See below *A v Governor of Arbour Hill* and *AG* v *X*; See R O'Connell, "Constitutional Interpretation" (2011).

sources. It has therefore been argued[86] that this grounds the legitimacy of reference to foreign and international materials and to other persuasive sources.[87] In addition to the text of the Constitution and relevant decisions of the Irish superior courts, other sources, though not binding, are indeed likely to have a persuasive role in constitutional interpretation. For example, work by legal writers, social and scientific work, political history and, although more rarely, custom have been used as guidance in defining the scope and meaning of constitutional provisions, as well as decisions of other national, foreign or international courts.[88] In particular, the reference to foreign and international case law and legal provisions has considerably enriched the Irish constitutional case law.[89]

Furthermore, as the Irish legal system is part of the common law system, Irish judges are likely to take into account as useful guides decisions made by courts in other common law countries—such as the US, Canada, England, Australia or New Zealand—and in countries whose legal systems have been heavily influenced by the common law—such as South Africa.

Moreover, certain fundamental rights might be said to stem from natural law, from what it means to behave morally or to be a human person and a rational being, as often expressly stated within the Irish Constitution.[90] Accordingly, one should acknowledge that they might transcend a specific legal system or a specific national constitution and therefore recognise the usefulness of looking at foreign law, and in particular at solutions adopted by other constitutional courts, when dealing with similar constitutional issues.[91] The Irish constitutional case law shows that the judiciary often recognised the value of considering foreign and international sources in interpreting constitutional rights and in dealing with values shared by other legal systems.

Among them, references to US case law are particularly frequent, as well as those to Canadian and European authorities.

Just to give a few examples, in *Quinn's Supermarket v Attorney General* [92], the court, addressing the question of state-imposed religious "positive discrimination" and thus dealing with the Church-State case law, looked at US precedents. In the

---

86 See, among others, R O'Connell, "Constitutional Interpretation" (2011).

87 Other constitutions contain a specific article providing for this kind of reference. In Spain, for instance, under Art 10: "The principles relating to the fundamental rights and liberties recognised by the Constitution shall be interpreted in conformity with the Universal Declaration of Human Rights and the international treaties and agreements thereon ratified by Spain". Art 39 of the South African Constitution, dealing with "Interpretation of Bill of Rights", expressly states that "When interpreting the Bill of Rights, a court, tribunal or forum … b) must consider international law; and c) may consider foreign law". For a critical analysis of the dialogue among constitutional courts, see G. De Vergottini, *Oltre il dialogo tra le Corti. Giudici, diritto straniero, comparazione* (Il Mulino, 2010).

88 R O'Connell, "Constitutional Interpretation" (2011).

89 P Gallagher, "The Irish Constitution: Its Unique Nature and the Relevance of International Jurisprudence" (2010) 45 *Irish Jurist* 22, 23.

90 See below section 4.

91 P Gallagher, "The Irish Constitution: Its Unique Nature and the Relevance of International Jurisprudence" (2010) 45 *Irish Jurist* 22, 33.

92 *Quinn's Supermarket Ltd. v Attorney General* [1972] IR 1.

case of *Re A Ward of Court* [93], as regards withholding medical treatments and the right to die, the Irish judges took into account US authorities too. In the *McGee case* relating to the use of contraceptives, the Irish Supreme Court, pointing out that the interpretation of the Constitution "is given in the light of prevailing ideas and concepts", which may be conditioned by the passage of time, held that "the development of the constitutional law of the United States of America is ample proof of it". Indeed, "while not professing to be governed by the precepts of Christianity", the US Constitution, in particular its Ninth Amendment, "recognises the existence of rights other than those referred to expressly in it and in its amendment". Thus, the Irish Supreme Court refers to "the development of the constitutional law of the United States" and to "the views of the United States Supreme Court, as reflected in the decisions interpreting that constitution and in the development of their constitutional law" which, as well as those of the Irish Supreme Court, "appear firmly to reject legal positivism as a jurisprudential guide".[94]

Decisions of the Canadian Supreme Court and of the European Court of Human Rights had also an interesting influence on the acknowledgement of the proportionality doctrine. The proportionality test was first applied in *Heaney v Ireland*,[95] citing explicitly the case law of these two courts, and it is now likely to become more frequent due to the growing influence of European developments. Again, in *Murphy v Attorney General*,[96] as regards the taxation of married couples and the constitutional protection of family and marriage, there is an analysis of the legal framework for this particular issue in the United States, Germany and Italy, as well as references to the decisions of the US Supreme Court and of the German and Italian Constitutional Courts. As to more recent cases, one can, for example, find citations of the South African Constitutional Court and of the Supreme Court of Zimbabwe in *McCann v Judges of Monaghan District Court*.[97] In this respect, it might be worth pointing out the different nature of the reference to German and Italian law or other civil law systems, because in this case the reference is to rules that are not part of the common law. Such a reference is also different from the one to, for instance, the law of the European Union, to the European Convention of Human Rights or to the Universal Declaration of Human Rights, since this kind of reference is related to international treaties and agreements ratified by Ireland, which is therefore party to them.

Another rather recent case in point is *A v Governor of Arbour Hill Prison*, where the Supreme Court used foreign law in deciding the intricate constitutional issue concerning the effects of the declaration of invalidity, in particular the retrospective effects of a declaration of unconstitutionality on conviction. In the opinion of the court, the acknowledgement of the distinction between the declaration of invalidity of an Act and the retrospective effects of this declaration on previous and finally decided cases is reinforced

93 *Re a Ward of Court* (withholding medical treatment)(No.2) [1996] 2 I.R. 79.

94 *McGee v Ireland* [1974] IR 284.

95 [1994] 3 IR 593. See P Gallagher, "The Irish Constitution: Its Unique Nature and the Relevance of International Jurisprudence" (2010) 45 *Irish Jurist* 22, 39.

96 [1982] IR 241.

97 [2010] 1 ILRM 17 at 50, see again P Gallagher, "The Irish Constitution: Its Unique Nature and the Relevance of International Jurisprudence" (2010) 45 *Irish Jurist* 22, 39–40.

> "by the fact that such a principled approach is consonant with the general principles of constitutional adjudication and interpretation in other legal systems generally but particularly in those where a judicial declaration of invalidity of law also applies *ab initio*".[98]

In his reasoning, the judge stressed the importance of looking at foreign authorities in dealing with such difficult constitutional issues and refers in particular to the European Court of Justice, the European Court of Human Rights, the Supreme Court of India and US and Canadian sources.[99]

Furthermore, international treaties might also be a legitimate guide to interpretation, although without normative force if not domestically incorporated by an Irish statute[100].

However, the reference to foreign case law is not unlimited and, as recently restated, "must have due regard to the institutional and contextual distinction which exists between all states". In addition, the Supreme Court stated that foreign case law might have a persuasive value "only to the extent that [it relates] to the interpretation of analogous provisions of our Constitution and are consistent with the approach of our courts to issues of interpretation".

It has then been argued that the relevance of foreign sources might actually depend on the level of uniqueness attributed by judges to the provision of the Irish Constitution that they have to interpret.[101]

4. Fundamental Rights and the Role of Constitutional Interpretation

Constitutional interpretation in the field of fundamental rights is consistent with what we already said on the main different interpretative approaches.

First, we should consider that many provisions of the Irish Constitution reflect in their actual text the idea of natural rights and contain explicit reference to Christian values.

For instance, in addition to the personal rights embodied in Art 40, according to Art 41, "the State recognises the Family ... as a moral institution possessing inalienable and imprescriptible rights, antecedent and superior to all positive law". As regards education, Art 42 acknowledging the family as the primary and natural educator of the child, "guarantees to respect the inalienable right and duty of parents to provide ... for the religious and moral, intellectual, physical and social education of their children". In exceptional cases the State, as guardian of the common good, shall endeavour to supply the place of parents "but always with due regard for the natural and imprescriptible rights of the child". Moreover, according to Art 43, concerning

98 *A v Governor of Arbour Hill Prison* [2006] 4 IR 88, 142.
99 *ibid* at 122, see also P Gallagher, "The Irish Constitution: Its Unique Nature and the Relevance of International Jurisprudence" (2010) 45 *Irish Jurist* 22, 43.
100 R O'Connell, "Constitutional Interpretation" (2011).
101 P Gallagher, "The Irish Constitution: Its Unique Nature and the Relevance of International Jurisprudence" (2010) 45 *Irish Jurist* 22, 23, 41.

private property "(t)he State acknowledges that man, in virtue of his rational being, has the natural right, antecedent to positive law, to the private ownership of external goods".

The Preamble itself begins with a clear and direct reference to God, declaring that the people of Éire adopt, enact and give to themselves the Constitution "[i] n the Name of the Most Holy Trinity, from Whom is all authority and to Whom, as our final end, all actions both of men and States must be referred". In addition, Art 6 states that "all powers of government, legislative, executive and judicial, derive, under God, from the people". It is therefore clear that the Irish Constitution acknowledges, both in its Preamble and in Art 6, God as the ultimate source of all authority.[102] Furthermore, according to the Preamble, the people of Éire, humbly acknowledge their "obligations to our Divine Lord, Jesus Christ, Who sustained our fathers through centuries of trial" and, above all, by means of the Constitution they seek "to promote the common good, with due observance of prudence, justice and charity, so that the dignity and freedom of the individual may be assured".

We have already seen how the judiciary does refer to natural law, extra-textual values and to general concepts such as prudence, justice and charity in interpreting the Constitution. As regards the role of religion, it is worth noting that the Irish constitutional case law contains references not only to the Christian nature of the State but also to other Christian sources, such as Encyclical Letters by the Head of the Roman Catholic Church, philosophers or theologians.

As already pointed out, unenumerated constitutional rights are considered to be, as stated by the High Court in the *Ryan* case, "those rights which result from the Christian and democratic nature of the State"[103]. In the same decision, the court found that the existence of a right to bodily integrity "gets support from a passage in the Encyclical Letter 'Peace on Earth'"[104] and quoted a passage of it. As another example, in *State (M) v Minister for Foreign Affairs*, the right to travel outside the State was also regarded as "arising from the Christian and democratic nature of the State—though not enumerated in the Constitution".[105] In *McGee*, Walsh J indicates charity as "the greatest additional virtue introduced by Christianity" and to justice as the highest human virtue in the opinion of Aristotle and Christian philosophers.[106]

As another case in point, in *Norris v Attorney General*, dealing with homosexuality, O'Higgins CJ considered that with the advent of Christianity the idea of homosexual conducts as contrary to the order of nature and as an affront to both society and God,

> "found clear expression in the teaching of St Paul and has been repeated over the centuries by the doctors and leaders of the Church in every land in which the Gospel of Christ has been preached".[107]

---

[102] See also Walsh J in *McGee v Ireland* [1974] IR 284.

[103] *Ryan v. Attorney General* [1965] IR 294 at 312.

[104] "Pacem in Terris", Encyclical of Pope John XXIII *On Establishing Universal Peace In Truth, Justice, Charity And Liberty*, promulgated on 11 April 1963.

[105] *State v Minister for Foreign Affairs* [1979] IR 73; see also B Doolan, *Constitutional Law and Constitutional Rights in Ireland* (Gill & Macmillan, 1988) 184.

[106] [1974] IR 284, 318–319.

[107] *Norris v AG* [1984] IR 36.

He further stated that although this strict view began to be questioned by individual Christian theologians, "it remains the teaching of all Christian Churches that homosexual acts are wrong".[108] Moreover, with particular reference to the Preamble of the Irish Constitution he explicitly found that

> "it cannot be doubted that the people, so asserting and acknowledging their obligations to our Divine Lord Jesus Christ, were proclaiming a deep religious conviction and faith and an intention to adopt a Constitution consistent with that conviction and faith and with Christian beliefs".

Therefore, despite the reference to the European Court of Human Rights in *Dudgeon*, he upheld the challenged Act considering a law that qualifies such conduct as criminal to be consistent with the Irish Constitution.

However, it is worth noting that such a strict religious approach is not that frequent and, above all, it is not unquestioned. In the same case, Henchy J, in his dissenting opinion, adopted a completely different approach,[109] stating that before entering on the question of unconstitutionality, it should be pointed out that judges were

> "not called upon in this case to express an opinion upon whether the law on this topic should be as it is or upon what the purpose of the law should be. Such considerations are for moral philosophers, legal theorists, lawmakers..."

Following a more secular approach, he then stated clearly:

> "the learned judge ... in substituting his own conclusions on the personal and societal effects of the questioned provisions, seems to have laid undue stress on the fact that the prohibited acts, especially sodomy, are contrary to the standards of morality advocated by the Christian Churches in this State. With respect, I do not think that should be treated as a guiding consideration".

He also stressed the importance of the necessary balance between the common good and the dignity and freedom of individuals, founding that what is considered to be necessary to one's dignity and freedom by a person might represent an exercise of immorality for another one. Therefore, in the opinion of the judge,

> "[t]he pluralism necessary for the preservation of constitutional requirements in the Christian, democratic State envisaged by the Constitution means that the sanctions of the criminal law may be attached to immoral acts only when the common good required their proscription as crimes".

Besides, notwithstanding the existence of religious references and the need to interpret constitutional rights in the light of the concepts of justice, prudence and charity, what clearly seems to emerge from a broader analysis of the Irish constitutional case law is the concept of evolving moral standards and therefore the importance of considering the Constitution as a living document.

---

108 *ibid.*

109 See also the opinion of McCarthy J.

In this respect, it is interesting to analyse the reasoning of Walsh J in *McGee*. On the one hand, he stated that, considering the acknowledgement of Christianity in the Preamble and the reference to God in Art 6, it must be accepted that the Constitution deals with human rights as belonging to the category of natural law as a theological concept, rather than simply as an ethical one. On the other hand, he stressed the difficulties related to the use of natural law[110] and found that

> "it falls finally upon the judges to interpret the Constitution and in doing so to determine, where necessary, the rights which are superior or antecedent to positive law or which are imprescriptible or inalienable".[111]

In doing so, one of the guidelines contained in the Constitution and useful in performing this difficult duty by judges is that "the very structure and content of the Articles dealing with fundamental rights clearly indicate that justice is not subordinated to the law"[112]. Thus, refusing legal positivism as an interpretative guide, the court stated, as already mentioned, that "the judges must [...] as best they can from their training and their experience interpret constitutional rights in accordance with their idea of prudence, justice and charity" and that it is natural that the prevailing ideas of these virtues might be conditioned by the passage of time.[113] Moreover, this case shows that the acknowledgement of the same right is possible even without any reference to religious elements, as Henchy J did in his concurring opinion.[114]

In any case, despite the reference to the values enshrined in the Preamble, according to the concept of evolving moral standards and to the dynamic nature of certain constitutional rights, judges are concerned with the need of a modern and pluralistic society to develop and thus to evolve its constitutional law. In this respect, constitutional interpretation might reveal its leading and even innovative role in the development of constitutional rights as regards both the meaning and scope of certain provisions and the identification of new unwritten rights. It should also be considered that the Constitution itself grants to the courts the power to give it an authoritative interpretation, and therefore "the Constitution means what the superior courts declare it to mean".[115] It follows that constitutional interpretation plays a vital role in adapting constitutional rights to contemporary values, thus preventing them from remaining linked to principles or to ideas of prudence, justice and charity perceived as outdated or even undesirable.

In this regard, one might acknowledge that exactly this "in-built capacity to evolve through judicial interpretation" might give the Irish Constitution "its lasting strength

110 "What exactly natural law is and what precisely it imports is a question which has exercised the minds of theologians for many centuries and on which they are not yet fully agreed. While the Constitution speaks of certain rights as being imprescriptible or being antecedent and superior to all positive law, it does not specify them.". *McGee v Attorney General* [1974] IR 284 at 318.

111 *ibid.*

112 *ibid.*

113 *Ibid*, at 319

114 *ibid.*, at 322

115 B Doolan, *Constitutional Law and Constitutional Rights in Ireland* (Gill & Macmillan, 1988) 5.

and the capacity to achieve justice and to protect the dignity and freedom of the individual – ideals specifically mentioned in its Preamble".[116]

The extensive development of fundamental rights by the Irish Superior Courts is therefore the result of the abovementioned doctrine of unenumerated rights which has been significantly strengthened by the view that constitutional rights have a dynamic nature, rather than a static one, thus allowing judges to follow changing conditions, mores and social needs.

This unenumerated constitutional rights doctrine leads us to the very core of the issue concerning the function of the High Court and the Supreme Court. Indeed, such a doctrine demonstrates the increasing significance of the role of courts in the development of Irish constitutional law—including the acknowledgement of the existence of further constitutional rights not expressly enumerated in the text of the Constitution—through an "evolutionary" interpretation. Thus, in *Ryan*, the court said:

> "if … [the general guarantee in Art 40.3] relates to personal rights other than those specified in Article 40, the High Court and the Supreme Court have the difficult and responsible duty of ascertaining and declaring what are the personal rights of citizens which are guaranteed by the Constitution".[117]

Although more recently courts have been less willing to identify new unenumerated rights, under this doctrine many important rights have been increasingly identified and thus constitutionally protected, including the right to free movement within the State, employment rights including the right to work and to earn one's livelihood, the right to due process of law, the right to justice and fair procedures, the right to communicate, and the rights of a non-marital child.[118] This wide range of fundamental rights is probably one of the reasons why judges do not need to identify other constitutional rights in order to cope with new challenging issues, which might be included in the protection of a list of unwritten constitutional rights which has been previously developed.

Particularly interesting is the role of constitutional interpretation in recognising and enlarging personal rights in the field of medical law and individual autonomy, in particular as regards the patient's right to consent to treatment and the right to refuse treatments, falling back on the unspecified constitutional right to bodily integrity or on the right to life.[119]

With reference to the development of fundamental rights and judicial activism, a leading role is also played by the doctrine of harmonious interpretation, which is

---

116 P Gallagher, "The Irish Constitution: Its Unique Nature and the Relevance of International Jurisprudence" (2010) 45 *Irish Jurist* 22, 32.

117 See G Casey, "Are There Unenumerated Rights in the Irish Constitution?" (http://www.ucd.ie/philosophy/staff/gerardcasey/casey/UnenRiIrCon.pdf) 5.

118 For reference to the relevant case law see JM Kelly *The Irish Constitution* (4th ed, Gerard W Hogan and Gerry Whyte ed, Lexis Nexis Butterworths, 2003) 755–789; RH Grimes and PT Horgan, *Introduction to Law in the Republic of Ireland* (Merlin Publishing, 1988) 174.

119 See for instance *Walsh v Family Planning Services Limited* [1992] 1 IR 496; *Geoghegan v Harris* [2000] 3 IR 536; In *Re a Ward of Court (No 2)* [1996] 2 IR 79.

likely to gain increasing importance, especially considering the wane of the natural law approach in Irish constitutional case law.[120]

To be more precise, there has been a significant change in the use of natural law since the 1990s, and in this respect it has been argued that "the issue that reoriented the debate was abortion".[121]

Without wishing to deeply analyse the evolution of the abortion debate in Irish constitutional law, it is worth making some preliminary remarks on the constitutional framework for abortion in order to show how courts tried to cope with challenging legal and ethical issues, through constitutional interpretation.

In particular, the Eighth Amendment to the Constitution acknowledged in 1983 the right to life of the unborn, with due regard to the equal right to life of the mother. In 1992 the Thirteenth Amendment to the Constitution provided that Art 40.3.3°, i.e. the right to life of the unborn, would not limit freedom to travel between Ireland and another state, and according to the Fourteenth Amendment, it would not limit freedom to obtain or make available information relating to services lawfully available in another state.

With reference to the role of natural law, a landmark case is *Re Regulation of Information Bill 1995*, i.e. the decision of the Supreme Court on the reference to it by the President of the Regulation of Information Bill 1995, concerning "Services Outside the State for Termination of Pregnancies".[122]

Counsel for the unborn argued that the Fourteenth Amendment was inconsistent with the Eighth Amendment because the provision of such information "would constitute assistance in the destruction of the life of the unborn".[123] Thus, in the argument of the counsel,

> "any provision in the Constitution or in any legislation which would permit or render lawful the giving or obtaining of such information was contrary to the natural law right to life of the unborn".[124]

Moreover, counsel expressly stated that "the natural law is the foundation upon which the Constitution was built and ranks superior to the Constitution" and therefore "no provision of the Constitution or of any Act enacted by the Legislature or any judicial interpretation thereof can be contrary to Natural Law, and if it is, cannot

[120] Coming back to the already mentioned *Norris* case, Henchy J's dissenting opinion seems to apply a harmonious approach pointing out that the essence of that case was whether the "right of privacy, construed in the context of the Constitution as a whole and given its true evaluation or standing in the hierarchy of constitutional priorities, excludes as constitutionally inconsistent the impugned statutory provisions".

[121] B Lewis, "Liberal Democracy, Natural Law and Jurisprudence: Thomistic Notes on an Irish Debate" in *Reassessing The Liberal State: Reading Maritain's "Man And The State"* (Catholic University of America Press, 2001) 141, quoted by J Jeffers, "Dead or Alive? The Fate of Natural Law in Irish Constitutional Jurisprudence" in (2003) 2 *Galway Student Law Review* 2, 8.

[122] [1995] 1 IR 1.

[123] *ibid*, 37.

[124] *ibid.*

be enforced".[125] Consequently, the Supreme Court was asked to deal with the role of natural law in the development of constitutional case law with particular regard to the identification of "the personal rights of the citizen" referred to in Art 40.3.1° of the Constitution. The court pinpointed the far-reaching implications of such an issue finding that

> "it is fundamental to this argument that, what is described as 'the natural law' is the fundamental law of this State and as such is antecedent and superior to all positive law, including the Constitution and that it is impermissible for the People to exercise the power of amendment of the Constitution by way of variation, addition or repeal, as permitted by Article 46 of the Constitution unless such amendment is compatible with the natural law and existing provisions of the Constitution and if they purport to do so, such amendment had no effect".

The Supreme Court expressly concluded that "[t]he Court does not accept this argument".[126]

The court went on to cite those constitutional provisions that illustrate the supremacy of the Constitution[127] and consider important case law involving unwritten personal rights, concluding that

> "the Courts, as they were and are bound to, recognised the Constitution as the fundamental law of the State to which the organs of the State were subject and at no stage recognised the provisions of the natural law as superior to the Constitution".[128]

The Supreme Court, through the consideration of cases recognising the existence of unwritten rights, acknowledged the unenumerated rights doctrine and the role of judges in interpreting such personal rights in accordance with the ideas of prudence, justice and charity in the light of changing moral standards. However, it clearly refused the recognition of the superiority of natural law on the Constitution and the idea of natural law as a limit to the amendment of the Constitution by referenda.

Coming back to harmonious interpretation, it can be found that as a general rule the idea that each constitutional provision should be interpreted with due regard to the Constitution as a whole, thus in harmonious relation with other constitutional rights, might now be said to be well entrenched in Irish constitutional case law.

In this respect, we should also mention that in relation to this doctrine, and actually with the purpose of coping with it, Irish case law began to acknowledge the idea of a hierarchy of constitutional rights. This was first accepted and clearly stated in *People v Shaw*: "there is a hierarchy of constitutional rights and, when a conflict

---

[125] *ibid*, 37–38.

[126] *ibid*, 38.

[127] The Supreme Court mentioned (*ibid*, 38–40) in particular Arts 5, 6, 15, 26, 28, 34 and 35.

[128] Accordingly: "(t)he people were entitled to amend the Constitution in accordance with the provisions of Article 46 of the Constitution and the Constitution as so amended by the Fourteenth Amendment is the fundamental and supreme law of the State representing as it does the will of the people". *ibid*, 43.

arises between them, that which ranks higher must prevail". According to Griffin J's opinion, when a harmonious application of constitutional rules is not possible "the hierarchy or priority of the conflicting rights must be examined, both as between themselves and in relation to the general welfare of society".[129] In the opinion of the Supreme Court, the decision on the priority of constitutional rights is to be made by the High and the Supreme Courts. It is therefore clear the role given to judges, through the duty to resolve conflicts of constitutional rights, by the harmonious doctrine and by the acknowledgement of a hierarchy of constitutional rules and rights.

The abortion case law is again a prime example, as in *Attorney General v X*, where such a decision on the priority of constitutional rights underlay the acknowledgement the right to life of the mother prevailed. In particular, in this case the threat to the mother's life was that of suicide. Finlay CJ considered the provision of the Eighth Amendment as addressing "the intimate human problem of the right to life of the unborn and its relationship to the right of the mother of an unborn child to her life".[130] He expressly accepted the principles set out in the *McGee* and *Donoghue* cases as correct and appropriate principles which must be followed in interpreting Art 40.3.3° and which are "particularly and peculiarly appropriate and illuminating in the interpretation of a sub-section of the Constitution" which deals with such an the intimate human problem.[131]

The judge also stressed the importance of "a harmonious interpretation of the Constitution carried out in accordance with concepts of prudence, justice and charity". In the opinion of the court, according to such harmonious approach, the judge "in vindicating and defending as far as practicable the right of the unborn to life but at the same time giving due regard to the right of the mother to life" must consider the position of the mother within the family, and the interrelation of her rights and obligation with those of the members of society in the areas in which her activities occur.[132]

As in this case an equal ranking of the two rights involved, i.e. the right to life of the unborn and that to life of the mother, was not possible, the court expressly decided to give preference to the right of the mother[133]. In particular, since, in the opinion of the court, the test proposed by the Attorney General

> "that the life of the unborn could only be terminated if it were established that an inevitable or immediate risk to the life of the mother existed, for the avoidance of which a termination of the pregnancy was necessary, insufficiently vindicates the mother's right to life",

---

[129] *People v Shaw* [1982] IR 1. See also, among others, JM Kelly, *The Irish Constitution* (4th ed, Gerard W Hogan and Gerry Whyte ed, Lexis Nexis Butterworths, 2003) cvi.

[130] [1992] 1 IR 1, 53.

[131] *ibid.*

[132] *ibid.*

[133] According to the court a balancing test would always result in favour of the right of the unborn, because the termination of pregnancy will always lead to the death of the unborn, whereas the continuation of pregnancy might not have this result, irrespective of the degree of this possibility. See also J M Kelly *The Irish Constitution* (4th ed, Gerard W Hogan and Gerry Whyte ed, Lexis Nexis Butterworths, 2003) cvii.

it concluded that, having regard to other provisions of the Constitution,

> "the proper test to be applied is that if it is established as a matter of probability that there is a real and substantial risk to the life, as distinct from the health, of the mother, which can only be avoided by the termination of her pregnancy, such termination is permissible".[134]

The abortion case law might lead us to mention another possible implication of the role of constitutional interpretation in the field of fundamental rights, with particular reference to the influence of European developments. Without entering into the wider framework of the interesting dialogue between the Irish Supreme Court and the European Court of Human Right, on the one hand, and the European Court of Justice, on the other, we ought to consider at least that the Irish system should coexist and be compatible to certain European standards and that constitutional interpretation may perform a leading role in this field.[135]

Despite the role performed by judicial interpretation, abortion is still a controversial and highly sensitive issue in Ireland. The Government has always been against the recognition of the right to abortion[136] and this policy is considered to be part of the national identity, with particular reference to a possible influence of European developments on it. This clearly emerges from the Maastricht Treaty Protocol No 35 on abortion, which is reproduced in the Lisbon Treaty. The protocol expressly mentions the present text of Art 40.3.3° of the Irish Constitution, stating that nothing in EU law affects the application of this article in Ireland.

However, it might be said that, notwithstanding the fact that the Irish system still takes a strong stand on the protection of the unborn and despite the reference to religious elements in its Constitution, through constitutional referenda and constitutional interpretation Ireland seems to be at least compatible with the path carved out by shared European standards.

5. Concluding Remarks

This overview of constitutional interpretation in Ireland has highlighted what the main interpretative approaches are and how the Irish courts use them, in particular

[134] [1992] 1 IR 1, 53–54. McCarthy, O'Flaherty and Egan JJ all agreed that this was the correct test: *ibid*, 80, 87, 92. Hederman J (dissenting) proposed an alternative, more restrictive test, under which "the evidence required to justify the choice being made must be of such a weight and cogency as to leave open no other conclusion but that the consequences of the continuance of the pregnancy will, to an extremely high degree of probability cost the mother her life and that any such opinion must be based on the most competent medical opinion available." *ibid*, 75.

[135] For instance, as regards the dialogue between the Irish Supreme Court and the European Court of Human Right, according to the ECtHR, Ireland can prohibit abortion, but if it does permit it in special cases then it must effectively allow for it. Reference needs to me made to the ECtHR case of *A B and C v Ireland* App No 25579/05, 16 December 2010. See, for example, L Busatta, "La sentenza A, B e C c. Irlanda: la complessa questione dell'aborto tra margine d'apprezzamento, consenso e (un possibile) monito", in *Diritto Pubblico Comparato ed Europeo*, 2011, 2, 445–454.

[136] Nevertheless, the Protection of Life During Pregnancy Act 2013 has recently allowed for abortion if there is a real and substantial risk to the woman's life, including the risk of suicide.

when dealing with fundamental rights. The analysis of the constitutional case law shows, as one might easily anticipate, that the five different approaches often overlap and that there is sometimes a lack of consistency among them.

Therefore, this overview allows us both to elaborate a comparative perspective and to stress the peculiar features of the constitutional interpretation in Ireland.

From the first point of view, these methods of interpretation prove to have elements in common with other legal systems, both in common and civil law countries.

For instance, the importance of looking at foreign law or of interpreting the Constitution in conformity with international treaties and agreements is expressly embodied in other Constitutions, as in South Africa and Spain. References, although less common, to the original understanding approach share elements with the debate on originalism in the US.

As a further example, the provision on "directive principles of social policy" influenced other common law countries, such as India, and contains a limit to all constitutional courts' review similar to the one embodied in the Spanish Constitution.

Unwritten rights have been recognised by the Swiss Tribunal Fédéral and by the Indian Supreme Court as well. Moreover, the concept of a living and dynamic constitution and the reference to general clauses, whose contents evolve according to prevailing contemporary ideas and sensitivities, are obviously common to many other legal systems, if not to all of them. The idea that personal rights are antecedent to the constitution, which recognises and protects them, reminds us of the provision embodied in Art 2 of the Italian Constitution, as well as, although with peculiarities, in the Ninth Amendment to the US Constitution.

The analysis of Irish constitutional case law shows significant references to natural law principles enshrined in the Constitution, as well as the combination of the Christian nature of the State and the original status of natural rights. However, on the one hand, the leading role of judicial interpretation allows judges to take into due account the evolving moral standards when interpreting constitutional rights in accordance with the concepts of "prudence, justice and charity" as conditioned by the passage of time and, on the other hand, the Constitution is considered to be superior to natural law.

Therefore, although natural rights are considered to be antecedent to the Constitution itself and reference to natural law, i.e. to extra-textual values, still remains a legitimate guide in the interpretation of constitutional fundamental rights, natural law cannot be considered as a limit to the amendment of the Constitution by the people through referenda.

With reference to the development of fundamental rights in the light of constitutional interpretation, we have highlighted the leading and innovative role of courts, especially due to the unenumerated rights doctrine and to harmonious interpretation. However, what is perceived as the unique nature of certain Irish constitutional rules, structures and rights proves to limit not only the influence of foreign law in the Irish legal system, but also the acknowledgement of evolving mores and complete compliance with European common standards, as the abortion debate, notwithstanding significant evolution, still shows.

CHAPTER 4

Evaluating the Judicial Role in Developing the Irish Constitution

Eoin Carolan[1]

1. INTRODUCTION

In reviewing the 75 years since the enactment of Bunreacht na hÉireann, it is plainly impossible to overlook the role that the judiciary have played in the development of Irish constitutional law. The story of Ireland's constitutional development is very much the story of an evolution in judicial attitudes over successive decades. In less than a century, Ireland's legal culture changed from one rooted in common law notions of judicial reticence and parliamentary supremacy to one at ease with ideas of strong judicial review by a distinct and unelected body that is functionally, politically and psychologically independent of the elected institutions of government.

Indeed, this shift from common law deference to a demand for inter-institutional respect occurred over a few short decades, thereby giving rise to the constitutional traditions associated with Irish jurisprudence today. The roots of contemporary Irish scholarship and of debates over the position and powers of the judiciary lie in these dramatic years of development starting around 1950.

2. THE ROLE OF COURTS IN DEVELOPING A CONSTITUTION: THE LESSONS OF 1922

In assessing the role and influence of the judiciary, it is instructive to compare the development and relative success of the 1937 text with the fate of the 1922 document which preceded it. While that document suffered from other difficulties associated with its efforts to balance nationalist aspirations with the residual legacies of imperialist politics, its failures in the realm of fundamental rights have been argued to owe much to the persistence among the legal and judicial classes of a common law tradition which regarded the judicial enforcement of rights as an alien and inexplicable concept.

It was not that the 1922 Constitution did not make provision for the sort of rights-oriented culture which now exists in Ireland. On the contrary, the committee responsible for the drafting of the 1922 Constitution made significant efforts to produce an innovative text which would consciously break with British legal culture. As Hogan J observed in a recent speech, at the launch of Ireland's current Constitutional Convention:

> "[The 1922 Free State Constitution] borrowed from the US Constitution the

[1] Lecturer, UCD School of Law.

idea of judicial review of legislation, i.e., the idea that laws which infringed human rights could be invalidated as unconstitutional by the courts. This was a radical idea, almost unknown in the Europe of its day. The Committee borrowed from Switzerland the idea of direct democracy and the idea that any fundamental changes in the rules governing our society could only be changed by referendum. Finally, the Committee borrowed from the inter-war constitutions of continental Europe for the contents of the human rights protections. In this regard, the Committee borrowed heavily from the much admired German Constitution ("Weimar Constitution") of 1919."[2]

However, these radical seedlings failed to flourish in a legal environment long nourished by Diceyan orthodoxy. Writing extra-judicially, the then Chief Justice Hugh Kennedy bemoaned how

> "Political and legal constitutional studies in this Country were in practice limited to the British Constitution and the working of the British Parliament. Professor Dicey's book became an evangel accepted reverently and without criticism or question in our schools (such as they were) of political philosophy and constitutional law."[3]

Similar views were expressed in more recent times by a later Chief Justice, Keane CJ, who again linked the demise of the Free State Constitution with the reluctance of judges trained in the common law tradition to contemplate making use of the more novel procedures adopted by the drafting committee.

> "The second [factor against judicial activism] was the innate reluctance of judges who had been bred in the English constitutional tradition to overstep what they saw as the traditional limitations on the role of the courts. Although a number of the judges in the Supreme and High Courts during that period were from a unionist background, some judges whose political sympathies before appointment had been regarded as nationalist were equally conservative in their approach, an outstanding example being James Murnaghan."[4]

In defence of the Free State judiciary, it should be noted that their relative unwillingness to make use of the powers of judicial review under the 1922 text may have been based in part on attitudes but also in part on doctrine and precedent. While the judges may have been more willing to exercise their authority as an independent and co-equal branch, it was obviously necessary to have tools available to the judiciary that were equipped for that purpose. From a standpoint 90 years later, when the doctrinal issues raised by the introduction of judicial review and the enforcement of rights have been subject to extensive litigation and judicial and

---

2 Gerard Hogan, *Address to the Constitutional Convention* (Dublin Castle, 1 December 2012) https://www.constitution.ie/AttachmentDownload.ashx?mid=d0e7d26f-283e-e211-a5a0-005056a32ee4 (last accessed 19 May 2013).

3 Hugh Kennedy, "Foreword" in Leo Kohn, *The Constitution of the Irish Free State* (George Allen & Unwin, 1932) xii–xiii.

4 Ronan Keane, "Across the Cherokee Frontier of Irish Constitutional Jurisprudence: The *Sinn Féin Funds* Case: *Buckley v Attorney General* (1950)" in *Leading Cases of the Twentieth Century* (Eoin O'Dell ed, Round Hall Sweet & Maxwell, 2000) 185, 188.

academic scrutiny, it is easy to underestimate the challenge posed by the development of wholly novel constitutional doctrines.

That is particularly so given the Free State judiciary operated at a time when these powers were—outside the United States of America—relatively unfamiliar. It was not open to these courts to draw on the sort of extended range of comparative material which is available to judges and scholars today. Nor can it be assumed that the courts were necessarily well served in this regard by those appearing before them. As Donal Coffey has observed in discussing this era:

> The common law system puts the judiciary at a disadvantage, in that if a case is not stated or argued, the judge cannot decide on that issue. Therefore, if the Bar did not produce Counsel who argued constitutional arguments forcefully and effectively, it was difficult for the bench to develop innovative new doctrines.[5]

Hogan J has also pointed out the relevance of the political background to the introduction and litigation of these new judicial competences concerning rights and judicial review—namely the existence of a Civil War and a subsequent ongoing level of politically inspired violence which led, at various points, to the introduction of forms of martial law. As he commented,

> "[t]here probably could not have been a more inauspicious time in which to introduce the novelties of a written Constitution with protections along with fundamental rights along with the power of judicial review of legislation".[6]

There are thus many reasons why the Free State Constitution may have failed in its evident aim of establishing a rights-based system of judicial review. What is relevant to note, however, is the extent to which this failure seems likely to have been linked, at least in part, with the prevailing culture and attitudes amongst lawyers and—in particular—judges at the time.

The corollary of this, of course, is that the subsequent success of the analogous provisions of the 1937 text must, accordingly, also be attributable in part to the attitudes and actions of a later generation of judges and jurists. This comparative experience underlines the importance and influence of the judicial role in developing the Irish constitution since 1937—whether for better or for worse.

3. Judiciary's Interpretation of the Constitution

3.1 Relevant Constitutional Provisions

By comparison with the common law traditions that predated it, the 1937 Constitution (like the 1922 document) incorporated some clear textual acknowledgments of the fact that there had been a fundamental change in the character of the courts' role in Ireland's government. Several of the concepts enshrined in the Constitution were alien to or, in some cases, inconsistent with the concept of a sovereign and supreme

5 Donal Coffey, "The Judiciary of the Irish Free State" (2011) 33 DULJ (ns) 61, 65.

6 Gerard Hogan, *The Origins of the Irish Constitution 1928–1941* (Royal Irish Academy, 2012) 3.

Parliament: the identification of the People as sovereign in the Preamble and in Art 6; the references to the legislative, executive and judicial powers of government as distinct functions in Art 6; the establishment and protection of an independent judicial branch under Arts 34 and 35; the endorsement of the notion of free-standing and fundamental rights in Arts 40–44; the description of some of these rights in terms such as "inalienable" and "imprescriptible", which made an implied assertion of pre-eminence over the constraints of legal instrument or political thought; and, perhaps most obviously, the conferring of an express jurisdiction on the High and Supreme Courts to invalidate legislation which was repugnant to the Constitution. These features, some of which were similar to those in the 1922 text, represented a considered break with the conventions of parliamentary supremacy in an effort to establish a system of democratic government that was more consonant with the themes of republicanism and popular sovereignty which had influenced much Irish nationalist thought.

The instructions given to the drafters by government included the specific requirements that the Draft Constitution should "contain certain basic Articles guaranteeing fundamental human rights" and that these Articles should be placed "in a specially protected position, i.e. to render them unalterable save by the people themselves or by an elaborate constitutional process".[7] The Secretary of the Department of Justice's evident horror at what was being proposed serves as an eloquent illustration of its novelty.

> "I believe that what the country wants at present and probably will continue to want for many years is a strong Executive, not liable, so long as it has the support of the people, to be delayed, hampered and humiliated at every step by long arguments in the Courts, or by propaganda of a threatening and seditious type. A Government should not allow itself to be insulted.
>
> Further I believe that the doctrines of 'judicial independence' and the 'separation of the functions' are being overdone and that the Courts have given or have assumed a position in our civic life to which they are not entitled. There was a time in England when the Judges job was to save the people from an irresponsible Executive: it may be necessary in turn for a responsible Executive to save the people from irresponsible Judges."[8]

That the desire for a rights-based system of judicial prevailed in the face of such express and trenchant internal opposition underscores the extent to which the final text represented a conscious rejection of inherited English orthodoxies. The defence of individual rights was not a task that the judiciary assumed for itself. Once it had been decided that rights would enjoy this "specially protected position", the judiciary, as the guardians of the Constitution and of the rights of those protected thereunder, could not but have had a significant role to play in the achievement of these constitutional objectives.

[7] Explanatory memorandum to the draft Heads of a Constitution of May 17th, 1935, quoted in Gerard Hogan, The *Origins of the Irish Constitution 1928–1941* (Royal Irish Academy, 2012), 154.

[8] *ibid.*

3.2 Implied Constitutional Doctrines

The courts' influence on the subsequent evolution of the constitutional regime was, however, also based in part on developments in judicial thinking, which provided them with additional interpretative, conceptual and remedial tools. These methods enjoyed varying degrees of support from the constitutional text which, unsurprisingly, generated controversy on occasions about the democratic or institutional legitimacy of the approach adopted.

For a period, especially in the 1980s and 1990s, it became common to acknowledge the alleged "activism" of the Irish judiciary—a tendency which was doubtlessly influenced by the courts' involvement in a number of high-profile and contentious decisions on social issues. However, it also seems likely that this wave of concern about "activism" was in part carried to Ireland by the currents of contemporary American controversies about counter-majoritarianism, Bork and abortion.[9]

The remainder of this piece reviews those developments with a view to providing a more context-sensitive assessment of the role of the judiciary, and of its interpretative armoury, in the development of the Irish constitutional system. The focus is on providing a descriptive account of the trends in Irish constitutional jurisprudence which places developments in the context of their time, of their political and social environment, and of the objectives of the constitutional drafters as outlined above. This, it is hoped, may assist in developing a more objective understanding of the influence of the judiciary on Ireland's constitutional development.

These other factors which affected the courts' influence included the existence of multiple permissible methods of textual interpretation, the recognition over several decades of a natural law basis for the Constitution's protection of rights, and the development of a doctrine of unenumerated rights.

For example, the Irish courts have on various occasions interpreted the text of the Constitution in a literal manner,[10] in a broad manner,[11] in accordance with historical norms at the time of its enactment,[12] or—perhaps most commonly—using a harmonious methodology, which assumes that:

> "Any single constitutional right or power is but a component in an ensemble of interconnected and interacting provisions which must be brought into play as part of a larger composition and which must be given such an integrated interpretation as will fit it harmoniously into the general constitutional order and modulation."[13]

---

9 It is a common feature of Ireland's linguistic bond with both the US and the UK that doctrines or debates about the quite different American or English system are transplanted into Irish law, whether through direct citation of comparative authorities or by the influence on the many Irish students, practitioners and judges who study in those systems. While this may be useful in some contexts, it can also generate confusion and incoherence when there is a failure to appreciate the significance of the distinct constitutional contexts.

10 *State (Browne) v Feran* [1967] IR 147 (SC).

11 *O'Byrne v Minister for Finance* [1959] IR 1 (SC).

12 *O'Donovan v AG* [1961] IR 114 (HC).

13 *People (DPP) v O'Shea* [1982] IR 384, 426.

The doctrine of natural law has also had an influence on the courts' approach to the construction of the constitutional text. Natural law suggests, of course, the existence of a body of principles that are superior to any written legal instrument. The Irish courts held for a considerable period that the Constitution endorsed this philosophy. This proposition enjoyed some support from the constitutional text, not least in terms of the strikingly religious language of the Preamble and, more directly, in the description of certain fundamental rights as being "antecedent and superior to all positive law". As Walsh J. explained in *McGee v Attorney General*:

> "Articles 41, 42 and 43 emphatically reject the theory that there are no rights without laws, no rights contrary to the law and no rights anterior to the law. They indicate that justice is placed above the law and acknowledge that natural rights, or human rights, are not created by law but that the Constitution confirms their existence and gives them protection. The individual has natural and human rights over which the State has no authority. The very structure and content of the Articles dealing with fundamental rights clearly indicate that justice is not subordinate to the law. In particular, the terms of s.3 of Article 40 expressly subordinate the law to justice."[14]

The third doctrine to note in this context is that of unenumerated rights. This, again, was a concept that was not expressly recognised by the text of the Constitution, but which was capable of deriving implicit support from it. The key provision in this regard was Art 40. 3, which provides that:

> "1° The State guarantees in its laws to respect, and, as far as practicable, by its laws to defend and vindicate the personal rights of the citizen.
> 2° The State shall, in particular, by its laws protect as best it may from unjust attack and, in the case of injustice done, vindicate the life, person, good name, and property rights of every citizen."

In *Ryan v Attorney General*, the High and Supreme Courts upheld the argument that the reference to "in particular" confirmed that the guarantee of "personal rights" in sub-section extended beyond those specifically identified in sub-section 2.[15] This effectively vested a power in the courts to confer protection on "new" rights in appropriate cases. Thus, in *Ryan*, for example, a right to bodily integrity was implied into the Constitution. This power was used in subsequent cases to protect, *inter alia*, the right to privacy,[16] the right to travel[17] and the right to die with dignity.[18].

For the purposes of this piece, what is pertinent about these theories is the extent to which they allowed the courts a certain level of residual flexibility in their approach to constitutional challenges. This left open the potential for the amendment, refinement or alteration of the constitutional jurisprudence as novel situations arose.

Yet, what one might see as valuable flexibility is often, for another, damaging

---

14 *McGee v AG* [1974] IR 284 (SC) 310, Walsh J.
15 [1965] IR 294, 313 (Kenny J), 344–345 (Ó Dálaigh CJ).
16 *McGee v AG* [1974] IR 284 (SC).
17 *State (M) v AG* [1979] IR 73 (HC).
18 *Re a Ward of Court (withholding medical treatment) (No 2)* [1996] 2 IR 79 (SC).

uncertainty. These doctrines have been criticised by various commentators on the basis that this ambiguity begets activism.

> "Since the early 1960s, Irish judges have been in the van of this wave of judicial activism. In interpreting statutes, they have been equipped not only with the common law presumptions in the public law field. They have also used— and sometimes even glossed—the Constitution. Laws have been struck down or interpreted in the light of the presumption of constitutionality so as to have a different effect from that intended by the legislature."[19]

A similar view was expressed more recently by Coffey:

> "The difficulty is that the doctrine of unenumerated rights is simply the engine used to pull the train of judicial activism, despite this activism throwing up constitutional difficulties."[20]

In truth, there may be merit in both these perspectives. It is certainly the case that the flexibility of these doctrines allowed the courts some latitude to adjust their approach to what remained a relatively novel jurisdiction. However, various judges also demonstrated a level of awareness of the problems that this ambiguity could pose. It is notable, for example, that the very first enunciation of the doctrine of unenumerated rights was immediately followed by a warning against an over-ready reliance upon it. In the High Court, the doctrine was explained as follows:

> "I think that the personal rights which may be involved to invalidate legislation are not confined to those specified in Article 40 but include all those rights which result from the Christian and democratic nature of the State. It is, however, a jurisdiction to be exercised with caution. None of the personal rights of the citizen are unlimited: their exercise may be regulated by the Oireachtas when the common good requires this. When dealing with controversial social, economic and medical matters on which it is notorious views change from generation to generation, the Oireachtas has to reconcile the exercise of personal rights with the claims of the common good and its decision on the reconciliation should prevail unless it was oppressive to all or some of the citizens or unless there is no reasonable proportion between the benefit which the legislation will confer on the citizens or a substantial body of them and the interference with the personal rights of the citizen. Moreover, the presumption that every Act of the Oireachtas is constitutional until the contrary is clearly established applies with particular force to this type of legislation."[21]

Ó Dalaigh CJ seemed similarly cognisant of the potential pitfalls of this approach on appeal:

> "the 'personal rights' mentioned in section 3, 1 are not exhausted by the

---

19 David Gwynn Morgan, "The Emergency Powers Bill Reference—II" (1979) 14 *Irish Jurist* 252, 260.

20 Donal Coffey, "Article 28.3.3, the Natural Law and the Judiciary: Three Easy Pieces" (2004) 22 *Irish Law Times* 310, 312.

21 [1965] IR 294 (HC) 312–313.

enumeration of 'life, person, good name, and property rights' in section 3, 2 as is shown by the use of the words 'in particular'; nor by the more detached treatment of specific rights in the subsequent sections of the Article. To attempt to make a list of all the rights which may properly fall within the category of 'personal rights' would be difficult and, fortunately, is unnecessary in this present case."[22]

The same caution can be seen in the case law on natural law. While natural law provided a powerful philosophical basis for the special protection of rights in the manner arguably anticipated by the drafters, it carried with it the inevitable danger of disagreement over the scope and extent of the protection it conferred. Once again, therefore, it is possible to identify efforts on the part of the judiciary in the early case law to impose some shape or limits on the potential scope of these doctrines. Henchy J's decision in *Norris* provides one example of this type of attempt to develop a unitary and internally coherent model of rights-protection.

> "Having regard to the purposive Christian ethos of the Constitution, particularly as set out in the preamble ("to promote the common good, with due observance of Prudence, Justice and Charity, so that the dignity and freedom of the individual may be assured, true social order attained, the unity of our country restored, and concord established with other nations"), to the denomination of the State as "sovereign, independent, democratic" in Article 5, and to the recognition, expressly or by necessary implication, of particular personal rights, such recognition being frequently hedged in by overriding requirements such as "public order and morality" or "the authority of the State" or "the exigencies of the common good", there is necessarily given to the citizen, within the required social, political and moral framework, such a range of personal freedoms or immunities as are necessary to ensure his dignity and freedom as an individual in the type of society envisaged. The essence of those rights is that they inhere in the individual personality of the citizen in his capacity as a vital human component of the social, political and moral order posited by the Constitution."[23]

These specific dicta have recently been endorsed by the Supreme Court as providing "valuable guidance" and Henchy J's approach as providing "a useful structure and focus for analysis" both in relation to "the identification of an unenumerated right, or the determination of the extent of an enumerated right".[24]

These notions of Christianity and democracy recurred across the case law on both natural law and unenumerated rights. Rights, it was suggested, would only be recognised where there were consistent with the Christian and democratic nature of the State.[25] But here, the problems of ambiguity and indeterminacy again arose. What was the relationship between the values of Christianity and democracy? Whose brand of Christianity? And what if the values came into conflict?

---

22 *ibid*, 344–345.

23 *Norris v AG* [1984] IR 36 (SC) 71 per Henchy J.

24 *Fleming v Ireland* [2013] IESC 19 (29 April 2013) para 113.

25 *Ryan v AG* [1965] IR 294 (HC) 312–313. Although the Supreme Court in *Ryan* did not address this aspect of Kenny J's reasoning, there are strong echoes of such an approach in later cases, such as the majority judgment in *Norris v AG* [1984] IR 36 (SC).

These difficulties were starkly highlighted by *McGee v Attorney General*, in which a constitutional challenge was brought to a prohibition on the importation and sale of contraceptives. Mrs McGee was a married mother of several children who had been warned that her health and life would be endangered by another pregnancy. Her case rested on her individual rights, including the right to bodily integrity and an asserted right to marital privacy. Both rights seem consistent with natural law—but the application of them to this case potentially ran counter to Roman Catholic teachings on contraception. Ultimately, the majority of the court upheld her challenge in a decision which strongly emphasised the role of the courts in determining these ambiguous cases of contested values. As Walsh J put it in his judgment:

> "In a pluralist society such as ours, the courts cannot as a matter of constitutional law be asked to choose between the differing views, where they exist, of experts on the interpretation by the different religious denominations of either the nature or extent of these natural rights as they are to be found in the natural law. The same considerations apply also to the question of ascertaining the nature and extent of the duties which flow from natural law; the Constitution speaks of one of them when it refers to the inalienable duty of parents to provide according to their means for the religious, moral, intellectual, physical and social education of their children: see s. 1 of Article 42. In this country it falls finally upon the judges to interpret the Constitution and in doing so to determine, where necessary, the rights which are superior or antecedent to positive law or which are imprescriptible or inalienable. In the performance of this difficult duty there are certain guidelines laid down in the Constitution for the judge. The very structure and content of the Articles dealing with fundamental rights clearly indicate that justice is not subordinate to the law. In particular, the terms of s. 3 of Article 40 expressly subordinate the law to justice. Both Aristotle and the Christian philosophers have regarded justice as the highest human virtue. The virtue of prudence was also esteemed by Aristotle as by the philosophers of the Christian world. But the great additional virtue introduced by Christianity was that of charity — not the charity which consists of giving to the deserving, for that is justice, but the charity which is also called mercy. According to the preamble, the people gave themselves the Constitution to promote the common good with due observance of prudence, justice and charity so that the dignity and freedom of the individual might be assured. The judges must, therefore, as best they can from their training and their experience interpret these rights in accordance with their ideas of prudence, justice and charity. It is but natural that from time to time the prevailing ideas of these virtues may be conditioned by the passage of time: no interpretation of the Constitution is intended to be final for all time. It is given in the light of prevailing ideas and concepts."[26]

This represented an acknowledgment of the inevitability of ambiguity about the natural law—an assertion that the determination of these ambiguities was a question for the courts—but also a concession about the inadequacy of such judicial determinations. These controversies were matters for best-efforts judicial adjudication rather than final resolution.

---

26 [1974] IR 284 (SC) 318.

As Kavanagh has pointed out, the decision in *Norris v Attorney General*, where the members of the Supreme Court presented differing philosophies of natural law in determining a case about the criminalisation of male homosexual conduct, demonstrates the limitations of this approach:

> "What this line of case law shows is that there were various strands of judicial thought emerging on the Irish Supreme Court on the role of Christian values when interpreting the Constitution. One line (pursued most explicitly by Henchy, McCarthy, Griffin, Budd JJ and, to some extent, Walsh J) gave pride of place to the dignity and freedom of the individual in the context of a judicial decision which was informed by the values of prudence, justice and charity which could change over time. The other gave greater emphasis to Christian values and the Christian ethos of the Irish people when they enacted the Irish Constitution in 1937. Of course, these Christian and dignitarian strands are not necessarily mutually exclusive, since the value of the dignity of the individual is part of Christian ethics. Therefore, whether a judge pursued one strand or another would not necessarily lead him or her to different outcomes. Nor is it the case that reliance on Christian values would necessarily lead to a "conservative" outcome or one which would align with Catholic social teaching relating to sexuality. For example, even in the trenchant dissents in *Norris*, Henchy and McCarthy JJ drew on some of the Christian elements in the Constitution to support their position which came down in favour of the liberty and freedom of the individual. And although the decision in *McGee* went against the Catholic Church's position on contraception, it was justified in part in terms of the importance of marriage and the Christian value of charity.
>
> Be that as it may, the *Norris* case showed that sometimes these different strands could come apart and therefore the general question about the appropriate approach to constitutional adjudication really mattered."[27]

3.3 An Activist Judiciary?

As explained above, the ambiguous and indeterminate character of much of the judicial reasoning in respect of these doctrines encouraged a general perception of the courts as aggressively activist in expanding their remit.[28]

It is arguable, however, that some of this criticism was, at the very least, overstated, with some coming close to a re-assertion of the Department of Justice's simplistic equation in the 1930s of democratic legitimacy with an English-style electoral supremacy. One factor to bear in mind when considering this criticism is the residual influence of such English orthodoxies. Indeed, this influence persists today, supported in part by the citation by domestic practitioners of English public law jurisprudence as if it were directly applicable to Ireland. One need only look to the reaction of elements of the British political class and press to the lesser role of their courts under the Human Rights Act 1998 to understand how such criticisms could be shaped by the political context and traditions to which these decisions

[27] Aileen Kavanagh, "The Irish Constitution at 75 years: Natural Law, Christian Values and The Ideal of Justice" (2012) 48 *Irish Jurist* 71, 85.

[28] David Gwynn Morgan, *A Judgment Too Far? Judicial Activism and the Constitution* (Cork University Press, 2001).

seemed alien. For some, it is questionable whether any exercise of an independent judicial review power would not have been seen as unduly "activist".

A second point to bear in mind is how many of the cases commonly cited as examples of activism involve striking down legislation or provisions which were seen by many as controversial, such as the ban on contraception in *McGee* or cases concerning the termination of pregnancies, such as *Attorney General v X*.[29] The contentious nature of such decisions may have served to amplify the perception of the courts as intervening in affairs beyond their remit.

This relates to a larger and more pertinent point about any assessment of the Irish courts as unusually aggressive or activist in expanding their role—namely that litigation, in the Irish constitutional context, has often been initiated only in response to a consistent failure on the part of the other organs of government to engage with controversial issues. The Irish political class has a particularly unfortunate history of failing to act on questions of social or moral controversy, a trait about which the courts have frequently complained when faced with the sort of controversial litigation that, once decided, subsequently sees them labelled by some as activist. McCarthy J's extended and eloquent description of the problems posed by the Oireachtas's failure to provide any legislative guidance as to how the Eighth Amendment on abortion should be implemented neatly encapsulates the courts' concerns.

> "In the context of the eight years that have passed since the Amendment was adopted and the two years since *Grogan's* case the failure by the legislature to enact the appropriate legislation is no longer just unfortunate; it is inexcusable. What are pregnant women to do? What are the parents of a pregnant girl under age to do? What are the medical profession to do? They have no guidelines save what may be gleaned from the judgments in this case. What additional considerations are there? Is the victim of rape, statutory or otherwise, or the victim of incest, finding herself pregnant, to be assessed in a manner different from others? The Amendment, born of public disquiet, historically divisive of our people, guaranteeing in its laws to respect and by its laws to defend the right to life of the unborn, remains bare of legislative direction. Does the right to bodily integrity, identified in *Ryan v Attorney General* [1965] IR 294 and adverted to by Walsh J in *SPUC v Grogan* [1989] IR 753 at p 767, involve the right to control one's own body? Walsh J. graphically describes part of the problem:
>
> > 'When a woman becomes pregnant she acquires rights which cannot be taken from her, namely, the right to protect the life of her unborn child and the right to protect her own bodily integrity against any effort to compel her by law or by persuasion to submit herself to an abortion. Such rights also carry obligations the foremost of which is not to endanger or to submit to or bring about the destruction of that unborn life. There is no doubt that, particularly in the case of an unmarried pregnant woman, intense pressures of a social kind may be brought to bear upon her to submit to an abortion, even from her peers or her parents. There may even be specious arguments of an economic nature ranging from those of the neo-Malthusian type to those which would seek to determine

[29] [1992] 1 IR 1 (SC).

for economic reasons that the population should be structured in a particular way even to the point of deciding that the birth of too many persons of one sex should be prevented. The destruction of life is not an acceptable method of birth control. The qualification of certain pregnancies as being "unwanted" is likewise a totally unacceptable criterion. The total abandonment of young children or old persons or of those who by reason of infirmity, mental or physical, or those who are unable to look after themselves too often occurs throughout the world. There is clear evidence that they are unwanted by those who abandon them. That would however provide no justification whatever for their elimination. On the economic plane there are, no doubt, some distorted minds which could make a case for the elimination of what they would regard as old useless and unproductive human units. To be unwanted is not justification for the destruction of one's life.'

Since the Amendment contemplates lawful abortion, how may the State still, as far as practicable, vindicate the right to life of the unborn? Legislation may be both negative and positive: negative, in prohibiting absolutely or at a given time, or without meeting stringent tests: positive by requiring positive action. The State may fulfil its role by providing necessary agencies to help, to counsel, to encourage, to comfort, to plan for the pregnant woman, the pregnant girl or her family. It is not for the courts to programme society; that is partly, at least, the role of the legislature. The courts are not equipped to regulate these procedures."[30]

Yet, almost 20 years later, a dispute between an estranged couple over the fate of the frozen embryos they had created during IVF treatment saw the Supreme Court again expressing disquiet at the failure of the political class to legislate on the implications of the Eighth Amendment. Fennelly J commented that

> "It is disturbing, to use no stronger word, that some four years after publication of the Report of the Commission on Assisted Human Reproduction, no legislative proposal has even been formulated. Counsel for the Attorney General argued before us that there is no law or public policy regarding the protection of frozen embryos, in short that they have no legal status. As I interpret these submissions, the organs of the State have no present intention to propose any legislation. It is obvious that this is extremely difficult and sensitive subject matter. It is controversial for all of the reasons mentioned by Hardiman and Geoghegan JJ. Nonetheless, it cannot be denied that the fertilisation of the ovum brings into existence, outside the womb, the essential unique components of a potential new individual human person. I agree with the judgments of Hardiman and Geoghegan JJ that the frozen embryo is entitled to respect. This is the least that can be said. Arguably there may be a constitutional obligation on the State to give concrete form to that respect. In default of any action by the executive and legislative organs of the State, it may be open to the courts in a future case to consider whether an embryo enjoys constitutional protection under other provisions of the Constitution."[31]

[30] [1992] 1 IR 1 (SC) 82–83.
[31] *Roche v Roche* [2010] 2 IR 321 (SC) 395–396.

This type of judicial legislation on controversial questions has been an unfortunate by-product of the political buck-passing that has been made possible by the judiciary's obligation to interpret and enforce the Constitution.

Where the costs of political decision-making are high, the incentive for politicians of having those costs borne by another institution may be too tempting to avoid. The reality is that a constitutional amendment that was argued to be necessary to prevent the judiciary from adjudicating on abortion has instead led to a situation in which difficult issues of policy have been almost entirely left to an unhappy Supreme Court to determine.[32]

As Desmond Clarke has observed, it seems peculiar to criticise the courts as activist for finding themselves forced into the position of unenthusiastic actors because of failures on the part of others.

> "This official reluctance to legislate rather than interpret the law has been frequently challenged by the failure of the Oireachtas to legislate, especially about moral issues that remain disputed among citizens. To mention only two examples: the courts had to decide that it was not illegal for married couples to import and use contraceptives, and that it is not illegal in Irish law in specific circumstances to have an abortion or to travel outside the jurisdiction of the courts for the purpose of having an abortion. One must therefore sympathise with the courts when they are requested to decide issues for which the Oireachtas has knowingly failed to legislate, rather than blame them for the creativity they exercise in order to provide some kind of reasoned judgment in such cases."[33]

A third institutional caveat to any characterisation of the judiciary as inappropriately driving constitutional change is the fact that the People, as sovereigns, are entitled to approve amendments to the text of the Constitution by way of a simple majority vote. That the power to initiate amendment proposals is confined to the political class does impose some practical limitations on the People's freedom to act in this regard. Nonetheless, experience in Ireland—especially in the period since the 1980s—has suggested that the political process will respond to popular demands in high profile or controversial cases. Nor, it has been suggested, is the lack of controversy necessarily indicative of a lack of popular support:

> "Those who argue that judicial activism negates democratic decision-making invariably assume that the People can only express their will through the proxy system of legislative deliberation or, more rarely, directly through referenda. However my argument here is that the People are not so restricted in the expression of their will. There is a third way. The silence of the People in the face of judicial activism does not have to be interpreted as the silence of impotent rage - it could be regarded as the approving silence of an electorate who are satisfied with the decisions of their judges, or, perhaps more accurately,

[32] Eoin Carolan, "Reviewing Ireland's abortion regime" I-Connect blog, 20 December 2012. http://www.iconnectblog.com/2012/12/reviewing-irelands-abortion-regime/ (last accessed 19 May 2013).

[33] Desmond Clarke, "Ireland: A Republican Democracy, a Theocracy or a Judicial Oligarchy?" (2011) 29 *Irish Law Times* 81, 82.

> the disinterested silence of an electorate (or their political representatives) who are not sufficiently antagonised by those decisions to wish to change them."[34]

In contrast to the US, therefore, it seems questionable whether a court decision that was substantially divergent from public opinion on an issue of political interest or controversy would survive in the long term. Imported American fears about anti-democratic judicial coups have less resonance in this framework. As Gerry Whyte has argued in addressing such concerns,

> "An interesting characteristic of the Irish Constitution, and one which marks it off quite significantly from its US counterpart, is the relative ease with which it may be amended. Articles 46 and 47 prescribe a three stage process for amendment - a bill proposing an amendment has to be passed by the two Houses of the Oireachtas and then approved by a simple majority of the votes cast at a referendum on the proposal, following which it is signed by the President. On a number of occasions, this process has been used to reverse, modify or otherwise circumvent judicial decisions or comments on different aspects of the Constitution.
>
> Perhaps the most spectacular example of this phenomenon, in terms of alacrity, was the Tenth Amendment to the Constitution, approved by the People on 26 May 1987, which permitted the State to ratify the Single European Act. This was in reaction to the Supreme Court decision in *Crotty v An Taoiseach* [1987] IR 713; [1987] ILRM 400 some six weeks earlier, holding that the Government was not entitled to enter into this international agreement. Seven other constitutional amendments were similarly provoked by decisions, actual or anticipated, of the judiciary. Thus the Sixth Amendment to the Constitution, giving express constitutional protection to the adoption process, was enacted in response to judicial misgivings expressed in the course of the hearing of *M v An Bord Uchtála* [1977] IR 287; the ostensible motivation behind the Eighth Amendment to the Constitution in 1983 was to pre-empt any judicial attempt to relax the existing ban on abortion; *In re Article 26 and the Electoral (Amendment) Bill 1983* [1984] IR 268; [1984] ILRM 539 dealing with the voting rights of non-citizens, was reversed by the Ninth Amendment to the Constitution in 1984; the Thirteenth and Fourteenth Amendments to the Constitution in 1992 were a reaction to the Supreme Court decisions in *Attorney General (SPUC (Irl) Ltd) v Open Door Counselling Ltd* [1988] IR 593; [1988] ILRM 19 and *Attorney General v X* [1992] 1 IR 1; [1992] ILRM 401; the Sixteenth Amendment to the Constitution in 1996 reversed the Supreme Court decision in *The People (Attorney General) v O'Callaghan* [1966] IR 501; (1968) 102 ILTR 45 on the availability of bail where there was a likelihood of the defendant committing further offences while on bail; and, in the following year, the doctrine of cabinet confidentiality first enunciated by the *Supreme Court in Attorney General v Hamilton (No 1)* [1993] 2 IR 250; [1993] ILRM 81 was modified by the Seventeenth Amendment to the Constitution.
>
> These examples suggest that the People (or, perhaps more accurately, the political elite) are quite prepared to take action to control judicial decision-

---

[34] Gerry Whyte, *Social Inclusion and the Legal System: Public Interest Law in Ireland* (IPA, 2002) 36

making with which they do not agree. Consequently, it is surely reasonable to infer from the People's passivity in the face of other judicial decisions that these decisions reflect popular sentiment (or perhaps more accurately in relation to some decisions, especially those of a technical nature, do not offend against that sentiment.) Thus one can argue that the whole corpus of implied fundamental rights identified by the courts since the 1960s carries with it implicit popular approval insofar as no attempt has ever been made to modify this development by way of constitutional amendment."[35]

Fourthly, and perhaps most tellingly, the image of the courts as pushing the boundaries of their powers is belied by the extensive number of decisions which emphasise, again and again, the limited role of the courts.

The most high-profile of recent decisions in this regard were those of the Supreme Court (by a majority) in *Sinnott v Minister for Education*[36] and *TD v Minister for Education*.[37] These attracted considerable comment[38] and have generally been seen as heralding a more conservative attitude to the role and function of the courts. The first of these cases concerned the right to free primary education which, somewhat unusually for its time, was made a justiciable and enforceable right in the 1937 text. The second related to a corollary of Art 42.5, identified by the High Court, under which a child with a severe behavioural disorder has a right that the State should provide the provision of such accommodation, services and arrangements as were required to deal with this condition.[39] More specifically, the cases concerned mandatory orders issued by the High Court requiring the construction under judicial supervision of certain educational or therapeutic facilities in accordance with plans previously created by the relevant government agency but from which they now proposed to depart. In finding these orders unwarranted, a majority of the Court in *TD* expressed concern that such remedies would inappropriately extend the power of the courts. For example, Murray J observed:

> "This would introduce a degree of judicial hegemony in the domain of policy formulation and implementation so as to disturb the balance of powers between the three great organs of state, the executive, the Oireachtas and the judiciary.
>
> It would involve the High Court in exercising its 'will' rather than its 'judgment' on justiciable issues between the parties. (In this regard see also the conclusion of Hardiman J. on the *locus standi* of the parties in this application to seek the order granted).
>
> It would offend against the underlying concept in the statement of Walsh J. in *Murphy v. Corporation of Dublin* [1972] IR 215 at p 234 that:- 'The division of powers do not give paramountcy in all circumstances to any one of the organs of State.' The proposition of the learned High Court Judge that "the court has to attempt to fill the vacuum which exists by reason of the failure

---

35 Gerry Whyte, "The Role of the Supreme Court in our Democracy: A Response to Mr Justice Hardiman" (2006) 28 *Dublin University Law Journal* 1, 12-13 (quoting Gerry Whyte, *Social Inclusion and the Legal System: Public Interest Law in Ireland* (IPA, 2002) 36-37).

36 [2001] 2 IR 545.

37 [2001] 4 IR 259.

38 Gerry Whyte, "Socio-Economic Rights in Ireland" (2006) 11 *Bar Review* 27; Mark de Blacam, "Children, Constitutional Rights and the Separation of Powers" (2002) 37 *Irish Jurist* 113.

39 *FN v Minister for Education* [1995] 1 IR 409.

> of the legislature and executive" would, it seems to me, arrogate to the courts a paramountcy in circumstances not envisaged in the separation of powers under the Constitution and undermine core functions of the executive and the legislature in a representative democracy where their primary answerability for policy matters is to the people. In my view the order goes beyond the boundaries envisaged in the *dictum* of this court in *Buckley and Others (Sinn Féin) v Attorney General and Another* [1950] IR 67, that justice shall be administered in the manner provided by the Constitution and 'in such a manner and not otherwise', and outside the 'particular ambit of functions under the Constitution' accorded to the judiciary as mentioned by Budd J. in *Boland v An Taoiseach* [1974] IR 338.
>
> The jurisdiction of the courts as envisaged by the Constitution is ample to defend and vindicate rights guaranteed by the Constitution, as the experience of many decades has demonstrated. Judicial statements as to the amplitude of the powers of the court in this regard in such cases as *The State (Quinn) v Ryan* [1965] IR 70 and *DG v Eastern Health Board* [1997] 3 IR 511, can only be interpreted and applied within the ambit of the role conferred by the Constitution on the courts with due respect to the role and function of the executive and the legislature. Any other approach would introduce incoherence into the concept of the separation of powers as delineated by the Constitution."[40]

Of course, the implications of these decisions are obscured to some extent by the unusual nature of the order with which the court was concerned. In a very real sense, the decisions of both majority and minority, while incorporating generalised dicta about judicial power and the separation of powers, were relevant only to the narrow issue of mandatory orders. Subsequent decisions confirming the power and entitlement of the courts to intervene in areas claimed by the legislative or executive as beyond the judicial remit[41] confirm that *TD* and *Sinnott* did not necessarily signal a retrenchment by the courts from their responsibility to uphold and defend the Constitution in all circumstances.

From the point of view of this piece, the point to note about *Sinnott* and *TD* is that the concerns expressed by the members of the court were—in Irish constitutional terms—neither novel nor unprecedented. As noted above, the Irish courts have at almost all stages in the evolution of their constitutional case law demonstrated an awareness of the limitations of the judicial role. The development of the doctrines of unenumerated rights and natural law was accompanied by judicial observations about the dangers of ambiguity, uncertainty and judicial creativity contained therein.

Furthermore, the same courts that developed these doctrines also adopted a number of principles which were intended to afford a degree of protection to the acts of other branches as a mark of "that respect which one great organ of the State owes to another"[42]. Rules requiring individual standing to challenge an Act of the legislature as unconstitutional, the presumption of unconstitutionality and the double-

---

[40] Per Murray J.

[41] *Maguire v Ardagh* [2002] 1 IR 385 (SC); *Doherty v Government of Ireland* [2011] 2 IR 222 (HC); *Callely v Moylan* [2011] 1 IR 676 (HC); *McCrystal v Ireland* [2012] IESC 53 (8 November 2012).

[42] *Buckley v AG* [1950] IR 67 (SC) 80.

construction rule all operate to increase the burden on those seeking to impugn an Act as unconstitutional.

Indeed, it is perhaps most instructive to note that the initial judicial enthusiasm for the more creative doctrines discussed above has gradually waned as the potential problems identified by the courts at the outset became more difficult to manage.

Most notably, the courts seem now to have abandoned the natural law philosophy once its creative potential became outweighed by the adverse implications of its indeterminacy. This became clear during one of Ireland's abortion controversies when, following litigation over the question of whether a young rape victim would be permitted to travel to the United Kingdom for an abortion,[43] a referendum was passed by the People to secure the right of persons to access information on abortions and to travel abroad for the purposes of obtaining a termination. However, the claim was made both extra-judicially and in argument before the Supreme Court that natural law—as a source of principles which was not dependent on, or subservient to, any positive law—ought to prevail over the will of the People as expressed in the referendum. While the logic of the argument was internally sound, the conflict created between natural law norms and the principle of popular sovereignty was only ever likely to be resolved one way. The Supreme Court thus dismissed both the specific argument and the general philosophy upon which it was premised:

> "From a consideration of all the cases which recognised the existence of a personal right which was not specifically enumerated in the Constitution, it is manifest that the Court in each such case had satisfied itself that such personal right was one which could be reasonably implied from and was guaranteed by the provisions of the Constitution, interpreted in accordance with its ideas of prudence, justice and charity.
>
> The courts, as they were and are bound to, recognised the Constitution as the fundamental law of the State to which the organs of the State were subject and at no stage recognised the provisions of the natural law as superior to the Constitution."[44]

Less starkly, the unenumerated rights doctrine has also been the subject of some judicial hesitation. While it has not been overruled—and presumably could not without requiring a wholesale revision of Irish jurisprudence on constitutional rights—Keane CJ for one has cast doubt on whether *Ryan v Attorney General* ought to have been followed in the manner it ultimately was, and has suggested that the courts should be very slow to recognise any further unenumerated rights.

> "There was no explicit endorsement of th[e subsequently accepted] view in this court, perhaps because the right under discussion in that case was conceded on behalf of the Attorney General to be such an unenumerated right. Whether the formulation adopted by Kenny J is an altogether satisfactory guide to the identification of such rights is at least debatable. Secondly, there was no discussion in the judgment of this court as to whether the duty of declaring

43 *AG v X* [1992] 1 IR 1 (SC).

44 *Re Regulation of Information (Services outside the State for Termination of Pregnancies) Bill, 1995* [1995] 1 IR 1 (SC) 43.

> the unenumerated rights, assuming them to exist, should be the function of the courts rather than the Oireachtas.

In my judgment in *I O'T v B* [1998] 2 IR 321, I said at p 370 that:-

> '... save where such an unenumerated right has been unequivocally established by precedent, as, for example, in the case of the right to travel and the right of privacy, some degree of judicial restraint is called for in identifying new rights of this nature.'"[45]

Other recent case law has provided further evidence of a willingness on the part of the courts to investigate intermediate remedies that stop short of invalidating governmental acts as unconstitutional,[46] demonstrating again the general instinct of the Irish judiciary to avoid interference with the work of the other branches of government if that can be avoided.

4. Conclusion

In conclusion, therefore, the Irish courts played a key role in ensuring the Constitution lived up to objectives of its drafters in importing a more rights-based form of review into a common law system. The vision of the drafters was one which—if it was to be implemented—required a break from inherited traditions and a degree of open-mindedness in approaching and applying its various innovations. As Paul Gallagher has argued, this new constitutional order was conceived in holistic terms.

> "The term 'unique' is perhaps most appositely applied to the 1937 Constitution not with reference to its individual provisions as such, but with reference to the vision and balance it demonstrated in the legal, political and social context which prevailed internationally at the time of its adoption, and with reference to the remarkable fact that it enshrined, as early as 1937, many principles which did not take root internationally until later. If the Directive Principles can be considered to be one example of this, the Bunreacht's provision for judicial review of the constitutionality of legislation can be considered to be another."[47]

Giving effect to a novel, wide-ranging and inter-related set of constitutional arrangements represented a significant challenge for which some degree of creativity and flexibility was essential. While the drafters provide tools to guide the courts, it is only with the experience of real-world practices that it becomes possible to identify the best routes to the ultimate constitutional direction. The way in which the Irish judiciary experimented with innovative, implied constitutional norms illustrates such creativity and flexibility in action. However, the fact that the courts have continued to refine their approach in a manner which places significant emphasis—both rhetorical and practical—on the democratic, constitutional and

---

45 *TD v Minister for Education* [2001] 1 IR 259 (SC) 281.

46 For a discussion, see Eoin Carolan, "The Relationship between Judicial Remedies and the Separation of Powers: Collaborative Constitutionalism and the Suspended Declaration of Invalidity" (2011) 46 *Irish Jurist* 180.

47 Paul Gallagher, "The Irish Constitution—Its Unique Nature and the Relevance of International Jurisprudence" (2010) 45 *Irish Jurist* 22, 28-29.

institutional limitations of the judicial branch also demonstrates their awareness of the importance of these real-world practices. It is only as the case law develops, and evidence of the impact of previous practices emerges, that the courts have an opportunity to review and adjust their approach.

This suggests that, contrary to the received wisdom in relation to an activist judiciary, a more nuanced assessment of the courts' role is required. It is unquestionable that the Irish courts post-1937 adopted a broad interpretation of their powers. Yet the fate of the 1922 Constitution, crippled in part by continued reliance on the common law orthodoxies that it was intended to replace, shows clearly how a reserved approach can also illegitimately frustrate the operation of a constitution in the manner intended. Arguably, in their evolving attempt to balance the vindication of rights and of the constitutional system with the limitations of the judicial process, the Irish courts were ultimately following the *Marbury v Madison* conception of the judicial role under a Constitution that entrusted them with powers that are "are as ample as the defence of the Constitution requires".

CHAPTER 5

Administrative Law in Ireland: Legitimacy of Administration under the Evolving Influence of Constitutional Law

Mario Comba[1]

1. INTRODUCTION

Judicial review of administration is the classical topic usually tackled by comparative administrative studies, in addition to the limitations to delegation of legislative power in favour of the administration. However, a reader expecting to find such issues directly addressed in the present chapter will be disappointed. In fact, the selection of Irish administrative law problems analysed in this chapter is different, due primarily to the peculiarities of Irish administrative law and also to the fact that this is a book about Irish constitutional law, which implies that administrative law should be approached from a constitutional standpoint

There is another reason that must be taken into account, which concerns the innovative method followed in the preparation of this book. Italian constitutional law scholars have been asked to write about Irish law (in my case, about Irish administrative law) and Irish colleagues are supposed to comment on those papers, thus highlighting the foreign lawyers' perceptions of their own legal system. According to this very challenging comparative exercise, it is supposed that the analysis of Irish administrative law should focus on the topics that are at the heart of Irish debate and not on the topics that are usually tackled in comparative law studies. This is why this chapter will deal with judicial review of administration and non-delegation doctrine only instrumentally, in the sense that those topics will be tackled in so far they are useful to explain and assess other problems.

In particular, the legitimacy of administration in the framework of the separation of powers theory has recently come to the fore due to the publication of the book by Eoin Carolan,[2] which, even though based on a sound theoretical and comparative framework, is rooted mainly in British and Irish legal systems. The legitimacy of the exercise of discretion by the administration is also a fundamental problem of constitutional law applied to the administration and thus constitutes an important issue forming the subject of analysis in Pt 2. It is evident that, in this discourse, judicial review of administrative action is a central issue and, in fact, it will be

---

1 Professor of Comparative Public Law, University of Turin.

2 E Carolan, *The New Separation of Powers* (OUP, 2009). For reviews of the book, see DG Morgan in (2009) 44 *Irish Jurist* 276 and NW Barber in 2011 *Public Law* 456 .

considered as an instrument in order to justify administrative discretion within the framework of a modern theory of the separation of powers.

In Pt 3, I will deal with the influence of Irish constitutional law on administrative law, in the light of Gerard Hogan's introduction to the Irish Constitution published in an Italian book about the constitutions of EU Member States.[3] The introduction to the former contains a short paragraph on the relationship between the Constitution and administrative law. In this context, Hogan's leading idea was that Irish administrative law—as distinct from Irish constitutional law—was still very much influenced by the common law (of course, the reference was to British common law and not to US or other common law jurisdictions), but that it was gradually moving towards new patterns under the influence of constitutional law and of European law. This seemed to me another interesting theme to be analysed here, because it implies an investigation about the trends of Irish administrative law under the influence of constitutional law. I will tackle this issue following the three paths suggested by Hogan: (1) the constitutionalisation of the right to impartial administrative procedures; (2) the right to damages for breach of constitutional rights; and (3) the legitimate expectations doctrine.

There is an inevitable overlap between issues in Pt 2 and Pt 3. In particular, it will be seen that the legitimate expectation doctrine, addressed in Pt 3.3 as an example of the influence of constitutional law on administrative law, is also central in the reconstruction of the legitimacy of the administration created by the Irish courts, in the framework of a new theory of separation of powers where the administration is subject to the duty of substantial fairness.

2. Legitimacy of Administration in the Separation of Powers Doctrine

In the first application of the Irish constitution—as of all other constitutions influenced by Montesquieu's doctrine of separation of powers—the legitimacy of administration was rooted exclusively within the theory of the so called "transmission belt", according to which the political legitimacy of the legislature is transferred to the administration in so far as the administration, being part of the executive power, limits itself to the execution of the will of the Parliament.[4] This theory necessarily relies on the fiction that the administration does not exercise any discretionary power (or only a very limited one): hence the centrality of the non-delegation doctrine, which was drawn by Irish courts from the interpretation of Art 15.2.1° of the Constitution.[5]

It is, however, recognised that Irish courts—and in particular the Supreme Court—while always reaffirming the principle of constitutional limits on the delegation of legislative power, have in practice upheld statutes which were, in reality, delegating substantial aspects of such power to the administration. For instance, as Casey wrote

[3] G Hogan, "Introduzione alla costituzione irlandese" in *Le Costituzioni dei Paesi dell'Unione Europea* (E Palici di Suni, F Cassella and M Comba ed, Cedam, 2001) 435, 475.

[4] Carolan, *The New Separation of Powers* (OUP, 2009) 49–52.

[5] "The sole and exclusive power of making laws for the State is hereby vested in the Oireachtas: no other legislative authority has power to make laws for the State".

in reference to the *City View Press* decision of the Supreme Court, upholding a statute which authorised a public authority to impose levies on firms without specifying the ceiling of levies and their calculation:[6] "If provisions of such vagueness can pass muster it is not easy to imagine what would not".[7]

The "transmission belt" theory implies that judicial review is admitted only when the administrative body is exercising a quasi-judicial power while, when it is acting as a non-judicial body, only *ultra vires* and non-delegation tests are admitted.[8] Again, this consequence relies on the fiction that the administration has no discretionary power when acting as part of the executive power, since it is subject to strict governmental control.

It is probable that in states where the separation of powers is incorporated into the constitution as in Ireland, the rigid application of the model elaborated by Montesquieu renders it more difficult to recognise the existence of the administrative power as a power separate from the executive, thus reinforcing the "transmission belt" doctrine. It is, however, evident that this justification of the exercise of public power by the administration is largely outdated in the present administrative state, in which unelected officials exercise broad discretionary powers.[9]

Even if the "transmission belt" doctrine remains predominant in Irish case law—at least as a general declaration (if not always as operational rule)—Irish courts have occasionally mentioned other possible reasons for the legitimacy of the administration. One of them is technical expertise, which was cited in a couple of cases to justify the exercise of discretionary power by administrative bodies, considering it was a question of complex technical problems.[10] This doctrine is also criticised,[11] however, since it attempts to neutralise recourse to administrative discretion through the fiction of a technical and impartial decision.

---

6 *Cityview Press Ltd v AnCO* [1980] IR 381.

7 J Casey, *Constitutional Law in Ireland* (3rd ed, Sweet & Maxwell, 2000) 223. A different interpretation of *Cityview Press* is expressed by Carolan, according to whom the decision shows that the "transmission belt" theory continues to feature prominently in the Irish approach to the issue of administrative delegation (*The New Separation of Powers* (OUP, 2009) 107). It is possible that the different position may be motivated by the ambiguity of the decision, which proclaims the persistence of the "transmission belt" doctrine, but then in practice allows a very wide delegation of power. The Supreme Court seems aware of the challenge of drawing the boundaries of the non-delegation doctrine, as is evident from O'Donnell J's attempt to distinguish *Cityview Press* in the recent decision of *McGowan v Labour Court* [2013] IESC 21 paras 21–23 (holding that Pt III of the Industrial Relations Act 1946 is invalid having regard to the provisions of Art 15.2.1°). See also *John Grace Fried Chicken v Labour Court* [2011] 3 IR 211 (HC) and the Industrial Relations (Amendment) Act 2012, which responded to that decision.

8 That was the position of Irish courts: see *Lynham v Butler* [1933] IR 74 (SC); *State (Crowley) v Irish Land Commission* [1951] IR 250 (SC); and more recently, even if within a different framework, *TD v Minister for Education* [2001] 4 IR 259 (SC).

9 For a reconstruction of the evolution of the separation of powers, particularly in relation to the birth of the administrative state, see M Comba, "The Evolving Concept of Separation of Powers and Independent Administrative Agencies" in *Independent Administrative Authorities* (R Caranta, M Andenas and D Faigrieve ed, BIICL, 2005) 225.

10 *Laurentiu v Minister for Justice* [1999] 4 IR 26 (SC); *Dunne v Minister for Environment* [2004] IEHC 304.

11 Carolan, *The New Separation of Powers* (OUP, 2009) 108–109.

The quest for a theory of autonomous legitimacy of the administration leads to a search for substantive values underlying the administrative activity that could be considered as objective criteria of administrative legitimacy. If the "transmission belt" doctrine imposes only procedural limits on the administration, to be checked by the judiciary through the *ultra vires* doctrine based on the fiction of the administration simply executing the will of parliament upon governmental instructions, the new legitimacy has to be grounded on more substantial values. The doctrine of legitimate expectations can be a sound answer to this question, because it consists of the duty of the administration to act fairly and as such it is beginning to be construed by Irish courts reviewing the activity of the administration.[12] The doctrine of legitimate expectations is more precisely analysed in Pt 3.3, but is mentioned here because it can help to reconstruct the evolution of doctrines on the legitimacy of the administration in Irish constitutional law.

In addition to the doctrine of legitimate expectations, the doctrine of proportionality can be considered as an instrument of autonomous legitimacy for the administration, since it is used by Irish courts to weigh the impact of the public interest against the position of the individual, and thus again constitutes a check on the substantive fairness of administrative activity.[13]

To a continental lawyer, it is surprising that the third element considered by Irish scholars as a new tool for legitimating the administration is the duty to give reasons.[14] This is because under the French model of administrative law, adopted throughout the European continent, this is a quite old assumption introduced by administrative courts and then often acknowledged by statute law. It is, however, reasonable to include this element among the tools created by Irish and British courts in order to impose a duty of substantial fairness on the administration, because in fact the duty to give reasons is a necessary condition for controlling the fairness of the administration.

Legitimate expectations and proportionality doctrines feature a duty on the part of the administration to act fairly, not only procedurally but also substantively, which softens the necessity for the administration to derive its legitimacy from the government, through the "transmission belt" of political representation and which enables it to be autonomously legitimated. The control of the courts over this substantive quality of the activity of the administration cannot be considered as an extension of judicial review of administrative discretion, because it should always be respectful of policy decisions and must act only in the context of an ever-evolving process of the inter-institutional model of decision-making.[15]

---

[12] *ibid*, 226–237.

[13] *Heaney v Ireland* [1996] 1 IR 580, where the Supreme Court imposed a specific test on the administration for justifying the infringment of the Art 40.6.1° constitutional right to silence, with particular reference to the proportionality to the objective of the effects on rights . See also *Re Article 26 and Part V of the Planning and Development Bill 1999* [2000] 2 IR 321. The extent to which proportionality review of administrative decisions does involve a test of their substantive fairness remains unclear, given the different readings of the decision in *Meadows v Minister for Justice* [2010] 2 IR 701 (SC).

[14] Carolan, *The New Separation of Powers* (OUP, 2009) 243–246. The broad scope of the duty to give reasons has now been confirmed by the decision in *Mallak v Minister for Justice Equality and Law Reform* [2012] IESC 59 (6 December 2012).

[15] Outlined in Carolan, *The New Separation of Powers* (OUP, 2009), particularly Ch 6.

The Irish debate about legitimacy of the administration can be well integrated into the European one, which is framed within almost the same terms.[16] In addition, in some EU Member States, the "transmission belt" doctrine, representing the typical instrument of "input" legitimacy, is considered anachronistic, and research is heading towards other forms of "input" legitimacy, such as direct participation in the administrative process by the people (administrative referenda, direct election of administrative officers and so on).

However, it is the "output" legitimacy that represents the more interesting and challenging issue in the present debate: from the Weberian model of good administration, which was the main legitimacy of European administration,[17] to many other emerging forms of legitimacy, among which is the substantive fairness of the administration.[18] This is, in fact, a point where "input" and "output" legitimacy converge: if control over the result of administrative activity (output) is performed also through the participation of interested citizens, or, more realistically, of different interest groups (input), a reconciliation between "input" and "output" legitimacy can be more easily discerned.

And here the connection with the Irish situation is evident, also taking into account the peculiarities of the Irish administrative system, which operates against the background of a common law jurisdiction. It is, however, noticeable that the development of the legitimate expectation and proportionality doctrines, as fostered by Irish courts, can also be considered as a model for the legitimacy process of the administration through inter-institutional dialogue in other EU Member States.

3. Irish Administrative Law: Towards a Civil Law Model Through the Influence of Constitutional Law?

As already explained in Pt 1, in his introduction to the Irish constitution, Gerard Hogan introduced the idea that Irish administrative law—still much influenced by British common law—was gradually moving towards new patterns under the influence of constitutional law and of European law.

This is a very interesting approach, especially for a comparativist: Irish administrative law is moving from a common law model towards a civil law model due to the influence of Irish constitutional law and European law. The phenomenon is of course easier to understand with regard to European law: it is, for example, well known that in the field of public procurement, and particularly with the Remedies Directive, the French model of *Contrat administratif* is influencing Member States with common law jurisdictions.[19] Another example could be shared administration,

---

16 The issue is accurately examined in M Ruffert ed, *Legitimacy in European Administrative Law: Reform and Reconstruction* (Europa Law Publishing, 2010). For an European law comparative overview, see R Caranta, "Democracy, Legitimacy and Accountability—Is There a Common European Theoretical Framework?" in Ruffert ed, 177.

17 P Craig, "Legitimacy in Adminstrative Law: European Union" in *ibid*, 197.

18 According to Rufert, "Judicial control is a special feature of the legitimacy of administrative law". See "Comparative Perspectives of Administrative Legitimacy" in *ibid*, 353, 360.

19 M Comba, "La direttiva ricorsi (2007/66/CE) e le sue conseguenze a livello sistematico: l'imposizione del modello francese di «contrat administratif»" in *Il recepimento della direttiva 2007/66/CE. Il rito speciale degli appalti nel nuovo codice del processo amministrativo e le*

or co-administration, of structural funds, where the administrative structure of the European Union influences the administrative organisation of Member States.[20]

The issue is more subtle when it comes to the influence of constitutional law as a driver for shifting Irish administrative law towards new models other than common law. At this point, one should question what is the common law model of administrative law—almost an oxymoron[21]— from which Irish administrative law is differentiating itself, but we do not have space enough here to deepen the issue. Another interesting field of comparative investigation could be to examine the evolution of administrative law in common law systems with a written constitution in order to check if there is any shared feature that differentiates it from the only one without such a constitution, i.e. the UK. But, again, that could perhaps be the subject for a future publication, because we do not have enough space here.

For the purposes of this chapter, I intend to take inspiration from the 2001 Introduction, in which Gerard Hogan listed three examples of the influence of Irish constitutional law on Irish administrative law, namely: (1) the constitutionalisation of the right to impartial administrative procedures; (2) the right to damages for the breach of constitutional rights; and (3) the principle of proportionality, from the perspective of the legitimate expectations doctrine. It is my intention to analyse these three examples with a comparativist approach, having in mind the Italian situation as a term of reference.

3.1 The Constitutionalisation of the Right to Impartial Administrative Procedures

In Hogan and Morgan's handbook on administrative law in Ireland,[22] the constitutionalisation of administrative procedures is labelled under the title "Constitutional Justice", which is quite striking for an Italian constitutional lawyer, since in current Italian terminology constitutional justice usually stands for the procedural law in front of the Constitutional Court, and has nothing to do with administrative procedure.

---

sue conseguenze sul processo di aggiudicazione (M Comba ed, Torino, IUSE Working Papers, 2011, 62) (www.workingpapers.iuse.it; last accessed 10 May 2013). For a classification of public procurement contracts in EU Member States, see JB Auby, "Comparative Approaches to the Rise of Contract in the Public Sphere" (2007) *Public Law* 40 and M Fromont, *Droit Administratif des Etats Européens*, (Presses Universitaires de France, 2006) 297. The influence of the French model on the British scheme of public procurement is recognised (and called for) also by English scholars: see ACL Davies, "English Law's Treatment of Governments Contracts: The Problem of Wider Public Interests" in *The Public Law/Private Law Divide: Une Entente Assez Cordiale?* (M Freeland and JB Auby ed, Hart, 2006) 113.

20 P Craig, "Shared Administration, Disbursment of Community Funds and the Regulatory State" in *Legal Challenges in EU Administrative Law* (HCH Hofman and AH Turk ed, Elgar, 2009) 34; JB Auby and R Dutheil de la Rochère ed, *Droit Administratif Européen: Partie 2 – L'Administration Indirecte et la Coadministration* (Bruylant, 2007) 235; P Craig, *EU Administrative Law* (Oxford University Press, 2006) 57; E Chiti and C Franchini, *L'integrazione amministrativa europea* (Il Mulino, 2003).

21 The reasons as to why administrative law was not developed in common law systems were explained in G Hogan and DG Morgan, *Administrative Law in Ireland* (3rd ed, Round Hall Sweet & Maxwell, 1998) 2.

22 *ibid.*

Having overcome this different characterisation, one has to recognise that Irish constitutional case law on administrative procedure has produced operational rules that are quite similar to those incorporated in the Italian administrative procedure act (Law 241 of 1990). Principles such as "a person affected must have notice", the "duty of the administration to give reasons" or the "promptness of the decision" are also relatively common in Italian law. However, Italian law lacks the right to an oral hearing, only providing for a right to send written memoranda and documents. Space does not permit a more definitive comparative analysis of specific cases, but one can refer to the comparative studies on fair administrative procedures[23] and to the models outlined in those studies.

What can be said, as a general point, is that in Italy the main source of the fair administrative procedure is contained in statute, specifically Law 241 of 1990 and regional laws (each specific region has enacted its own administrative procedure act), which are usually very similar to the national law. However, there is also a constitutional principle that the Constitutional Court derives from Art 97 of the Constitution, declaring the duty of impartiality of the administration.[24] The constitutional source in Ireland seems to be Art 40.3.1° of the Constitution,[25] interpreted in both procedural and substantive terms.[26] The main difference is that in Italy the principle of fair administrative procedure stems from a duty of the administration to be impartial, while in Ireland it is part of a fundamental right of the citizen, in its procedural dimension.

If the operational rules in Italy and Ireland do not seem so different, the legal debate is very different, because of the different backgrounds against which the constitutionalisation of procedural rights was introduced.

In Italy, the reference to Art 97 of the Constitution, which is not in Pt I (fundamental rights) but in Pt II (organisation of the Republic), prompted a debate as to whether the administrative procedure law was aimed at protecting the interests of the administration, in order to foster its efficiency, or the interests of the citizen, in order to protect his or her rights. The two positions often concur, but sometimes they can be differentiated. The duty of the administration to examine the citizen's written memoranda and documents before issuing the administrative decision can be seen as being aimed at letting the administration take the best possible decision, even if contrary to the citizen's interests, or to protect the citizen's interests.

This kind of debate does not seem to exist in Ireland. This is probably due to the fact that the constitutional basis for administrative procedure is rooted in Art 40.3, which deals with fundamental rights. The cultural roots of the Italian position could be, at

---

23 E Palici di Suni, *I diritti al procedimento. Profili di diritto comparato* (Giappichelli, 1994): the two main models of administrative procedure are the Austrian one, after the 1925 Austrian law on administrative procedure, and the US one, after the 1946 US Administrative Procedure Act.

24 Corte costituzionale, sentenza 28 novembre 2008, n. 390.

25 Art 40.3.1° of Irish Constitution: "The State guarantees in its laws to respect, and, as far as practicable, by its laws to defend and vindicate the personal rights of the citizen".

26 Hogan and Morgan, *Administrative Law in Ireland* (3rd ed, Round Hall Sweet & Maxwell, 1998) 503.

least partially, traced back to Jellinek's theory of public subjective rights, while the Irish tradition of constitutional rights is free from that influence.

On the contrary, Irish constitutional lawyers have discussed at length the distinction between natural justice and constitutional justice as the source for fair administrative procedure. The Supreme Court stated its position in the *McDonald* decision of 1965,[27] with the consequence that fair procedure rules could not be modified by statute, as they could if grounded in common law; but it seems the debate was not conclusively resolved by then. In Italy that was not a problem, for the obvious reason that Italy does not have a common law background. But the debate is interesting for understanding Gerard Hogan's ideas about constitutional law as a tool for softening the links between Irish administrative law and the common law. In fact, if the principle of fair administrative procedure finds its legal basis in the Constitution instead of the common law, the whole matter is subject to constitutional law rules rather than common law ones, with all the theoretical and practical consequences this entails.

3.2 The Right to Damages for Breach of Constitutional Rights

Remedies for breach of constitutional rights[28] are another example of the influence that Irish constitutional law has exerted on Irish administrative law in order to loosen its ties with the common law. Here, it is meaningful to recall the judgment of Justice Walsh in the leading 1973 case of *Meskell*,[29] in which he stated that constitutional rights can be protected or enforced by action "even though such action may not fit into any of the ordinary forms of action in either common law or equity".[30]

It can thus be said that there exists in Ireland an action for damages directly based on the Constitution, at least in those cases where common law remedies are inadequate or inexistent.

This is something unknown to Italian law, because in Italy (like the other civil law systems)[31] there are not different actions for damages according to the different substantial rights in issue, and thus there is no residual action for damages deriving from the breach of constitutional rights. In civil law jurisdictions the legal basis for damages is usually applicable, without distinction, to the unjust breach of any right, be it statutory or constitutional. The burden of proof required is the same, as are the principles for the quantification of damages, and it is well known that punitive (or

27 *McDonald v Bord na gCon* [1965] IR 217, 242: "In the context of the Constitution, natural justice might be more appropriately termed constitutional justice and must be understood to import more than the two well-established principles that no man shall be judge in his own cause and *audi alteram partem*". It can be said that after 1965 in Ireland the principle of fair administrative procedure has lost its ties with common law under the influence of constitutional law.

28 See for instance JM Kelly, *The Irish Constitution* (4th ed, Gerard W Hogan and Gerry Whyte ed, Lexis Nexis Butterworths, 2003) 1302–1315; Hogan and Morgan *Administrative Law in Ireland* (3rd ed, Round Hall Sweet & Maxwell, 1998) 819–827.

29 *Meskell v CIE* [1973] IR 121 (SC) 132–133.

30 *ibid.*

31 See for instance, s 24(1) of the Canadian Charter of Rights and Freedoms, which empowers courts to order any remedy that the court considers "appropriate and just in the circumstances for breach of rights and freedoms guaranteed by the Charter". See Supreme Court of Canada in *Vancouver (City) v Ward* 2010 SCC 27.

exemplary) damages do not exist (with a new and limited exception introduced by the EU Remedies Directive in public procurement).[32]

In my view, the main point is another one. Under the Italian theory of "legitimate interest" (*interesse legittimo*), when the administration is exercising its discretionary power against a person, the latter is not entitled to a right against the administration, but only to a legitimate interest. A legitimate interest is something less than a right and is given legal protection in front of special courts called administrative tribunals (not to be confused with UK or Irish administrative tribunals). For example, if a person asks the administration for a taxi-driver licence, he or she does not have a right but rather a legitimate interest, just as when he or she is opposing the expropriation of land from the local road agency. On the other hand, the administration does not have a discretionary power when liberty or privacy rights are concerned, which means that a person has a right, and not only a legitimate interest, against illegal arrest or telephone tapping, for example.

Until 1999, Italian case law ruled out the possibility of claiming damages for breach of legitimate interest, the only remedy being the nullification of the illegitimate act of the administration. Only in 1999 did the Corte di Cassazione admit such a remedy, albeit with certain limitations which cannot be explained here. It follows that until 1999 a case like *Conway v INTO*[33] would have resulted in a completely different outcome in Italy from that reached by the Irish Supreme Court in 1991.

Conway arose out of the interruption of primary schooling in certain schools as a result of an industrial dispute; the plaintiff asked for damages for the breach of the constitutional right to education. The Supreme Court awarded the plaintiff both compensatory damages and punitive or exemplary damages. An Italian court, prior to 1999, probably would not have awarded any damages, on the basis that schooling is a public service which does not generate a right but only a legitimate interest, even if it is recognised by the Constitution. Post-1999, damages could be awarded only if the plaintiff could prove (1) a real pecuniary damage and (2) the negligence of the administration. No punitive or exemplary damages could be awarded.

In addition, it must be remembered that in the 1987 case of *PH v Murphy* the Irish High Court ruled that constitutional rights must be applied also against other private parties:

> "Uniquely, the Irish Constitution confers a right of action for breach of constitutionally protected rights against persons other than the State and its officials."[34]

---

32 Directive 2007/66 on remedies in public procurement procedures, which introduces art 2f to Directive 89/665.

33 *Conway v INTO* [1991] 2 IR 305.

34 *PH v Murphy (John) and Sons Ltd* [1987] IR 621 (HC) 626. For comments, see JM Kelly, *The Irish Constitution* (4th ed, Gerard W Hogan and Gerry Whyte ed, Lexis Nexis Butterworths, 2003) 1293; Hogan and Morgan *Administrative Law in Ireland* (3rd ed, Round Hall Sweet & Maxwell, 1998) 822 n116; C O'Cinneide, "Irish Constitutional Law and Direct Effect–A Succesful Experiment" in *Human Rights in the Private Sphere: A Comparative Study* (J Fedtke and D Oliver ed, Routledge-Cavendish, 2007) 213 and "Taking Horizontal Effect Seriously: Private Law, Constitutional Rights and the European Convention on Human Rights" (2003) *Hibernian Law Journal* 77; C Donnelly, "Problems of Legitimacy in Contracting Out and

Even if, in reality, it seems that subsequent case law has limited the possible consequences of *PH v Murphy,* it nevertheless provides an interesting issue for comparison, considering the difficulties which the Italian Constitutional Court—as well as other European constitutional courts—have experienced in recognising the horizontal effect of constitutional rights.[35]

3.3 The Legitimate Expectations Doctrine

The doctrine of legitimate expectation has already been partially examined in Pt 2 of this chapter as a feature of the legitimacy of the administration in a new theory of separation of powers. The same doctrine is analysed in this part but from a different perspective outlined in Gerard Hogan's Introduction, namely that it represents one of the main evolutions of Irish administrative law under the influence of constitutional law.

The doctrine of legitimate expectation should be framed in Irish constitutional law as a consequence of the seminal 1972 decision in *Byrne v. Ireland*,[36] in which the Irish Supreme Court, after an accurate comparative analysis of state immunity from suit for wrongs, concluded that immunity from suit is not a necessary ingredient of state sovereignty. Building on these grounds, the Supreme Court went on to state that the Irish Constitution does not grant any immunity for State activity, since it has not absorbed the common law principle by which "[t]he king can do no wrong". Therefore, the Supreme Court recognised that in Ireland, contrary to the general assumption of the common law, the State is liable for the torts of its servants.

Having opened the way to State liability, the doctrine of legitimate expectations received its imprimatur in Ireland in 1988 with the decision *Webb v Ireland*,[37] in which the Supreme Court ruled that the plaintiff, who had found treasure containing exceptionally valuable ancient artistic objects and had conferred them to the National Museum, had a legitimate expectation to receive a reward, since it was a long-standing practice of the Museum to pay rewards to treasury finders.[38]

In 2001, with *Glencar Exploration plc v Mayo County Council*[39] the doctrine was

Privatisation" in *Legitimacy in European Administrative Law: Reform and Reconstruction* (Ruffert ed, Europa Law Publishing, 2010) 278–280.

35 Even though Italian comparativist scholars recognised the importance of the issue many years ago: see G Lombardi, *Potere privato e diritti fondamentali* (Giappichelli, 1967).

36 *Byrne v Ireland* [1972] IR 241 (SC). The majority opinion written by Walsh J is a great example of recourse to comparative arguments in judicial decisions. In particular, Walsh J examined extensively the legal systems of France, Germany, Australia, Canada, New Zeland, South Africa and the US in order to demonstrate that "immunity from suit for wrongs is not a necessary ingredient of State sovereignty" (*ibid*, 269).

37 *Webb v Ireland* [1988] IR 353 (SC). In England, the doctrine of legitimate expectation was introduced 20 years earlier than in Ireland in an *obiter dictum* by Lord Denning MR in *Schmidt v Secretary for Home Affairs* [1969] 2 WLR 337, but on a common law basis rather than a constitutional law basis, as in Ireland.

38 Hogan and Morgan, *Administrative Law in Ireland* (3rd ed, Round Hall Sweet & Maxwell, 1998) 860 ff; JP Casey, *Constitutional Law in Ireland* (3rd ed, Round Hall Sweet & Maxwell, 2000) 49–50; H Delany, "The Future of the Doctrine of Legitimate Expectations in Irish Administrative Law" (1997) *Irish Jurist* 217.

39 *Glencar Exploration plc v Mayo County Council (No 2)* [2002] IR 84 (SC).

more widely defined, since the court listed the requirements necessary in order to have the doctrine applied.

> "Firstly, the public authority must have made a statement or adopted a position amounting to a promise or representation, express or implied as to how it will act in respect of an identifiable area of its activity. I will call this the representation. Secondly, the representation must be addressed or conveyed either directly or indirectly to an identifiable person or group of persons, affected actually or potentially, in such a way that it forms part of a transaction definitively entered into or a relationship between that person or group and the public authority or that the person or group has acted upon the faith of the representation. Thirdly, it must be such as to create an expectation reasonably entertained by the person or group that the public authority will abide by the representation to the extent that it would be unjust to permit the public authority to resile from it. Refinements are extensions of these propositions are obviously possible. Equally they are qualified by considerations of the public interest including the principle that freedom to exercise a statutory power properly is to be respected. However, the propositions I have endeavoured to formulate seem to me to be preconditions for the right to invoke the doctrine."[40]

The doctrine of legitimate expectations in essence imposes a duty on the administration to act fairly[41] in order to avoid the frustration of legitimate expectations it has created with its behaviour. There are, however, many possible diverging contents of the doctrine. For instance, it is debated whether it is justified by a commitment to good administration or to the protection of an individual's position and, in the latter case, whether it refers only to procedural or also to substantial claims of the individual against the administration.[42]

In Italy, a similar rule was introduced by the Constitutional Court[43] as a limit on the legislator against retroactive legislation (which is explicitly forbidden by the Constitution in criminal issues only) on the basis of the constitutional principle of reasonableness (which the Constitutional Court has drawn from Art 3.1 of the Constitution[44]), and it is also admitted in the case law of the Consiglio di Stato (the higher administrative court). The connection between retroactive legislation and legitimate expectations relies on the assumption that the citizen may expect the legislature not to modify retroactively laws unreasonably, and therefore his or her expectation is protected by the Constitution when retroactivity of the new law is not reasonable. The Italian Constitutional Court construed the doctrine as committed to the protection of an individual's position, not only procedural but also substantive.

It would be interesting to analyse the specific cases in which Irish and Italian case

40 *ibid*, 162–163.
41 E Carolan, *The New Separation of Powers* (OUP, 2009) 226.
42 *ibid*, 227.
43 Corte Cost., 17 dicembre 1985, n. 349; Corte Cost., 14 luglio 1988, n. 822; Corte Cost., 26 luglio 1995, n. 390; Corte Cost., 4 novembre 1999, n. 416; Corte Cost., 22 novembre 2000, n. 525,; Corte Cost., 12 novembre 2002, n. 446.
44 Art 3.1 of Italian Constitution: "All citizens have equal social dignity and are equal before the law, without distinction of sex, race, language, religion, political opinion, personal and social conditions."

law recognise the presence of a legitimate expectation, but it is not possible to do so here. It is, however, important to stress that the theoretical problem underlying the legitimate expectation doctrine seems to be similar in Italy and in Ireland. The problem has two main aspects: (1) legitimate expectations can bind the administration to do something which is not within its legitimate discretion to do and (2) legitimate expectations can bind the administration to do something that is in its discretionary power to do, but that perhaps it is not convenient to do in the future.

The first problem is considered by Irish case law[45] on the assumption that the legitimate expectation doctrine cannot force the administration to act illegally, because in this case the expectation is not legitimate. If the administration promises to do something illegal, it cannot be forced to do so; neither can it be forced to act illegally only because it did so on a previous occasion. The rule is similar in Italy, but there is an exception when the administration acted illegally in favour of someone and after some time it realises the situation and wants to self-annul the illegal measure. In this case, Italian law says that the illegal measure can be nullified only if there is a specific public interest reason other than the simple elimination of illegality and taking into consideration the legitimate expectations of the affected person in relation to the elapsed time. In other words, if it is true that the administration is not bound to act illegally in the future only because it promised to do so or because it did so in another occasion, it is also true that, if the administration actually acted illegally in the past, it cannot always self-nullify its illegal act. Rather, it has to evaluate the time elapsed and the public interest and weigh them against the legitimate expectation that it created in the recipient of the illegal act.

The second problem is more difficult. It includes the consideration that it would be *ultra vires* to fetter the administration's discretionary powers by an agreement of any kind because they have to remain discretionary.[46] If we take it literally, no legitimate expectation doctrine could exist, under any circumstances, and nobody could trust an obligation concluded with the administration.

In Italy, the problem is approached through a distinction between the administration acting in a private-law rather than in a public-law capacity: in the first case fettering is permitted, while in the second it is more problematic.[47] In Hogan and Morgan's book on Irish administrative law, there is a hint of this distinction but only through a reference to Paul Craig's book on UK administrative law.[48] It therefore remains

---

[45] Hogan and Morgan, *Administrative Law in Ireland* (3rd ed, Round Hall Sweet & Maxwell, 1998) 860–862.

[46] *ibid*, 860–865.

[47] Italian scholars have addressed the problem particularly with reference to contracts of the administration. See for instance G Greco, *I contratti dell'Amministrazione tra diritto pubblico e privato. I contratti ad evidenza pubblica* (Giuffré, 1986); *Accordi amministrativi tra provvedimento e contratto* (Giappichelli, 2003); C Cicero, *Contratto pubblico e principi di diritto privato* (Cedam, 2011). A comparative approach, with reference to the British common law, can be found in A Benedetti, *I contratti della pubblica amministrazione tra specialità e diritto comune* (Giappichelli, 1999).

[48] Hogan and Morgan, *Administrative Law in Ireland* (3rd ed, Round Hall Sweet & Maxwell, 1998) 864, citing P Craig, *Administrative Law* (2nd ed, Sweet & Maxwell, 1983). Later editions of Craig's *Administrative Law* do not deepen the distinction: in the last edition (2008), the ability of the administration to exercise its contractual capacity infringing the no-fettering rule is limited to a short paragraph (p 527, para 16.030).

open as to whether an Italian-type approach will be followed in future Irish case law on the subject.

A typical application of this distinction between the administration acting in a private-law and public-law capacity can be found in the execution phase of public procurement after the award of the contract, where the contracting authority acts as an economic operator and is therefore bound by obligation assumed with the contract (even if an accurate comparative analysis can show that in this phase the administration also retains some relevant public powers).[49]

On the other hand, if the administration acts in its public-law capacity, the general rule is that it can always modify its position in the exercise of its public power, if it demonstrates that the public interest has changed. However, the Italian legislator allows the administration to bind itself, even when acting in its public-law capacity, with a special legal device called a "contract additional to or substituting for an administrative act", which is a binding contract, ruled by the civil code, but with the possibility for the administration to cancel it for public interest reasons. However, this is subject to a very strict burden of proof concerning the modification of public interest and involves the payment of an indemnity. It is a compromise between the protection of legitimate expectations and the no-fettering rule, which was introduced in Italy with Law 241 of 1990 and was not much used until an amendment of 2005, which permitted its invocation in a wider range of cases.

49 M Fromont, "L'Évolution du Droit des Contrats de l'Administration–Differences Thèoriques et Convergences de Fait" in *Comparative Law of Public Contracts Treatise/Traité de Droit Comparé des Contrats Publics* (R Noguellou and U Stelkens ed, Bruylant, 2010) 263.

CHAPTER 6

Rights and Freedoms in the Domestic Context – Fair Procedures in Difficult Times

Dr Ailbhe O'Neill[1]

1. Introduction and Scope

Faced with producing a paper with the title "Rights and Freedoms in the Domestic Context," the scholar of Irish constitutional law has a number of enticing options from which to choose. The fundamental rights provisions of Bunreacht na hÉireann have generated a volume of case law that provides rich source material and sufficient idiosyncrasies to keep the interest of even the most jaded of comparative legal scholars. One could devote an entire paper, for example, to the evolution (and uneven application) of the proportionality doctrine as a means of analysing claims of unconstitutionality.[2] Remedies for breaches of constitutional rights provide another fruitful source of material. The acceptance that constitutional rights are applicable horizontally in Ireland often surprises the outside observer—as does the fact that this development has not led to a flood of successful litigation.[3]

While these are all interesting areas of analysis, the topic of this paper is slightly different. It focuses instead on the development by the Irish courts of the right to fair procedures in administrative decision-making. Recent cases suggest that the Supreme Court sees fair procedures as an important right to be strictly defended even in the context of legislation enacted in order to deal with the financial crisis.[4]

The right to fair procedures is one of the unenumerated rights read into the Constitution by the judiciary. Before looking at fair procedures specifically, some background on the development of unenumerated rights—itself an interesting aspect of Irish constitutional jurisprudence—is provided.

2. Fundamental Rights under Arts 40–44

The personal rights and freedoms of the citizen are stated in Arts 40–44 of the Irish Constitution.[5] The list of rights and freedoms contained in those provisions

---

1 Assistant Professor in Law, Trinity College Dublin.

2 See, for example, Foley, *Deference and the Presumption of Constitutionality* (Institute of Public Administration, Dublin, 2008).

3 See Hogan and Whyte ed, *Kelly: The Irish Constitution* (Lexis Nexis Butterworths, 3rd ed, Dublin, 2003), pp 1291–1294 and 1311–1315.

4 *Dellway v National Asset Management Agency* [2011] 4 IR 1; [2011] IESC 4. Murphy CJ, Denham, Hardiman, Fennelly, Macken, Finnegan and McKechnie JJ.

5 In addition to Arts 40–44, it is worth noting that Art 38.1, which concerns the trial of criminal

includes guarantees relating to life, liberty, equality before the law, private property, freedom of expression, freedom of association and freedom of assembly, freedom of conscience, and free practice and profession of religion. Rights to education and the protection of the family are also set out in these provisions. The right to one's good name set out in Art 40.3.2° has been a vehicle for the recognition of a variety of important procedural protections where the reputation of the individual is at stake.[6] These are part of a broader requirement of fair procedures that has been identified by the Irish courts as part of the evolution of unenumerated rights.

3. Unenumerated Rights

In addition to the rights specifically set out in the text, Art 40.3 of the Constitution has been read as implying that there are other rights protected under the Constitution that are not explicitly listed in the text. The relevant constitutional provisions read as follows:

> "1° The State guarantees in its laws to respect, and, as far as practicable, by its laws to defend and vindicate the personal rights of the citizen.
>
> 2° The State shall, *in particular*, by its laws protect as best it may from unjust attack and, in the case of injustice done, vindicate the life, person, good name, and property rights of every citizen."[7]

This potential of the emphasised text to serve as the basis for implying additional rights into the Constitution was first realised in the seminal case of *Ryan v Attorney General*,[8] in which Kenny J held that the words "in particular" in Art 40.3.2° implied that there were other rights protected under the Constitution, additional to the "personal rights" listed in Art 40.3.1°. Referring to the "Christian and democratic nature of the State", Kenny J indicated that there was a range of unenumerated rights protected under the Constitution. Referring to a papal encyclical,[9] he found that one of the rights that were so protected was the right to "bodily integrity".

The approach taken by Kenny J in *Ryan*, while it can be seen as an example of judicial activism,[10] had some support in the text of the Constitution, additional to the provisions of Art 40.3 itself. Certain of the provisions of the Constitution refer to the rights protected therein as being "natural", "inalienable" and "imprescriptible" rights that are "antecedent and superior to all natural law".[11] The use of this language suggests that the Constitution is merely declaratory of rights that exist as a matter of natural law.[12] The Constitution also contains evidence of the influence of the Roman Catholic Church. The Preamble invokes

offences, has been interpreted to require a variety of procedural protections for accused persons. See Hogan and Whyte, *op. cit*, pp 1039–1239.

6 *Re Haughey* [1971] IR 217 (SC) was the first such case.

7 Emphasis added.

8 [1965] IR 294.

9 *Pacem in Terris*.

10 It is worth noting that the plaintiff in the case, who was challenging a decision to add fluoride to the water supply, was ultimately unsuccessful. The right to bodily integrity identified by Kenny J was found not be have been violated, because she had failed to prove that the process had a harmful effect on her or her children.

11 See Art 41.1.1°, Art 42.1, Art 42.5 and Art 43.1.1°.

12 The Constitution Review Group took the view that "the drafters of the 1937 Constitution clearly

> "the Most Holy Trinity, from Whom is all authority and to Whom, as our final end, all actions both of men and States must be referred"

and acknowledges the people's "obligations to our Divine Lord, Jesus Christ, Who sustained our fathers through centuries of trial". Art 6.1 provides that: "All powers of government, legislative, executive and judicial, derive, under God, from the people." In Art 44.1:

> "The State acknowledges that the homage of public worship is due to Almighty God. It shall hold His Name in reverence, and shall respect and honour religion."

Despite these theocratic references, the use of natural law has not consistently been identified with Roman Catholic moral teaching. In *McGee v Attorney General*,[13] natural law was relied on to ground a constitutional right to "marital privacy", which rendered a ban on the importation of contraceptives unconstitutional—a finding that contradicted the position of the Vatican as set out in *Humanae Vitae*.

While the practice of reading rights into the Constitution raises difficult questions, the courts continued to do so, recognising a panoply of constitutional rights in Art 40.3, including the right to individual privacy,[14] the right to work and to earn a livelihood,[15] the right of autonomy,[16] the right to dignity,[17] the right to litigate and the right of access to the courts,[18] the right to justice and fair procedures,[19] the right to travel within the State,[20] the right to travel outside the State[21] and the right to communicate.[22] The courts have also identified a number of rights that affect individuals in the context of their family relationships, such as the right to marry,[23] the right to beget children,[24] the right to independent domicile,[25] the right to maintenance[26] and the rights of children.[27]

There are many criticisms that can be and have been made of the natural law approach and the practice of creating new rights.[28] These include the lack of certainty about

---

held natural law principles"; *The Report of the Constitution Review Group* (Stationery Office, Dublin, 1996), p 249.

13 [1974] IR 284.

14 *Norris v A.G.* [1984] IR 36; *Kennedy v Ireland* [1987] IR 587; [1988] ILRM 472.

15 *Murtagh Properties v Cleary* [1972] IR 466

16 *Re a Ward of Court (withholding medical treatment) (No.2)* [1996] 2 IR 79; [1995] 2 ILRM 401.

17 *Re a Ward of Court (withholding medical treatment) (No.2)* [1996] 2 IR 79; [1995] 2 ILRM 401.

18 *State (Quinn) v Ryan* [1965] IR 70; (1966) 100 ILTR 105; *Macauley v Minister for Posts and Telegraphs* [1966] IR 345; *Tuohy v Courtney* [1994] 3 IR 1; [1994] 2 ILRM 503.

19 *Glover v BLN Ltd.* [1973] IR 388.

20 *Ryan v Attorney General* [1965] IR 294.

21 *State (M) v Attorney General* [1979] IR 73.

22 *Murphy v Independent Radio and Television Commission* [1999] 1 IR 12; [1998] 2 ILRM 360.

23 *Ryan v Attorney General* [1965] IR 294; *McGee v Attorney General* [1974] IR 284; (1974) ILTR 29.

24 *Murray v Ireland* [1985] IR 532; [1985] ILRM 124.

25 *CM v TM (No.2)* [1990] 2 IR 52; [1991] ILRM 268.

26 *CM v TM (No.2)* [1990] 2 IR 52; [1991] ILRM 268.

27 *Re Article 26 and the Adoption (No.2) Bill 1987* [1989] IR 656; [1989] ILRM 266.

28 Hogan, "Unenumerated Personal Rights: Ryan's Case Re-evaluated" (1990–1992) *Irish Jurist*

the source of natural law as well as its content, which arguably leaves judges (who are unelected in Ireland) to choose what natural law to apply. In the context of the enumerated right to life of the unborn (which is protected in Art 40.3.3° of the Constitution), there was also a debate about the hierarchical relationship between natural law and the Constitution, the suggestion being that natural law might constrain the extent to which the Constitution could be amended.[29]

That argument was explicitly rejected by the Supreme Court in *Re the Regulation of Information (Services outside the State for Termination of Pregnancies) Bill 1995*.[30] The Supreme Court pointed out that Arts 5 and 6 of the Constitution established that Ireland was a sovereign and democratic state, in which all powers of Government derive under God from the people. Going further than a simple rejection of the argument that the Constitution was subject to a form of higher law which would preclude its amendment, the court also went on to analyse the case law concerning unenumerated rights, holding that it was

> "manifest that the Court in each such case had satisfied itself that such personal right was one which could reasonably be implied from and was guaranteed by the provisions of the Constitution, interpreted in accordance with the ideas of prudence, justice and charity. The Courts, as they were and are bound to do, recognised the Constitution as the fundamental law of the State to which the organs of the State were subject and at no stage recognised the provisions of the natural law as superior to the Constitution."[31]

In *TD v Minister for Education*[32] and *O'T v B*,[33] Keane CJ advocated judicial self-restraint when it came to the identification of new unenumerated rights, and the courts have not declared any "new" rights in recent years.

4. Fair Procedures

One of the existing unenumerated rights that has enjoyed a high level of protection and generous judicial interpretation is the right to fair procedures in civil matters.[34] This procedural protection appears to be seen by the Irish courts as a critical

---

95. For some of the most trenchant criticism, by two philosophers, of Kenny J's interpretation of Art 40.3 in *Ryan*, see Casey, "'Logically Faultless' Argument for Unenumerated Rights in the Constitution" (2004) 22 *Irish Law Times* 246 and Clarke, "Unenumerated Rights in Constitutional Law" (2011) 18 *Dublin University Law Journal* 101.

29 The procedure for amending the Irish Constitution—which involves a referendum proposal being passed by a simple majority vote—is set out in Art 46. For the view that judges are bound by natural law even where inconsistent with a provision in the Constitution, see O'Hanlon, "Natural Law and the Constitution" (1993) 11 ILT 8 and "The Judiciary and the Moral Law" (1993) 11 ILT 129. See also Clarke, "The Constitution and Natural Law: A Reply to Mr Justice O'Hanlon" (1993) 11 ILT 177; Murphy, "Democracy, Natural Law and the Irish Constitution" (1993) 11 ILT 81.

30 [1995] 1 IR 1; [1995] 2 ILRM 81.

31 [1995] 2 ILRM 81, 107.

32 [2001] 4 IR 259.

33 [1998] 2 IR 321.

34 In the context of criminal matters, Art 38.1 provides for a trial "in due course of law" and this has been read as importing a number of procedural protections, some of which existed before 1937 at common law but which now have the force of constitutional requirements. An accused person has the right to be represented, the right to silence, the right to a trial without undue

protection for the citizen as against the State. The common law principles that no man shall be judge in his own cause and that one must "hear the other side" were stated to be constitutional requirements in the administration of justice in *McDonald v Bord na gCon*,[35] where Walsh J held that, in the context of the Constitution,

> "natural justice might be more appropriately termed 'constitutional justice' and that constitutional justice must be understood to import more than the well-established common law principles that no one shall be judge in his own cause and *audi alteram partem.*"[36]

This was followed in *Re Haughey*,[37] in which the Supreme Court found that the right to basic fairness of procedures was one of the unenumerated rights guaranteed to the citizen by Art 40.3. Ó Dálaigh CJ (for the court) held that rules of procedure which might be acceptable when an ordinary witness gave evidence before the Public Accounts Committee of the Dáil would not be sufficient to safeguard the applicant. Certain serious allegations had been made against him by another witnesses based on hearsay evidence in circumstances where that witness enjoyed immunity. He objected to participating in the inquiry on the basis that, *inter alia*, his entitlement to fair procedures was not protected and was found guilty by the High Court of an offence of refusing to answer questions.[38] It was accepted by Ó Dálaigh CJ that the applicant had been entitled to cross-examine his accusers and to address the Committee *via* counsel in his own defence. Ó Dálaigh CJ held that:

> "The provisions of Article 38, s. 1, of the Constitution apply only to trials of criminal charges in accordance with Article 38; but in proceedings before any tribunal where a party to the proceedings is on risk of having his good name, or his person or property, or any of his personal rights jeopardised, the proceedings may be correctly classed as proceedings which may affect his rights, and in compliance with the Constitution the State, either by its enactments or through the Courts, must outlaw any procedures which will restrict or prevent the party concerned from vindicating these rights".[39]

Re Haughey, of course, considered the right to fair procedures as playing a supporting role in the vindication of the right to one's good name under Art 40.3.2°. As has been pointed out by O'Donnell J (writing prior to his appointment to the Supreme Court):

> "The Article treats the right to a good name in the same name as the rights to

---

delay and the right to a trial without such publicity as would render a fair trial impossible. For an account of what is covered, see Hogan and Whyte, *op. cit*, pp 1039–1194.

35 [1965] IR 217.

36 *ibid* at 242.

37 [1971] IR 217.

38 As a separate matter, the power of this parliamentary committee to "certify" to the High Court that a person in the applicant's position as guilty of an offence was found to be unconstitutional since—even if it could be interpreted merely sending the person for trial in that court—no provision could properly be read into the statute for that trial to take place with a jury, as would be required in the case of an offence carrying an unlimited penalty: *ibid* at 246–255. However, the court ruled on the question of the procedures that a parliamentary committee must generally be adopted in such a situation, independently of the issue of the validity of the impugned statutory provision.

39 [1971] IR 217 at 264.

life, property and person. Once this is the case, it must also be recognised that a report does affect good name (unlike life or property) and if the evidence and report are absolutely privileged, may do so unjustly since there is no other method of challenging the correctness or fairness of the statement or thereby vindicating the right to good name of the citizen. It is hard to see therefore, how the Supreme Court could properly come to any other conclusion that it did i.e. that due process was required."[40]

5. The Double Construction Rule

One consequence of constitutionalising the right to fair procedures was the application of the double construction rule,[41] so as to require administrators to observe fair procedures when exercising their powers and functions under legislation.[42] In that context, in the *Dellway* case, the Supreme Court refused to accept at face value arguments as to the policy justifications for excluding a right to make representations.

6. *Dellway*: The High Court

Dellway came before the Supreme Court following an appeal[43] from the judgment of the Divisional High Court.[44] The case concerned, *inter alia*, the right to fair procedures in the context of the National Asset Management Agency Act 2009. The Act established the National Asset Management Agency ("NAMA"), which had the power to acquire certain loans from certain financial institutions. The applicants in the case were an individual property developer and a number of companies controlled by him whose loans NAMA decided to acquire pursuant to s 84 of the Act.

Section 84 did not specifically provide for any opportunity for borrowers whose loans were being acquired to make representations to NAMA prior to a decision to acquire being made.[45] The applicants argued that they were entitled to make representations

---

40 O'Donnell, "A Comparison of Article 6 of European Convention on Human Rights and the Due Process Requirements of the Constitution of Ireland" (2004) 4 *Judicial Studies Institute Journal* 37 at 52.

41 *McDonald v Bord na gCon* [1965] IR 217 (SC); *East Donegal Co-Operative Livestock Mart Ltd v Attorney General* [1970] IR 317 (SC). This rule was developed as an aspect of the presumption of constitutionality that applies to legislation enacted after 1937. The double construction rule requires a court to interpret a statute in a manner consistent with the Constitution where possible.

42 A point made presciently by Gerard Hogan, writing in 1984 in "Natural and Constitutional Justice–Adieu to Laissez-Faire" (1984) 19 *Irish Jurist* 309.

43 The National Asset Management Agency Act 2009, s 194 limits the right of appeal from the Supreme Court to situations where the High Court certifies that "its decision involves a point of law of exceptional public importance and that it is desirable in the public interest that an appeal should be taken to the Supreme Court" (s 194(2)). The restriction does not apply in respect of a determination of the High Court involving a question as to the validity of any law having regard to the provisions of the Constitution (s 194(3)).

44 *Dellway Investments Ltd v National Asset Management Agency* [2011] 4 IR 1; [2010] IEHC 364. The Divisional High Court consisted of Kearns P, Kelly and Clarke JJ.

45 Section 84(1) provided as follows:

> "NAMA may acquire an eligible bank asset of a participating institution if NAMA considers it necessary or desirable to do so having regard to the purposes of this Act

to NAMA before it made a decision to acquire the loans and that this requirement should be read into s 84 pursuant to the double construction rule[46] or, if that was not possible, that the statutory provision should be found to be unconstitutional.

The Divisional High Court had found that there was no requirement to give the applicants an opportunity to make representations because no constitutionally protected rights of the applicants were affected by the decision to acquire their loans.[47] Kearns P., considering when the right to fair procedures might arise, held that:

> "There must be a real risk that a party's rights will be interfered with in the event that there is an adverse decision. The adverse decision must be such as would directly interfere with those rights, or at least any interference must be so closely connected with any adverse decision so as to warrant that the party concerned be entitled to invoke a right to fair procedures. Obviously, the precise application of that general principle requires an analysis of the right which it is said might be interfered with and the manner in which it is said that an adverse decision would interfere with that right."[48]

7. The Supreme Court and the Threshold for Fair Procedures

The judgments delivered by the Supreme Court[49] on appeal took a different view and the majority seemed to be in agreement that it is not necessary that some constitutionally protected right be threatened in order for a right to fair procedures to arise.

Hardiman J gave the strongest judgment in favour of an independent right to fair procedures, which he characterised as a freestanding right under Art 40.3, as opposed to a right that derives from or supplements other constitutional rights.[50] Fennelly J took a broad approach, which fell short of Hardiman J.'s position, finding that it was not necessary to demonstrate an interference with the substance of constitutionally protected rights, as opposed to an interference with the enjoyment or exercise of them.[51]

Finnegan J agreed with the judgment of Fennelly J, stating:

> "In particular I agree that a person whose interests are capable of being affected directly by decision of a public body exercising statutory powers is ordinarily

and in particular the resources available to the Minister. NAMA is not obliged to acquire any particular, or any, eligible bank asset of such an institution on any grounds."

46 *East Donegal Co-operative Ltd v Attorney General* [1970] IR 317 (SC).

47 The Divisional Court rejected the arguments that the constitutionally protected right to earn a livelihood, property rights or reputational rights of the applicants would be affected by the acquisition of their loans.

48 [2011] 4 IR 1, 63 Kearns P.

49 Judgments were delivered by Murray CJ (who delivered two judgments) Fennelly, Denham, Finnegan, Macken, and Hardiman JJ. McKechnie J did not deliver a judgment.

50 *ibid* at 283–285 (paras 316–320). Macken J concurred with Hardiman J. Although note that Hardiman J does not seem to have accepted that the applicants had no constitutionally protected rights in this case; *ibid* at 285 (para 320).

51 *ibid* at 326 (para 455). See also *ibid* at 327–329 (paras 457–460) and *ibid* at 331 (para 466) and the discussion of *Haughey v Moriarty* [1999] 3 IR 1 (SC).

> entitled to have notice of the intention to consider the making of the decision and have his representations considered by the decision maker."[52]

The Chief Justice stated that he agreed with the analysis in the judgments of Fennelly and Finnegan JJ of the potential practical impact on the applicants of the decision to acquire their loans. Murray CJ did not specifically state whether or not there must be interference with constitutional rights to give rise to a right to fair procedures. It seems, however, from the authorities referred to, and some of the dicta in his judgment, that he did not believe that it is necessary to demonstrate a potential interference with constitutional rights in order to give rise to a right to fair procedures. For example, he refers to the "well established principles of statutory interpretation according to which fair procedures must be observed by decision makers exercising discretionary statutory powers."[53]

Both Macken and Denham JJ,[54] on the other hand, gave judgments that suggest that a constitutional right to fair procedures is available only where a constitutional right is interfered with. Macken J, for example, interpreted the submissions of the appellants as being to the effect that "the right to be heard flows from the fact that several constitutionally protected rights are being interfered with."[55] She stated that she was

> "in agreement with the analysis of Irish case law on the right to be heard, as an element in the right to fair procedures or natural justice, found in other judgments".[56]

However, her judgment appears to take the view, in its analysis of the authorities, that there must be an underlying constitutional right for there to be a right to fair procedures. She stated that she was

> "satisfied that each of the claimed right of the appellants, as in both by them, when properly considered, is a genuinely serious right which they are justified in invoking for the purpose of asserting the right to be heard."[57]

It seems, however, that a majority of the Supreme Court tended towards the view that the right to fair procedures or at least that version of it that requires merely a right to make representations—is one that applies regardless of the implication of an "underlying" constitutional right.

8. Fair Procedures: An Absolute Entitlement in all Circumstances?

One of the questions raised by the approach of the Supreme Court in *Dellway* is the extent to which the enjoyment of the right to fair procedures can be excluded without

---

52 *ibid* at 359 (para 528).
53 *ibid* at 204 (para 33).
54 See para 79 of the judgment of Denham J.
55 *ibid* at 342 (para 493).
56 *ibid.*
57 *ibid* at 344 (para 499). She refers in that paragraph to property rights and right to earn a living.

violating the Constitution. It had previously been observed by Hogan, discussing *McDonald v Bord na gCon*,[58] that:

> "It does not, of course, automatically follow that every statutory provision which authorises the taking of an administrative decision affecting legal (or even constitutional) rights or legitimate interests without prior notice is in itself unconstitutional. The guarantee of fair procedures is not absolute, and the terms of Article 40.3 are qualified by considerations of practicability. Thus, legislation which excluded the rules of natural justice might very well be upheld if peremptory administrative action taken pursuant to these statutory provisions was justifiable on the grounds of urgency or necessity."[59]

While that proposition seemed accurate and supported by the case law[60] at the time at which it was stated, the approach taken by the Supreme Court in *Dellway* seems to suggest that the range of circumstances in which the State may dispense with the requirement to observe fair procedures is very limited.

As noted above, the approach taken in *Dellway* was to read into s 84 of the NAMA Act an entitlement to make representations prior to a decision to acquire being made. The wording of the legislation did not *preclude* such an opportunity being provided and the double construction rule enabled the court to read into the Act this requirement in order to render it constitutional.

9. Implications of *Dellway*

Two related themes emerge from the judgments in this context. The first is the idea that the right to fair procedures is a fundamental principle closely allied to the rule of law. The second is a concern to ensure that at times of crisis such fundamental rules are observed.

It is noteworthy that the court was unreceptive to the argument that the context in which the NAMA Act was passed—namely the financial crisis—was such as to justify departure from the requirements of fair procedures. The Chief Justice firmly refused to accept that this would justify abrogating the right to fair procedures. He stated:

> "In the course of hearing it was at one point argued on behalf of the State that the exclusion of a right to a hearing might be justified by reason of the crisis affecting the national banking system and the urgency of the measures needed to counter systemic threats to that system. I have to say that there was no evidence or material before the High Court to suggest that the time involved in permitting persons such as the appellants to make representations to NAMA before it made a final decision would impinge on, let alone be fatal for, its effective functioning. Moreover I find it difficult to envisage circumstances

---

58 [1965] IR 217.

59 Hogan, "Natural and Constitutional Justice" *op. cit* at 309 (footnote 35).

60 Hogan refers to *State (Lynch) v Cooney* [1982] IR 337 (SC) and *O'Callaghan v Commissioners of Public Works* [1985] ILRM 364.

> where the principles of constitutional justice ensuring that decisions are fair for the individual could be overridden. To do so would be to abrogate a constitutional protection which every citizen enjoys when the State decides to exercise any power which encroaches on individual rights."[61]

Hardiman J similarly rejected the argument that the economic circumstances in which the NAMA Act was passed were such that the State was entitled to exclude the right to fair procedures in the Act, drawing attention to the fact that it was only in an emergency as defined by Art 28 of the Constitution that the Oireachtas could suspend rights.[62]

The approach taken by the Chief Justice in the part of his judgment considered above can be usefully contrasted with that taken in the part of his (separate) judgment where he dealt with the question of whether the definition of eligible assets in the NAMA Act was so overbroad as to constitute an unjustified interference with property rights. Here, he placed much more emphasis on the purposes of the NAMA Act and the circumstances in which it was passed. He referred to the purposes of the Act in s 2 and in the preamble and found that the adoption of a broader definition was inevitable:

> "Given that the instability of the financial system and loss of confidence in the viability of the banking sector stemmed primarily from borrowings related directly or indirectly to development land and borrowers from the banks with a very substantial investment on the basis of property values which are subsequently collapsed, it was inevitable that a broad definition of an eligible bank asset would be adopted so as to ensure that NAMA would be in a position, and be perceived to be in a position, to deal with all bank assets of systemic importance ... The policy decision of the Oireachtas, as reflected in the Act, (and as the Divisional Court pointed out it is not for the Courts to express approval or disapproval of a lawful policy choice), includes the restoration of confidence in the banking sector by providing a statutory mechanism by which bank assets of specified classes were eligible to be acquired by NAMA, not on any basis but only for the stated purposes of the Act. Public confidence, but particularly confidence in the financial banking sector, may be profoundly influenced by perception and it seems to the Court entirely rational that the Oireachtas would provide for a broad definition of eligible bank assets to avoid any risk that any bank borrowings which posed a systemic risk to the economy and in particular the banking sector might be considered to fall outside the remit of the statutory provisions."[63]

The difference in approach—which is far more deferential to the policy choice of the Oireachtas and its calibration of the legislation—is of interest because it suggests that the right to fair procedures is in some way different to other constitutional rights and that it deserves particular protection.

Fennelly J in his judgment pointed out:

61 [2011] 4 IR 1 at 208 (para 52).
62 *ibid* at 289 (para 337). Denham J made a similar observation: *ibid* at 229 (para 123).
63 *ibid* at 192–193 (para 33).

> "NAMA also relies on the general economic and banking crisis. It says that the appellants' banking relationship was never going to be the same following the crisis which led to the ground by the State of the banking guarantee in September, 2008. It has to be acknowledged that there is great force in that argument which was accepted by the High Court in the following terms at paragraph [43]:
>
> > '[43]… in the absence of some significant executive and legislative response to these problems, it is almost certain that the existing banks operating in Ireland (including those with whom Mr. McKillen had long standing banking relationships) would have ceased to function or, at least, function in any way remotely resembling the traditional model of a bank.'[64]

In considering counterarguments put by Mr McKillen, Fennelly J noted that there were points which he should be entitled to put to NAMA and further:

> "the banking crisis does not deprive him of that right. In some respects, it strengthened that: he wishes to say that his position is different from the borrowers."[65]

Denham J, after referring to the long title of the NAMA Act, which states that it is an Act "to address a serious threat to the economy and to the systemic stability of credit institutions in the State generally," held that

> "The State is addressing a financial crisis principally arising out of the failure of the banks. In a democratic society, where the rule of law governs, the right of a state institution to interfere with the rights or vested interests of a person on the basis that there is an emergency, is a matter for very careful consideration. Certainly, while the Act of 2009 addresses issues of a financial crisis, there is no suggestion in the legislation that the Oireachtas was abandoning the rule of law."[66]

She went on to state:

> "Clearly the Act of 2009 was part of a government policy introduced to meet the very serious banking crisis within the State. However, this does not exempt it from the provisions of the Constitution."[67]

Denham J.'s judgment, which links the right to fair procedures with the rule of law itself, is echoed also in the approach taken by the Chief Justice.

> "The State in exercising its powers to the organs of government designated by the Constitution have extensive powers to regulate and limit the exercise of individual rights in the interest of the common good and this may be relevant where the State is faced with a national crisis, such as one of a fiscal nature.

---

64 *ibid* at 332 (para 469).
65 *ibid* at 333 (para 470).
66 *ibid* at 229–230 (para 124).
67 *ibid* at 230 (para 125).

> The State has the power to act in the interests of the common good because the Constitution, in its provisions, expressly envisages that. It also envisages that in exercising such powers the State must act within the ambit of the Constitution as a whole. In a democratic State founded on the rule of law there are definite limits to the extent to which the State can interfere with or restrict constitutional rights or rights vested in or acquired by individuals—freedom of expression, assembly, freedom of religion, right to education, right to earn a livelihood, property rights (including contractual rights), right to strike—to name but some, even when it is acting or purporting to act in the interest of the common good in a national crisis. In common with international instruments, such as the Covenant of the United Nations and the European Convention on Human Rights, the Constitution envisages that rights may be regulated and limited but not to an extent that is disproportionate or in a manner which is arbitrary or discriminatory in an invidious sense. In particular the State cannot act in a manner which would abrogate a right or deprive it of its very essence.

If the State were to succeed in its argument, namely that the Act of 2009 prohibits NAMA from giving any consideration to representations from persons in the position of the appellants, it would be denying the very essence of a right to a hearing, a concept at the core of the principle of constitutional justice and due process."[68]

The judgments of the Supreme Court in *Dellway* represent a robust defence of the right to fair procedures and one which seems to view procedural fairness as falling outside the usual proportionality analysis applicable to constitutional rights. Denham J alone seemed to hint that the right was less than absolute, noting that:

> "The right to be heard, as with other constitutional rights, is not absolute. In referring to the personal rights under Art 40, Kenny J in *Ryan v Attorney General* [1965] IR 294 stated at pp.312 to 313—
>
>> 'None of the personal rights of the citizen are unlimited: their exercise may be regulated by the Oireachtas when the common good requires this. When dealing with controversial social, economic and medical matters on which it is notorious views change from generation to generation, the Oireachtas has to reconcile the exercise of personal rights with the claims of the common good and its decision on the reconciliation should prevail unless it was oppressive to all or some of the citizens or unless there is no reasonable proportion between the benefit which the legislation will confer on the citizens or a substantial body of them and the interference with the personal rights of the citizen.'"[69]

It is fair to say, however, that the remainder of her judgment took an approach which was less flexible than that taken in *Ryan* and which was strongly protective of the right to be heard. She was not alone in this approach. A number of the Supreme Court judgments seemed to take the view that the circumstances in which the right to make representations could be excluded were limited.

Hardiman J., for example, seemed to limit the exclusion of such a right to

---

[68] *ibid* at 208–209 (paras 53–54).

[69] *ibid* at 225 (para 110).

"circumstances of extreme urgency, combined, perhaps, with an intrinsic difficulty in the giving of notice."[70]

Denham J similarly made reference to and distinguished *O'Callaghan v Commissioners of Public Works*,[71] where O'Higgins CJ had referred to the urgency in that case:

> "Here, an emergency had been created by the plaintiff's own action in defiance of his legal obligations. If the Commissioners had hesitated in acting as they did, the monument which it was their duty to preserve would have been seriously damaged or destroyed. Further, it was not possible to contact the plaintiff because his address was not then known and did not become known to the Commissioners until some time later."[72]

Denham J noted that in *Dellway*, no evidence of similar urgency had been given. Similarly, Hardiman J noted that arguments based on urgency were undermined by the facts of the case and also by the fact that: "a method was found, apparently without too much difficulty, to give a hearing to the banks, but not to their customers."[73] A similar point was made by the Chief Justice:

> "there was no evidence or material before the High Court to suggest that the time involved in permitting persons such as the appellants to make representations to NAMA before it made a final decision would impinge on, let alone be fatal for, its effective functioning."[74]

This aspect of *Dellway* is of interest because it suggests that the right to fair procedures is one that can be interfered with only in exceptional circumstances. It also suggests that there is little room for a proportionality-based analysis of interferences with the right. The idea that there is no room for proportionality in the context of due process was strongly endorsed by Barrington J in the context of Art 38.1 in *Re National Irish Bank Ltd (No 1)*,[75] where he stated that

> "The phrases 'due course of law' and 'due process of law' like the phrase 'equality before the law' embody dynamic constitutional concepts into which lawyers have obtained deeper insights as society has evolved. But it is doubtful if the principle of proportionality—so important in other branches of constitutional law—can have any useful application here. A criminal trial is conducted 'in due course of law' or 'with due process of law' or it is not."[76]

The exclusion of a proportionality analysis from the due process or criminal law context is perhaps explicable on the basis of the liberty interests at stake, but where lesser interests are concerned in the civil context it seems extraordinary to allow no balancing of the interests of the individual and those of the State. In this context,

---

70 *ibid* at 292 (para 347).
71 [1985] ILRM 364 (SC).
72 *ibid* at 373–374.
73 [2011] 4 IR 1 at 296 (para 357).
74 *ibid* at 208 (para 52).
75 [1999] 3 IR 145 (SC).
76 ibid at 180.

the approach developed by the United States Supreme Court provides a point of comparison. In *Mathews v Eldridge*,[77] the court developed a test for fair procedures under the Due Process Clause of the Fourteenth Amendment to the United States Constitution whereby the court considers:

> "First, the private interest that will be affected by the official action; second, the risk of an erroneous deprivation of such interest through the procedures used, and the probable value, if any, of additional or substitute procedural safeguards; and finally, the Government's interest, including the function involved and the fiscal and administrative burdens that the additional or substitute procedural requirement would entail."[78]

10. The Right to Make Representations: An Empty Formula?

As noted above, the right to fair procedures varies with the context in which it arises from the full panoply of rights set out in *Re Haughey*, including an oral hearing and an opportunity to cross-examine to more limited rights to make representations. As Barron J noted in *Flanagan v UCD*[79]:

> "Procedures which might afford a sufficient protection to a person concerned in one case, and so be acceptable, might not be acceptable in a more serious case."[80]

All the judges in *Dellway* took the view that the entitlement was limited in the context of that case. Fennelly J put it thus:

> "A person whose interests are capable of being affected by a decision of a public body exercising statutory powers, is ordinarily entitled to have notice of the intention to consider the making of the decision and to have his representations heard by the decision maker with regard to those effects."[81]

Finnegan J, concurring with Fennelly J, agreed

> "that a person whose interests are capable of being affected directly by a decision of a public body exercising statutory powers is ordinarily entitled to have notice of the intention to consider the making of the decision and to have his representations considered by the decision maker."[82]

---

77 424 US 319 (1976).

78 *Mathews* itself concerned an entitlement to an oral hearing which is, of course, a different level of procedural entitlement to that discussed in *Dellway*. As discussed further below, the entitlement read into s 84 was the far weaker one of an entitlement to notice and to make representations.

79 [1988] IR 724 (HC).

80 *ibid* at 730–731. The Irish courts have clearly distinguished between the different types of requirements that fall under the general heading of *audi alteram partem*, for example, in *Doupe v Limerick Corporation* [1981] ILRM 456 (HC) and *Gallagher v Revenue Commissioners (No 2)* [1995] 1 IR 55 (SC).

81 [2011] 4 IR 1 at 321 (para 434).

82 *ibid* at 359 (para 528).

The judgments thus do not require a great deal in terms of the content of the fair procedures guarantee and allow a significant degree of latitude as to how that process might be conducted.

The breadth of the discretion enjoyed by NAMA was a matter which Macken J saw as increasing the entitlement of the citizen to have an opportunity to make representations. After referring to *Haughey v Moriarty*,[83] she pointed out:

> "The fact that a decision is one which is going to be taken in the exercise of the discretion, even a very wide discretion, is not a ground, in itself, from departing from the basic principle of *audi alteram partem*. Neither the breadth of the discretion, nor the fact that it is described as the 'sole' discretion of the Tribunal, and thus may only be reviewed in very limited circumstances, can, in law, lead to the conclusion that if that decision is one very affecting the interest of a party, does not attract the rules of natural justice. Indeed, it might be said that the discretion afforded is very broad, as here, and the limits on possible review may therefore be narrow, this makes it all the more important that an affected party should have the right to make submissions to the decision maker before a decision is made. If anything, the scale of the NAMA statutory discretion and statutory powers, and the fact that there is no appeal from its decision, emphasises the importance of scrupulous adherence to the rules of natural justice."[84]

The lack of any entitlement to appeal is a matter to which Denham J also made specific reference. She noted that s 103 of the NAMA Act precluded a subsequent cause of action against NAMA arising solely from the fact of that acquisition:

> "once an acquisition schedule has been served, litigation is limited. This places the prior decision under s. 84 in critical perspective and the limitation of litigation is a relevant factor in analysing rights and section 84."[85]

Further, it seems to have been recognised that the availability of the entitlement to make representations might not have made any difference to the outcome of the decision making process. Thus, Murray CJ noted:

> "It could indeed transpire that NAMA, having taken into account all relevant representations made on behalf of the appellants and other relevant factors would decide to acquire the assets in any event. But at least, as a matter of constitutional justice, the appellants would have had an opportunity to make their own case before the relevant assets are taken into the NAMA scheme."[86]

One cannot help but wonder what purpose is served by a bare requirement to consider representations in circumstances where the decision-making body had

---

83 [1999] 3 IR 1.

84 [2011] 4 IR 1 at 343 (para 498).

85 *ibid* at 218 (para 83). Hardiman J described the provision as "confusing" in its scope but noted that the appellant was "afflicted with a limitation, of uncertain scope, on his right of access to the Courts arising from the NAMA acquisition of his loans; *ibid* at 245 (para 171). See also the judgment of Macken J; *ibid* at 338 (para 483).

86 *ibid* at 207 (para 49).

such a broad discretion. Requiring an entitlement to make representations in such circumstances seems apt to create a culture of box-ticking in the public service and a level of protection for the individual that is more apparent than real. The approach of the Supreme Court in *Dellway* prompts one to reflect on the observation that

> "there is an inevitable tendency when considering human rights to consider that, like Mae West, you can't get too much of a good thing. It is easy to assume that the greater the reach of fundamental right provisions and the more exacting their interpretation, the better it is for everyone. However, the creation or expansion of rights creates correlative duties, in the first place, on society and the State as a whole, and if constitutional rights are given horizontal enforcement (as they are in Ireland) on other citizens which necessarily restricts the liberty of others."[87]

11. Why Guarantee Fair Procedures? Some Reflections on Dellway

One of the most important developments in Irish administrative law was the recognition that all administrative decision-making gave rise to fair procedures—not just the decisions of courts or other bodies carrying out judicial functions.[88] A requirement that public bodies should be under a general obligation to act fairly fits with the origins of the principles of natural justice as explained by O'Higgins CJ in *Garvey v Ireland*, where he noted that those principles

> "came to be recognised ... at a time when society was emerging from the rule of might and force and when men looked for the protection of their rights in the moral sphere of fairness and justice. Natural justice, imprecise though the term may be, was something which came to be regarded as each man's protection against the arbitrary use of power."[89]

The protection of the citizen through the interposition of fair procedures between him or her and the State was also characterised by O'Higgins CJ as a critical aspect

---

87 O'Donnell, *op. cit*, at 38.

88 Where courts are concerned, the right to fair procedures can be seen as part of the administration of justice pursuant to Art 34.1 of the Constitution. Thus in *Orange Ltd v Director of Telecoms (No 2)* [2000] 4 IR 159 (SC) 189 it was noted that:

"... [A] judge may conduct a case in such a manner as to violate the requirements of natural justice or fair procedures: if he does so his decision will be set aside on that ground whether the failure was due to fatigue in the hearing of a case at the end of a long and crowded list, an innate and sometimes regrettably irreversible tendency to rudeness or bad manners, or hostility, overt or covert, to one of the party's based on race, religion or gender or simply because the judge did not like the appearance of the litigant in question. No doubt, the last two examples will readily attract the description of bias. But in any such instance the decision is set aside not on the ground of objective or even actual bias, but because, under our Constitution and law, natural justice and fair procedures must at all times be observed in the administration of justice and in proceedings before quasi-judicial tribunals and the Superior Courts will not tolerate breaches of these canons, whatever the motive and whether indeed any particular motive on the part of the adjudicating tribunal which has fallen into error has been established."

89 *Garvey v Ireland* [1981] IR 75 at 91. See *Ridge v Baldwin* [1964] AC 40 for the evolution of this limitation on administrative action in the United Kingdom prior to the introduction of the Human Rights Act 1998.

of the constitutional and democratic State established by the 1937 Constitution in which the old immunities of executive privilege had been dismantled:

> "I do not propose to consider the older judicial authorities for, in the main, they exemplify or are derived from the concept in British constitutional theory that the King can do no wrong and that offices held at royal pleasure are outside the reach of natural justice: to hold the Crown to be thus limited would have been an unwarrantable invasion of an absolute and unjusticiable exercise of the royal discretion. This is a theory of immunity and executive absolutism that has been steadily crumbling in modern times ... Judicial precedents resting on it are of little value today, particularly in a State such as this where constitutional guarantees compel the recognition of personal fundamental rights which, prior to the Constitution, could have been overborne by theories of executive prerogative or public policy."[90]

Viewed in this way, the right to fair procedures can be seen as forming part of a series of developments in Irish law which have evolved so as to ameliorate the imbalance of power between the individual citizen and the State. It is important to recall that these are all relatively recent developments, and while they reflect the same trends as have been demonstrated in other Western constitutional democracies, the entitlement to sue the State for wrongdoing as a matter of private law[91] or to review its actions and obtain a remedy are all important and still evolving areas of the law. Some significant questions in this area remain unanswered and some areas are still being incrementally mapped out[92] as cases come before the Courts.

Viewed from an individual perspective, the right to procedural fairness can also be seen as supporting other substantive rights. The approach taken to due process in *Re Haughey*, for example, characterises the right to fair procedures as a derivative or secondary right which is protected due to its instrumental value in ensuring the vindication of other rights.[93]

It is clear from *Dellway*, however, that the right to make representations at least does not require the invocation of some underlying constitutional entitlement, provided some *interest* of the applicant is affected. In fact, this aspect of the judgment may not be as significant in terms of extending the scope of procedural fairness as first appears. The facts of the case were unusual in that the decision-making process

---

90 *Garvey v Ireland* [1981] IR 75 at 99.

91 *Byrne v Ireland* [1972] IR 241 (SC). See contemporary commentary in Osborough, 'The Demise of the State's Immunity in Tort' (1973) 8 *Irish Jurist* 275 and "The State's Tortious Liability: Further Reflections on Byrne v Ireland" (1976) 11 *Irish Jurist* 279. For a critique of the manner in which *Byrne* and *Webb v Ireland* [1988] IR 353 removed benign powers previously enjoyed by the executive see Costello, '"The Expulsion of Prerogative Doctrine from Irish Law' (1997) 32 *Irish Jurist* 145.

92 The evolving jurisprudence on legitimate expectations is a prime example of this. See Hilary Delany, "Recent Developments Relating to the Doctrine of Legitimate Expectations" (1993) 11 ILT 192, Hilary Delany, "The Future of the Doctrine of Legitimate Expectations in Irish Law" (1997) 32 *Irish Jurist* 217, James McDermott and Niall Buckley, "Managing Expectations" (2007) 42 *Irish Jurist* 29, Hilary Delany, "Legitimate Expectations and Substantive Effect–Recent Developments" (2007) 14 DULJ 423.

93 For the viewpoint that due process rights constitute "rights against risks," see Alexander, "Are procedural rights derivative substantive rights?" (1998) 17 *Law and Philosophy* 19.

affected contractual rights of such a nature and in such a way that it could plausibly be argued that they fell outside the rubric of constitutional protection altogether.[94] That argument arose because of the nature of the property rights (contractual entitlements that arose in connection with loans) and the nature of the State action (which was the acquisition of those loans by NAMA by way of assignment). Few cases concerning the State acquisition of contractual rights would be likely to give rise to the argument that there were *no* constitutionally protected property rights at stake.

On the other hand, there are many other situations in which interests of citizens that do not give rise to constitutionally protected property rights might call for procedural fairness. The modern welfare and regulatory state gives rise to many entitlements which may not be considered worthy of substantive constitutional protection extending to compensation but interference with which rightly requires the observation of fair procedures. This issue was faced by the United States Supreme Court in *Goldberg v Kelly*,[95] where it held that the termination of enrolment in a state-administered welfare programme required a full hearing under the Due Process Clause of the Fourteenth Amendment. Where a citizen's property interests are created by the State—whether via a welfare system or perhaps by way of a licensing regime[96]—the lack of any prima facie entitlement to compensation for deprivation of value does not mean that there are *no* limitations on what the State may do in respect of such property-related interests.[97]

Where the right to fair procedures arises in the absence of a link to another constitutionally protected right, it may nonetheless be justified on an individualistic basis on what has been described as a "dignitarian" rationale[98]—the idea that as individuals, litigants are entitled to be treated fairly and that it is the process of this treatment, as opposed to any outcome of it, that is important. This approach seems closest to the natural law origins of the right to fair procedures and explains its status as a free-standing, non-instrumental right.

It also explains why arguments that "the greater includes the lesser" are of no application to fair procedures. The fact that the State is entitled to do something, e.g. acquire one's property compulsorily, does not entail the entitlement to do so in a manner which breaches fair procedures. That the remedy in such circumstances

---

94 This argument was not accepted by all of the judges who made up the majority in respect of the scope of fair procedures.

95 397 US 254 (1970). Due to the wording of the Fourteenth Amendment it was necessary in that case to find that the welfare benefits constituted "property" for the limited purpose of due process protection.

96 *Hempenstall v Minister for the Environment* [1994] 2 IR 20 (HC).

97 The principle of equality might be thought to apply in a similar way. While attempts to rely on Art 40.1 in the context of social welfare have been unsuccessful—see *Lowth v Minister for Social Welfare* [1998] 4 IR 321 and *Dennehy v Minister for Social Welfare*, High Court, 26 July 1984—there is some scope in those judgments for a understanding of equality which would apply notwithstanding the lack of any underlying constitutionally protected property right. See also *Re Article 26 and the Employment Equality Bill* [1997] 3 IR 321, which is perhaps best understood in this light. See also the judgment of Murray CJ in *Dellway* referring to arbitrariness and discrimination. The doctrine of legitimate expectations is also a significant development in the relationship between the citizen and the State, which can give rise to substantive entitlements on the basis of representations by the State which would not otherwise arise.

98 Paul Craig, "The Human Rights Act, Article 6 and procedural rights" [2003] *Public Law* 753 at 758.

may be simply a remittal of the same decision to the decision maker with a rhetorical requirement to consider the interests of the individual, it is nonetheless the position under Irish law and seems unlikely to change.[99]

The true impact of *Dellway* is that it raises the prospect of reading into all decision-making powers a requirement to consider representations, no matter how wide the discretion of the decision maker.[100] It also suggests that any attempts to exclude such entitlements run the risk of being found to be unconstitutional—at least in the absence of some form of appeal that would give rise to an entitlement to make representations. The emphasis in the decision on the necessity for evidence of the need to exclude representations suggests that there may be some circumstances in which representations may be excluded. It is difficult, however, to conceive of a fact scenario in which such urgency would extend to exclude a right of appeal. The judgments in *Dellway* did not accept that the decision concerning the applicants had no effect on their interests.

Perhaps the most interesting subsequent jurisprudential developments will be those in which other interests are canvassed as attracting the right to make representations. The decision is a clear indication that the current Supreme Court sees itself as the guardian of this important protection for the citizen. It is interesting that the proposal to amend the Constitution to allow for parliamentary committees of inquiry to investigate matters of public interest was rejected by the people in a referendum held only a few months after the *Dellway* decision.[101] One of the main concerns that arose in the context of the proposal was that the wording of the amendment suggested that the parliament itself would decide on the balance between the rights of the individual and the public interest. Concerns that this would exclude the possibility of judicial review seem to have a played a large part in the rejection of this referendum proposal, suggesting that the Supreme Court is not alone in considering the judicial defence of procedural fairness to be an essential protection for the citizen.

---

99 See *Caldwell v Mahon* [2011] IESC 21 (28 July 2011).

100 There is an obvious parallel here with the development of a duty for decision-makers to give reasons for their decisions, which seems have come close, at the very least, to being of general application, as result of *Mallak v Minister for Justice, Equality and Law Reform* [2012] IESC 59 (6 December 2012). In particular, it is not a ground upon which the decision-maker can resist giving reasons that the decision was one for him or her to take in his or her "absolute discretion" (*ibid*, para 45, Fennelly J).

101 De Bréadún, "Judicial pay issue drew 79% support: State to reflect on close vote on inquiries" *Irish Times*, 31 October 2011, p 5; McGee, "Five reasons why referendum was lost" *Irish Times*, 1 November 2011, p 6.

Part II

Elements of the Constitutional Design

CHAPTER 7

The Irish Constitutional Preamble in a Comparative Perspective

Angelo Rinella[1]

1. INTRODUCTION

The constitutional preamble—where one exists—usually introduces the articles of the constitutional text, revealing the basic purposes, inspiration, historical peculiarities and signs of the identity of the people who approve that Constitution.

It is quite clear that the language used in preambles has tones and shades that are different from those typical of a statutory provision. Nevertheless, preambles offer some keys for interpreting constitutional rules and, to the that extent, it makes these preambles part of the nature and legal value of the constitutional text.

The Preamble to the Constitution of Ireland is quite peculiar in that it includes some features not easily found elsewhere. In fact, it contains an *invocatio Dei*, along with an explicit reference to a specific religion by the invocation to the Holy Trinity and the Divine Lord Jesus Christ and the reference to values such as prudence, justice and charity.

If we look at the preambles to the democratic constitutions of Western Europe, the *invocatio Dei* is to be found in a few limited cases, primarily in Ireland, Greece, Germany, Poland and, most recently, the Hungarian Constitution of 2011.

In fact, the issue has to be framed in a proper legal and comparative perspective, starting from the origin, namely the relationships between state and religion and, hence, the role of the religious factor in the Constitution.

This paper intends to analyse:

- first, the framework of models of the state-religion relationship, from which the character of that between the Constitution and the religious factor directly derives;
- secondly, the different examples of constitutional preambles in a comparative panorama and their legal meaning and function;
- thirdly, the constitutional preambles that contain an *invocatio Dei*, including the Preamble to the Irish constitution of 1937.

---

1 Professor of Comparative Public Law at the University of Rome LUMSA.

2. State and Religions: Patterns and Classifications

The classification of states according to the position taken with respect to religious phenomena has been the subject of numerous historical, legal and political studies.[2] Particular attention has been paid to the relationship between religion and politics and to the system of relations between state and religions.

2.1 Legal Status of Religions

The legal status of religions results directly from the type of political relations between the state and religious confessions. According to the best-known and most widespread classifications, it is possible to distinguish between systems of relations based on the principles of subordination, separation and coordination.

Systems Based on Subordination

Systems based on the principle of subordination can be further subdivided into those providing for the subordination of churches as regards the state (including caesaropapism[3] and jurisdictionalism) and those that put the state in a subordinate position to the dominant religion.

Caesaropapism combines the power of secular government with the spiritual authority of the church; in other words, it is based on a status of union between the civil and religious power or otherwise on a system in which the state dominates the church by law. There are traces of caesaropapism in the role that the English crown and parliament play in the internal affairs of the Anglican religion and, of course, in the Vatican State and the Polyteia of Athos, in Greece.

The clearest example of the systems that subordinate the state to a religion is represented by the theocratic state.

Jurisdictionalism—which spread throughout Europe in the age of absolutism—denotes a situation in which religions are directly controlled by the state. The state intervenes directly with laws and administrative acts in the religious life of its subjects, protecting the official church on the one hand and defending the state from the interference of religion in public life on the other hand.

Systems Based on Separation

Systems based on the principle of separation distinguish the state legal system from religious confessions, ensuring state neutrality in religious matters, the independence

---

2 See J Martinez-Torròn, *Separatismo y cooperaciòn en los acuerdos del Estado con las minorias religiosas* (Granada, 1994); F Margiotta Broglio, C Mirabelli and F Onida, *Religioni e sistemi giuridici* (Il Mulino, 1997) 114ff.

3 The term caesaropapism was coined by Max Weber, who defined "a secular, Caesaropapist ruler" as one who "exercises supreme authority in ecclesiastic matters by virtue of his autonomous legitimacy". According to Weber's political sociology, caesaropapism entails "the complete subordination of priests to secular power." See M Weber, *Economy and Society*, cited by R Swedberg and O Agevall, *The Max Weber Dictionary: Key Words and Central Concepts* (Stanford University Press, 2005) 22.

and autonomy of religions, and equal treatment before the law, like the other forms of association. Generally these systems also demand that religious groups do not intervene directly in public affairs.

This approach emerged in some Western European states in the first half of the 20th century; however, it became difficult to keep the religious dimension removed from public life. In fact, some parties were founded in connection with the religions in order to represent and defend the confessional interests. In general, even in those states (France, Portugal, Germany, the Netherlands, Ireland, Belgium, Austria, Luxembourg and Italy) where the principle of separation was proclaimed, it is extremely difficult to keep the religious dimension out of public life.

Systems Based on Coordination/Collaboration

Systems based on the principle of coordination and/or collaboration between state and religious confessions provide for the existence of agreements or arrangements designed to regulate aspects of religious phenomena that have significant effects on the legal system of the state (Italy, Germany, Portugal, Austria and, in France, the Alsace-Moselle).

Finally, there are states that have maintained a close relationship with a particular church, without setting any conditions of subordination; in other words, these are states that formally define the main and historically established church as the national church or the official, dominant state church (Denmark, Sweden, Finland and the United Kingdom, where the Anglican Church is, however, the official church only in England, and not in Wales or Northern Ireland, while Scotland has its own "national" church).

2.2 Hirschl Taxonomy

Nowadays, the framework that determine the relations between state and religions includes a set of very complex political and institutional elements; in certain contexts not only legal factors but also ideological, social, economic and political elements are relevant.

Therefore, the classification of the state with reference to the system of relations with religions derives from the observation of empirical and contingent features that characterise the relationships between civil and religious society.

A recent taxonomy of different contemporary approaches to state-religion relations has been suggested by Ran Hirschl[4] (a Canadian scholar). According to Hirschl, it is possible to distinguish at least nine models which include the most important experiences of state-religion relations.

Atheism and the Proactive Elimination of Religion: Typical Antireligious Approach of Communist Regimes

These regimes generally consider religion, at the level of both private and public

[4] R Hirschl, *Constitutional Theocracy* (Harvard University Press, 2010) 26ff.

spheres, as the expression of a false consciousness. Consequently, from the Communist-atheist perspective, the state has to make every effort to eliminate religion. The People's Republic of China tried to eradicate religion from Chinese life and culture between its establishment in 1949 and the 1982 Constitution, which formally recognises and guarantees religious freedom, within the limits of public order and without interfering with the state education system (Art 36, Chinese Constitution).

Assertive Form of Secularism or Separationist Reformism, Often Established as a Modernist Reaction to Backwardness and Religious Dominance

The French policy of *laicité* represents the clearest expression of the will to avoid any religious influence over the public life of the state and, at the same time, to establish a religion-free citizenship.[5]

As Hirschl underlines, French *laicité* expresses "a form of assertive, even militant secularism that goes beyond neutrality towards religion or even a declared a-religiosity to advance an explicitly secular civic religion"; it considers secularism "as a core element of the modern nation and its members' collective identity".[6]

Another example of assertive and militant secularism is to be found in Turkey. The secularisation of the Turkish state by Mustafa Kemal Atatürk is perhaps the most important example of separationist reformism of the 20th century.

Separation as State Neutrality towards Religion

This is the case of those countries where a formal separation of religion and state is established, and secularism emphasises the state neutrality and impartiality towards religions. The prototype of this model is the First Amendment to the United States Constitution, which provides that "Congress shall make no law respecting an establishment of religion, or prohibiting the free exercise thereof". On the one hand, the Constitution prohibits the State from adopting, preferring or endorsing a religion; on the other hand, the State cannot interfere with the religious freedom of its citizens and inhibit religious practice.

Separation with De Facto Approach to Diversity and Religious Differences

This formal separation between state and religion exists in some "immigrant society" democracies, like Canada and post-apartheid South Africa. In these countries, the formal separation is joined to a serious multicultural policy according to a mosaic or assimilationist approach. In other words, although state and religion are separated, the concept of citizenship is not strictly based on secularism or state neutrality. It includes also differences based on religious traditions, language and cultural background.

---

5 See R Ahdar and I Leigh, *Religious Freedom in the Liberal State* (Oxford University Press, 2005) 73ff; AT Kuru, *Secularism and State Policies toward Religion: The United States, France, and Turkey* (Cambridge University Press, 2009) 11ff.

6 R Hirschl, *Constitutional Theocracy* (Harvard University Press, 2010) 26-27.

Separation with De Facto Pre-Eminence of a Given Religion and its Moral Vision

This is the case in those countries where the constitution guarantees the formal separation of church and state, "but where longstanding patterns of politically systemised church hegemony and religion-centric morality continue to loom large over the constitutional arena".[7]

Good examples of this model are offered by Ireland, Poland, Hungary and, to a lesser extent, Slovakia and Italy.

Weak Form of a "State Religion" Designation

In these countries, the formal and mainly ceremonial designation of a given religion as official religion of the state has few or no implications in public life.

Several European countries can be classified under this model. Norway, Denmark, Finland and Iceland designate the Evangelical Lutheran Church as the "state church" in their constitutions; Norway's head of state is the leader of the church.

Similarly, Greece and Cyprus designate the Greek Orthodox Church as their state church.

In England, the monarch is the "supreme governor" of the Church of England and the "defender of faith"; between the crown and the church there are several forms of reciprocal interference.

In a minor form, this model is also used in Germany, where the institutional apparatuses of the Evangelical, Catholic and Jewish religious communities are treated as public corporations and consequently worthy of public financial support.

Selective Interference of Religion in Areas of Law: "Religious Jurisdictional Enclaves"

In these cases, the legal system provides for the enforcement of religious rules in some fields, such as personal status. This is the case in India, Israel, Kenya, Afghanistan, etc.

Selective Interference of Non-Religious Rules in Areas of Law: "Secular Jurisdictional Enclaves"

This is the mirror of the previous model. In these legal systems, most of the laws originate from the state religion; but a few areas of the law are insulated from the religion's influence, such as economic law (Indonesia and parts of Nigeria).

Mixed Systems of Religious Law and General Legal Principles

These legal systems are the expression of the ideal type of constitutional theocracy.

---

7 R Hirschl, *Constitutional Theocracy* (Harvard University Press, 2010) 29.

Here, the entire legal and constitutional system is based on religious fundamental and constitutional principles that are entrenched in sacred texts and religious authority (Afghanistan Iraq, Yemen and Iran, just to mention the most important cases).

The last two models (highlighted by Hirschl) could be classified under the constitutional theocracies pattern; obviously, there are in practice various degrees of influence of religion over the legal system, which originates from the degree of separation between state and religion.

3. The Constitutional Preambles and Their Legal Status

A preamble is part of the constitution and with summary formulas expresses the fundamental ideas and constitutional aims that the founding fathers wanted to embed in the constitutional text. The preambles to the constitutions have seen their role grow in the constitutional context. From a global and comparative perspective, it is possible to note that constitutional preambles have been increasingly used to interpret and enforce the constitutional rules. They are used quite frequently to constitutionalise unenumerated rights, too.

To focus on the legal status of preambles to the constitutions, we need to consider briefly what kind of content it is possible to find in preambles and what their functions are.

3.1 Content of Preambles

From the point of view of the content of preambles, comparative legal doctrine[8] distinguishes five different categories, based on the subjects at their core.

The Sovereign

Generally, preambles recall the origin of the sovereignty. It could be identified in "the people", which is a relatively neutral term; or it could be a particular national group from which the sovereignty stems. Some preambles refer to representative bodies or—in the case of federations—to the constituent states.

Historical Narrative

This focuses on the history of a people, a nation or a state and includes the traditions, the culture and the heritage that identify that people.

---

[8] See L Orgad, "The Preamble in Constitutional Interpretation" (2010) 8 *I-CON*714-738; M Handler, B Leiter and CE Handler, "A Reconsideration of the Relevance and Materiality of the Preamble in Constitutional Interpretation" (1990–1991) 12 Cardozo Law Review fn. 14, 117 ff.; D Himmelfarb, "The Preamble in Constitutional Interpretation" (1990–1991) 2 *Seton Hall Constitutional Law Journal* n. 127, 160 ff.; K Roach, "The Uses and Audiences of Preambles in Legislation" (2001) 47 *McGill Law Journal* n. 47, 129 ff.; A Winkel "The Contextual Role of a Preamble in Statutory Interpretation" (1999) 23 *Melbourne Law Review* 184 ff.; AV Bogdandy, "The European Constitution and the European Identity: a Critical Analysis of the Convention's Draft Preamble" in *Altneuland: The EU Constitution in a Contextual Perspective* (JHH Weiler and CL Eisgruber ed, NYU, 2004).

Supreme Aims

Very often, the preambles contain the fundamental aims of the society, not only from a political point of view, but also from an economic, social and moral perspective. Sometimes the preambles refer to universal values such as fraternity, peace and human rights.

National Identity

Frequently the preambles to constitutions include a statement about the national creed and aspirations, the constitutional faith or philosophy.

Reference to God and Religion

Some preambles invoke the supremacy of God (Canada) or the Name of God (Switzerland); some others refer to a religion and its moral authority (Ireland, Greece, Poland and Hungary). In contrast, the preamble may also underline the separation of state and religion or its secular character (Turkey and India).

3.2 Functions of Preambles

From the point of view of the possible functions that preambles may perform, comparative constitutional scholars have identified three main categories.

Ceremonial-Symbolic

This kind of preamble adheres to the concept of preambles that the Greek philosopher Plato asserted in *The Laws*. According to Plato, laws are intended to guarantee a self-controlled society; the preamble to the law has the aim of justifying the law to the people, convincing the people that the law is morally good and virtuous, and persuading the people to obey it.

The preamble of the US Constitution belongs to this category: it is persuasive, symbolic and generally has no legal force.

Interpretive

The use of preambles as a key in constitutional interpretation is quite usual in common law and civil law systems. This role of preambles is particularly emphasised when they include keynotes or guidelines for constitutional interpretation. A good example of this is the South African Constitution, whose preamble is considered by the Constitutional Court as a guide to interpreting the Bill of Rights.

Similarly, the Irish constitutional preamble has been invoked by courts as a tool in constitutional interpretation. The German constitutional preamble, which generally has no legal force, has been invoked in some seminal decisions of the Constitutional Court (recently, in the Treaty of Lisbon decision, 2009).

Substantive

A preamble is substantive when it contains legally binding clauses and represents a source of rights and obligations.

Generally speaking, the preamble's legal substantive force depends on its use in constitutional interpretation; in other words, it depends on the binding value that the courts accord it.

There is only one case in which the constitution expressly recognises a binding effect of the preamble, Art 116.1 of the Constitution of Nepal.[9]

4. God and the Religious Factor in the Constitutional Preamble

In this section, we will focus our attention on the references to God and religion in constitutional preambles, in particular those of the Western democracies.

Among the constitutions of the Member States of the European Union (noting that the United Kingdom has no written constitution and Sweden has four fundamental laws), ten have no preamble. Among the remaining 15 constitutions having preambles, nine do not contain any reference to God or religion. Six preambles thus remain where it is possible to find a religious reference: in the case of the German constitution, the reference in the preamble is generally addressed to God; the five other constitutions, however, refer to a specific religion in the preamble.

Concerning the six countries that have included a reference of a religious nature in their constitutional preambles, we can distinguish at least two types. The first encompasses Germany and Poland.

The German constitution of 1949 opens with this statement:

> "Conscious of their responsibility before God and man the German people, in the exercise of their constituent power, have adopted this Basic Law."

The Polish Constitution of 1997 uses a more complex formula:

> "We, the Polish Nation—all citizens of the Republic, both those who believe in God as the source of truth, justice, good and beauty, as well as those not sharing such faith but respecting those universal values as arising from other sources".

Both these constitutions were written when the countries had just come out of totalitarian and atheistic regimes. The invocation of God, then, seems like a signal of discontinuity with the previous regimes. In the case of Poland, the joint reference to God is highlighted, and then to the believers and the conscience of the individual regardless of their religious or philosophical and existential belief.

---

9 "A bill to amend or repeal any article of this Constitution, without prejudicing the spirit of the Preamble of this Constitution, may be introduced in either House of parliament".

The second type of preamble that contains a reference to the religious dimension is found in the cases of Slovakia, Hungary, Greece, Ireland and, once again, Poland. The characteristic of these preambles is that they contain a reference to a particular religion.

In the preamble to the Polish Constitution, we read:

> "Poland, beholden to our ancestors for their labours, their struggle for independence achieved at great sacrifice, for our culture rooted in the Christian heritage of the Nation and in universal human values ... Hereby establish this Constitution of the Republic of Poland as the basic law for the State".

The preamble of the recent Hungarian Constitution of 2011 states:

> "We are proud that our King St Stephan established the Hungarian State on firm foundations a thousand years ago and made our country a part of Christian Europe. ... We recognize the role of Christianity in preserving our nationhood."

As to the Slovak Constitution of 1992, the preamble states:

> "We, the Slovak nation, mindful of the political and cultural heritage of our forebears, and of the centuries of experience from the struggle for national existence and our own statehood, in the sense of the spiritual heritage of Cyril and Methodius ... adopt through our representatives the following Constitution".

Thus, the preambles to the Polish, Hungarian and Slovak constitutions contain an explicit reference to the Christian religion, which is indicated as part of the historical and cultural heritage of the people. These references are mainly intended to reconstruct the elements of an identity that is a foundation stone of the new constitution.

In the case of the preambles to the constitutions of Greece and Ireland, the reference to the Christian religion seems to grant this the same value as the constitution.

The Greek Constitution opens with the following invocation:

> "In the name of the Holy and Consubstantial and Indivisible Trinity".

The Irish Constitution contains the following invocation:

> "In the Name of the Most Holy Trinity, from Whom is all authority and to Whom, as our final end, all actions both of men and States must be referred ... Humbly acknowledging all our obligations to our Divine Lord, Jesus Christ, Who sustained our fathers through centuries of trial".

It is quite clear that these invocations express a strong confessional choice that finds its origin in very specific historical reasons.

Besides the Member States of the European Union, the Swiss constitution of 2000, proclaimed "in the name of God Almighty", deserves a special mention, as do those of Albania and Ukraine, which contain a specific reference to God.

If we take a broader view and look at the global landscape, we can observe that preambles to constitutions frequently contain references to God and religion; rarely is the secular state proclaimed. The most widespread model is limited to invoking or mentioning the name of God, without defining it in a confessional sense, of course with the exception of Muslim countries, where the frequent references to religion specifically refer to the God of Islam or Islamic tradition.[10]

5. Christian and Democratic Nature of the Irish State Arising from the Constitutional Preamble: Implications for Personal Rights not Expressly Enumerated

The religious reference in the preamble of the Irish constitution has resulted in a number of implications for the Irish legal system.

From the standpoint of freedom of religion and freedom of conscience, Art 44 of the Constitution establishes the principle of protection by the State of the religious factor and, consequently, the freedom of conscience and freedom to profess one's faith.

Article 44.1 refers to Almighty God, without any specification of a confessional nature, in order to affirm the attitude of respect and deference to the religious dimension the Irish State intends to take.

More closely related to the confessional statement of the constitutional preamble was the recognition, in the same Art 44, of a special mention for the Roman Catholic Church and other specific Christian religious confessions existing in Ireland at the date of the coming into force of the Constitution.

Although the Roman Catholic Church was not given a position of privilege, the constitutional provision was considered discriminatory against other religious communities and not respectful of religious freedom. For this reason, the provision was repealed as a result of the approval of the Fifth Amendment to the Constitution Act 1972, confirmed by a large majority in a popular referendum.

The current provisions of Art 44 have satisfactorily completed the task of ensuring freedom of religion and conscience and the principle of non-discrimination. This does not in itself mean that the State has renounced its confessional ethos to promote the religion of the majority of the Irish people, sometimes at the expense of the religious minorities.

Article 40.3 of the Irish constitution makes the State responsible for guaranteeing

---

[10] For a global perspective, see AM Vega Gutierrez ed, *Religiòn y libertades fundamentales en los paìses de Naiones Unidas: Textos constitucionales* (Comares, 2003); S Ferrari "Dio, religione e Costituzione, in *Osservatorio delle libertà e delle istituzioni religiose* (www.olir.it, 2004).

the personal rights of its citizens; "in particular" the State intends to protect and guarantee the life, person, good name and property rights of every citizen.

The fact that Art 40.3.2° enumerates a specific number of rights to be protected, using the formula "in particular", has formed the basis of the unenumerated rights doctrine,[11] rights which would be protected by Art 40.3.1°.

This interpretation was adopted for first time in *Ryan v Attorney General*.[12] According to the interpretation proposed by Kenny J, the personal rights that can be invoked to declare the unconstitutionality of a law are not only those mentioned in Art 40 of the Constitution, but also all those rights that may result from the nature of the Christian and democratic state, even if not expressly mentioned by the constitutional provisions.

More precisely, Kenny J identified three different arguments in support of the constitutional protection of individual rights, even if not expressly mentioned: the wording of Art 40.3, which clearly suggests the existence of rights protected by the Constitution beyond the textual references; the derivation of the protection of personal rights by the Christian and democratic nature of the state, and the teachings of the Catholic Church's social doctrine in the field of human rights.

The reference to the Christian and democratic nature of the State requires some attention. As far as the democratic nature of the Irish State is concerned, there are no doubts that the framework of constitutional provisions ensures a democratic system. Nevertheless, there is no doubt that the rights pertaining to the dignity of the human person cannot be adequately protected except in the context of a democratic order; the rules of democracy, in fact, ensure full respect for human dignity.

The reference to the Christian nature of the State does not seem as well-founded. In fact, if the Preamble suggests that the State has adopted a confessional choice in favour of Christianity, other parts of the Irish constitution instead show a state open to religious freedom and the protection of religious confessions without discrimination.

Adopting the Christian nature of the State as a source for the protection of human rights introduces an element of crisis as regards the principle of state secularism; nor can the use of Catholic Church documents and papal encyclicals in constitutional interpretation be considered consistent with the principle of state secularism.[13]

---

[11] See O Doyle, *Constitutional Law: Text, Cases and Materials* (Clarus Press, 2008) 85 ff.

[12] [1965] IR 294 (HC) 313–314.

[13] It should be noted, however, that in the *Ryan* case itself, the Supreme Court did not endorse the second or third reasons that Kenny J employed to reach the conclusion that there are "unenumerated" personal rights, confining itself to approval of his textual analysis of Art 40.3 itself. Indeed, the Supreme Court was silent as to what criteria could be employed to decide what these unenumerated rights are ([1965] IR 294 at 344–345). The most recent case law from the Supreme Court suggests that it inclines to a somewhat more secular mode of reasoning than was evident either in Kenny J's decision in *Ryan* or, for example, in the majority decision in *Norris v AG* [1984] IR 36 (SC). It seems to prefer, instead, the to treat"the purposive Christian ethos of the Constitution" no more one factor among several that might be relevant to identifying the implications of the "human personality" of each citizen for the personal rights that he or she enjoys, as was proposed by Henchy J in his dissent in *Norris*. See *Fleming v Ireland* [2013] IESC 19 (29 April 2013) paras 109–115.

6. Conclusion

Based on the aspects examined, a number of conclusions can be reached.

A first quite obvious fact is that a preamble does not represent an essential element of modern constitutions. The presence of the preamble is usually justified by the need felt by the constituents to proclaim their identity traits, which are summarised by reference to values, ideals and symbols. Elsewhere, where there is no preamble, these features are outlined in the constitutional text.

From the literary point of view, preambles generally contain references to national identity and to the fate of that people, reproduce the main features of the history of that people, and contain exhortations, commemorations, aspirations and, as we have seen, appeals to God.

The *invocatio Dei* is an element of connection between what is purely human, even if relevant as a fundamental law, and the religious and spiritual dimension of human life.

Since the time of archaic human communities, religion and religious activity have represented an element of social aggregation. In particular, religion has always played a crucial role in unification and social identification; frequently adhering to a common faith has allowed the group to recognise itself as a community, their faith being the symbol of a certain social order.

In other words, religion has always been a strong element of social cohesion, placing itself as an essential and instrumental bonding element of the very structure of a community.[14]

With reference to the ideals of the Enlightenment, even though the presence of God could not be proved, it was postulated that He was an infallible entity, and the *invocatio Dei* had essentially the purpose of submitting the political community to the supervision of an abstract entity in order to ensure a certain moral order.

The reference to God or a religion in the constitutional preamble can be found in the constitutions of Western democracies based both on the pluralist principle and on state secularism. Therefore, the reference to God or religion cannot be understood as preclusive of any other faith or religious worship, nor as an implicit form of discrimination on religious grounds. Religious freedom is not called into question by a constitutional reference to a specific religion.

On the other hand, the principle of the secularity of the state does not require the constitution to mention God and religion, nor that the constitution may make provisions about the relationships between the state and religions.

If we consider the Italian constitution, during the work of the Constituent Assembly

---

14 BR Wilson, *La religione nel mondo contemporaneo* (Il Mulino, 1996) 47; P Lillo, *Globalizzazione del diritto e fenomeno religioso* (Giappichelli, 2002).

a proposal made by Giorgio La Pira[15] was discussed concerning the introduction of an *invocatio Dei* at the beginning of the constitutional text: "in the name of God the Italian people adopt this constitution".

It is evident that this reference did not preclude religious freedom in any way nor implicitly impose the domination of a certain religion on others. However, La Pira withdrew the proposal after hearing the first objections, realising the impossibility of creating and consequently strengthening the sense of unity of the Italian people around the *invocatio Dei*. The reference to God was supposed to be used exclusively to express the reasons for unity, but this function would have failed if it had been understood as an expression of diversity.

In the case of the Preamble to the Irish Constitution, the *invocatio Dei* expressly refers to the Catholic faith and reflects the cultural climate of the 1930s. It is quite clear that the reference to the symbols of the Roman Catholic Church is linked to the strong nationalist demands that accompanied the advent of the 1937 Constitution.

Since the Preamble forms part of the legal nature of the constitutional text, it can be used by the courts as an interpretive key of constitutional provisions and laws which are enacted. The content and literary style of the Preamble to the Constitution of Ireland should encourage interpreters to consider it a preamble of a symbolic nature, which uses some terms in order to evoke a certain tradition and identity.

The use of the Preamble to the Constitution of Ireland as a key of legal interpretation is the result of a political choice rather than a hermeneutic option.

The tones of the Preamble to the Irish Constitution, besides the symbolic and historical value, do not seem aligned with the features of a constitution of liberal democracy which the Irish constitution is. It declares the separation between state and religion, the principle of pluralism and religious freedom.

The situation on the basis of which the Catholic religion played a *de facto* leading role among the religions for a certain period—or, rather, for political and ideological reasons—now seems entirely surpassed as a consequence of the changes that Ireland went through, especially in the last quarter of the 20th century.

What some scholars are keen to define as the "moral civil war" which, especially between 1973 and 1995, pitted social conservatives against social liberals, led Ireland to a substantial emancipation from Catholic morals and a profound change of social climate. Suffice it to mention the referendum in 1972, which removed the reference to the Catholic Church from Art 44 of the Constitution, which had explicitly reserved it a special place.

In this process, the courts have fulfilled a vital role in their activism aimed at pressing for important social changes. Here it is sufficient to refer to the Supreme Court

15 Member of the Constituent Assembly, catholic, La Pira performs an appreciated work in the context of the "Committee of 75", especially in the drafting of the Fundamental Principles.

ruling in *McGee v Attorney General* (relating to the import of contraceptives, until then considered to be unconstitutional).[16]

In the 1990s almost all the remaining Catholic influences specifically introduced in the 1930s, were removed from the Constitution, reinforcing the liberal-democratic and secular nature of the Constitution itself.

Today, we would have to ask if an *invocatio Dei* is an appropriate element of contemporary democratic constitutions. From a legal point of view, the answer to this question must clearly be "no". This is owing to the risk of the interpretation of constitutional rules being used as a political expedient.

If we consider it as a symbol of historical identity, we would conclude that the *invocatio Dei* represents a sort of warning about the limitation of human thought and action.

Traditional *invocationes Dei* can stand today for the claim that human laws, human authority and human rights are not without limitations and conditions. The human being cannot be the measure of all things.

16 [1974] IR 284 (SC). It is of some interest that it is to Henchy J's concurring opinion in *McGee* that the Supreme Court reverts in *Fleming v Ireland*, in order to help establish the proper criteria for assessing a claim for the existence of an unenumerated personal right: [2013] IESC 19 (29 April 2013) para 112.

CHAPTER 8

The Dialogue among Constitutional Judges, Parliaments and Executives[1]

Nino Olivetti Rason[2] and Pier Luigi Petrillo[3]

1. INTRODUCTION

How can constitutional courts influence the evolution of the form of government? In what way can they—courts that have to judge the constitutionality of a law approved by Parliament—create, promote, stimulate a dialogue among others constitutional organs? Our essay tries to answer these questions.

Historically, scholars distinguish two different models of judicial review: the "decentralised model", originating in the United States, based on the power of each court at any level to analyse the conformity of a law with the Constitution; and the "centralised model", originating in Austria, based the concentration of this kind of question in one special court at central level.

These two models reflect, historically, two different conceptions of the principle of separation of powers and of the role of the judiciary: while in the United States the judge took up the role of "liberator" from the oppression of the British Parliament, in Europe, the judiciary represented the armed wing of the absolute sovereign, the instrument through which the sovereign could oppose the resolutions of the Parliament (which was the expression of popular sovereignty).[4] Consequently, in Europe, the idea of a diffuse constitutional legitimacy review of the laws approved by Parliament was rejected, because the tendency was to affirm the exceptionality of a judgment on the "product" of the legislative power.

So-called "parliamentary sovereignty" or, in other words, the supremacy of the legislative power and thus of the law considered as an expression of general will,[5]

---

[1] Even though they are the outcome of a joint work, Pier Luigi Petrillo wrote sections 1 and 3, Nino Olivetti Rason wrote section 2, and they wrote the conclusion (section 4) together.

[2] Honorary Professor of Comparative Public Law, University of Padua.

[3] Lecturer of Comparative Public Law, Unitelma Sapienza, University of Rome.

[4] A Pizzorusso, "I sistemi di giustizia costituzionale dai modelli alla prassi" in *Quaderni costituzionali* (1982) (3) 523; L Elia, "Giustizia costituzionale e diritto comparator" in *Quaderni costituzionali* (1984) (1) 9; L Favoreu, "Constitutional Review in Europe" in *Constitutionalism and Rights, the Influence of the United States Constitution Abroad* (L Henkin and AJ Rosenthal ed, Columbia University Press], 1990); T Groppi, "Introduzione" in *La giustizia costituzionale in Europa* (T Groppi and M Olivetti ed, Giuffrè, 2003) 13.

[5] See R Carre' De Malberg, *La legge espressione della volontà generale* (1931), ed by M Calamo Specchia, Giuffrè (2008) and EJ Sieyès , *Che cos'è il Terzo Stato?* (1789), in id, *Opere e testimonianze politiche*, I, 1, ed by G Troisi Spagnoli (Giuffrè, 1993).

could not, in that context, be questioned by a simple judge (expression of the sovereign will).

In this sense, it has been observed that the European civil law context rejects diffuse judicial review

> "on the basis of 'lawmaker's privilege': the law is a product of Parliament ... and cannot be put in the hands of a career judge, but requires its own special judge ... characterised by a special political sensitivity derived from his professional profile."[6]

However, down the years, and with the development of the democratic systems, the characteristics of the "concentrated" model have been somehow mixed with the features of the "diffuse" model, thus giving rise to new classifications.

The analysis of constitutional justice in Ireland or Italy, for instance, clearly shows this hybridisation process: the Irish and the Italian models of constitutional justice cannot be reconciled either with a diffuse system or with a centralised one, as they present elements of both.

For this reason, doctrine has long adopted a new set of models of constitutional justice, based on the object of the review and on how the "judge of the laws" is activated. Thus the "abstract" models have been separated from the "concrete" ones: the former are characterised by the fact that the judicial review is issued independently from the factual application in a specific case or situation of the law subjected to the review; the latter are identified by the fact that the judicial review of a law originates from the need to apply that specific law to a specific, "concrete", as it were, situation.

However, this classification also seems limited by the fact that often the judicial review can be both "concrete" and "abstract" (as is indeed the case in Italy and Ireland). Therefore, in this case, too, elements of the first model can coexist with elements of the second model.[7]

For this reason, and for the purpose of approaching how the constitutional judges converse with the legislative and executive powers by developing a comparative analysis, it seems appropriate to proceed by distinguishing between civil law and common law systems.

This is the framework to be taken into account in analysing the relationship among the constitutional courts and parliaments and executives.

Thus, notwithstanding the fact that the traditional models are now obsolete, the

---

6 T Groppi and M Olivetti ed, *La giustizia costituzionale in Europa* (Giuffrè, 2003) 14, as widely mentioned in VE Lambert, *Il governo dei giudici e la lotta contro la legislazione sociale negli Stati Uniti (1921)* (Giuffré, 1996).

7 M Cappelletti, *Il controllo giudiziario di costituzionalità delle leggi nel diritto comparato* (Giuffré, 1968); A Pizzorusso, *I sistemi di giustizia costituzionale: dai modelli alla prassi* in Quaderni Costituzionali, 1982, 521; L Pegoraro, *Lineamenti di giustizia costituzionale comparata* (Giappichelli, 1998) 27.

issue of the relationship between the "judge of the laws" (the constitutional court) and the authority constitutionally entrusted with the making of law (the parliament) continues to be a relevant subject, due to the constant tension between constitutional justice and democratic practice.

Our essay analyses this theme, with a comparative approach to the instruments through which the supreme or constitutional courts have built a dialogue with parliaments and the executive powers.

First, one thing must be taken in consideration: the terms "relationship" and "dialogue" are used to describe different legal situations.

In democratic systems, the existence of a relationship among the constitutional bodies (courts, parliament and the executive) is considered a given. In fact, the nature, scope and contents of such a relationship between the constitutional organs define the form of *the* government (presidential, parliamentary, semi-presidential, directorial, etc). While the existence of a relationship among constitutional bodies is at the root of the democratic nature of the state, the existence of a dialogue among those bodies is not to be taken equally for granted.

The term "dialogue", indeed, implies a constant conversation between two or more subjects "which makes it possible to reduce the causes of dissent, and favours mutual understanding."[8]

So, how can constitutional courts create this *dialogue*?

In some systems, constitutions specify the proper tools needed to turn the relation between courts and parliaments into a real dialogue: in this way, in some respects, the Constitution of Ireland introduces specific legal instruments for "building" a dialogue among the President of Ireland, the Parliament and the Supreme Court.[9]

In other systems, like the Italian one, such a tools are not provided by constitutions, and they are introduced by the constitutional court's case law. In this manner, dialogue is a judicial product, created by the constitutional court through models of judgments forged by the same court, such as "*sentenze interpretative, manipolative, additive, additive di principio e monito*" (judgements that interpret the law; or that manipulate it; or add new principels or rules to it; or, as we will explain after, make a warning to the Legislator), all of them more complex than a simple decision that may override the statute under scrutiny. In particular, we will focus our attention to the group of "*sentenze monito*" ("warning decisions"), which represents—in our opinion—the more effective and transparent way of dialogue between legislators

8 *Dizionario Garzanti di Lingua Italiana* (2010) 541.

9 For now, see DG Morgan, *Lineamenti di diritto costituzionale irlandese* (Giappichelli, 1998) 216; R Toniatti, "Irlanda (Repubblica d'Eire)" in *Digesto delle discipline privatistiche—sezione civile* (Utet, 1993) 187; JP Casey, *Constitutional Law in Ireland* (2nd ed, Sweet & Maxwell, 1992) 269; D Deener, "Judicial Review in Modern Constitutional Systems" (1952) 3 American Political Science Review, 1087; B Doolan, *Constitutional Law and Constitutional Rights in Ireland* (Gill and Macmillan, 1984) 75; V Tamburrini, "I paesi con controllo diffuso di costituzionalità delle leggi" in *La giustizia costituzionale in Europa* (T Groppi and M Olivetti ed, Giuffrè, 2003) 375.

and constitutional courts. The *sentenze monito* are "double decisions", in that the court first declares that the constitutionality argument is not admissible, but then considers the issue founded and invites the lawmaker to intervene.

It is our opinion that the constitutional courts are legitimated mainly through the ongoing dialogue with the lawmaker and the creation of a public space for debate, as well described by the discursive theories of democracy.[10]

2. "Judicial Review of Legislation" and "Reference Jurisdiction" in Ireland: The Study of "Dialogue" in Comparative Law

The aim of this section is to present some observations on the theory of dialogue to Irish colleagues, as it has been developed in the United Stated, Canada, and, finally, Italy, and to check whether—and how—it can be or has been applied in the Irish constitutional system.[11]

Looking at Ireland from this perspective must take into account the fact[12] that the Irish legal system can be considered a derivation of the British one and belongs to the *common law* family. However, especially with regard to judicial control in its widest sense, the Irish Constitution is slightly different from those of Commonwealth countries, having more in common with the Constitution of the United States of America. It could be said[13] that the constitutional text here reflects the intentions of those who led the country at the time of its introduction in 1937. The reference here is to the then Prime Minister Éamon de Valera, who wished to depart from the traditions of the United Kingdom.

Before expounding in these topics, it is necessary to distinguish between strong and weak judicial review. According to Mark Tushnet,

> "strong —and weak—form systems operate on the level of constitutional design, in the sense that their characteristics are specified in constitutional documents or in deep-rooted constitutional traditions … in strong form judicial review the Courts and in the end, the Supreme Court, have general authority to determine what the Constitution means."[14]

This is the system adopted in the United States, where the Supreme Court has can dispose of several instruments, not necessarily available to other similar courts: to

---

[10] Illustrated by J Habermas, *Fatti e norme, Contributi a una teoria discorsiva del diritto e della democrazia* (Guerini e associati, 1996) 285.

[11] The theory of dialogue among powers has been largely developed in Canada and was also discussed in some Supreme Court cases. In Italy, the topic was explored in a book by S Gerotto, *Premesse metodologiche ad una teoria del dialogo tra giudice costituzionale e legislatore* (Cleup, 2008).

[12] Widely explored by S O'Tuama, "Judicial Review under the Irish Constitution: more American than Commonwealth" (2008) 12 Electronic J of Comparative Law 1.

[13] See in this regard *ibid*, 1–2.

[14] M Tushnet, "Symposium: Judging Judicial Review: Marbury in the Modern Era: Alternative Forms of Judicial Review" (2003) 101 Mich L Rev, 2781.

avoid pronouncing on judicial review cases, to defer the effects of the ruling, or to invoke the theory of deferential review.[15]

Commonwealth countries are more familiar with the weak form of judicial review. As Tushnet says, "the mark of weak form review is that ordinary legislative majorities can displace judicial interpretation on the Constitution in relative short run".[16]

If we focus the attention on the Irish experience, we notice that the Irish Free State, under the 1922 Constitution, which still looked more to the British model, had in practice weak judicial review.[17] The Irish system under the 1937 Constitution migrates from the weak to the strong system. We may say[18] that the new model attempts to create a new balance of powers: it empowers the courts to face down legislature over the constitutionality of the law.

Thus, a brief analysis on the role of the judiciary in Ireland—as regulated by Arts 34 and 26 of the Constitution—is appropriate to highlight how, in terms of judicial review, the courts interact and therefore "dialogue" with legislative and executive powers.

The specificity of Irish judicial review is, first of all, written into the Irish Constitution.

After a general examination of judicial organisation[19], Art 34.3.2° is dedicated to the principles of judicial review. This provision does not follow the rules of decentralised jurisdiction adopted in other common law systems, where they are connected to the principle of *stare decisis*, but states that jurisdiction must be entrusted solely and exclusively to two bodies: the High Court and, ultimately, the Supreme Court.

The Constitution determines the role of the various participants, without dictating specific behaviours, although in practice there is some continuity in the way judicial review is carried out.

The Irish Supreme Court must express its judgments as though unanimously, with a *single* opinion: the hypothesis of concurring and dissenting opinions, which is common in American and Canadian case law, is not even considered here.[20]

---

15 The theory of deferential review was developed at the end of the 19th century by J Thayer, "The Origin and Scope of the American Doctrine of Constitutional Law" (1893) 7 Harvard L Rev 17, and states that a law whose constitutionality might be in doubt but that is not manifestly inconsistent with the Constitution may survive.

16 M Tushnet, "Symposium: Judging Judicial Review: Marbury in the Modern Era: Alternative Forms of Judicial Review" (2003) 101 Mich L Rev 2786.

17 For the failure of the system of judicial review (very similar to the current one) envisaged by Arts 65 and 66 of the 1922 Constitution to take effect, largely due to lack of judicial receptivity to it, see JM Kelly, *The Irish Constitution* (4th ed, G Hogan and G Whyte ed, Lexis Nexis Butterworths, 2003) 2160–2163.

18 Following, S Gardbaum, "The New Commonwealth Model of Constitutionalism" (2001) 49 American J of Comparative Law 707.

19 Not without encountering doubts expressed by various scholars and by judges alike: suffice it to mention JM Kelly, *The Irish Constitution* (4th ed, G Hogan and G Whyte ed, Lexis Nexis Butterworths, 2003) xii–xiii.

20 Art 34.4.5°. There is no similar restriction on a Divisional High Court (consisting typically of three judges) from expressing concurring or dissenting opinions in such a case, although the convocation of a Divisional Court is relatively rare. For example, in *State (Nicolaou) v*

The single opinion rule has been criticised, especially by those who consider it the expression of conservatism, contrasting with the country's natural development.

It is therefore right to wonder whether, in the Irish experience, it is possible—as it is in the Italian case, where the single opinion principle is also applied—to see, or at least sense, the presence of different orientations within the judging panel. This would compromise the false feeling of a consensus that some commentators (O'Tuama, in particular) have criticised

Judges start from one hypothesis: the law must be considered compliant with the Constitution until it can be proved otherwise. The presumption of constitutionality entails that among the various possible interpretations the judge must follow the one that better complies with the fundamental law.

The invalidity on an unconstitutional law is "declared" by the judges and implies its disapplication. Given the flexibility that is usually attributed to "precedent", it cannot be excluded that a judicial body may change its mind in the course of time; for this reason, the disapplied law may come back into force again without any need for the legislative power to intervene.[21]

The constitutional validity of laws is controlled following different criteria of interpretation; Kelly[22] emphasises that the courts have shown no consistency in their choice. In a case where the court follows the literal approach, the Constitution, as the fundamental law of the State, should be accepted, interpreted and construed according to the literal meaning of words used.[23] Using the broad approach, the High Court rejected excessive literalism and considered the Constitution to be a political instrument as well as a legal document.[24] The doctrine of harmonious interpretation was considered in cases which required (where possible) that relevant constitutional provisions be construed and applied so that each will be given due weight in the circumstances of the case. This interpretation seems to open the door—more than others—to judicial policy-making. The importance of history and the influence of natural law in interpretation should also be taken in consideration. Kelly remarks that the natural law approach will continue to be employed as a mechanism of avoiding an unpalatable result in any case where this might be produced by a stark literalist interpretation of the Constitution; however, as far as the day-to-day routine of constitutional adjudication is concerned, the natural law method will prove to have only limited application.[25]

Another useful tool that can be used to promote the dialogue between the powers is what is commonly referred to as reference jurisdiction, which manifests itself through

An Bord Uchtála [1966] IR 567, three lengthy judgments were delivered in the High Court, whereas the one-judgment rule applied in the Supreme Court.

21 No actual example of this can be given in Ireland. The Oireachtas will often have responded to the court's decision by a repeal or amendment that confirms the effect of the finding of invalidity in respect of the earlier provision.

22 JM Kelly, *The Irish Constitution* (4th ed, G Hogan and G Whyte ed, Lexis Nexis Butterworths, 2003) 3–46

23 *People (Director of Public Prosecution) v O'Shea* [1982] IR 384 (SC).

24 *AG v Paperlink Ltd* [1984] IR 373 (HC).

25 JM Kelly, *The Irish Constitution* (4th ed, G Hogan and G Whyte ed, Lexis Nexis Butterworths, 2003) 32.

advisory opinions expressed in various forms and with different consequences, according to the judicial system under consideration.

While the American system, at federal level, prevents the legislative or the executive power from addressing the Supreme Court to request an advisory opinion or an abstract ruling, this procedure is admitted in Canada and Ireland, albeit in different forms and with different consequences in the two countries.

It cannot be excluded, however—and indeed it is quite frequent—that the American Supreme Court, in drafting its opinion, will clearly divide the *ratio decidendi* from *obiter dicta* and use the later to admonish and counsel the executive or the legislature or both.

In other words, the United States rejected the (formal) use of the advisory opinions at federal level, whereas Canada accepted them and considers them with respect. Ireland, instead, has been using references as a form of preventive control, to be performed according to a rather complex procedure.

This process is regulated by Art 26, which (as observed by Kelly[26]) "was a relative innovation […] the inspiration for its inclusion [in the Constitution] was […] probably drawn from […] other […] legislative models".

This procedure applies to a Bill that has been passed (or is deemed to have been passed) by the two legislative chambers and has been presented by the Taoiseach to the President of Ireland for signature. During this final phase of the *iter legis*, the President who has doubts concerning the constitutionality of all or part of the Bill, after hearing the Council of State (whose opinion must be obtained, but is not binding) can suspend the legislative procedure and ask the Supreme Court to decide on the possible formal and material defects of the Bill.[27]

One commentator[28] on Art 26 has stated:

> "to the students of comparative constitutional law the power of the Irish President to refer bills to the Supreme Court for an advisory opinion under Article 26 is a most striking feature of the Constitution."[29]

However, more recent interpretations seem to hold that the President's power to make an Art 26 reference is limited by the existence of quite strong constitutional conventions that dictate when a reference should be made to the Court.

---

26 *ibid*, 399.

27 Certain types of Bills are excluded from the power of reference given by Art 26: Money Bills, Bills for which the time for consideration by the Seanad (Senate) has been abridged under Art 24 (which itself requires that the President concur) and Bills expressed to contain a proposal for an amendment of the Constitution.

28 J Jaconelli, "Reference of Bill to the Supreme Court—A Comparative Perspective" (1983) 18 *Irish Jurist* 322

29 *ibid*, 322 "Advisory opinion" is something of a misnomer, as the President has, apart from the provisions of Art 27, no further discretion once the Supreme Court's ruling has been given: if it is one of repugnancy, he or she must not sign the Bill; otherwise he or she must sign it.

An assessment of Art 26 must take into account that several types of Bill are exempt from reference: so-called money Bills, Bills containing a proposal to amend the Constitution and Bills for which the President has authorised the abbreviated procedure.

From the very first reference, dating back to 1940, the Supreme Court adopted the presumption of constitutionality of a Bill as a criterion. Lately, the court added the proviso, included in the fourth reference, made in 1975:

> "the Court does not accept that any distinction should be drawn in relation to the presumption of constitutionality between an Act of the Oireachtas and a Bill referred by the President under Article 26."[30]

A provision of Art 26 that has been much criticised concerns the alternatives that ensue from the decision of the Court: if the Bill is considered unconstitutional, it shall not become law; but "if no repugnancy is found, the decision may never be questioned again in any Court". The consequence of this is "the permanent immunity of any Act or provision which has successfully passed an Art 26 Reference at Bill phase".[31]

The President (alone) has the power of initiating the reference procedure; the subsequent consultation phases involve several subjects; the judgment of the Supreme Court concludes the procedure, with a decision on the constitutionality of the Bill.

Here are some examples.

With regard to the Employment Equality Bill 1996, then President Mary Robinson (who used the reference jurisdiction more than any other President)

> "referred the Bill to the Supreme Court pursuant to the provision of Article 26 … of the Constitution of Ireland for a decision as to whether the provisions of the Bill, or any of them, are repugnant to the provisions of the Constitution or any provisions thereof."[32]

The review was quite far-reaching, as is usual in these cases. In the end, the court declared that several of the Bill's provisions were repugnant to the Constitution. The President was informed of this.[33] A similar procedure was adopted for the Equal Status Bill 1997, and in this case the court, on the basis of the decision it had given concerning the Employment Equality Bill 1996, "found itself confronted by a Bill which contains two sections which were and are indisputably repugnant to the Constitution".[34] Again—a third example among many others—"Having been passed by both Houses of the Oireachtas, Part V of the Planning and Development

---

30 *Re Criminal Law (Jurisdiction) Bill, 1975* [1977] IR 129, 144.

31 JM Kelly, *The Irish Constitution* (4th ed, G Hogan and G Whyte ed, Lexis Nexis Butterworths, 2003) 407.

32 *Re Employment Equality Bill, 1996* [1997] 2 IR 321, 328–329.

33 *ibid* at 385.

34 *Re Equal Status Bill, 1997* [1997] 2 IR 387, 402. It was notable that, this being the case, the court refused to conduct a review of any of the Bill's other provisions.

Bill, was referred to the Supreme Court by the President".[35] After examining the more significant aspects of the Bill, and after discussing the matter extensively, the court decided that "none of the provisions of Part V of the Bill are repugnant to the Constitution".[36]

It seems that the Irish reference procedure follows ancient models. Indeed, it has many similarities with the procedure regulated by the Judicial Committee Act 1833, which authorised the British Sovereign ("it shall be lawful for his Majesty") to use the reference procedure to obtain a hearing by the Privy Council, which would consider the matter and provide an answer to the question posed.

Similar reviews to those foreseen in the Irish Constitution exist also in other current Constitutions. Suffice it to remember that Art 61 of the French Constitution, as repeatedly amended over the years, establishes that any organic laws and any regulations of the parliamentary assemblies, before being passed and coming into force, must be submitted to the preliminary enquiry and control of the Conseil Constitutionnel, which decides whether or not they comply with the Constitution. It also establishes that a request for preliminary enquiry of any Bills can be referred to the Conseil for an opinion. In the latter case, the initiative may come from the President of the Republic, the Prime Minister, the chairpersons of the legislative assemblies, and also by the appropriate number (60) of members of one of the two assemblies.

The reference jurisdiction in Canada is different, but equally worthy of consideration for the purposes of this analysis. In this case, the procedure is less rigorous than the Irish one, and the advisory opinion of the Supreme Court, given in terms of a judgment, does not concern the constitutionality of a Bill, but rather the assessment of a programme or reform. The advisory opinion may also deal with a provincial demand for autonomy or independence. Even though the opinion expressed by the court does not constitute a binding precedent, it is valued because of the issuing body's prestige, the suggestions that other judges may subsequently take from it and recommendations for the legislative and/or executive power, with consequences that affect the dynamics of the legal system.

While in the past the Canadian Supreme Court preferred to adopt a certain self-restraint in its advisory opinions, this instrument has become much more relevant with regard to the reform of 1982, on which the court gave its favourable opinion (engendering perplexity and even antagonism among the French-speaking minority.) The active and creative role of the Supreme Court of Canada through the reference jurisdiction may be found in the Secession Reference of 1998.[37] The court invoked unwritten principles of democracy, federalism, constitutionalism and protection of minorities to hold that if Quebec (or any other province) wanted to secede, it had to follow the appropriate procedure (and submit the question to a referendum). The federal government and the other provinces come under a legal duty to enter into a dialogue on the problem of secession.

---

35 *Re Part V of the Planning and Development Bill, 1999* [2000] 2 IR 321.

36 *ibid* at 359.

37 *Reference re Secession of Quebec* [1998] 2 SCR 217.

With the judicial review of legislation, and with the reference jurisdiction, the courts mentioned here, before deciding, are required to interpret and, in interpreting, to intervene, admonish and counsel. Each decision must take into account the relevant context.

3. An Original Dialogue: The Italian Case

In Italy, the Constitutional Court's competences are regulated by Arts 134–137 of the Constitution, by constitutional laws n. 1 of 1948 and n. 1 of 1953, and by ordinary law n. 87 of 1953.

Neither the Constitution nor other laws define the types of judicial review, apart from determining that the court can decide only in two senses: accepting or rejecting the question. However, notwithstanding the absence of specific provisions, the court, in time, introduced several degrees in its decisions. It seems as if the court had introduced other colours between white (decision that void the law) and black (decision that reject the question), thus creating a some *nuances* of grey in order to develop an ongoing and permanent dialogue with the legislative power.[38]

This dialogue finds an anchor point in Art 28 of law n. 87 of 1953, where it is stated that the

> "judicial review of the Constitutional Court with regard to a law or an act with force of law excludes all judgements of a political nature and all questions on the use of Parliament's discretionary power".

This rule, even were it not stated in the law mentioned, could have been inferred by the very constitutional provisions (Art 64 and following articles) that define the parliamentary form of government in a democratic state. And yet, if the (ordinary) lawmaker found it necessary to detail the scope and contents thereof, this was clearly done in order to underscore the clear separation between a decision of this court and the discretion of politics.

The court, therefore, during a review, is asked not only to take into account such discretionary power, but also to somehow protect and guarantee it, in its capacity as a "negative legislator" (according to Kelsen's doctrine), but also, more importantly, as the ultimate guarantor of constitutionally defined order.

In this framework, the doctrine has identified the category of the so-called "warning decisions" issued by the court "when it does not feel that the raised issue can be accepted, but there is uncertainty with regard to the implementation of the constitutional values".[39] In such cases, the decision with which the court rejects the issue of constitutional legitimacy also invites the lawmaker to intervene, reforming the subject matter under review, including pursuant to the suggestions sometimes provided by the court itself.

---

38 V Crisafulli, "La Corte costituzionale tra magistratura e Parlamento" in AA.VV, *Scritti giuridici in memoria di Calamandrei*, IV, Padova (Cedam 1958)273 and A Cerri, *Corso di giustizia costituzionale* (Giuffre, 2001) 242.

39 A Cerri, *Corso di giustizia costituzionale* (Giuffre, 2001) 242.

In this way, legal theory has identified three sub-categories of warning decisions, with different effects.

1. The law subject to judicial review is unconstitutional, but this cannot be declared by the court, as "there is no single way to remedy that"[40] (see, for example, decision on health care assistance, n. 431 of 1987).
2. The law subject to judicial review is unconstitutional, but there are incidental reasons that justify the maintenance of the law, and yet the court is asked to intervene within a certain deadline (defined as the "breaking point"; see decision n. 179 of 1998 and decision n. 826 of 1988 on the transitional arrangements on television).
3. The law subject to judicial review is unconstitutional, but if the court should declare as much, other constitutional principles would be damaged and only the legislator can intervene (such as, for instance, in budgetary matters, when a decision might compromise the principle stated in Art 81 of the Constitution, e.g. decisions 9, 15, 27, 45, 268 of 1988; 141, 292 of 1999).

In these cases, the court weighs the different constitutional principles and values against one another, and through such decisions "exercises an increasing pressure on the recipients, with the co-operation of the Judiciary, so as to ensure a maximum of pluralism and of participation in this delicate matter".[41] With these decisions, the court warns the legislator of a need for action; if the legislator does not intervene in a timely fashion, the court, should a similar case be presented for review, shall be obliged to act and declare the full unconstitutionality of the general law, with an additive judgment.

Over time, the "warning" of the court has taken four forms:

1. *exhortation*, where the court simply invites the legislator to act;
2. *integration*, where the court not only asks the legislator to act, but also integrates this exhortation with punctual instructions on the way to do that;
3. *admonition*, where the court invites the legislator to act under the penalty to void the law on a second occasion (if we can use a football metaphor, the court first gives a yellow card to the parliament and then gives the red one);
4. *statement of temporary legitimacy*, where the court states that although the norm under review is certainly unconstitutional, it shall nevertheless retain its force of law, provided that the legislator intervenes soon.

There are some more or less relevant examples of this.

With regard to *exhortation-warnings*, one of the first, historic judgments of the court

[40] *ibid*, 243.

[41] *ibid*, 249. See P Carnevale and F Modugno, "Sentenze additive, soluzioni costituzionalmente obbligate e declaratoria di inammissibilità per mancata indicazione del "verso" della richiesta addizione" in (1990) (1) Giur Cost 519. R Romboli, "Il giudizio di costituzionalità delle leggi in via incidentale" in *Aggiornamenti in tema di processo costituzionale (1996–1998)* ([ed.R. Romboli, Giappichelli, 1999) 185, speaks of a "threat".

is Decision n. 8 of 1957. The decision concerned the constitutionality of Art 2 of the then Consolidated Act on public security (TULPS) promulgated by the Fascist Regime, which conferred on the Prefect special powers to arrest people that were clearly in conflict with the Republican Constitution.

Should the court have declared the clear unconstitutionality of the law, the decision would have created a material regulatory vacuum, depriving the state of an instrument that was considered essential. At the same time, however, had the court simply rejected the issue, it would have automatically admitted that the law complied with the new constitutional provisions. Therefore, in order to escape the simple accepted/rejected dichotomy, the court introduced what we now call "warning decisions". Indeed the court, while rejecting the constitutional legitimacy issue regarding Art 2 of TULPS, appealed to the legislator to adjust the Consolidated Act to the new constitutional provisions "so as to make it formally more compliant with the powers attributed to the Prefect".[42]

Similarly, decision n. 188/1996 reviews the military codes, "a task that should have long been addressed by the legislator", so that

> "this Court feels that it should exhort the legislator once more, to intervene, also taking into account the implementation issues that are further highlighted by the constitutionality issues raised by the military judges".

Again, see also decision n. 52/1997 on the consideration for the mayors of municipalities with a population of less than 10,000 people, where the Court, after rejecting the issue submitted for review, warns the legislator that

> "there is a need for the relevant regulations, in line with the modern legislation that is inclined to mitigate the gratuitousness of public functions, to comply with adequacy criteria and fulfil the need, often pointed out, to facilitate the participation of workers to the organisation of the Country".

The court reasoned that "in the presence of considerable unease regarding the implementation of the constitutional principles",[43] it would not decide negatively on the issue brought to its attention, so as to give the legislator time to act.

With regard to *integration-warnings*, for example, we can consider the decision n. 225 of 1974 on the matter of broadcasting monopoly, where the court, while maintaining the validity of the discipline under review, provides the legislator with a sort of "decalogue" for the maintenance of the public broadcasting monopoly.

---

42 On this issue, see A D'Atena, *Intepretazione adeguatrice, diritto vivente e sentenze interpretative della Corte costituzionale*, Speech at the Seminar organized by the Italian Constitutional Court on "Constitutional Courts, judges and interpretations of the legal text", Rome, 6th November 2009, in www.cortecostituzionale.it/documenti/convegni_seminari/06_11_09_DAtena.pdf (Last accessed 7 April 2013).[The author would also like to recall the "second act" in the affair concerning Art 2 TULPS, when the court, with decision n. 26 of 1961, declared the relevant law illegitimate thanks to an interpretation of the "provision" (the written text) and of the "rule" (the principles that can be inferred from the provision).

43 R Romboli, "Il giudizio di costituzionalità delle leggi in via incidentale" in R. Romboli (ed.) *Aggiornamenti in tema di processo costituzionale (1996–1998)* (Giappichelli, 1999) 185.

In particular, the court, while confirming the legitimacy of leaving the state as the sole subject able to use the broadcasting structures, considers it needful for the legislator to introduce in the legal system eight principles, aimed at ensuring the impartiality of the broadcasts, the maximum degree of pluralism, the right of access, the objectivity of journalists and a limitation to advertising.

With this ruling the Court "while respecting the discretionary power of the legislator in choosing the most appropriate instruments to attain the two fundamental goals [pluralism and impartiality]"(see Decision n. 225 of 1974, page 8), formulates a decalogue that the legislator must take into account in order to preserve the broadcasting monopoly, as "the current legislation does not reach so far, in that ... nothing therein is even similar to the kind of regulation mentioned above" (ibidem)[44]

With regard to *admonition-warnings*, an example may be found in decision n. 114 of 1994, where the court, while recognising the legitimacy of the rules on the collective abstention of lawyers from hearings, invited the legislator to amend them in order to guarantee the right of the accused to a defence, even though later on, with decision n. 171 of 1996, the court declared the unconstitutionality of the same rules as the legislator had not intervened in the meanwhile.

Finally, with regard to *decisions on temporary legitimacy*, an example is decision n. 826 of 1988 on the transitional arrangements regarding television.

The issue, too complex to be summarised here appropriately, starts with some District Judges blacking out several local private broadcasting stations which, by broadcasting the same show at the same hour had effectively created a state-wide private broadcasting station, thus breaking the public monopoly.

To go beyond the blackout ordered by the judge, the government has issued a decree-law, which was not subsequently converted, and a second one (n. 807 of 1984), which was subsequently converted into law n. 10 of 11 February 1985; this decree made it possible for private concerns in the sector to continue their activity, while waiting for the passing of an organic law on broadcasting, but only for a period of six months after the date of coming into force of the decree-law.

After three years from the expiration of the extension, and in the absence of any legislative action, the court, while admitting to the unconstitutionality of several articles of law n. 10 of 1985, declared the relevant issue not admissible and warned the legislator that

> "should the approval of the new law be unreasonably delayed, it would no longer be possible to consider ... the contested discipline temporary, and it would automatically acquire a permanent status: in that case, this Court, if asked to review the same issue again, would inevitably adopt a different opinion, with all the relevant consequences" (see Decision n. 826 of 1988, page 24).

---

[44] For the sake of completeness: after the quoted ruling, Parliament intervened by approving law n. 103 of 1975, which provided a certain measure of information pluralism within state television.

With the same technique, the court, with its decision n. 243 of 1993 declared the unconstitutionality of some legal provisions that excluded a cost-of-living adjustment from the calculation of severance pay benefits. It did not annul the contested provisions or interpret them pursuant to the Constitution, but rather invited the legislator to intervene to choose the most appropriate instruments to ensure the country's economic stability and the effectiveness of the social rights granted by the Constitution.

In this latter case, the court needed to balance several constitutional principles: on the one hand, the principles on the social rights of the citizens; on the other hand, those on the coverage of expenditure and the balance sheet break-even pursuant to Art 81 of the Constitution (which states that "Any other law involving new or increased expenditures must specify the resources to meet these expenditures"). To balance these two goals, and to avoid the "nullification" of a constitutional right as well as the creation of a sort of "hole" in the state budget, the court has developed, especially at the beginning of the 1990s, these innovative decision instruments, which, as has been mentioned, can be classified among the so-called "warning" decisions[45].

Indeed, as it has been observed, the court found itself between the Scylla and Charybdis of Greek mythology, that is to say, between the risk of abdicating its role as last guarantor of the Constitution and the risk of causing serious economic repercussions due to its decisions.[46]

These four categories of "warning" decisions must, however, be kept separate from the so-called additive judgments, with which the Court, in its judicial review, introduces a new principle that can be derived from the contested provisions and with which the *a quo* judge must comply.[47]

In its warning decisions the court, while sometimes spelling out a principle of the contested provision and thus saving the provision itself, adds something more, because it invites the legislator to give effect to it with statutes that are universally effective, indicating a deadline within which the legislature must act. In its opinions in such decisions, the court indicates a deadline within which the legislature must act and sets forth the principles it must follow. In this way, a single decisional tool manages to combine the contents of an "additive" judgment with a sort of "delegation" order, in order to reconcile the immediacy of the court's "acceptance" of the constitutional challenge with the preservation of the legislature's discretion: "the Constitutional Court strives to strike a balance between safeguarding the Constitution and preserving the discretionary powers of the legislator."[48] In other words, "these decisions differentiate themselves from the 'additive judgments'

---

45 See R Pinardi, *L'horror vacui nel giudizio sulle leggi. Prassi e tecniche decisionali utilizzate dalla Corte costituzionale allo scopo di ovviare all'inerzia del legislatore* (Giuffre, 2007) 76.

46 T Groppi, "The Italian Constitutional Court: Towards a 'Multilevel System' of Constitutional Review?" (2008) 3 Journal of Comparative Law 100, especially at 114.

47 The additive judgment is considered by some a "telum imbelle sine ictu", an "effete debate which nobody is going to take seriously" (Zagrebelsky, *La giustizia costituzionale* (Il Mulino, 1988) 311).

48 T Groppi, "The Italian Constitutional Court: Towards a 'Multilevel System' of Constitutional Review?" (2008) 3 Journal of Comparative Law 100 at 108.

in that they do not introduce a new principle in a specific discipline subjected to the Court's review; instead, they show the legislator where to go to draft future, constitutionally legitimated regulations."[49]

While with the warning decisions the court invites the legislator to adjust an existing law so that it becomes compatible with the Constitution (even though it does not declare it unconstitutional), with additive judgments the court itself makes the necessary adjustments to the contested provision, so that by interpreting it according to a different principle it will comply with the constitutional dictates.[50]

---

[49] T Martines, *Diritto costituzionale* (Giuffre, 2000) 495.

[50] The issue of the warning decisions of the Italian Constitutional Court is strictly connected with the theme of the time effectiveness of the court's decisions and with the lack of inclusion, in our system, of mechanisms similar to those in the Austrian Constitution or the German Fundamental Law, according to which the court may defer the effects of the decision. R Pinardi, *La corte, i giudici ed il legislatore. Il problema degli effetti temporali delle sentenze di incostituzionalitá* (Giuffré, 1993). Worried about the immediate practical consequences that its decisions may produce, the court has used the "warnings" to the legislator to overcome any "political obstacles", as they have been defined by the most authoritative authors (A Pace, "Effetti temporali delle decisioni di accoglimento e tutela costituzionale del diritto di agire nei rapporti pendenti, in AA.VV., *Effetti temporali delle sentenze della Corte costituzionale anche con riferimento alle esperienze straniere, Atti del Seminario della Corte costituzionale. Roma 23-24 ottobre 1988* (Giuffre, 1989) 54. In Germany, indeed, the Fundamental Law recognises the possibility for the Constitutional Court to conclude a judicial review of a law using, among others, decisions of incompatibility or warning-decisions (*Appellentscheidungen*). The decisions of incompatibility subordinate the annulment effects to the condition that Parliament fails to amend the legislation within a set deadline and therefore, at least in theory, they compel the legislator to amend the law. Warning decisions express only an invitation for the legislator, sometimes with a deadline for the amendment, but the expiration of that deadline does not automatically render the law void (it is approximate, not binding as it is in the first case). The doctrine looks on favourably at this second type of decision, because they are deemed more compatible with the role of this court and with the Parliament's discretionary power, to the extent that warning decisions are considered a positive example of institutional co-operation between the two bodies.

The case of Portugal is certainly very interesting in this context, especially since the Portuguese Constitution expressly requires the court to intervene with warning decisions (*decisiones apelativas*), in particular when the legislator fails in its duty. Indeed, Art 283 of the Constitution states that "A requerimento do Presidente da República, do Provedor de Justiça ou, com fundamento em violação de direitos das regiões autónomas, dos presidentes das Assembleias Legislativas das regiões autónomas, o Tribunal Constitucional aprecia e verifica o não cumprimento da Constituição por omissão das medidas legislativas necessárias para tornar exequíveis as normas constitucionais.", specifying, in the following paragraph, that "[q] uando o Tribunal Constitucional verificar a existência de inconstitucionalidade por omissão, dará disso conhecimento ao órgão legislativo competente".. In these cases, the Portuguese Constitutional Court invites the legislator to act and, if after a set time the legislator has failed to do so, issues (provided that a case concerning the same issue is presented to it) an integrative or substitutive decision (e.g. decision n. 143 of 1985 and decision n. 203 of 1986). For these reasons, such decisions (whose efficacy is left to the will of the legislator) are comparable to the warning decisions. Next to this type of warning decisions in the event of a regulatory void, Portugal recognises also exhortation-decisions, which the court issues "se porventura a declaração de inconstitucionalidade viesse a implicar a necessidade de qualquer providência normativa" (decision n. 154 del 1986). On these topics, see C De Caro Bonella, "Sviluppi della forma di governo in Portogallo dal 1974 al 1982" in (1982) (2) *Quaderni costituzionali* 330; R Orru', "Vicende e giurisprudenza del Tribunal constitutional portoghese negli anni 1999 e 2000" in *Giurisprudenza costituzionale*, 2001) 3225; M Ruotolo, *La dimensione temporale dell'invalidità della legge* (Cedam, 2000) 328–329. As observed by G Fontana, *La giustizia costituzionale in Portogallo* in *La giustizia costituzionale in Europa* (T Groppi and M Olivetti ed, Giuffre, 2003) 179 at 201: "il controllo di costituzionalità per omissione, dunque, none

4. Conclusion

Judges who are invested with the power to strike down laws (as in Ireland the High Court and the Supreme Court, or in Italy the Constitutional Court) have a great deal of discretion in interpreting the Constitution. We wonder how they may now use their discretion. The famous aphorism of Justice Holmes, "the Constitution is what the judges say it is", no longer applies to modern democratic society. One is more interested in exploring the possibility of an interaction of the constitutional judges with the bodies that exercise the legislative or the executive power. We are aware (following the words of Justice Iacobucci of the Supreme Court of Canada)[51] that the legislative power (or, we may add, the executive power) can react to a decision by passing of (or suggesting) a new legislation. Such interplay is at the origin of what has been called a dialogue.[52]

Dialogue can be characterised by a confrontation, a debate or a weak acceptance of the proposal of the other party; but it can also degenerate into a challenge and a provocation.

We are now considering the interaction among constitutional organs of one state, and not the possibility that courts of different systems (be they states or international organisations) may influence each other.[53] The problem with which we are dealing suggests that we explore the evolution of judicial review and of reference jurisdiction in Ireland, on the basis of recent and important decisions. This will be our programme for the near future. For now, it may be noted that, when interpreting the Constitution, Irish judges consider foreign decisions as "persuasive authorities". They look mainly to the United States, but lately even German and Italian materials were deemed apposite. This is why we venture to say that our research on Irish experience may draw suggestions from two other common law countries.

The American experience shows that, in some cases involving national politics (recent judgments with regard to terrorism are proof of this), the Supreme Court makes its decisions in accordance with the line adopted by the Government, even more than it does with Congress.

---

idoneo a ripristinare l'ordine costituzionale violato, atteggiandosi, piuttosto, a strumento di vigile tutela dell'attuazione costituzionale nel rispetto della separazione dei poteri". LN De Almeida, "El tribunal constitucional y el contenido, vinculatoriedad y efectos de sus decisions" in (60–61) (1988) *Rivista de Estudio Politicos* 859, especially at 876. This point is treated extensively by G Vagli, "Controllo di costituzionalità per omissione in Portogallo" in *Diritto e società* (1997) (3) 575.

51 *Vriend v Alberta* [1998] 1 SCR 493, 566 (para 139).

52 On the concept of dialogue, see PW Hogg and AA Bushell, "The Charter Dialogue Between Courts and Legislatures" (1997) 35 Osgoode Hall LJ 75; CB Manfredi and JB Kelly, "Six Degrees of Dialogue: A Response to Hogg and Bushell" (1999) 37 Osgoode Hall LJ 513; PW Hogg and AA Thornton, "Reply to 'Six Degrees of Dialogue'" (1999) 37 Osgoode Hall LJ 529. For a confrontation between the judiciary and the elected members of government, see K Roach, "Dialogue or Defiance: Legislative Reversals of Supreme Court Decisions in Canada and the United States" (2006) 4 Internat J of Constitutional Law 347. On the theory of dialogue, see S Gerotto, *Premesse metodologiche ad una teoria del dialogo tra giudice costituzionale e legislatore* (Cleup, 2008).

53 G De Vergottini, *Oltre il dialogo tra le Corti. Giudici, diritto straniero, comparazione* (Il Mulino, 2010) *passim* and M Gobbo, *La funzione consultiva delle Corti negli ordinamenti anglosassoni* (Bonomo editore, 2004).

This is evidenced by the long period (2001–2004) in which the Supreme Court decided to stay silent rather than undertaking judicial review of the actions of the executive. When it finally intervened, it did so to guarantee the due process of law on the one hand, and to recognise the weight and importance of the Government's decisions in security matters on the other hand. Even when it sends strong signals to the political forces, such as in the *Hamdan v Rumsfeld*,[54] the Supreme Court leaves the road open for the executive that, together with the legislative power, can bypass the decision.

When, rather than tackling wide-ranging political issues, the court focuses on specific individual rights, the judges do not hesitate to make themselves heard, sometimes even in an aggressive kind of way.

A very well-known instance of this is around *Miranda v Arizona*[55] Which frequently mentioned in the mass media. In reviewing the rules followed by police forces in handling people whom they wished to interrogate, the Supreme Court ruled by a narrow majority that informing suspects of their three basic rights—the right to remain silent, the right to be informed that anything that they say may be used against them in court, and the right to be assisted by a lawyer—were an absolute prerequisite to interrogation. It should be remembered that among the minority judges, some thought that "the social costs of crime are too great to call the new rules anything but an hazardous experimentation"[56] and how, within the majority itself, the idea prevailed that the provision "in no way creates a constitutional straightjacket".[57] The latter words might be considered an opening for dialogue; a first reaction came two years later in 1968, when Congress included a clause in the Omnibus Crime Control and Safe Streets Act that, while accepting the principles and formulations of the court with regard to *Miranda*, made the applicable rules more relaxed. As a member of the Senate commented, that was "a response to a judicial oligarchy composed of five Supreme Court justices".[58]

On reflection, the new legal provisions were not especially significant, as shown by the fact that in the following 30 years the court never felt the need to respond. However, in the relationship between powers, the fact that the decision of the court no longer represented "an absolute prerequisite to interrogation"[59] diminished the importance of the *Miranda* case. It is therefore understandable that the court, when called to judicially review the 1968 law in 2000, decided by wide majority and with a lot of energy that "Congress may not legislatively supersede our decisions interpreting and applying the Constitution".[60]

The abovementioned events lead to the "theory of dialogue" between the

---

54 548 US 557 (2006). See, C Bassu, *Terrorismo e costituzionalismo. Percorsi comparati* (Giappichelli, 2010) *passim*.

55 384 US 436 (1966).

56 *ibid* at 517 Harlan J (diss).

57 *ibid* at 467.

58 Senator Sam Ervin, 114 Cong Rec 14, 155 (May 21, 1968), cited by Y Kamisar, "The Rise, Decline and Fall(?) of *Miranda*" (2012) 87 Washington L Rev 965, 973.

59 384 US 436 (1966), 471

60 *Dickerson v US* 530 US 428, 437 (2000)

constitutional justice and the legislator, developed by Gerotto[61] on the basis of the evolution of the American doctrine on this point. The purpose is to dilute conflicts arising from the judicial activism, to try to go beyond the moments in which judicial supremacy manifests itself and to recognise the existence of mechanisms that allow the legislative and executive power to respond to the decisions of the judges.

With regard to judicial activism, it is maybe appropriate to quote President Roosevelt: "the Court has been acting not as a judicial body, but as a policy making body".[62] But it is also well known that President Roosevelt had many instruments to go beyond the rulings of the court and made good use of them. However, the principle of judicial supremacy is not so deeply rooted in the United States as some claim. In its decisions on terrorism, the Supreme Court has followed, perhaps excessively, the rule of self-restraint.

Therefore, we think that the theory according to which dialogue is antithetical to the American experience should be rejected. Dialogue can include a discussion, including a lively one, where one of the participants—the Supreme Court—may see its ideas prevail over another's. Dialogue is not necessarily an exchange of words between peers; dialogue exists as long as one speaks and the other answers.

In Canada, too, judicial review caused problems after the 1982 constitutional reform, in connection with the increasing militancy of the courts and of the Supreme Court in particular. However, in contrast with the United States, the Canadian system provides some rules for the review and some limitations on its exercise, as well as the possibility of suspending the availability of charter-based review in relation to legislation for a certain period of time (five years). These provisions, and more generally, the form traditionally adopted by the relationship between the powers, lead Canada to lean towards joint solutions.

Although Canadian constitutional law experts have different opinions on the number and type of possible dialogues and on the relationships between the participating subjects, it is widely felt that dialogue is an important facet of the free and democratic society which the Canadian Charter of Rights and Freedoms wishes to guarantee. We may add that reasonableness is very important for the theory of dialogue in Canada.

For example, *Re Manitoba Language Rights*[63] concerned the constitutional legitimacy of a Manitoba law that states that the official language of the province is English, any statute or law to the contrary notwithstanding. This law did not respect the bilingualism guarantees established in the Manitoba Act 1870 that became part of the current Constitution of Canada after its reform in 1982. Thus, the use of French and English in official documents is mandatory in Manitoba and the provisions passed to support the exclusive use of English are unconstitutional and, in the words of the court, void of any force and effect. However, the court realised that the immediate implementation of this judicial finding of unconstitutionality might have had severe consequences, not only for the province, but for the whole

---

[61] S Gerotto, *Premesse metodologiche ad una teoria del dialogo tra giudice costituzionale e legislatore* (Cleup, 2008).

[62] Franklin Delano Roosevelt, *Fireside Chat 9: On "Court-Packing"* (9 March 1937) (available at http://millercenter.org/president/speeches/detail/3309; last accessed 7 April 2013).

[63] *Re Manitoba Language Rights* [1985] 1 SCR 721.

Canadian system. Therefore it stated: "the current Acts of the Legislature will be deemed to have temporary force and effect for the minimum period of time necessary for their translation, re-enactment, printing and publication".[64] This was a triumph of common sense.

A dialogue is always a relationship between two or more subjects, but there is no dialogue if one speaks and the other listens but does not react. In this case, we have a monologue.

For the system to work, it is necessary for the legislator to answer the court's warning with concrete action. What happens if there is no response? This, in our opinion, is the issue on which we should concentrate, now that we have reached the end of the analysis.

Nowadays, we are often compelled to witness a dialogue of the deaf: both participants speak, neither listens to the other, and both are convinced that they have performed their institutional duty. See what has happened in Italy, where the Senate expressly decided not to follow the Constitutional Court's judgment no. 277 of 2011, which stated the incompatibility between the role of members of parliament and the mayor's office in cities where there are more than 20,000 inhabitants.[65]

It has been seen that, if the legislator omits to act, or to address the warning, the courts sometimes have the necessary instruments to act directly, by reviewing the same situation again and excluding it from the legal structure.

However, it seems that the legislators' failure to address the courts' warnings depends also on the role that the legislative power has assumed in the last few decades in the democratic systems.

As the literature has been observing for some time now (for instance, the volumes edited by Poguntke and Webb[66] and, in Italy, by Di Giovine and Mastromarino[67]) there is an ongoing *presidentialisation* of the democratic systems, characterised by a loss of power to influence the decision-making processes of assemblies, a power that is being shifted to the executive power and, even more, on the head of the executive. In other words, the recipients of the warnings of the constitutional courts are the parliaments, in their capacity as holders of the legislative power and as producers of the subject matter of the judicial review.

However, nowadays, parliaments seem to have lost their traditional activities and have not yet understood what is happening albeit they remain with significant powers, in the democratic circuit.

---

64 *ibid* at 783.

65 See the report of the meeting of 21 December 2011, Giunta delle Elezioni, Senato della Repubblica (www.senato.it/japp/bgt/showdoc/frame.jsp?tipodoc=SommComm&leg=16&id=623237).

66 T Poguntke and P Webb ed, *The Presidentialization of Politics: A Comparative Study of Modem Democracies* (Oxford University Press, 2005).

67 A Di Giovine and A Mastromarino ed, *La presidenzializzazione degli esecutivi nelle democrazie contemporanee* (Giappichelli, 2007).

As some evidence of that, one may recall the role assumed by the president of the republic towards parliament and the executive, in Italy as well as in Ireland.

In regard to Italy, see for example the practice introduced by the President of the Republic, on 2009, in occasion of the enactment of the laws, or the approval of the acts of the Council of Ministers, or parliamentary activity.

In particular, the head of the state has added to the enactment of the laws approved by Parliament a declaration where he distances himself from such laws. In this way, he introduced a sort of enactment "with reservation", stressing on the other hand the reasons for the possible invalidity of such laws, which could legitimate their return to Parliament.[68]

In addition, bear in mind the unusual communications that have been made by him to the President of the Council of Ministers during the work of this institution, in order to prevent the Government from taking a certain decision (i.e. the approval of a decree law adopted just to fill a gap in the legislation concerning the voluntary interruption of life).

Thirdly, direct interventions in the Parliament's debate on a Bill, in order to push the amendment of its content, must be recalled (this has occurred during the vote on the Bill converting the so-called *milleproroghe* decree-law in December 2010, or during the debate concerning a proposal for constitutional reform in May 2010).

In all of these cases, the President of the Italian Republic has believed that it would be convenient to introduce new and original practices, or to reinterpret old ones, far from using the powers established by the Constitution, to make possible the dialogue with other constitutional organs, perhaps because he has considered such powers to be inadequate.

A similar reasoning can be made in the Irish context.

Of course, this depends undoubtedly also on the personality of the head of the executive (as the institutional and political history of Canada shows clearly).

In any case, one thing is clear: parliaments, when faced with judicial review that present warnings, do not exactly turn a deaf ear, but seem to tackle them completely inadequately.

The tendency to *presidentialisation* of executive powers in contemporary democracies has changed the dialogue between the courts and parliaments, transforming it into a dialogue between the courts and the executive power. Now it is necessary to understand how and with what instruments the judges will carry out dialogue with the executive. This is the new challenge for those courts; it will probably no longer be possible to call them the "judges of the laws", as they are now required to build a relationship, as well as a true dialogue, with the holders of a new, different "legislative-executive" power.

68 See A Ruggeri, "Ancora un caso di promulgazione con motivazione .... 'contraria'" (a proposito del mancato rinvio della legge sulla sicurezza)" in *Forum di Quaderni costituzionali* 24 July 2009 (www.forumcostituzionale.it; last accessed 7 April 2013).

CHAPTER 9

Ireland, Europe, and the Partial Eclipse of Constitutional Authority

Dr Maria Cahill[1]

1. INTRODUCTION

Ireland's legal relationship with the European Union has developed, I would like to suggest, against the backdrop of some non-legal concerns in relation to fundamental rights. The first concern emerges from a consciousness that Ireland is a little different with regard to fundamental rights protection, this difference being typified, but not exhausted, by the fact that, unusually, the Irish Constitution enumerates the right to life of unborn children. The second concern is that Ireland will not be able to convince other Member States that its position on these fundamental rights issues should be adopted also by them and become the harmonised standards across the European Union and that therefore Ireland must seek, in the alternative, to derogate from common European standards on these issues. This combined concern that Ireland's "difference" with regard to fundamental rights protection must be protected as a minority position within the European Union has led to the kinds of politico-legal solutions that take the form of derogations or exceptions, such as the Protocol to the Maastricht Treaty[2] or the so-called Lisbon Guarantees.[3]

My argument will be that, in approaching fundamental rights protection in this way, whereby exemptions from substantive provisions of EU law must be carved out in pressurised political discussions in order to protect national constitutional provisions on fundamental rights, we undermine the very important concept of constitutional authority. Indeed, I will suggest that the concept of constitutional authority has been at least partially eclipsed in both judicial and academic writing on Ireland's relationship with the European Union. My interest here is therefore to examine the interaction between the Irish constitutional order and the European legal spheres in terms of the implications for the constitutional frame, rather than simply in terms of their implications for fundamental rights protection. By constitutional authority, I mean the lawful mandate and limited power vested in the organs of government, through the mechanism of the constitutional text, by those who hold that authority originally, viz. the constituent power.

The chapter will deal in Part I with Art 29.4 of the Irish Constitution, which mandates Ireland's accession to the European Union, and the manner in which it has been interpreted. Part II looks at the (in)famous *Crotty* decision and the manner in which it has been received and interpreted subsequently. Finally, Part III deals with what

---

[1] Lecture, Faculty of Law, University College Cork.

[2] Protocol No. 17 annexed to the Treaty on European Union and to the Treaties establishing the European Communities.

[3] Presidency Conclusions of the Brussels European Council, 18–19 June 2009.

I consider to be the most fascinating and most pertinent decision on the question of the relationship between European law and Irish constitutional law: the case of *SPUC v Grogan*.

2. Part I

The particularity of Ireland's relationship with European Union law must be traced back to the inclusion, within the constitutional provision that allowed Ireland to accede, of what came to be known as the "immunity clause". In 1972, the Irish Constitution was amended prior to accession, in order to include this text as Art 29.4.3°:

> "The State may become a member of the European Coal and Steel Community (established by Treaty signed at Paris on the 18th day of April, 1951), the European Economic Community (established by Treaty signed at Rome on the 25th day of March, 1957) and the European Atomic Energy Community (established by Treaty signed at Rome on the 25th day of March, 1957). No provision of this Constitution invalidates laws enacted, acts done or measures adopted by the State necessitated by the obligations of membership of the Communities or prevents laws enacted, acts done or measures adopted by the Communities, or institutions thereof, from having the force of law in the State."

Unfortunately, during the parliamentary debates on the legal provisions adopted to accommodate Ireland's accession to the European Union, discussion centred on the implementing legislation, the European Communities Act 1973, rather than the wording of the constitutional amendment. The Fianna Fáil Government of the day, under Taoiseach Jack Lynch, did not argue for either the substance or the wording of the provision with any notable depth or rigor, and so it remains unclear why the Government considered in necessary to propose such a sweeping immunity clause. Opposition deputies who challenged the proposal, questioning why Ireland should amend its Constitution in such a far-reaching way, when no other Member State made such an amendment to its national constitution, were not given an answer; Mr Lynch merely remarked very briefly that a blanket immunity was needed because it would be impractical to go through each article of the Constitution, making the necessary adjustments to each provision in order to make them compatible with membership.[4] One opposition parliamentarian, Deputy Keating, vigorously attacked the proposed amendment throughout the legislative process:

> "In one sentence, we have this incredible and extraordinarily comprehensive sweeping aside of very large parts of our Constitution on the one hand, while on the other hand there is an extraordinary and comprehensive acceptance of laws, or rules and of actions taken by the Communities which were not responsible to any democratic organisation. We are rubber-stamping undemocratic and bureaucratic decisions. I find the fact that this major change, the most fundamental change in national policy and direction since the foundation of

4 Statement by Taoiseach Jack Lynch of the Fianna Fáil Party in Dáil Éireann on 2 December 1971, as the Bill to amend the constitution to provide for membership of the European Economic Community passed through the second stage of the legislative process. Available at: http://historical-debates.oireachtas.ie/D/0257/D.0257.197112020003.html.

> the State, should be wrapped up in four vague lines profoundly scandalous and shocking, but it is entirely in line with the determination to settle things by preventing the real issues coming before the people."[5]

Later in the debate, Deputy Keating reiterated his objection to

> "the aspects of the Bill which enable not just sections of the Constitution to be rendered invalid but which effectively negate the Constitution. So much of it is swept away that what is left is hard to describe as being the original document."[6]

His colleague Deputy Desmond agreed that "[i]n effect the electorate are being asked to sign what can be described only as a constitutional blank cheque" because they would be sanctioning the altering and negating of constitutional provisions without having specified in advance which provisions would be altered or negated and in which circumstances this would occur. "If it were to be accepted as it stands," he concluded, "it would effectively bring Ireland under the rule of a new constitution, namely, under the laws enacted by the Communities at any time in the future. We would finish up with a new constitution."[7]

This provision has been renumbered four times in the intervening years since 1973,[8] and has undergone some small changes in wording (mostly to account for the changes in the nomenclature of the European polity itself) although its essential substance remains entirely the same. It is now Art 29.4.6°, and it reads:

> "No provision of this Constitution invalidates laws enacted, acts done or measures adopted by the State, before, on or after the entry into force of the Treaty of Lisbon, that are necessitated by the obligations of membership of the European Union referred to in subsection 5 of this section or of the European Atomic Energy Community, or prevents laws enacted, acts done or measures adopted by –
>
> - the said European Union or the European Atomic Energy Community, or by institutions thereof,
> - the European Communities or European Union existing immediately before the entry into force of the Treaty of Lisbon, or by institutions thereof, or
> - bodies competent under the treaties referred to in this section,
>
> from having the force of law in the State."

---

5 Justin Keating TD (Labour Party), 2 December 1971, *Third Amendment of the Constitution Bill, 1971: Second Stage* 257 *Dáil Debates*, col 1076 (available at: http://historical-debates.oireachtas.ie/D/0257/D.0257.197112020003.html; last accessed 14 May 2013).

6 Justin Keating TD (Labour Party), 25 January 1972 *Third Amendment of the Constitution Bill, 1971: Committee Stage* 257 *Dáil Debates*, col 400 (available at: http://historical-debates.oireachtas.ie/D/0258/D.0258.197201250023.html; last accessed 14 May 2013).

7 Barry Desmond TD (Labour Party), 2 December 1971 *Third Amendment of the Constitution Bill, 1971: Second Stage* 257 *Dáil Debates*, cols 1126, 1133 (available at: http://historical-debates.oireachtas.ie/D/0257/D.0257.197112020003.html; last accessed 14 May 2013).

8 Between 1973 and 1993, it was numbered Art 29.4.3°; between 1993 and 1999, it was numbered Art 29.4.5°; between 1999 and 2002, it was numbered Art 29.4.7°; between 2002 and 2009, it was numbered Art 29.4.10°, and since October 2009, it has been Art 29.4.6°.

It has been described by Hogan and Whelan as "an astonishingly wide immunity clause ... wide in terms both of the class of measures to which it applied, and of the breadth of immediate or potential application of those measures."[9] The wide class of measures to which the clause applies can be usefully broken down into two broad categories, along the lines outlined by the structure of the provision itself: in effect, two separate "immunity clauses", or, as I have elsewhere termed them, "constitutional exclusion clauses".[10] The first constitutional exclusion clause provides that no provision of the Constitution invalidates measures "adopted by the State which are necessitated by the obligations of membership".[11] The second provides that no provision of the Constitution prevents measures "adopted by [European institutions] from having the force of law in the State."

Astonishing and imprudent the provision may well be; however, I have sought to defend the proposition that the scope of the immunity provided to European law via Art 29.4.6° may not in fact be at all as wide or as deep as might be imagined at first glance.[12] In any case, whatever the scope of immunity provided, the provision does not surrender constitutional authority to the European Court of Justice. Quite the opposite, in fact; since Art 29.4.6° is the mechanism by which it is possible for European law to enter into the Irish legal system at all, it is the *sine qua non* of European law in Ireland. The mere fact of having a constitutional provision that is designed to regulate the legal relationship between Irish law and European law is conclusive evidence for the proposition that, as a matter of Irish constitutional law, the relationship between Irish law and European law is to be established on the terms prescribed by Irish law, and specifically Art 29.4.6°. As Phelan and Whelan put it: "[a]lthough Article [29.4.6] of the Constitution of Ireland is 'receptive' to Community law, it remains an Irish constitutional provision."[13]

On this basis, I argue that judicial statements by the Irish courts which adopt an extremely supine approach to the incorporation of European Union law cannot, in fact, find a mandate in Art 29.4.6°. As examples of these, I would point to such statements as that of Blayney J:

> "It is well established that Community law takes precedence over our domestic law. Where they are in conflict, it is the Community law that prevails. See *Marleasing S.A. v La Commercial Internacional de Alimentacion S.A.* Case

[9] Gerard Hogan and Anthony Whelan, *Ireland and the European Union: Constitutional and Statutory Texts and Commentary* (Sweet and Maxwell, 1995) 7.

[10] Maria Cahill "Constitutional Exclusion Clauses, Article 29.4.6, and the Constitutional Reception of European Law" (2011) 34 *Dublin University Law Journal* 74.

[11] It may be noted that the words "necessitated by the obligations of" replaced the wording originally proposed, which referred to law, acts or measures "consequent on the obligations" of membership of the Communities (as they then were). This change resulted from an amendment moved by Dr Garret FitzGerald TD, on behalf of Fine Gael, an intervention that he later regretted: JM Kelly, *The Irish Constitution* (4th ed, Gerard W Hogan and Gerry Whyte ed, Lexis Nexis Butterworths, 2003) 523 at n132; Garret FitzGerald, *Reflections on the Irish State* (Irish Academic Press, 2002) 49-50.

[12] *ibid*, 96ff; Diarmuid Rossa Phelan, *Revolt or Revolution: The Constitutional Boundaries of the European Community* (Round Hall Sweet and Maxwell, 1997) 350ff.

[13] Diarmuid Rossa Phelan and Anthony Whelan, "National Constitutional Law and European Integration" (1997) 6 *Irish Journal of European Law* 24 at 42.

> C-106/89 [1990] ECR 1-4135, and *Francovich v Italy* (Case C-6/90) [1991] ECR 1-5357."[14]

See also Keane J, who stated:

> "The jurisprudence of the Court of Justice of the European Communities has of course, established that the law of the Communities, whether embodied in the regulations or directives, must be given primacy where it is applicable, over the domestic law of the member states"[15]

Denham J wrote quite provocatively:

> "The democratic system in Ireland functions through three branches of government. However, in addition, the State is subject to the European institutions and provisions made therein".[16]

Interestingly, the judges' reasoning in order to reach these conclusions focuses on statements made in the case law of the European Court of Justice, rather than interpretations of Art 29.4.6°.

These statements do seem to confirm, however, that many Irish judges work under the assumption that exclusive decisional jurisdiction on the question of the conflict of laws between Irish and European law belongs to the European Court of Justice. This is evident from their recourse to decisions of the ECJ in support of the conclusion that European law is supreme over Irish law. Other rulings that follow the same pattern include the case of *Pigs and Bacon Commission v McCarron*, in which Costello J ruled in the High Court that the conclusion that

> "Community law enjoys precedence over a conflicting national law has been made clear in a number of decisions of the European Court and most recently in Case 106/77 *Simmenthal* ..."[17]

---

14 *Meaghar v Minister for Agriculture and Food* [1994] 1 IR 329 at 360. This has been affirmed and often expressly endorsed in numerous other judgments, of which the more notable include *Murphy v Bord Telecom Éireann* [1988] ILRM 53, *Society for the Protection of Unborn Children (Ire) Ltd. v Grogan (No. 3)* [1993] 1 ILRM 197, *Nathan v Bailey Gibson Ltd.* [1998] 2 IR 162, and *Society for the Protection of Unborn Children (Ire) Ltd. v Grogan (No. 5)* [1998] 4 IR 343. In the last case, the Supreme Court stated that "[t]he ruling of the European Court of Justice is binding on the national court"; [1998] 4 IR 343, 351. This position was played out in practical terms in the case of *Campus Oil v Minister for Industry and Energy*, in which Walsh J ruled that the right of appeal to the Supreme Court from any decision of the High Court (guaranteed by Art 43.4.3) "must yield to the primacy of [European law]"; [1983] IR 82 at 87. This decision was referred to as a "questionable interpretation of the Constitution" by Hogan and Whyte (JM Kelly, *The Irish Constitution* (4th ed, Gerard W Hogan and Gerry Whyte ed, Lexis Nexis Butterworths, 2003) 521). While I would agree that the decision is indeed a questionable interpretation of the Constitution, it does seem to be logically coherent with the other rulings mentioned in this section that represent the dominant view on the constitutional reception of European law. For additional commentary on the decision, see David O'Keefe, "Preliminary Deference: The Supreme Court and Community Law" (1983) 5 DULJ 286.

15 *Maher v Minister for Agriculture and Rural Development* [2001] 2 IR 139 at 167–168, Keane CJ.

16 *ibid*, 222; Denham J. Emphasis added.

17 *Pigs and Bacon Commission v McCarron* (unreported, High Court, Costello J, 30 June 1978).

In the case of *Lawlor v Minister for Agriculture*, Murphy J ruled that "it is no part of the function of this Court to determine whether or not any part of the EEC regulations were invalid ..."[18]

It is very noticeable that the dicta used by the courts in arriving at these conclusions are not grounded in interpretations of the provisions of the Irish Constitution—not even in an expansive interpretation of Art 29.4.6°. Instead, and rather inexplicably, the conclusion that national law has been displaced by European law, has been grounded exclusively in very cursory references to the case law of the European Court of Justice. Needless to say, this is an unconventional approach for a supreme court and a constitutional court to take in any matter, most especially in a situation where the resulting legal outcome is the displacement of national (constitutional) law.

It should be noted, moreover, that in none of these cases are the courts actually faced with a conflict between a provision of Irish constitutional law and European law. Moreover, many of these dicta were included in judgments handed down after 1989, which disregard an available Supreme Court precedent which deals precisely with the question of a conflict between Irish constitutional law and European law, and which interprets Art 29.4.6° as establishing that the Irish courts must have the responsibility to review European law by reference to the provisions of the Irish Constitution. That decision will be dealt with in Part III of this chapter; it is enough for now to reiterate that although Art 29.4.6° may have been unnecessary in its wantonly expansive terms, it cannot be understood to have abdicated the competence to determine the constitutional reception of European law in favour of the European Court of Justice. If it establishes nothing else, Art 29.4.6° establishes at least that this question remains a matter over which the Irish courts retain constitutional authority.

3. Part II

This section will deal with what must surely be one of the most well-known decisions of the Irish Supreme Court, *Crotty v An Taoiseach*, which arose in the context of the ratification of the Single European Act in 1986.[19] The Supreme Court confirmed that the Irish Constitution requires that the Government must arrange for a referendum when it proposes to ratify a European treaty that requires an amendment to the Irish Constitution. However, although the name of the case is well-known, and the political implications of the decision infamous, the reasoning for the decision is rarely discussed. Finlay CJ opened the discussion by holding that the Irish people had signed up to a particular vision of the European project when they voted in the 1972 referendum to agree that Ireland should become a member of the European Economic Communities. He therefore construed the first sentence of Art 29.4.3° (as it was then) as entailing, in his words:

> "an authorisation given to the State not only to join the Communities as they stood in 1973, but also to join in amendments of the Treaties so long as such amendments do not alter the essential scope or objectives of the Communities. To hold that the first sentence of Article 29.4.3 .... does not authorise any form of amendment to the Treaties after 1973 without a further amendment

[18] *Lawlor v Minister for Agriculture* [1990] 1 IR 356 at 378.
[19] *Crotty v An Taoiseach* [1987] IR 713.

> of the Constitution would be too narrow a construction; to construe it as an open-ended authority to agree, without further amendment of the Constitution, to any amendment of the Treaties would be too broad".[20]

The Supreme Court went on to apply that test in the instant case, ruling that the creation of a Court of First Instance was within the essential scope and objectives of the Communities as they stood in 1973. Similarly, the extension of competences regarding environmental protection and other miscellaneous provisions under Title II of the Single European Act were within the scope and objectives of the Treaties as originally ratified. However, Title III of the Single European Act contained, the Court ruled, the

> "possible ultimate objective of a form of European political union between the Member States of the Communities as an addition to the existing economic union between them ... [which] if that aim were ever achieved ... would constitute an alteration in the essential scope and objectives of the Communities to which Ireland could not agree without an amendment of the Constitution."[21]

The rationale behind this conclusion is also explained by the other judgments handed down in the case. In the words of Walsh J:

> "It is not within the competence of the Government, or indeed of the Oireachtas, to free themselves from the restraints of the Constitution or to transfer their powers to other bodies unless expressly empowered so to do by the Constitution. They are both creatures of the Constitution and are not empowered to act free from the restraints of the Constitution".[22]

Hederman J concurred, providing succinct summary of the ruling:

> "[T]he essential point at issue is whether the State can by any act on the part of its various organs of government enter into binding agreements with other states, or groups of states, to subordinate, or to submit, the exercise of the powers bestowed by the Constitution to the advice or interests of other states ... The State's organs cannot contract ... in any way to fetter powers bestowed unfettered by the Constitution. They are the guardians of these powers – not the disposers of them."[23]

The reason that the People must be consulted when the Government wishes to transfer certain of its powers to the European institutions is because the powers vested in the Government do not belong to the Government, but belong rather, in the first instance and in the final analysis, to the People. It is not possible, therefore, for the Government to divest itself of those powers without the approval of the people in accordance with the Constitution.

---

[20] *ibid*, 767.
[21] *ibid*, 771.
[22] *ibid*, 778.
[23] *ibid*, 794.

Reaction to the *Crotty* decision has, with one or two exceptions, been quite negative. Elaine Fahey describes it as "a legal and political noose on the nation",[24] John Temple Lang surveys the High Court and Supreme Court judgments without much enthusiasm,[25] and Hogan and Whyte question its precedential value:

> "The breadth of the majority's reasoning is such, however, that it could plausibly be regarded as casting doubt on the State's general treaty-making powers. Consequently it may be appropriate to take a less than sanguine view of its prospects for survival".[26]

In an article on the decision, "The Supreme Court and the Single European Act", Gerard Hogan describes the decision as "one of the most extraordinary" decisions of the Supreme Court, and a "remarkable display of judicial activism".[27] He considers that it is probably best regarded as a unique case, and that it is likely that its precedential value would be very narrowly construed in any future case.[28] While reiterating that he found the reasoning in the decision "less than compelling", he concludes by noting that the result is "at least arguably consistent with the concepts of popular sovereignty which underlie the Constitution".[29]

More recently, and also in a critical vein, Gavin Barrett, examined "the legal landscape" regarding ratification of European treaties and writes that he is "unconvinced" of the correctness of the *Crotty* decision.[30] His criticism of the Supreme Court in *Crotty* is that "it is as if for the Supreme Court the EEC Treaty was no more than a treaty on economic co-operation", whereas, he argues,

> "[t]here is nothing self-evident about such an approach. Arguably, it does not accurately reflect the historical origins of the Treaties or the intention underlying them or the reality that from its inception European integration was intended to be, and has been an ongoing process".[31]

Furthermore, he says that the "essential scope and objectives" test "would better suit a situation in which Ireland had joined a static unchanging entity, not a constantly evolving organisation like the European Union".[32] Furthermore, he argues:

> "It is difficult to form an opinion about *Crotty* without also considering a more fundamental question raised implicitly by the case, which is that of in what circumstances referendums are to be viewed as an appropriate decision-

24 Elaine Fahey, *EU Law in Ireland* (Clarus Press, 2010) 8.

25 John Temple Lang, "The Irish Court Case which delayed the Single European Act: *Crotty v. An Taoiseach and others*" [1987] *Common Market Law Review* 709.

26 JM Kelly, *The Irish Constitution* (4th ed, Gerard W Hogan and Gerry Whyte ed, Lexis Nexis Butterworths, 2003) 97.

27 Gerard Hogan, "The Supreme Court and the Single European Act" (1987) 22 *Irish Jurist* 55.

28 *ibid*, 69.

29 *ibid*, 70.

30 Gavin Barrett, "Building a Swiss Chalet in an Irish Legal Landscape? Referendums on European Union Treaties in Ireland &the Impact of Supreme Court Jurisprudence" (2009) 5 *European Constitutional Law Review* 32 at 68.

31 *ibid*, 42.

32 *ibid.*

> making method, particularly (although not exclusively) in the context of European treaties".[33]

He concludes that more thought needs to be applied to the questions of when and how referendums on European treaties should be held in Ireland.[34]

To a similar end, Laurent Pech raises the possibility that the question of whether ratification by constitutional amendment actually is legally required in any individual treaty ratification is not asked as conscientiously or answered as rigorously as it might be, based on the test laid down in the *Crotty* case.[35] In effect, it is now almost customary for any new treaty to be put before the Irish people in constitutional referendum.

While these contributions centre on the decisions without the context of the Nice I, Nice II, Lisbon I and Lisbon II sagas, there are others which document and critically engage with the political and constitutional crises which resulted from the rejection of the Nice Treaty and the Lisbon Treaty by Irish voters. Concerning Nice, a typically lucid contribution has been made by Gerard Hogan and published in *European Public Law*,[36] along with a very provocative piece by Cathryn Costello entitled "People's Vengeances: Ireland's Nice Referenda".[37] The timing of her piece is interesting in that it was a look back at the Nice saga (the reasons for the "no" vote in Nice I as well as an assessment of the "yes" vote in Nice II) against the contemporary backdrop of the double rejection of the Constitutional Treaty by French and Dutch voters. The significance of this implicit point of comparison is heightened by the fact that while the Nice Treaty required unanimous ratification by all Member States, the Constitutional Treaty explicitly provided for the possibility of progress if only four-fifths (20 of the 25) Member States ratified it.

In Costello's assessment, the Nice II referendum in Ireland is a positive example of popular participation in decision-making on the programme for European integration. She suggests:

> "[t]he *Nice II* referendum in Ireland illustrates that citizens acting in a national context, indeed in the Irish constitutional setting, exercising a sacrosanct popular sovereignty, can make decisions taking into account needs and interests beyond the statist paradigm. ... The subtle but significant shift from *Nice I* to *Nice II* related to a *national* taking of responsibility for the manner of engagement with the EU, and yet a Europeanisation of the frame of reference of the debate".[38]

---

33 *ibid*, 45.

34 *ibid*, 68.

35 Laurent Pech, "Le référendum en Irlande pour ratifier les traités européens: obligatoire ou coutumier?" *Revista de Estudos Europeus*, no. 4, July–December 2008 99–113. (Available at: http://www.robert-schuman.eu/doc/actualites/QE-Irlande-referendum_25_09_2008_3.pdf; last accessed 14 May 2013).

36 Gerard Hogan, "The Nice Treaty and the Irish Constitution" (2001) *European Public Law* 565.

37 Cathryn Costello, "People's Vengeances: Ireland's Nice Referenda" (2005) 1 *European Constitutional Law Review* 357.

38 *ibid*, 375.

To her mind, then, Nice II illustrates that is not necessarily the case that ratification based on national constitutional procedures "undermines attempts at creating a European public space"; in fact, it could be that the opposite is true.[39]

In defence of *Crotty*, there are fewer scholars. Gerard Casey attempted to respond to the early wave of criticism of *Crotty*, noting that the case is "significant in that it sets constitutional limits on the conduct of foreign affairs—which is also why it generated so much apparent astonishment and concern".[40] The purpose of his essay is to put the case in comparative perspective, because by so doing it becomes apparent, as he says, that "it is not the constitutional anomaly some seem to think".[41] Casey's comparative work is comprehensive and incisive, referring to the constitutional legal orders of Australia, Canada, France, West Germany (as it then was), Portugal, Spain, and the United States. His conclusion from this analysis is that it is untrue to say that the decision is truly distinctive, since

> "constitutional limitations on the executive *are* enforceable through the judicial process, whether they relate to procedural or substantive matters ... From the decided cases there surely emerges a general principle – that the citizen has a right to insist upon constitutional restrictions, a right ... to require that the government be administered according to law."[42]

In support of this interpretation, he points to the following dicta. Walsh J ruled:

> "one of the functions of the Court is to uphold the Constitution. That includes restraining the Government from freeing themselves or purporting to free themselves from the restraints of the Constitution".[43]

Henchy J states in his judgment:

> "in the conduct of the State's external relations, *as in the exercise of the executive power in other respects*, the Government is not immune from judicial control if it acts in a manner or for a purpose which is inconsistent with the Constitution ... any attempt by the Government to alienate in whole or in part to other states the conduct of foreign relations would be *inconsistent with the Government's duty to conduct those relations in accordance with the Constitution.*"[44]

More recently, I have sought myself to defend, or at least to promote a more careful reading of, the judgment in *Crotty*.[45] It seems to me that the decision can be

---

39 *ibid*, 380.

40 Gerard Casey, "*Crotty v. An Taoiseach*: A Comparative Perspective" in *Human Rights and Constitutional Law: Essays in Honour of Brian Walsh* (James O'Reilly ed, Round Hall Press, Dublin, 1992) 189.

41 *ibid*, 190.

42 *ibid*, 199.

43 *Crotty v. An Taoiseach* [1987] IR 713 at 799.

44 *ibid*, 786–787. Quoted in Gerard Casey, "*Crotty v. An Taoiseach*: A Comparative Perspective" in *Human Rights and Constitutional Law: Essays in Honour of Brian Walsh* (James O'Reilly ed, Round Hall Press, Dublin, 1992), p.189, 199–200. Emphasis in Casey.

45 Maria Cahill, "Ireland's Constitutional Amendability and Europe's Constitutional Ambition: the Lisbon Referendum in Context" (2008) 9 *German Law Journal* 1191.

fully understood only as a decision about constitutional authority, rather than one motivated by political expediency, and in terms of its foundation in three inter-linked principles of constitutionalism.

First, and as noted above, the judgment endorses the position that executive power is limited. The Government as a whole and the Minister for Foreign Affairs in particular do have plenipotentiary status in the sense that they are the rightful representatives of the Irish people at such negotiations on international agreements and they negotiate on behalf of and with the authority of the Irish people; but they cannot through those agreements give away their constitutionally granted powers, because those powers do not belong to them, but belong rather, and ultimately, to the Irish people. They only hold the powers and competences they are vested with on trust for the constituent power, according to the terms of the Constitution.

Secondly, the role of the People in the ratification on European treaties is determined as a matter of Irish constitutional law. It goes without saying that we do not have referendums on European treaties in Ireland because the Irish people are fixated with the minutiae of European policies, but rather when European treaties propose a change to the terms of the Irish constitutional order because they require that we delegate to the European Union certain competences that the Constitution has delegated to a branch of government in Ireland.

Thirdly, throughout the judgments, the judges work on the basis of a foundational presumption that it is the Supreme Court, and not, for example, the European Court of Justice, which rightfully decides the question of the extent to which, and the terms under which, the Irish Constitution receives European law. It would perhaps be trite to mention this, were it not for the cases noted in the previous section, which appear to give the opposite impression.

4. Part III

In the third part of this chapter, I wish to deal in some depth with a case that has been alluded to previously. It is the only example that we have where the Supreme Court considers what the legal position under the Constitution might be if Irish constitutional law and European law were to lead to conflicting legal solutions to the same legal problem. The case, *SPUC v Grogan*,[46] deals with the possibility of conflict between European law and the constitutionally protected right to life.

Article 40.3.3° protects "the right to life of the unborn ... with due regard to the equal right to life of the mother". The Supreme Court had ruled in 1988 that the State's duty to vindicate the right to life of the unborn made it constitutionally impermissible for the State to allow for the dissemination of information that promoted abortion services available abroad.[47] Nevertheless, some groups continued to distribute information promoting abortion, and so the 1989 case arose because the applicants sought an injunction preventing such promotion. This time, the defendants added a European dimension to their argument; hypothesising that pregnant women had

---

46 *Society for the Protection of Unborn Children v Grogan* [1989] IR 753.

47 *AG (Society for the Protection of Unborn Children) v Open Door Counselling Ltd.* [1988] IR 593.

a right under European law to travel to another Member State in order to have an abortion, and that they therefore had a corollary right under European law to have information about abortion clinics in another Member State, and that the defendants therefore had a further corollary right under European law to publish and distribute that information.[48] These European law rights, they suggested, were so all-pervasive that they should negate the constitutional protection of the right to life guaranteed in Art 40.3.3°.

By any standards, it was a very hard-headed and recalcitrant argument; if only for the fact that this particular series of European law "rights" had not even been recognised at European level; neither in the body of treaties and legislation nor in the case law of the European Court of Justice. (In fact, at this point, the European Union did not possess a charter of fundamental rights.) Moreover, the contumacious nature of the defendants' argument is present also in the assumption that these putative European law rights should trump national constitutional provisions' expressly entitled fundamental rights.

The High Court judge, Carroll J, accepted the defendants' argument. On appeal, however, the defendants lost and, in arriving at their conclusion, the Supreme Court judges took a different approach to constitutional authority: the three judgments handed down by the Supreme Court judges in this case each defend the Irish constitutional legal order, on almost exactly the same terms as the constitutional courts in other Member States defend their national constitutional orders, *vis-à-vis* European law. The German *Bundesverfassungsgericht* (Federal Constitutional Court) is, of course, the primary example of such a court, and the *Lisbon* decision is the most recent and most powerful defence of this position,[49] but the equivalent courts in

48 Their arguments were noted in the judgment of Finlay CJ and summarised as follows: "pregnant women in Ireland had a right under European Community law to travel to any other member state where abortion was legal in order to have the service of an abortion performed on them; that a corollary to that legal right was a right to information about the identity, location and method of communication with abortion clinics in the United Kingdom. Having regard to that right vested in pregnant women in Ireland, it was argued that the defendants had a corresponding right vested in them by European Community law to publish and distribute that information." *Society for the Protection of Unborn Children v Grogan* [1989] IR 753 at 761.

49 *Lisbon Decision*, BVerfG, 2 be 2/08, 30 June 2009. Available at: http://www.bundesverfassungsgericht.de/entscheidungen/es20090630_2bve000208.html (last accessed 14 May 2013; German-language text.) The *Lisbon* decision builds on the previous case law of the Bundesverfassungsgericht dealing with the same question in the cases of *Internationale Handelsgesellschaft* [1974] 2 CMLR 540; *Re Wünsche Handelsgesellschaft* [1987] 3 CMLR 225 (commonly known respectively as the *Solange I* and *Solange II* decisions), and Cases 2 BvR 2134/92 & 2159/92, *Brunner v the European Union Treaty* [1994] 1 CMLR 57 (the so-called Maastricht decision of the court).

the Czech Republic,[50] Denmark,[51] Italy,[52] Poland,[53] and Spain[54] have made similarly powerful pronouncements on the organic power of the national constitutional order.

The shape of their argument is similar, despite the nuances of national specificity and judicial style: (1) since it is the national constitution that has been constituted by the people of the nation in virtue of their constituent power, and (2) since it is on the basis of the national constitution that the Member States interact with each other at the international level, thereby establishing international institutions to whom competences—even very specific competences over a wide range of subject-areas—can be devolved, and (3) since it is therefore only by virtue of the national constitution that the laws emanating from these institutions become applicable at all in the national legal order, (4) it is also the national constitution that circumscribes the terms of the entry of those laws, and (5) therefore it is the job of the supreme court or constitutional court as guardian of the constitution to ensure that the measures emanating from those international institutions do not exceed the scope of their defined mandate and do not undermine the essence of the national constitution.[55]

In *SPUC v Grogan*, Finlay CJ, with whom Griffin and Hederman JJ concurred, pointed out in his judgment that, whatever about the putative European law "rights" relied on by the defendants, "the right to life of an unborn child [is] a right acknowledged and protected under the Constitution;" and therefore "[t]hat constitutionally guaranteed right must be fully and effectively protected by the courts."[56] In the light of the one-year-old precedent, he ruled that the injunction sought by the applicants in this case, "consists of an application to restrain an activity which has been clearly declared by this Court to be unconstitutional and therefore unlawful."[57] While there was no actual conflict between Irish constitutional law and European law in this case (because the European "rights" relied on by the defendants had not actually been recognised by the European law) Finlay CJ went on to consider what would happen if the ECJ recognised a right under Community law to engage in activity which could assist and is intended to assist in the destruction of the right to life of an unborn child. He ruled:

---

50 *See* Decision Pl. ÚS 50/04 *Sugar Quota Regulation II*, 8 March 2006, available at http://www.usoud.cz/en/decisions/?tx_ttnews%5Btt_news%5D=516&cHash=9dec62b1eff2cd2f1323808674355cac8 (last accessed 21 January 2014).

51 *Carlsen v Prime Minister* [1999] 3 CMLR 854 at 861.

52 *Frontini v Ministero delle Finanze* [1974] 2 CMLR 372; *SpA Granital v Amministrazione delle Finanze* Judgment of 8 June 1984 [1984] 1 Giui It 1521, noted by Gaja (1984) 21 CMLRev, 756–772; *Fragd v Ammistrazione delle Finanze* (1989) 72 Revista di Diritto Internationale 103.

53 Judgement of 11 May 2005 in the case K 18/04 (Wyrok z dnia 11 maja 2005 r. Sygn. Akt K 18/04) OTK Z. R 2005/5A, item 49. A summary of the judgment is available in English at http://www.trybunal.gov.pl/eng/summaries/documents/K_18_04_GB.pdf (last accessed 14 May 2013).

54 Declaration 1/2004, Case 6603-2004, *Re the EU Constitutional Treaty and the Spanish Constitution*, 13 December 2004, reported in [2005] 1 CMLR 981.

55 For discussion of the common themes of the judgments of these courts, see Maria Cahill, "European Integration and European Constitutionalism: Consonances and Dissonances" in "*Integration through Law" Revisited: The Making of the European Polity* (Daniel Augenstein and Mark Dawson ed, Ashgate, 2012).

56 *Society for the Protection of Unborn Children v Grogan* [1989] IR 753 at 765.

57 *ibid*, 764.

> "If and when a decision of the Court of Justice of the European Communities rules that some aspect of European Community law affects the activities of the defendants impugned in this case, the consequence of that decision on these constitutional guaranteed rights and their protection by the courts will then fall to be considered by these courts."[58]

The Chief Justice thereby expressly acknowledged and reserved for the Irish courts the power to review a decision of the European Court of Justice on the grounds that it was contrary to a fundamental right protected by the Irish Constitution.

Walsh and McCarthy JJ both delivered their own statements of reasons for concurring with the decision of the Chief Justice. McCarthy J was unequivocal in his statement that "[t]he sole authority for the construction of the Constitution lies in the Irish courts, the final authority being this Court."[59] If the Supreme Court were to accept the argument of the defendants, and therefore fail to guarantee protection of a fundamental right recognised in the Irish Constitution, and thereby also to fail to follow its own one-year-old precedent then, as he bluntly put it, "the rule of law would be set at nought".[60]

Walsh J, with whom Hederman J also concurred, was similarly unambiguous in his assertion that "[t]he interpretation of the Constitution of Ireland is within the exclusive competence of the courts of Ireland".[61] This authority, which was vested in the courts of Ireland by the Constitution, he recognised, also comes with a responsibility that is held personally by each individual judge, such that, according to Walsh J, "[i]t is not open to any judge to do anything which in effect suspends any provisions of the Constitution for any period whatsoever".[62]

It was not necessary in the instant case to make a determination on the interaction between a constitutional right and a European law right when those come into conflict with each other, because the European law right in question was never determined to exist, but this case clearly establishes that the Supreme Court retains the right to finally determine these kinds of questions because the job of finally interpreting the Irish Constitution is the exclusive mandate of the Supreme Court.[63]

As with the *Crotty* decision, this *SPUC v Grogan* decision has been received with opprobrium in academic circles. Hogan and Whelan refer to the dicta of the judges as "rumblings in the Supreme Court in *Grogan*", which are considered by them to be "too moot" to have any real precedential value.[64] Hogan and Whyte similarly express the view that "these remarks must be regarded as isolated ones and entirely confined to an area of great sensitivity and it is unlikely that they would nowadays be

58 765.
59 770.
60 771.
61 766.
62 767–768.
63 768–769.
64 Gerard Hogan and Anthony Whelan, *Ireland and the European Union: Constitutional and Statutory Texts and Commentary* (Sweet and Maxwell, 1995) 142.

followed".[65] These remarks appear to have been justified by the plethora of judicial cases, the most important of which were discussed above, that have followed in the wake of the *SPUC v Grogan* decision and do appear to ignore its precedential value and rule to the contrary that the Irish courts unequivocally endorse the supremacy of European law on the basis of the decisions that have been handed down by the European Court of Justice.[66] Even Phelan and Whelan, who hold back from such unequivocal support for the supremacy of European law, only tentatively suggest that

> "[i]t is probably only in situations of profound normative conflict, which threatens directly the Constitution's fundamental principles or legitimation, that the Irish Courts will consider the non-application of a Community law rule as part of domestic law".[67]

They go on to point out that

> "abandonment of constitutional protection of natural rights of the individual in the light of the exigencies of the common good in favour of an externally imposed and differently legitimated conception of rights and of the general interest is argued to amount to ... a constitutional revolution".[68]

While I think that it is regrettable that the judges in this case do not engage in a very careful and rigorous analysis of the terms of Art 29.4.6°, which would have strengthened the rational basis for their conclusions, nonetheless it seems to me that their decision is constitutionally sound. Indeed, any lawyer would rightly be alarmed if the judges of any supreme or constitutional court were to do anything other than uphold the fundamental rights protected by the Constitution when they came into "conflict" with putative rights that were not acknowledged or recognised by the European legal order.

Moreover, even if those rights were not hypothetical, one would rightly be concerned if the judges of any supreme or constitutional court were to allow European law to undermine the level of protection of fundamental rights guaranteed by the national constitution. Political difficulties might consequentially arise, perhaps even a constitutional crisis or a European crisis might ensue; but from the perspective that values constitutional authority, the only legal outcome one can expect, in such a

---

65 JM Kelly, *The Irish Constitution* (4th ed, Gerard W Hogan and Gerry Whyte ed, (Lexis Nexis Butterworths, 2003) 535.

66 *Meagher v Minister for Agriculture and Food* [1994] 1 IR 329 (SC); *Murphy v Bord Telecom Éireann* [1988] ILRM 53 (HC); *Society for the Protection of Unborn Children (Ire) Ltd. v Grogan (No. 3)* [1993] 1 ILRM 197 (HC); *Nathan v Bailey Gibson Ltd.*, [1998] 2 IR 162 (SC); *Society for the Protection of Unborn Children (Ire) Ltd. v Grogan (No. 5)* [1998] 4 IR 343 (SC); *Maher v Minister for Agriculture and Rural Development* [2001] 2 IR 139 (SC).

67 Diarmuid Rossa Phelan and Anthony Whelan, "National Constitutional Law and European Integration" (1997) 6 *Irish Journal of European Law* 24 at 45.

68 Diarmuid Rossa Phelan and Anthony Whelan, "National Constitutional Law and European Integration" (1997) 6 *Irish Journal of European Law* 24 at 55. In order to avoid such a revolution, they propose that the application of European law in Ireland should be "subject ... to compliance with the fundamental commitments, though not with all the detailed positive provisions, of Irish constitutional law". It would, of course, be a matter for Irish constitutional law to differentiate between "fundamental and contingent constitutional commitments", and the authors suggest that the courts would be assisted in this task by "external references to inalienable rights antecedent to positive law"; *ibid*, 55.

situation, is that the national judges will honour the oath they swore to uphold the national constitution. It seems to me, therefore, that although it has, to all intents and purposes, been dismissed by commentators, the 1989 Supreme Court ruling of *SPUC v Grogan*[69] should not be understood as an abortion-specific emotional knee-jerk reaction ruling, but rather as one that espouses the most accurate reading of the terms of the constitutional mandate that European law has within the Irish legal order.

5. Conclusion

It seems to me that it is regrettable that the concept of constitutional authority has been left in the shadows in much of our discussion of the terms by which the Irish constitutional order can receive European Union law, as evidenced in the judicial decisions that appear to avoid the concept entirely, and in the unfavourable reaction to those few decisions in which the judges advert to constitutional authority and let themselves be guided by it. Nonetheless, it is, I think, still possible, by means of a closer reading of Art 29.4.6° itself and by relying on the authorities of *Crotty* and *SPUC v Grogan*, to clear away the shadows that prevent us from engaging with constitutional authority and allow ourselves be guided in the future by its light.

---

[69] *Society for the Protection of Unborn Children v. Grogan* [1989] IR 753.

Chapter 10

The Irish Form of Government: A Merely Apparent Semi-Presidentialism

Luca Mezzetti[1]

1. The Category of Semi-Presidentialism within the Classifications of the Forms of Government

Classical constitutional doctrine has always affirmed the existence of two different ways to achieve harmony and equilibrium in the framework of a form of government: the presidential regime, which has established a rigid separation of powers, and the parliamentary regime, which has realised a cooperative relationship among the powers of the State. The use of ideal models for interpreting the social phenomena serves to obtain auxiliary elements, points of reference for a rational construction of historical, concrete and contingent reality. Therefore, in discussing the effectiveness of the forms of government, considering the ideal models can bring about serious theoretical and practical distortions.

The performance of a form of government depends on its adaptation within the ideal model, but following political and social demands. According to Nohlen, when you proceed to a comparison between parliamentarism and presidentialism, you can commit serious methodological errors: when you refer to the form of parliamentary government you are thinking of the countries of post-war Western Europe; the same happens when in relationship to presidentialism you are thinking of the Latin American reality of the last decade.[2] You are comparing very distant experiences in reality.

As is well known, besides the parliamentary and presidential traditional forms of government, Duverger coined and promoted the category of the semi-presidentialism, particularly on the basis of the system of government of the Fifth French Republic, built between 1958 and 1962.[3] The individualisation of the constitutive elements of the semi-presidential form of government has resulted in a long and unresolved doctrinal debate, from which seems to emerge a certain overlap between the semi-presidential "model" and the form of government of the French Fifth Republic. Such overlap often involves the generalisation, almost up to the objectification, of peculiar characteristics of that determined historical-political order, and therefore

---

1 Full professor of Constitutional Law, Faculty of Law, University of Bologna.

2 D Nohlen, *Presidencialismo vs. Parlamentarismo en America Latina* (Nueva Sociedad, 1991) 46ff.

3 M Duverger, "A New Political System Model: Semi-Presidential Government" (1980) 8 *European Journal of Political Research* 165–187.

the assumption that the mechanisms that characterise the French experience are typical elements of the form of semi-presidential government *tout court*.

It has been specified that it is necessary not to confuse the semi-presidential "model" with the French "prototype"; in other words, the heuristic representation of the institutional phenomenon with the description of that commonly considered as the exemplar of the same phenomenon. Faced with the difficulties in reaching a shared doctrinal definition, a pragmatic approach could lead one to take the experience of the Fifth Republic as model and prototype at the same time. With such a formulation, the semi-presidential model would be adopted only insofar as the model was accurately reproduced.

A part of the doctrine does not share the formulation according to which the actual French experience represents the full and exclusive expression of the form of semi-presidential government, but it considers it rather to be one of the forms of expression, one of the subtypes of semi-presidentialism.

Two motivations have been proposed to explain the overlap between semi-presidentialism and French regime. The first is certainly based on the role that France occupies both in the history of the democratic constitutionalism and in the actual comparative-institutional context, a role that offers a high degree of visibility to the French institutions compared with those of other states with analogous form of government. The second one is based on the theoretical difficulties that a categorisation of the semi-presidential form of government raises, compared with which the French experience, particularly in the "simplified" literature predominantly diffused, can allow a reassuring reduction of complexity.

Including the semi-presidential form of government in the traditional forms of classifying government raises various problems, and the doctrine cannot agree on the conceptual autonomy of the category itself. The main difficulties arise from the fact that the essence of semi-presidentialism is based on a mixture between dualism and monism, with aporetic characteristics in comparison with the principles of forms of government theory.

In reality, semi-presidentialism applies parliamentarism (the centrality of the confidence relationship) without monism; it uses typical institutions of presidentialism without combining them with a structural separation of the powers; and, a greater difficulty for the construction of a model, it is characterised by a prevalence of functional elements over structural ones. Such theoretical contradictions make a solution difficult. Various attempts have been tried to resolve the problem through clever *escamotages*: classification in the final analysis into presidentialism or parliamentarism, or the most refined attempt of Duverger to consider semi-presidentialism as a system essentially characterised by alternate phases of parliamentary and presidential regime. Such definition should be applied to those regimes that exhibit "the coexistence of a parliamentary-type government with a presidential-type head of state".[4]

[4] Maurice Duverger, *Échec au roi* (Albin Michel, 1978) 18, cited by C Skach, *Borrowing Constitutional Designs: Constitutional Law in Weimar Germany and the French Fifth Republic* (Princeton UP, 2005) 4.

Various doctrinal positions have been taken, in a negative sense, toward the opportunity to give the semi-presidential regime an autonomous scientific value.

Such formulations do not emerge from a single interpretative position: in fact, these orientations, although reaching the result of excluding the semi-presidential system from the classification of the forms of government, according to which elements defining the model are considered to prevail, include it within parliamentarism or presidentialism. Authors who characterise such an experience by calling it a parliamentary regime with a "presidential corrective" or with a "presidential tendency" belong to the theory favourable to placing the semi-presidential regime in the category of parliamentarism.

The first definition just mentioned has been introduced by Colliard, who, referring to the Constitution of the Fifth French Republic, has affirmed that the difference between this constitutional order and other parliamentary regimes would not reside in the institutional elements, but rather in the form of the political game determined by the position of the president towards the parties.[5] This interpretation, which has been welcomed by other French scholars and authors (among others, by Le Divellec),[6] is based on the evaluation of the potentialities of the head of state, which are, however, subordinate to the different combination of variables of a political type. In fact, in the hypothesis in which the party that has the parliamentary majority recognises in the president its own leader, the prevalence of the will of the head of state over that of the prime minister will be inevitable due to the determination of the political direction. In the opposite case, the prime minister will become the true head of the government, removing the difference from other parliamentary systems.

The configuration of a parliamentary regime with a "presidential tendency" has been delineated by Italian doctrine which, similarly comparing with the French system—although recognising the prominence of the President of the Republic—has underlined the permanence of the typical relationships of the parliamentary government formed between the legislative and executive organs, based on the confidence relationship.

In particular, G de Vergottini[7] has affirmed that constitutions described as semi-presidential, even if attributing wider competences of political direction to the head of state, also formally envisage the separation of powers between the president of the republic and the prime minister, as well as diffused forms of collaboration and influence between government and parliament, rejecting therefore the classical scheme of presidential government of the United States of America. For this reason, discarding the presidentialist hypothesis and privileging the relationship of confidence between the executive organ and legislative organ, the dualism that subsists between the parliamentary and presidential components is destined to turn most frequently in favour of the first institution, so that also semi-presidential

5 JC Colliard, *Les régimes parlementaires contemporains* (Presses Universitaires de France, 1978).

6 For Divellec's views, see: A Le Divellec "Die dualistische Variante des Parlamentarismus—Eine französische Ansicht zur wissenschaftlichen Fata Morgana des semipräsidentiellen Systems" Zeitschrift für Parlamentsfragen, 27(1) (1996) 145–151.

7 G de Vergottini, *Diritto costituzionale comparato* (Cedam, 2011).

experiences have to be classified according to the paradigm of the parliamentary forms of government.

A similar conclusion, even if based on substantially different parameters, has been reached by Cadart who, having ascertained it to be impossible to classify semi-presidential government within the category of monistic parliamentarism, has recalled the figure of the dualistic parliamentarism of Orleanist type, attempted in France during the kingdom of Louis Philippe of Orleans (1830–1848).[8] Indeed, this form of government, characterised by a dualist structure (double responsibility of the government towards the parliament and the sovereign), according to the scheme of three organs (head of state, government and parliament) and two powers (executive and legislative), has been considered by this researcher as the most suitable to describe the semi-presidential regime. Besides the relationship between government and parliament, it is based on the presence of a president of the republic as an integrating part of the executive power and holder of his or her own specific powers.

Nevertheless, the reference to the Orleanist parliamentarism has raised various objections, since in such an experience dualism assumed not only an institutional character but also historical-social character, therefore giving rise to a precarious equilibrium among opposed social forces that turned into the retrenchment of the organ expressive of the nobility (the head of state of monarchical derivation) and the corresponding prevalence of the government-parliament axis (representing the interests of the middle class). This specification, if it explains the transitoriness of such dualism (Mortati), allows us to detach the semi-presidential system from the framework of the liberal state and to bring it to the democratic-pluralist state, in which the head of state and the parliament both have popular legitimation and express the normal dialectics among the different political and social forces.[9]

Trying then to identify the theories that classify semi-presidential government in the category of presidentialism, it is necessary to specify that such orientations—besides making almost exclusively reference to the Fifth French Republic, given its great visibility—have the tendency to capsize the relationship of strength established between parliament and head of state in favour of the latter, so according him a position of prominence.

In Italy, the first author who expressed such remarks was Mortati, even if in reality he affirmed that the French experience can only improperly be considered presidential, as it is corrected by the survival of elements typical of the parliamentary regime, such as the relationship of confidence between government and parliament and the presence of ministers with their own competences. On the one hand, the existence of such elements prevents us from speaking of a presidential regime. On the other hand, in the hypothesis in which there is homogeneity between the president and a strong majority party, the head of state will be accorded a power of political direction that is superior to that of the President of the United States of America, also considering that the latter is not endowed with the power to dissolve the parliament.

The presidential character of such experience has been examined also by Leclercq,

[8] J Cadart, *Institutions politiques et droit constitutionnel*, Tome 2 (3rd ed, Économica, 1991).
[9] C Mortati, *Le forme di governo* (Cedam, 1973).

while other authors, Gicquel, Hariou and Decaumont, have preferred to define the French system as "presidentialist", as based on the phenomenon of the concentration of powers in the hands of the head of the state, who is elected by the people with universal suffrage and enjoys the support of an unconditional majority, with the consequence that such a situation breaks the system of the countervailing powers assigned to the parliament and the government, which therefore are no longer able to balance in a proper way the political-institutional position of the president of the republic.[10]

Again, Quermonne has spoken of "majoritarian presidentialism", setting the accent on the supremacy of the head of state, but at the same time has underlined that such status implies the necessary coincidence of the parliamentary and presidential majorities.[11] Similarly, Mény has coined for the French experience the expression "presidentialist with cohabitationist exception",[12] while for Vedel the Fifth Republic has to be considered as a "ultrapresidential" regime, as usually the French president, thanks to the coincidence of the majorities, accumulates the powers of the American president with those of the British prime minister who is supported by the parliamentary majority.[13]

With reference to the theories that have identified semi-presidentialism as a *tertium genus* of the forms of government classifications, one must emphasise the position assumed by Elia, who has coined the expression "form of government with presidential and parliamentary components".[14] In particular, the author affirmed that the constitutions of the countries that introduce the double peculiarity of a president of the republic elected by the people and of a confidence relationship between government and parliament, as far as the form of government is concerned, display "multiple virtualities", as they are able to create situations that can be identified either with parliamentary government or with a presidential one: the first condition occurs when the head of state loses or does not have the power to determine the government, while the other hypothesis applies when the president faces fluid majorities in the parliament.

Despite these considerations, and even as some constitutional orders can be classified only with a certain difficulty in the traditional categories, Elia has affirmed the possibility of individualising a new form of government, on the basis of the experience of the French Fifth Republic. Such a constitutional order should be defined as existing "with presidential and parliamentary components", as provided with a head of state who, besides being chosen by the people, is also leader of the parliamentary majority and therefore the head of the executive, while, in contrast, the parliamentary majority has the power to remove the government.

---

10 C Leclercq "La Ve République : primauté présidentielle ou fait majoritaire?" *Pouvoirs*, 4, 1982, 123–131; J Gicquel and J-E Gicquel, *Droit constitutionnel et institutions politiques* (26th ed, Montchrestien, 2012); F Decaumont, *La présidence de Georges Pompidou: Essai sur le régime présidentialiste français* (Économica, 1978).

11 See J-L Quermonne, "Le Président de la République: quelle place et quel rôle dans l'organisation des pouvoirs publics?", *Cahiers Français*, no. 332, 2006, 4.

12 Y Mény, *Le système politique français* (6th ed, Montchrestien, 2008).

13 See G Vedel, "Variations et Cohabitations" *Pouvoirs*, 83, 1997, 101–129.

14 L Elia, "Governo (forme di)" in *Enciclopedia del diritto* (1970).

Therefore, this dual structure would have the merit of containing "the best of the two worlds". On the one hand, popular election of the true head of the executive would avoid the dangers typical of the mediatisation of multiparty systems. On the other hand, this leader would have the parliamentary means to realise his or her programme because he or she would have a majority in parliament, which holds votes of confidence in the government emanating from him or her and approves the main legislative measures on the basis of ministerial initiative. This assessment is supported by further elements. First, the operation of the French electoral system has been significant: being majoritarian with two rounds for both elections, it reduces the risk of opposite political conjunctures. Secondly, it has been noticed that during the first two presidencies of the Fifth Republic cohesive majorities always emerged, which therefore allowed this new form of government.

Moulin has also preferred to define the Fifth Republic as a separate category within the classification of the forms of government, explaining that the systems equipped with a presidential head of state, with the confidence relationship and with the power of dissolving the parliament, even if normally inserted in an intermediate category, in reality can be classified neither within the parliamentary scheme nor within the presidential one. Theoretically, the rigid separation of powers typical of the presidential regime and the flexible separation typical of the parliamentary model, due to the particular relationship between executive and legislative, are not superimposable. To this extent, because of this incompatibility, these constitutional orders cannot be considered at the same time parliamentary and presidential; on the contrary, they must be qualified as neither parliamentary nor presidential, with the consequence that they constitute an autonomous category.[15]

Similarly, Rescigno has expressed his preference for the semi-presidential model, affirming that the prerogatives of this form of government should not be sought in the structural-formal elements but in the real dynamics of the system, which are influenced by a condition and by a variable. The condition postulates the existence of political parties disciplined according to the European model, so the model works only if the party of the president is the party that has (the decisive part of) the majority. In different situations, two consequences can arise: political-institutional paralysis and therefore the crisis of the system or the formation of a government that has the confidence of the parliament and is of opposite political colour to that of the president, which however succeeds in governing, forcing the head of state to follow it, working as a parliamentary government.[16]

The variable pertains to the relationships established among the president of the republic, the government and the parliamentary majority, with the consequence that all depends on the real allocation of the political authority. In conclusion, it is not possible not to consider it as a separate type, since such a scheme of government does not belong—in its working and in the popular election of the head of state—to the parliamentary form, and it is different from presidential government because it presupposes the relationship of confidence and the anticipated dissolution of the parliament.

[15] R Moulin, *Le Présidentialisme et la classification des régimes politiques* (Librairie Générale de Droit et de Jurisprudence, 1978); " Election présidentielle et classification des régimes" *Pouvoirs*, 14, 1980, 129–140.

[16] GU Rescigno, "Forma di Stato e forma di governo" in *Enciclopedia giuridica Treccani* (1989).

Massari has likewise set the accent on the flexibility of the semi-presidential system, affirming that the main prerogative of this model is to be able to realise different equilibriums inside the diarchic structure. Therefore, to determine the centre of the power of gravity, you need to refer to the different combinations between the position of the president of the republic and the parliamentary majority, rather than to the formal attributions accorded to the head of state and the prime minister. The nature of their relationships within the executive is essentially political, and therefore subject to the determinations of the variables connected with it.[17]

With reference to the flexibility of the semi-presidential model, Volpi on the one hand agrees in believing that such flexibility can orient the system in the direction of the prevalence of the president or the prime minister, according to the weight of the presidential component or of the parliamentary one. On the other hand, he firmly rejects the idea that within the same constitutional order you may have phases in which the real head of the executive is the president and phases in which such a position is assigned to the prime minister.[18]

To support his own opinion, the author specifies that, apart the French case, in other constitutional orders qualified as semi-presidential the legal ownership of executive power never oscillated between president and prime minister. The characteristic of flexibility, if intended in such a sense, cannot be considered as a typical criterion with the purpose of individualising the semi-presidential form of government, because it seems to be a prerogative of the Fifth Republic. Likewise, Volpi affirms the lack of legitimacy of those criteria that make reference to the presidential power of anticipated dissolution of the parliament or those that formulate the hypothesis of the cohabitation, as these parameters also are indebted to the French experience. Therefore—if they were used—the semi-presidential nature of those constitutional orders in which the routine does not correspond to that verified in France should be excluded.

To this extent, on these bases, the author affirms that—if you do not want to take the risk of an undue and inaccurate generalisation of the experience of the Fifth French Republic—you must distinguish the example constituted by the Fifth Republic from the heuristic model that instead individualises the leading characteristics common to all semi-presidential constitutional orders.

Therefore, only after such an operation is it possible to recognise the lines defining the semi-presidential form of government, which besides being founded on the popular election of the president of the republic and on the institution of the confidence relationship between government and parliament, introduces as its own particularity the ability to create a mixed system, which can realise very different orders of government in its concrete operation, with a prevalence of the presidential or parliamentary component, without putting again in discussion the peculiarity and the autonomy of the model.

---

17 S Ceccanti, O Massari and G Pasquino, *Semipresidenzialismo. Analisi delle esperienze europee* (il Mulino, 1996).

18 M Volpi, *Le forme di governo* in *Diritto pubblico comparato* (G Morbidelli, L Pegoraro, A Reposo and M Volpi ed, Giappichelli, 2009).

The unity of the category of semi-presidentialisms is contested by Ieraci, who, having undertaken an investigation of the relationships between the institutional and political system within "difficult democracies", divides the systems with bipolar or dual executives in two separate models: the denominated semi-presidential system and the semi-parliamentary system.[19] Considering that semi-presidentialism is a system whose equilibrium must be sought in the political routine or in the material constitution rather than in the separation of powers, he declares that Duverger's model does not produce a homogeneous type, in which you could track down two subtypes. The first regime is represented by the proper semi-presidential system, in which relationships of strength favourable to the president in his or her relationships with the government correspond to favourable analogous relationships of strength towards the parliament. The second is constituted by the semi-parliamentary system, in which the relationships of strength are favourable to the president, or not disadvantageous to him or her, only towards the government, but not towards the parliament.

Nevertheless, such a formulation has the defect of being based not on the individualisation of the characters common to a series of constitutional orders with a dualist structure, but on the evaluation of the different output of such experiences. For this reason some authors (for example, Volpi) have manifested perplexity, as in this way the scientific category, built on the base of formal and structural criteria, is confused with its practical operation, which represents an important variable, but not such to imprint itself on the nature of the forms of government. In fact, if such an operation took place in respect of the parliamentary form of government, the autonomy of this model would also be put in crisis, given the difference of output of the constitutional orders referable to this category (thinking of the British and Italian experiences).

Barbera and Fusaro also seem to favour the configuration of the semi-presidential form of government as a separate category. Moving from a historical perspective, they affirm that such a form of government, even with some substantial difference, is the direct evolution of the dualist 19th-century (or Orleanist) parliamentarism. In fact, while dualist parliamentarism was based on the figure of the hereditary sovereign, the semi-presidential system is marked by the presence of a head of state with representative character and a direct popular mandate. Unlike dualist parliamentarism, which has had origin at the beginning of the liberal state, semi-presidentialism also historically asserted itself in the pluralist state, as the experiences of Weimar Germany and Finland testify, both regulated by a constitution that entered into force in 1919.[20]

Moreover, such authors have confirmed that one may properly speak of a semi-presidential form of government only starting from the end of World War II. The need to assure greater stability to those constitutional orders emerging from negative experiences of parliamentary government or in transit toward more democratic forms of state gave the framers the opportunity to experiment with "the virtues of the dualist parliamentarism". This new form of government was characterised on the one

[19] G Ieraci, "Presidenzialismo e parlamentarismo nelle democrazie difficili" in *Quaderni di scienza politica*, 1/1, 1994, 35–90.

[20] A Barbera and C Fusaro, *Il governo delle democrazie* (il Mulino, 1997).

hand by the presence of the typical institutions of the rationalised parliamentarism and on the other hand by a tempering of the role of the president of the republic in comparison with the presidential model.

Adhering to the theories of Duverger and examining the system of the Fifth Republic, Gambino has specified that—including the 1958 Constitution in the semi-presidential typology—it is necessary to consider how far the juridical-formal model appears sensitive to variables of another nature, able to influence the working of the form of government.[21] To this extent, according to Gambino, in addition to analysing the juridical-formal constants of the constitutional order, to understand the complexity of the relationships between legislative and executive and the relationships between the president of the republic and the government, one must use the indications that spring from the political system and from constitutional routines, which constitute the key to reading the different *modus vivendi* of the Constitution.

In fact, an investigation of the Fifth Republic limited to evaluation of the constitutional text, while allowing one to individualise the presence of a diarchic structure of the executive and a strengthening of the powers attributed to the president of the republic and the government in comparison with those of the parliament, nevertheless appears unproductive. The form of government of the French constitutional order is constantly exposed to the variability of the political situation, which has a decisive role in defining the equilibria between the two heads of the executive, and in developing constitutional routines, directed to filling the spaces left empty by the formal norms. Mény, referring to the French Constitution, has described it as "formally ambiguous in its text, plural in its readings, evolutionary in its interpretations."[22]

A substantially similar orientation, directed to the evaluation of the factors that condition the working of the French model, has been expressed by Rinella. Even while recognising the autonomous scientific value of the semi-presidential form of government, Rinella diverged from the interpretative lines elaborated by Duverger, opting instead for the thesis elaborated by Sartori, according to which the constitutional order of the Fifth Republic, rather than shaping an elementary alternation between presidential and parliamentary phases, constitutes a mixed system that owes its own peculiarity to the potential oscillations that can take place inside the diarchy in the executive power.[23] Therefore, as the prominence of the presidential or parliamentary component depends on the coincidence of electoral majorities, the author lingered on the juridical-formal criteria that are thus more sensitive to the phenomenon of the oscillations.

The first element to be recalled pertains to the election by popular vote of the president of the republic, as well as the sphere of the powers attributed to him or her. If the majority that has elected the president also dominates the parliament, the democratic legitimation of the head of state works as a constitutional lockpick, fit to widen the sphere of the attributions of the president beyond the formal text of the constitution.

---

21 S Gambino ed, *Democrazia e forma di governo. Modelli stranieri e riforma costituzionale* (Maggioli, 1997); S Gambino ed, *Forme di governo* (Giuffré, 2007).

22 Y Mény. *Le système politique français* (6th ed, Montchrestien, 2008), p.89.

23 A Rinella, *La forma di governo semi-presidenziale della V Repubblica. Profili metodologici della circolazione di un modello nell'Europa centro-orientale* (Giappichelli, 1997).

In the case of a contrary parliamentary majority, the democratic legitimation of the president is valuable in avoiding his or her complete neutralisation, even if the powers of the head of state are reduced to a more contained *facultè d'empecher*, except for his or her prerogatives obviously.

Similarly, the confidence relationship between the parliament and the government, as well as the role and the powers of the prime minister, show a mutable intensity according to electoral majorities. In the case of harmonious majorities, the prime minister and the government substantially issue from the head of state and the activity of the government is converted in a mere faculty of execution of presidential directives. Under the opposite hypothesis, political confidence obtains the whole weight of the parliamentary tradition, as the parliament chooses a prime minister and a government able to assume a position of prominence towards the head of state.

To this extent, on the basis of these considerations, this author has affirmed that only through an examination of the connections between the complex of the juridical-formal characters of the French form of government and the political variables that influence the constitutional order is it possible to show the "amphidromic profile of the prototype", in other words, the ability of the model to work, according to the conditions, alternately under the guide of the head of state or the prime minister.

Pegoraro also inclines towards recognising the semi-presidential form of government. Having examined the problems that can occur at the classificatory level because of the missed distinction between heuristic model and exemplary model, Pegoraro has affirmed that currently the term "semi-presidential" evokes a form of government with its own characteristics, in which the model with a strong president appears recessive. This is despite the term having been object of a slow process of change, due on the one hand to the evolution of the French constitutional order and on the other hand to further differentiations of other semi-presidential experiences.[24]

Finally, for Ceccanti, Massari and Pasquino semi-presidentialism seems to constitute a better institutional formula than presidentialism or parliamentarism. Based on power-sharing, even creating a leadership, it results in mixed systems in which either the president of the republic or the prime minister can prevail.[25] Compared with presidentialism, semi-presidentialism also guarantees a better working of the institutional system in cases in which the presidential majority does not coincide with the parliamentary one, considering that any cohabitation is not converted into the stalemate that characterises the American government, divided between a president in whom confidence cannot be revoked and a Congress that cannot be dissolved.

As far as parliamentarism is concerned, semi-presidentialism has the advantage of not posing any risk of "assemblyarism" or any danger of decisional impotence. A strong majoritarian position can, in the medium to long term, facilitate the achievement of bipolar mechanics inside the political system, so simplifying the relationships between parliament and government. To this extent, these authors believe that the semi-presidential form of government, given its attitude towards resolving the

[24] L Pegoraro and A Rinella ed, *Semipresidenzialismi* (Cedam, 1997).

[25] S Ceccanti, O Massari and G Pasquino, *Semipresidenzialismo. Analisi delle esperienze europee* (il Mulino, 1996).

negative aspects that can bring the presidential and parliamentary regimes to a political-institutional blockage, with a consequent crisis of the system, represents the model to be imitated for constitutional orders that have as primary objective to reach political stability and decisional effectiveness.

According to Sartori, semi-presidentialism can be defined as a form of government that jointly introduces the following characteristics: (1) inside the system, there is a head of state directly chosen with popular vote or indirectly for a fixed period; (2) the head of state shares the executive power with the prime minister, as a member of a dual or bicephalous executive; (3) the president is independent from the parliament, but his or her government must mediate and be receptive to parliamentary directives; and (4) the prime minister and his cabinet are independent from the president, in as far as they depend upon the parliament, they are subject to parliamentary confidence and they need the support of a parliamentary majority.[26]

The particularity of the executive of this mixed system can be symbolised, according to Duverger, as "an eagle with two heads",[27] or rather as a structure with a dual or diarchic or bipolar authority. This means not only shared executive power—as there are two leaderships or authority centres holding or participating in the executive power—but also, as Sartori warns, that such structure "allows different equilibriums and also mutable orders inside the executive, if the potential autonomy of every unity or component of the executive always subsists".[28]

Operating a more systematic classification of political forms, Shugart and Carey contest the unitary character of semi-presidentialism and divide the category into two separate types of regime: the "presidentialism with premier" and the "parliamentarism with president." The first one is defined as a type of regime in which the president has notable powers, but the cabinet is responsible only towards the parliament.[29] The notion of "presidentialism with premier" is assimilated therefore to that of "semi-presidentialism" given by Duverger, even if the two authors do not share his definition of this term. Such a regime has three peculiar characteristics: (1) the president is chosen by popular vote; (2) the president has notable powers; and (3) a premier and a cabinet coexist, which exercise executive functions and are subject to the confidence of the parliament.

Therefore, the "presidentialism with premier" is different, first from presidentialism, as the president is not necessarily head of the executive, but must coexist with a prime minister who is the head of the government. Secondly, in this form of government presidential powers are not necessarily legislative; more typical are the powers related to the formation of governments. Such differences are at the base of the Shugart and Carey's theory, according to which this form of government can also compensate for some of the criticisms of presidential systems, while maintaining the advantage of having two representatives of the electorate.

The second type of regime is defined as "parliamentarism with president" and is

---

26 G Sartori, *Ingegneria costituzionale comparata* (il Mulino, 2004).

27 M Duverger, *Échec au roi* (Albin Michel, 1978).

28 G Sartori, *Ingegneria costituzionale comparata* (il Mulino, 2004), p 74.

29 M Shugart and J Carey, *Presidenti e assemblee. Disegno costituzionale e dinamiche elettorali* (il Mulino, 1995).

characterised by a division of responsibility between president and assembly, with a position of supremacy for the president and with the dependence of the cabinet upon the parliament. Essential elements of this form of government are as follows: (1) the president is popularly elected; (2) the president nominates and removes the ministers of the cabinet; (3) the ministers of the cabinet are subject to the parliament's confidence; and (4) the president has the power to dissolve the parliament or has legislative powers or both. Such elements explain why such a regime is different both from presidentialism and from the presidentialism with premier. First of all, an equal authority emerges as regards the power to remove the members of the cabinet. Secondly, there is no independent survival of the parliament and of the executive, despite the great power of the president over the cabinet.

The parliament's prerogative of expressing a vote of no confidence in ministers means that the survival of the executive power is not separate. Presidents themselves reconstruct the government, which is naturally subject to the possibility of further votes of no confidence. The latter is a further element of differentiation compared with the presidentialism with a premier. According to Shugart and Carey, this latter type of regime often encounters serious crises, as far as the power of the presidents and the parliaments is concerned.

Part of the political and constitutional doctrine nevertheless does not seem to share this further distinction operated by the authors. According to Sartori, in fact, the last category would result in a nearly empty container, as the authors include a much-discussed case—the Weimar Republic—and entirely "evanescent" (unstable) cases (such as Ecuador, Korea, Peru and Sri Lanka), while in the first, they would include Austria and Ireland, losing every differentiating power.

The same French case should be distinguished into two separate systems, given "the alternation" (according to Duverger's expression) among phases of presidential prominence and of parliamentary prominence (during cohabitation, for instance).

The doctrine finds more adherents to the notion of semi-presidentialism, as a system with a diarchic structure, adopting a unitary definition as a real mixed system, thus subject not to "alternations" but to "oscillations", according to Sartori's expression, that maintains intact its unitary structure.

However, due to its empirical diffusion, doctrine seems today more prepared to accord scientific value and conceptual autonomy to semi-presidentialism and to look out upon it as one of the possible solutions of the constitutional engineering. It has been observed that such a form of government, which has been adopted in so different and distant social and political contexts, shows elevated high degree of applicability and adaptability.

Duverger, in his list (drafted in 1978) of the countries that have adopted such a form of government, included seven cases in decreasing order on the basis of the purely formal criterion of the constitutional prerogatives of the president: Finland (1919 constitution), Iceland (1944), Republic of Weimar (1919), Portugal (1976), Austria (1929), France (1958) and Ireland (1937).

With reference to the diffusion of the semi-presidential model, the promoters of such form of government, apart from the undisputed case of the Fifth French Republic, for which an unanimity of opinions is manifested, do not agree upon which experiences are to be included in that category. Duverger, as observed above, enumerates in his list, drafted in 1978, seven cases of semi-presidentialism. Shugart and Carey modify this list in two respects: they assign Ireland to the category of parliamentary systems and identify a new category, denominated as "presidential with premier", that would absorb constitutional experiences as the Weimar Republic, Sri Lanka, Ecuador, Peru and South Korea. Some authors (Linz and Valenzuela) have emphasised that the semi-presidential solution has been proposed in numerous Latin American states dissatisfied with presidentialism, especially in Argentina, Brazil and Colombia.[30]

Blondel[31] has also noted that the Gaullist scheme has inspired the institution of other dualistic systems in Third World area (Algeria, Tunisia, Somalia, Senegal, Zaire, Lebanon and Burma), while Rinella, Bartole and Ganino have analysed the constitutional and regime transformations of former socialist countries of Central and Eastern Europe that took place starting from the 1989.[32]

On the basis of the positions mentioned, one might think that semi-presidentialism includes cases that are not referable to any unitary definition, since—paraphrasing Sartori—either one reduces the list of the countries whose political structure has indeed a common nucleus, or semi-presidentialism is a name that does not designate anything, or only a residual category.

A first selection should immediately eliminate the dualistic experiences in the Third World, as such constitutional orders still seem distant from attaining a political-institutional framework in line with the principles of the democratic-pluralist state, and therefore with the bases of the rule of law.

The direct election of the president has been adopted in Russia, Bulgaria, Poland, Romania and partially in Estonia (where the choice is up to the parliament if no candidate reaches the majority in the first round of the direct popular election). However, even if direct election is not enough to define a semi-presidential system, we can affirm that the semi-presidential model has inspired the constitutions of Romania (1991) and Poland (1992–1997), while in Russia the presidency is decidedly a ruling organ and predominant over the government and the parliament, enough to unbalance the system toward an impure form of presidentialism (Ganino). In Bulgaria, after an initial period of strong role of the president, a parliamentary evolution of the system has prevailed, proclaimed in Art 1 of the 1991 Constitution, according to which Bulgaria is "a parliamentary regime".

Nevertheless, the objective circumstance of the oscillating experience of those

---

30 JJ Linz and A Valenzuela, *Il fallimento del presidenzialismo* (il Mulino, 1995).

31 J Blondel, *Types of Party System*, in P. Mair (ed.) *The West European Party System* (Oxford: Oxford University Press, 1990), pp 302-310.

32 A Rinella, *La forma di governo semi-presidenziale della V Repubblica. Profili metodologici della circolazione di un modello nell'Europa centro-orientale* (Giappichelli, 1997); S Bartole, *Riforme costituzionali nell'Europa centro orientale* (il Mulino, 1993); M Ganino "Le forme di governo dei Paesi dell'Europa centro-orientale" in *Presidenzialismi, semipresidenzialismi, parlamentarismi: modelli comparati e riforme istituzionali in Italia* (L Mezzetti and V Piergigli ed, Giappichelli, 1997).

democracies still does not make fully decipherable the concrete political-institutional formula. The uncertainty of the meta-legal data and the intervening reforms of electoral systems suggest that we exclude such constitutional orders from the analysis concerning the working of the various semi-presidential experiences.

As far as the classification introduced by Shugart and Carey is concerned, the objections of Sartori and Volpi to the category of presidentialism with a premier seem well made. On the one hand, it is a category that includes unstable cases, whose reception in different contexts by democratic states puts in doubt their affiliation to the semi-presidential form of government. On the other hand, despite the practice held until now, with a clear predominance of the head of state, the French Fifth Republic is in a category characterised by the supremacy of the prime minister over the president within the executive power.

Furthermore, the list proposed by Duverger has not escaped criticism. In fact, both Massari and Sartori exclude from the group of semi-presidential systems three countries: Austria, Ireland and Iceland. According to Duverger, a practice of exclusively parliamentary power has developed in these constitutional orders outside the constitutional rules, with the effect of reducing the role of the heads of state to that of "façade presidents". On this basis, Massari and Sartori have put these experiences outside the circle of semi-presidentialisms. The reasons for this exclusion should be sought in two different motivations: in the adoption of a dualistic structure of the executive more through *force majeure* than from real conviction about the good results of such an ordering, and in the impossibility of reviving the formal constitution on the material level.

As to the first point, we have to note that in Ireland and in Iceland the direct election of the president of the republic was proposed not to realise a dual executive but to confirm national independence from, respectively, Great Britain in 1937 and Denmark in 1944, while in Austria the attempt to create a "presidential-parliamentary Republic", founded on a dual structure of the executive, failed because of the explicit decision of the political parties to sterilise presidential powers, which since 1930 have never been exercised. Such considerations offer an important reading key in a historical-political perspective and seem enough to exclude these constitutional orders from the category of semi-presidential regimes.

The constitutional norms that formally invest the Austrian and Icelandic presidents (but not the Irish one) with notable powers have atrophied as the material constitution has developed. Sartori has affirmed that in the Irish and Icelandic cases there is no possibility of revival of the formal constitution. The Irish Constitution does not attribute to the president any relevant power and there is nothing to revive. In Iceland, the atrophy of the presidential position has reached its point of no return both with the routine of the automatic renewal of the presidential mandate when any candidate opposes the former president and because the Constitution can be amended through a simple majority, so a president interested in intervening in the political game can easily be deprived of the powers that he or she does not exercise. According to this author, some remote hope can be seen in the Austrian case, where the figure of the "notarial president" is a fruit of the long tenure of the "great coalition", during which a 90 per cent parliamentary majority made concretely impossible any presidential intervention in government affairs. Nevertheless, even if today Austria has turned its original bipartisan system into a three-party system, this new order can stop any presidential activism as well it could as in the past.

Although its results are founded upon correct premises, a formulation of this type cannot be taken to extremes, ultimately eliminating the aforesaid experiences from the group of semi-presidentialisms, as once more you would confuse the classificatory profile with the performance of the various constitutional orders with a dual structure. Nevertheless, the circumstance that the routine in these countries has provoked a stasis about the application of the constitutional norms related to presidential prerogatives cannot lead to the conclusion that such norms have been repealed: in fact, recognising the importance and the dissuasive ability of material constitutional rules, it is necessary to keep in mind that a possibility of revival, even though remote, must be granted to constitutional norms, as in theory their restoration could always happen.

The list formulated by Duverger has met further criticisms, because of the insertion of Portugal and the Weimar Republic among the experiences that are assumed as semi-presidential.

The system of government introduced in Portugal in 1976 after the revolution has been nearly unanimously qualified as semi-presidential. However, after the constitutional revision of 1982 some scholars have suggested excluding the new regime from the category of semi-presidentialisms or to qualify it as "semi-parliamentary" (Sartori, Ieraci). Nevertheless, the permanence of the direct election of the president of the republic, endowed with remarkable powers, and the confidence relationship between government and parliament, allows us to maintain the reference to a semi-presidential model in respect to both 1976–1982 and the post-1982 period. In fact, we have two different expressions of semi-presidentialism: the first nearer to the Fifth French Republic model, given the arsenal of powers accorded to the head of state in relation to other constitutional organs, and the second more attenuated, as the relationships of the president of the republic with other organs of government have redrawn in a logic of better balancing.

Major problems are raised the classification of the Weimar Republic. It was characterised not only by an institutional dualism that corresponds to the theoretical scheme of the semi-presidentialism, but also by a political-social dualism that could allow us to classify such an experience as dualistic parliamentarism. Two principal centres of authority, the president and the parliament, were expressions of opposing political and social forces as well as of two different principles (respectively of the principle of unity and continuity of the Prussian bureaucratic-military State and the democrat-pluralist principle). Nevertheless, in Weimar the origin of two separate centres of power was represented by the popular vote and the parliament had a pluralist nature and was not an organ expressing the hegemony of a social class. This experience constituted at the same time the last meaningful example of dualistic parliamentary government and the first democratic order of a semi-presidential nature (Volpi, Rinella).

Even keeping in mind that there is no accord among the constitutional law scholars on the cases to include in the category, in no case has semi-presidentialism (unlike presidentialism, when exported) constituted a threat to democracy, with the exception of Weimar. In effect, the Weimar Republic is the only negative case, as far as the stability of the democratic regime is concerned.

Compared with the past, semi-presidential experiences today originate no longer from ideological options, but from functional considerations and also from conditions imposed by the necessity of institutional compromises in a phase of transition. It is also significant that the semi-presidential option has survived even when the conditions that had brought it about have disappeared. In Latin America, the semi-presidential solution has been studied in Brazil, in the 1987–1988 Constituent Assembly and in the 1993 plebiscite. In Argentina it was officially proposed in the framework of the *Consejo the Consolidación de la Democracia*, founded by President Alfonsin in December 1985, with the purpose of mitigating the much-criticised "hegemonic Argentinian hyperpresidentialism". In this last case the intention of transforming the Argentinian system into a parliamentary one was evident and this was looked upon as a semi-presidential or semi-parliamentary solution.

Such projects, nevertheless, have not been institutionalised in real constitutional reforms. In a Latin American context, with its strong presidentialist tradition, the introduction of semi-presidentialism appears to many to be an indirect way of approaching parliamentarism, without, however, showing a full openness to radical change in the constitutional tradition.

2. Semi-Presidential Form of Government and Alternatives to Presidentialism

Semi-presidentialism or, to use the categories of Shugart and Carey, presidentialism with a premier, has been seen by some authors as a possible alternative to presidentialism, in as far as it would attenuate some of the difficulties that presidential systems introduce.

The problem of double legitimation between legislative and executive, typical of presidential systems, is replaced in semi-presidential regimes by the potential presence of competitive legitimations inside the executive itself, or in other words by the problem of cohabitation.

The substitution of the president as head of the government with a prime minister with legislative confidence constitutes an institutional means of resolving legislative immobilism between president and parliament. Also, a majoritarian president will have a great incentive in semi-presidentialism, compared with pure presidentialism, to support the policies applied his or her coalition, since his or her status within the executive directly depends on the coalition's cohesion.

As for the possibility that an outsider is elected as president, it has been observed that this can happen in semi-presidentialism also, but it would not introduce the problems that arise in such situation in presidentialism. In fact, the prime minister in a semi-presidential regime enjoys a constitutional protection in respect to a possible predominance by the president, so when the president is not the leader of the prime minister's party, the latter may be able to act in a sufficiently independent way.

The duration of a presidential mandate in semi-presidentialism is normally fixed, as in presidentialism. Nevertheless, it has been observed that the problem of a president and a parliamentary majority of opposite political orientations is not marked by the same temporal rigidity as in pure presidentialism. Where the president is not the head of the government, when the assembly does not support the president's party or coalition of parties, the president must name a prime minister to form an "opposition" government. Besides, in semi-presidentialism it is not required that the president, when he or she enjoys a majority in the parliament, should dominate the prime minister.

The fixed duration of presidential mandate does not implicate, therefore, the possibility of crisis due to the temporal rigidity. Linz has observed that a system with a dual executive depends, as much or more than in a presidential system, on the president's personality and abilities. At the same time, responsibility becomes diffused and it is possible that further conflicts start, which may be increased by the fixed duration of the presidential mandate. The supporters of the opposite thesis remark that, even if presidents dominate the executive, a possible loss of legislative support in the medium term will not be a sign of crisis, if the president names a cabinet of the "opposition", supported by the assembly.

A further way of avoiding the problems of the fixed-duration mandate in many systems is to equip the president with the power to dissolve the parliament and to call new elections. Such a tool is useful, above all, when a new president faces a previously elected parliament (when the duration of the mandates is not synchronised) that is dominated by the opposition.

In contrast to what happens in presidential systems, in most semi-presidential regimes there is a presidential power of veto that requires a qualified majority to be overridden. Legislative control over the executive, nevertheless, is possible in some measure thanks to the mechanism of parliamentary confidence. The legislators in a majority coalition are discouraged from jeopardising the stability of the cabinet, as happens in parliamentarism.

If the president dominates the prime minister, the vote of no confidence threatens such a position but not the mandate of the president as head of state. In so far as meaningful political power is in the hands of a minority president, independent opposition by legislators to the government's initiatives does not involve as high risks as in a parliamentary regime. It has been observed, however, that there is little data to support the conclusion that the legislators under semi-presidentialism have greater independence than the legislators of parliamentary regimes.

If presidents predominate in a semi-presidential system it is because they have the support of the majority in parliament. Some have observed that when the president dominates the executive, the prime minister becomes a sort of arbiter or, as Duverger defines him, "the chief of the staff." If the president and the prime minister share a similar political programme, then the prime minister acts as a connecting link between the executive and the assembly. On the other hand, the president can act as arbiter of conflicts in a divided government. When presidents face an opposition government, or when they are not the leaders of the party, they are necessarily somewhat distant from the politics of legislative coalition formation. Lijphart and

Rogowoski have underlined that it is exactly such distance that allows the president to be an umpire in disputes between parties.[33]

First, the president has the power to designate the prime minister who must form a cabinet. The president as arbiter can use his or her discretion in the choice of the candidate who must form a government, for the purpose of ensuring concessions by the future prime minister and eventually of guaranteeing ample representation of interests in the cabinet.

Secondly, minority presidents can exercise formal powers constitutionally accorded to them to influence the result of a legislative struggle, including that of submitting the government's legislation to constitutional review or to a referendum. Finally, whereas presidents have the power to dissolve the assembly, they can use such tool to push ministers to accept compromises with coalition partners or to face the electorate.

One scholar has questioned whether democratic stability arises from semi-presidentialism itself, maintaining rather that "the relationship between this type of system and the stability of the democracy is not quite deprived of ambiguity".[34] For Linz, the installation of such a form of government has always been enabled by particular historical circumstances, as in the case of Germany, which, having abolished the monarchy, chose the road of political innovation. Max Weber and others opted for a solution that envisaged a directly elected president, without abandoning at the same time the parliamentary tradition. The new democracy needed a strong leader, but the solution of a pure presidentialism, with separation of powers, was not kept in consideration.

Such a complex of factors led to the 1919 German (Weimar) Constitution, which established a semi-presidential system. Peculiar conditions also led in Finland to the particular compromise that has continued to this day. In France, an important factor in the introduction of a dual executive has been mistrust towards political parties. The idea of a neutral power serving as arbiter among the parties or above them was very tempting in countries in which the polarisation of parties made the parliamentarism difficult. As Bartolini remarks, systems with a dual executive were introduced in countries that got their independence from another country or from a dominant power and that were looking for a symbol of the new nation.[35] This was the case of Finland and above all of Ireland and Iceland after independence. Popular legitimation was considered essential to give the aura of the monarch to the president of a new democracy.

For Linz it is possible that a bipolar scheme works, but not always and everywhere, as its supporters desire.[36] According to the author, it works when it becomes a *de*

---

33 A Lijphart and R Rogowski, "Separation of Powers and Management of Political Cleavages" in *Political Insitutions and Their Consequences* (K Weaver and B Rockman ed, Brookings Institution, 1991).

34 J Linz, Presidential or parliamentary democracy: does it make a difference', in J Linz and A. Valenzuela (eds), *The Failure of Presidential Democracy*, (The Johns Hopkins University Press 1994), pp 3-87.

35 S Bartolini, "Sistema partitico ed elezione diretta del Capo dello Stato in Europa" in *Rivista Italiana di Scienza Politica*, 14(2), 1984, 223–243

36 JJ Linz and A Valenzuela, *Il fallimento del presidenzialismo* (il Mulino, 1995).

facto parliamentary system, as has happened in Ireland, Iceland and Austria, or when the party or the parties that sustain the president and those that have the majority in the parliament are the same. In conclusion, for Linz the thesis that bipolarism can produce stability depends on the same conditions that assure a stable parliamentary government, in other words, a parliament in which the parties are able to sustain the prime minister. The problem comes from the existence of a further condition: consensus between prime minister and president.

3. Final Remarks

The Irish system can be described as an anomalous semi-presidential regime. If, on the one hand, the Constitution welcomes the inspiring principles of the parliamentary form of government, adopting the confidence relationship between Government and Parliament, on the other hand it envisages the direct election of the head of state, who is nevertheless a President endowed with powers of inferior degree compared with some presidents elected by parliaments. The Irish Constitution relegates the President to a practically ceremonial role only, excluding therefore his or her active participation in the political arena.

A first explanation of such an anomaly can be sought in the genesis of the constitutional text. Observing the whole plan traced by the Irish founding fathers, subsequently adjusted to the needs of the times, two conflicting elements come in relief: the influence of the British matrix and the wish to become emancipated, distinguishing themselves from the legal order of the United Kingdom.

Irish constitutional history is based on two main documents: the 1922 Constitution and the 1937 Constitution, each of which marks the attainment of important objectives connected to the procedure of independence from the United Kingdom.

The first step was represented by the conclusion in 1921 of the Treaty, signed by the delegates of British and Irish governments, under which the Irish Free State was founded. After centuries of dependence on Great Britain, the agreement gave Ireland the status of a "self-governing dominion", with recognition of wide autonomy. Based on this negotiation, in December 1922 the first Irish constitution went into effect, substantially reproducing in written form the traditional British model, even if the resulting Westminster model was corrected through three essential elements: the written nature of the constitution, the adoption of a proportional electoral system and the institution of a supreme court with a power of judicial review of acts of parliament. The Executive Council (government) in practice held the executive power and was responsible to the lower house (Dáil Éireann), while a symbolic role was accorded to the British Crown. It emerges that in this Constitution two principles cohabited, contradictory to each other: it attributed sovereignty to the people, but confirmed, at least formally, a "foreign" king at the top of the executive, even if such incoherence can be explained by considering the process the gradual of independence from the United Kingdom.

With the 1937 Constitution Ireland reached full autonomy and independence, which was sealed not only with the approval of the new text through popular plebiscite (1 July 1937), but also through notable changes, among which was the direct election of President of Ireland by the people for a seven-year period. Such a choice by the

Irish framers reveals the intention of contrasting a charismatic figure with the British sovereign, who—being supported by popular legitimation—would guarantee the unity of the nation and its complete independence.

The configuration of such constitutional organ was subject to much debate in the constituent assembly, where the supporters of Fine Gael, the main party in the opposition, stated that it feared that the legitimacy emerging from direct election could lead to a more "presidentialist" than presidential working of the constitution, allowing De Valera, leader of the dominant Fianna Fáil party, if elected, to convert himself in a dictator, supported by the popular vote and by the parliamentary majority. In fact, an expansive interpretation of the provision made in Art 13.10, according to which additional powers and functions can be conferred to the President by law, would have been able to widen notably his or her sphere of intervention.

Nevertheless, these fears, which may have been justified in the initial debate, lost any basis as the definitive text of the Constitution was settled, essentially for two reasons. First, because the few competences assigned to the head of state immediately would have confined him or her to a marginal role. Moreover, the norms regulating presidential elections, according to which nobody is able in practice to compete for the position if not supported by one of the main parties or by a coalition of smaller parties, allowed the parties to agree on a candidate, so activating Art 12.4.5° of the Constitution, which prescribes that in the case in which only one person is a candidate at the presidential election, there is no need to proceed to the vote, so emptying direct election of any meaning. This second reason partly explains why some Irish Presidents have been deprived of popular charisma and of the weight in their relationships with other constitutional organs that can be used by presidents elected by the people.[37]

The Irish Constitution determines with precision the presidential functions, which scholars divide in two separate categories. To the first category belong the functions that the President exercises, in a purely formal way, on direction ("advice"), designation (nomination) or recommendation from other organs, which are included in the ordinary sphere of attribution of the heads of state. To the second category belong the faculties that the Constitution expressly accords him or her as proper to his or office, either if the President acts in full autonomy (in his or her absolute discretion), or if he or she exercises them after having heard the opinion (after consultation with) of the Council of State, a merely advisory organ.

From the constitutional scheme emerges a weak presidential figure, in a largely subservient position *vis-à-vis* other organs. In fact, the head of state simply assumes a role "of façade" when, according to Art 13.1.1° of the Constitution on the designation of the Dáil Éireann, he or she appoints the Taoiseach (the prime minister), who must necessarily be a member of the Dáil and the choice of the majority in that chamber. An analogous position can be attributed to the President when, according on the nomination of the Taoiseach and with the Dáil's approval, he or she appoints the other members of the Government (Art 13.1.2°) or, on the advice of the prime minister, accepts the latter's resignation or revokes his or her

37 R Olivetti Rason, "La forma di governo in Irlanda" in *Studi in onore di Leopoldo Elia* (Milano, 1999).

mandate (Art 13.1.3°). Similarly symbolic is his or her function as commander-in-chief of the armed forces, as although holding formal direction of them, decisions on these matters are assumed by the Minister for Defence (Art 13.5.1°).

Nevertheless, despite the President's apparently only nominal functions, he or she is conferred with two important prerogatives: the first is the discretionary power to refuse the anticipated dissolution of the parliament to a prime minister who no longer enjoy the support of the majority in Dáil Éireann (Art 13.2.2°); the second is the power, having consulted the Council of State, to refer a Bill to the Supreme Court for constitutional review (Art 26.1.1°).

As far as the faculty of dissolving the popular chamber is concerned, the presidential "power of refusal" has never been exercised, and doctrine does not agree on the exact meaning of the constitutional provision. Indeed, some scholars believe that, for the sub-section to be applicable, an express vote of no confidence is necessary, while for others defeat on a confidence question would be enough, above all if related to proposed legislation that reflects basic aspects of government policy. Some scholars, finally, wonder on the attitude of this norm towards a Taoiseach as the head of a minority government.[38]

The second meaningful power granted to the President, the possibility of going to the Supreme Court with the purpose of verifying the constitutionality of a Bill, has been exercised in various circumstances, even if in only one case was it the cause of a serious institutional crisis.[39] In fact, in 1976, President Ó Dálaigh's decision to refer to the Supreme Court the Emergency Powers Bill, pertaining to the treatment to be given to IRA members, provoked a sharp conflict with the Government, which led to the resignation of the President. This crisis would have been aggravated had the President been open to the charge of not maintaining a *super partes* attitude, that is, if he could have been seen as supporting his former party, Fianna Fáil, in opposition at the time, so looking to intervene in political life. However, President Ó Dálaigh's resignation did not respond to any public call from either government or opposition parties that he should do so. Instead, it arose from his own personal decision that his position was untenable, given that Taoiseach Liam Cosgrave refused to dismiss a minister (the Minister for Defence) who had cast aspersions on the President personally (for which he subsequently apologised) in course of strongly criticising the decision to refer the Bill.[40]

Faced with the weak competences accorded to the presidential figure, the dominant position of the Taoiseach emerges. By virtue of the substantial bipolarity and in spite of the proportional electoral system, the Taoiseach is invariably likely to be the leader of the party or the coalition that wins the elections, enjoying a legitimacy superior to that that enjoyed by the President through direct election. Such evident

38 JP Casey, *Constitutional Law in Ireland* (3rd ed, Sweet & Maxwell, 2000) 83–87; JM Kelly, *The Irish Constitution* (4th ed, Gerard W Hogan and Gerry Whyte ed, Lexis Nexis Butterworths, 2003) 208–209.

39 JP Casey, *Constitutional Law in Ireland* (3rd ed, Sweet & Maxwell, 2000) 88–90; JM Kelly, *The Irish Constitution* (4th ed, Gerard W Hogan and Gerry Whyte ed, Lexis Nexis Butterworths, 2003) 399–401.

40 JP Casey *Constitutional Law in Ireland* (3rd ed, Sweet & Maxwell, 2000) 93.

prominence eliminates any possibility of recognising a really dual executive in the Irish system.

To this extent, a putative bicephalous structure of the executive cannot be inferred without difficulty from the constitutional text, according to which (Art 28.1.2°) the Government is the exclusive holder of the executive power but—above all—it is extraneous to Irish political practice, which assures the supremacy of the prime minister. In other words, from the constitutional scheme it emerges that the choice to found the presidential office on (and to equip it with) a direct popular legitimation was not dictated by the determination of Irish framers to adopt a semi-presidential form of government as more fit to guarantee the stability and the effectiveness of the system, but by the need to definitely enact Irish independence, aiming to affirm and "visually" to represent the will of the nation to decide its own national life autonomously. But, born as a substitute for an historically rejected monarch, the *de facto* "head of the Irish state" has been accorded extremely reduced powers. On the base of such considerations, it seems possible to describe the Irish constitutional order as a parliamentary regime corrected by the anomaly of the direct popular election of the President, rejecting the description of "intermittent" semi-presidentialism attributed to the Irish experience by some scholars and preferring the definition of *merely apparent semi-presidentialism*.

CHAPTER 11

The 2013 Irish Constitutional Convention: A Bold Step or a Damp Squib?

David M Farrell[1]

In late 2012, the Irish government finally took the long-anticipated step of establishing the Irish Constitutional Convention (www.constitution.ie), whose first formal session was held on the weekend of 26–27 January 2013. Ireland now joins a small but growing band of countries to have gone down the route of using people's conventions as a means of considering big questions of institutional design.

Needless to say, this is not the first time that Irish constitutional reform has been on the agenda. Despite its relative rigidity, Ireland's Constitution (enacted in 1937) has not been immune from change, although much of this has been relatively recent. After a three-year period of settling in during which time some tweaks were made (for the most part of a "housekeeping" nature[2]), the first successful moves to amend the document were not until the early 1970s, in each instance requiring a referendum.[3] Since that time, Irish citizens have voted on 31 proposals for amendment, 23 of which have been accepted.

There has also been plenty of talk (and ink) devoted to the possibility of further constitutional reform, not least in the various reports of Joint Committees of the Oireachtas (Parliament): the 1967 Committee on the Constitution; the 1996 Constitution Review Group (arguably the most comprehensive of these); the 1998 All-Party Committee on the Constitution; and most recently the four reports of the Joint Committee on the Constitution whose work preceded the 2011 general election. All these reviews shared in common two things: (1) the membership comprised members of the establishment (politicians and legal and academic experts); and (2) hardly any of what they proposed ever saw the light of day as an actual constitutional reform.[4] It is too early to tell whether the current Constitutional Convention will overcome the second hurdle, but certainly it does override the first.

---

1 The author is supporting the work of the Irish Constitutional Convention as its research director. All views expressed in this chapter are the personal views of the author.

2 See Michael Gallagher, "The Changing Constitution" in *Politics in the Republic of Ireland* (5th ed, John Coakley and Michael Gallagher ed, Routledge/PSAI Press, 2010) 78–84.

3 There were three earlier unsuccessful proposals to amend the Constitution, one in 1959 and two in 1968, each of which was defeated at a referendum. All three related to changes in the Dáil electoral system: Cornelius O'Leary, *Irish Elections, 1918–1977: Parties, Voters and Proportional Representation* (St Martin's Press, 1979) 46–58, 66–70 (discussed by Arend Lijphart, "Advances in the Comparative Study of Electoral Systems" (1984) 36 *World Politics* 424, 427).

4 The restatement of the law on cabinet confidentiality (Seventeenth Amendment of the Constitution Act 1997), the constitutional recognition of local government (Twentieth

The issue to be considered in this chapter is just how a significant a move is the establishment of the Constitutional Convention. The chapter is arranged in three parts. I start by outlining the origins and nature of the Convention. I then briefly review how the Irish initiative compares with other examples of people's conventions that have occurred over the past decade. Finally, I provide a preliminary assessment of the significance of the Irish Constitutional Convention.

1. The Irish Constitutional Convention

Arguably, the origins of the Irish Constitutional Convention were in late 2009 to early 2010 in the deliberations of the Oireachtas Joint Committee on the Constitution, whose report in July 2010[5] proposed the establishment of a Citizens' Assembly (modelled on the British Columbia Citizens' Assembly) to consider the question of electoral reform. In the discussions leading up to this report, the Joint Committee had been given evidence from a number of expert witnesses (the current author included) informing the committee membership of the merits of such an approach, and it is likely that this may have had some bearing on the proposal.

The work of the Joint Committee coincided with a major policy review by Ireland's then largest opposition party, Fine Gael, whose long-standing leader, Enda Kenny, sought to make his mark with significant policy proposals. In late 2009 to early 2010, Kenny made a number of speeches on new policy areas that attracted considerable media attention and the ire of some of his frontbench colleagues who were not happy with the leader's efforts to produce party policy on the fly without input from party colleagues. Among the policy proposals that Kenny sought to bounce his colleagues into was electoral reform. Like many commentators at the time, Kenny proposed replacing Ireland's single transferable vote (STV) electoral system with a variant of the German mixed-member electoral system, his rationale being that this would help to reduce the excessive localism in Irish representative politics.[6]

Electoral reform was not the only reform proposed by Enda Kenny; he also promised gender quotas and the abolition of the Seanad. In the ensuing backlash from his parliamentary colleagues, he found himself forced to backtrack on a number of his proposals. It is apparent that some of his advisors were aware of the deliberations of the Joint Committee, which might explain why in Fine Gael's subsequent *New Politics* policy document, published in March 2010, a specific proposal for a new electoral system was replaced by one proposing instead the establishment of a

---

Amendment of the Constitution Act 1999) and the abolition of the death penalty (Twenty-First Amendment of the Constitution Act 2001) all owe at least something to the recommendations made by one of more of these previous reviews, particularly the *Report of the Constitution Review Group* (Pn 2632, Stationery Office 1996), which recommended each of them; see respectively (10 September 1997) 480 *Dáil Debates*, cols 640–641; (11 May 1999) 504 *Dáil Debates*, col 652 and (11 April 2001) 534 *Dáil Debates*, col 839.

5 Joint Committee on the Constitution *Fourth Report – Article 16: Review of the Electoral System for the Election of Members to Dáil Éireann – July 2010* http://www.oireachtas.ie/viewdoc.asp?fn=/documents/Committees30thDail/J-Constitution/Report_2008/20100722.pdf (last accessed 16 May 2013).

6 For discussion, see D Farrell, *Irish Electoral Reform: Three Myths and a Proposal*, paper presented at the *MacGill Summer School*, Glenties, July 2010, http://politicalreformireland.files.wordpress.com/2010/07/irish_electoral_reform-2.pdf (last accessed 21 January 2014).

Citizens' Assembly to deliberate on options for electoral reform.[7] The Citizens' Assembly proposal was retained for the party's election manifesto in the 2011 general election, a manifesto that included a suite of other constitutional reform proposals.

Within a few months of the launch of Fine Gael's *New Politics* document, the Labour Party—soon to become Fine Gael's coalition partner as a result of the outcome of the 2011 election—also published an ambitious agenda for constitutional reform.[8] Indeed, the Labour Party's proposals for change were even more ambitious and wide-ranging than Fine Gael's. At the heart of their proposals was the establishment of a Constitutional Convention to consider root-and-branch reform of the entire Irish Constitution. The party proposed that the membership of the Constitutional Convention should comprise one-third politicians, one-third experts and one-third ordinary citizens. As in Fine Gael's case, these proposals were retained in the party's election manifesto.

The outcome of the 2011 general election was the formation of a Fine Gael/ Labour coalition government, whose programme for government[9] sought to marry the sometimes quite disparate manifesto promises of both parties. In relation to the parties' respective proposals on Citizens' Assemblies and Constitutional Conventions, this coalition marriage resulted in the following wording:

> "We will establish a Constitutional Convention to consider comprehensive constitutional reform, with a brief to consider, as a whole or in sub-groups, and report within 12 months on the following:
>
> - Review of our Dáil electoral system.
> - Reducing the presidential term to 5 years and aligning it with the local and European elections.
> - Provision for same-sex marriage.
> - Amending the clause on women in the home and encourage greater participation of women in public life.
> - Removing blasphemy from the Constitution.
> - Possible reduction of the voting age.
> - Other relevant constitutional amendments that may be recommended by the Convention."[10]

There were no details about the membership of the Convention (most observers

---

7 *New Politics*, March 2010; subsequently revised in 2011, see http://electioncamp.eu/sites/default/files/NewPolitics.pdf (last accessed 16 May 2013).

8 *New Government, Better Government: Changing a Broken System. Labour's 140 Proposals to Transform Government, Politics and the Public Services* (Labour, January 2011). By the time of the election, it is safe to say that political and constitutional reform was very high on the agenda of all Irish political parties, without exception (Jane Suiter and David Farrell, "The Parties' Manifestos" in *How Ireland Voted 2011: The Full Story of Ireland's Earthquake Election* (Michael Gallagher and Michael Marsh ed, Houndmills, Basingstoke, 2011).

9 Department of An Taoiseach, *Programme for Government 2011* http://www.taoiseach.gov.ie/eng/Publications/Publications_Archive/Publications_2011/Programme_for_Government_2011.pdf (last accessed 16 May 2013).

10 By the time of its launch, 18 months or so later, the Convention's list of items was extended to include the issue of whether to give voting rights in presidential elections to Irish citizens living abroad (voting at the embassies).

assumed that this would most likely be based on the Labour Party's tripartite model), nor was anything said about its modus operandi.

The expectation was that the Convention would start work soon after the election; both parties' manifestos indicated their desire to move quickly on their reform proposals. It was in this context, therefore, that a group of us[11] decided to mobilise to start an initiative, promoted by the Irish political science community, to extol the virtues of deliberative approaches, seeking to influence the government's plans relating to the Constitutional Convention. To that end we secured a generous donation from a philanthropic organisation based in Dublin, Atlantic Philanthropies, to fund a year-long set of activities under the banner of "We the Citizens",[12] which culminated in a pilot Citizens' Assembly held over a summer weekend in 2011. A final report presented to government included survey evidence (drawn from the deliberative poll underlying the Citizens' Assembly) demonstrating the success of the deliberative process in terms of its impact on the citizen participants.[13]

While we cannot be certain of this, there is good reason to believe, nevertheless, that the *We the Citizens* report was influential in the move by the government to launch the Constitutional Convention—albeit 18 months later than envisaged—as well as in the decision over how it should be comprised (notably the decision to increase the citizen membership to two-thirds of the total and to dispense with expert members) and how it should operate, namely along deliberative lines.

The Convention held its inaugural (launch) event in the historic venue of Dublin Castle on 1 December 2012, with opening speeches by the Taoiseach, Tánaiste and opposition party leaders. Chaired by Tom Arnold, the outgoing chief executive of Concern, a leading international charity, the other 99 members of the Convention are 66 citizens selected at random by the survey company Behaviour and Attitudes, and 33 elected members of the Oireachtas (29 members) and Northern Ireland Assembly (four members). To allow for the possibility of members not being available for all meetings, a list of substitute members was drawn up at the same time.

2. People's Conventions in Comparative Perspective

Ireland is not the first country to include citizens at the heart of discussions over possible constitutional reform in a process that follows deliberative practice. We can refer to these entities generically as "people's conventions", which share the following traits.

- They address big, national questions of constitutional/institutional design.
- They are established by government to meet a certain objective in time-delimited fashion.
- They are quite deliberately and distinctly treated as a supplement (rather than competitor) to the existing system of representative democracy.

---

11 The other colleagues involved included Eoin O'Malley, Jane Suiter and Elaine Byrne.

12 http://www.WetheCitizens.ie (last accessed 16 May 2013).

13 For more, see David Farrell, Eoin O'Malley and Jane Suiter, "Deliberative Democracy in Action Irish-Style: The 2011 We The Citizens Pilot Citizens' Assembly" (2013) 28 *Irish Political Studies* 99–113.

- Ordinary citizens are at their core (though on occasions working side-by-side with elected politicians).
- For the most part, the membership is based on random selection rather than election.
- For the most part, the outcome of their deliberations is generally made clear at the point of establishment (e.g. whether to have their recommendations go straight to referendum or back to government).
- At the heart of the enterprise is deliberation—"the process by which individuals sincerely weigh the merits of competing arguments in discussions together".[14]

Table 1: Variations in people's conventions in the modern era

	Membership	Appointment of citizen members	Agenda	Mode of discussion	Promised outcome
Australia	Mixed	Election	Limited	Debate	Referendum
British Columbia	Citizens only	Selection	Limited	Deliberation	Referendum
Iceland	Citizens only	Election	Broad	Deliberation	Non-binding referendum
Ireland	Mixed	Selection	Broad	Deliberation	Parliament
Netherlands	Citizens only	Selection	Limited	Deliberation	Parliament
Ontario	Citizens only	Selection	Limited	Deliberation	Referendum

Table 1 summarises the main features of variation among the principal examples of people's conventions that have been established to date. Of the six cases presented in the table, the Australian constitutional convention established by John Howard in 1998 to consider whether Australia might become a republic did not follow the usual principles associated with deliberative processes: notably, election rather than random selection was used to pick the citizen members,[15] and the mode of discussion followed parliamentary norms of debate and position-taking rather than deliberation and dialogue.[16] Nevertheless, the fact that ordinary citizens were included in the membership was a striking departure from previous practice for Australian constitutional review.[17] The convention's recommendation that Australia become a republic was defeated in the subsequent referendum.

[14] James Fishkin, *When the People Speak: Deliberative Democracy and Public Consultation* (Oxford University Press, 2009) 33.

[15] For discussion on the virtues of random selection (or "sortition") in democratic politics, see Oliver Dowlen, *The Political Potential of Sortition* (Imprint Academic, 2009) and Peter Stone, *The Luck of the Draw: The Role of Lotteries in Decision Making* (Oxford University Press, 2011).

[16] *Constitutional Convention 2–13 February 1998, Transcripts of Proceedings* (Parliament of Australia, 2008) (http://www.aph.gov.au/Parliamentary_Business/Hansard/HANCON (last accessed 16 May 2013); John Warhurst, *From Constitutional Convention to Republic Referendum: A Guide to the Processes, the Issues and the Participants* (Australian Parliamentary Library Paper, No. 25. Canberra, 1999) (http://www.aph.gov.au/binaries/library/pubs/rp/1998-99/99rp25.pdf; last accessed 16 May 2013); George Williams, *The 1998 Constitutional Convention: First Impressions*, Parliament of Australia, Current Issues Brief, 1998 (http://www.aph.gov.au/About_Parliament/Parliamentary_Departments/Parliamentary_Library/Publications_Archive/CIB/CIB9798/98cib11; last accessed 16 May 2013).

[17] Heather McRae and Anne Mullins, *Australian Constitutional Convention 1973–1985: A Guide*

The membership of the 2011 Icelandic Constitutional Council was also elected.[18] Established in the heat of the country's economic and financial meltdown, it was tasked with considering root-and-branch reform of the country's constitution. It met full time over an intensive four-month period, and produced a series of detailed constitutional reforms, all of which received widespread public support (two-thirds majority votes) in the subsequent indicative referendums. At the time of writing, the parliament has yet to formally ratify these results and the results of the 2013 Icelandic general election have put the adoption of a new constitution in grave doubt.[19]

It is our next three cases that have attracted the most scholarly attention: the citizens' assemblies on electoral reform in the Canadian provinces of British Columbia (2004) and Ontario (2007) and the Dutch citizens' forum (*BürgerForum*) of 2006.[20] Only ordinary citizens were involved in these cases. They were selected at random. These assemblies/fora met at weekends over a number of months: 11 months in British Columbia, eight months in Ontario and nine months in the Netherlands. The two Canadian cases resulted in referendum questions that went directly to the citizens, which in both instances were defeated (though in British Columbia, which held two successive votes on this, on the first occasion the proposition actually received majority support but failed to pass a super-majority threshold). In the case of the Dutch citizens' forum, the recommendation was for only minor changes to the existing electoral system. This was to have been discussed by the government, but the process disintegrated with the collapse of the coalition government.

Ireland is the latest entrant to this group. While the Irish case bears some similarity to the Australian one in mixing ordinary citizens with professional politicians, the decision to select the citizen members at random rather than by election and to seek to operate the convention along deliberative lines puts it more on a par with the Canadian and Dutch cases.

---

to the Archives (University of Melbourne, Centre for Comparative Constitutional Studies, 1998) (http://dtl.unimelb.edu.au/dtl_publish/research/4/124747.html; last accessed 16 May 2013). Furthermore, judging by some of the citizen participants' reflections on the experience, there is evidence of a sense of empowerment and engagement that is often associated with deliberation (http://www.abc.net.au/concon/diaries/default.htm; last accessed 16 May 2013).

18 Erikur Bergmann, "Reconstituting Iceland: from an economic collapse to a new 'post-revolutionary' 'crowd-sourced' constitution", paper presented at *Political Legitimacy and the Paradox of Regulation* conference, workshop title: "Crowd-pleasers or key janglers? The impact of drops in political legitimacy on democratic reform and their consequences" (Leiden University, 24–25 January 2013; http://www.academia.edu/2463798/Reconstituting_Iceland_-_constitutional_reform_caught_in_a_new_critical_order_in_the_wake_of_crisis; last accessed 16 May 2013). The election result was declared null and void on legal grounds by the courts. In response, the parliament appointed the 25 citizen members who had been successful in that election.

19 Thorvaldur Gylfason, "Putsch: Iceland's Crowd-Sourced Constitution Killed by Parliament" *Verfassungsblog*, 30 March 2013 (http://www.verfassungsblog.de/putsch-icelands-crowd-sourced-constitution-killed-by-parliament; last accessed 16 May 2013); Giulia Dessi, "When Politics Strike Back: The End of the Icelandic Constitutional Experiment?" *Open Democracy.net*, 26 April 2013 (http://www.opendemocracy.net/giulia-dessi/when-politics-strike-back-end-of-icelandic-constitutional-experiment; last accessed 16 May 2013).

20 Patrick Fournier, Henk van der Kolk, Kenneth Carty, André Blais and Jonathan Rose, *When Citizens Decide: Lessons from Citizen Assemblies on Electoral Reform*. (Oxford University Press, 2011); Mark Warren and Hilary Pearse ed, *Designing Deliberative Democracy: The British Columbia Citizens' Assembly* (Cambridge University Press, 2008).

3. Bold Step or Damp Squib?

It is safe to say that the launch of the Irish Constitutional Convention attracted little by way of positive reaction. On the contrary, it was met with a mix of indifference from the mass public, cynicism from the ranks of those members of the media commentariat who were bothered to pay any attention to it,[21] and howls of derision across most social media circles.

From the outset, there were three main sets of criticisms of it, relating to its composition, its agenda, and its limited advisory role. While it clearly is far too early to pass definitive judgment on the success or otherwise of the Convention, the fact that it has been operating for several months and has already deliberated over and made recommendations on four of the themes on its agenda provides an opportunity to take early stock of it.[22] Some of the criticisms that have been made can only be assessed in the fullness of time, after the Convention has completed its work and after we know how government and—if asked—citizens have reacted to its recommendations. At this early stage in its life, it is possible to make some preliminary remarks relating to the three areas of criticism.

We can start with the criticisms made about how the Convention membership has been constituted. The main point of contention here is over the mixing of ordinary citizens with elected politicians,[23] the argument being that the latter are likely to dominate the discussions and intimidate the citizen members.[24] Based on

---

21 For a sample, see Fintan O'Toole, "We ourselves are fit to make a new republic" *Irish Times*, 11 September 2012 (http://www.irishtimes.com/debate/we-ourselves-are-fit-to-make-a-new-republic-1.528385; last accessed 16 May 2013); Editorial, "Constitutional Convention chief needs some savvy" *Irish Independent*, 3 December 2012 (http://www.independent.ie/irish-news/constitutional-convention-chief-needs-some-savvy-28942535.html; last accessed 16 May 2013).

22 Its first and second reports are available: *First Report of the Convention on the Constitution* [Voting Age & Presidential Term] (26 March 2013) https://www.constitution.ie/AttachmentDownload.ashx?mid=e1f8e128-2496-e211-a5a0-005056a32ee4 (last accessed 16 May 2013) and *Second Report of the Convention on the Constitution* [Role of women] (8 May 2013) https://www.constitution.ie/AttachmentDownload.ashx?mid=268d9308-c9b7-e211-a5a0-005056a32ee4 (last accessed 16 May 2013).

23 Journalistic fears of citizen members being too easily open to intimidation seemed quickly realised over an issue that emerged even before the launch of the Convention, when it became apparent that the citizen members' identities were to be kept anonymous. This particular matter was quickly dissipated when at the launch meeting the Convention members agreed to release their names and county locations: *Convention on the Constitution: List of Members* (April 2013 version) https://www.constitution.ie/Documents/ListOfMembers.pdf (last accessed 16 May 2013).

24 There was a related criticism by some elements of civil society that it was wrong to exclude experts as members. For example, Donncha O'Connell "Constitutional Convention — a missed opportunity for radical appraisal by citizens" *Galway Advertiser*, 9 August 2012 (http://www.advertiser.ie/galway/article/54182/constitutional-convention-a-missed-opportunity-for-radical-appraisal-by-citizens; last accessed 16 May 2013). This criticism misses the point behind deliberative approaches (as shown by the other cases of people's conventions discussed in the previous section), where experts are given a prominent role in their capacity as "experts" to advise, brief and give witness to the members of the convention. The objective behind selecting a random group of ordinary citizens is to ensure that there is a decent sample of citizens (as representative as possible) who are selected as members purely on the basis of chance and not because of representing any set of vested interests or because of any particular area of expertise that they may have (for more, see Fishkin, *When the People Speak: Deliberative Democracy and Public Consultation* (Oxford University Press, 2009)).

observations of the meetings to date (and coverage by journalists), this fear that politicians would dominate the proceedings seems unfounded. A point of detail that many of the critics may not have picked up on is the modus operandi that surrounds deliberative processes such as this, namely the practice of having the members distributed in tables of seven to eight each with a trained facilitator whose role is to ensure that all members are given an equal right to participate in discussions in an atmosphere of mutual respect. By its very nature, this ensures equal opportunity for all.

It should also be pointed out that the politician members have made every effort not to steal the limelight, particularly in the plenary discussions: as can be seen from the streamed video feed of these discussions, on regular occasions politician members can be seen encouraging other members of their table to contribute.[25]

A further advantage of having politicians among the ranks of the members is that it could prove useful in helping to minimise the risks of a "disconnect" between the Convention and the political class—a problem that was apparent in the case of the Canadian and Dutch citizens' assemblies, where the political class quite deliberately stayed clear of the work of the assemblies, making it difficult for these assemblies to gain much political purchase.[26]

The second area of criticism is over the agenda of the Constitutional Convention, which is seen at the same time as too limited and overly crowded. The first point relates to the fact that the list of eight matters is too restrictive, not dealing with the fundamental issues of constitutional reform that many called for.[27] More to the point, specific matters of constitutional reform that were also on the government agenda (e.g. children's rights and the abolition of the Senate) were not included on the list of items. The criticism of the crowded nature of the agenda relates to the fact that the Convention has been given just 12 months to conclude its work, with space and resources for just eight weekends of meetings.

While detailed consideration of these points will have to wait another day, it is possible to make some preliminary remarks that deal with some of the matters raised. First, in the Oireachtas Resolution of July 2012 proposing the establishment of the Convention it is explicitly stated that its work is not only confined to the eight themes it has been asked to consider:

> "following completion of [its] reports [on those eight themes it may consider]

---

25 The archive of video of the public plenary sessions of the Convention can be viewed online at https://www.constitution.ie/Meetings.aspx#video-archive (last accessed 16 May 2013).

26 Patrick Fournier, Henk van der Kolk, Kenneth Carty, André Blais and Jonathan Rose, *When Citizens Decide: Lessons from Citizen Assemblies on Electoral Reform* (Oxford University Press, 2011). For good discussion of this point, see Ken Carty's speculations on how the Irish Constitutional Convention might operate, in a web interview several months before the launch of the Convention (http://www.youtube.com/watch?v=3E6Z_AW3CRk&feature=youtu.be; last accessed 16 May 2013). See about 50 seconds into the video.

27 Elaine Byrne, "The Democracy of a Republic" in *Up the Republic!* (Fintan O'Toole ed, Faber and Faber, 2012).

> such other relevant constitutional amendments that may be recommended by it".[28]

Who can say what other themes the Convention members may wish to deliberate on that might result in additional recommendations for constitutional reform?

Second, it is already apparent that the Convention members are minded to read their brief quite liberally, moving beyond the confines of the specific questions posed in the July 2012 Oireachtas Resolution. In its January 2013 weekend meeting, for instance—its first full meeting—the Convention considered two themes: whether to reduce the voting age to 17 and whether to reduce the President's term of office from seven years to five (with a supplementary question over whether a reduced term of office might then lead to aligning presidential elections with local and European Parliament elections). Having read the briefing materials, heard from experts and advocacy groups, and deliberated over the details of the relevant arguments, the Convention members took two key decisions that undoubtedly went beyond their brief.

Specifically, the Convention voted in favour of

- Reducing the voting age to 16 (the age proposed by many of the advocacy groups promoting a reduced voting age) not 17 (the age they were asked to consider); and
- Giving citizens a direct role in the process of nominating presidential candidates, an issue that was arguably entirely beyond their remit. The Convention voted against the proposal to reduce the presidential term.[29]

The third main area of criticism relates to the fact that the Convention can only make recommendations: i.e. its role is advisory rather than declaratory. Unlike the example shown by the Canadian citizens' assemblies, in the Irish case the proposal is that the recommendations of the Convention will be sent back to government to consider rather than going directly to the people as referendum proposals. This leaves the final power with government to determine whether or not its recommendations will ever see the light of day in the form of referendum questions.

Again, we have to wait and see what transpires, but a point of detail that appears not to have been taken on board is the fact that the Government has given a specific undertaking to respond in timely fashion. As it made clear in the July 2012 terms of reference,

> "the Government will provide in the Oireachtas a response to each recommendation of the Convention within four months and, if accepting the

---

[28] *Resolution of the Houses of the Oireachtas of July, 2012* https://www.constitution.ie/Documents/Terms_of_Reference.pdf (last accessed 16 May 2013).

[29] Another instance of the Convention moving beyond its remit was in the decision at its second weekend of deliberations to recommend that the text of the Constitution should be amended to include "gender-inclusive language". *Second Report of the Convention on the Constitution* [Role of women] (8 May 2013) 8–9 (https://www.constitution.ie/AttachmentDownload.ashx?mid=268d9308-c9b7-e211-a5a0-005056a32ee4; last accessed 16 May 2013).

> recommendation, will indicate the timeframe it envisages for the holding of any related referendum."[30]

This means ruling out the common practice of simply ignoring unpalatable reports, of letting worthy documents gather dust in a damp civil service cellar—the Government has said it will respond. Furthermore, even before the Convention has completed its work at the end of 2013 it can expect to have received government responses to its earlier reports. This should provide some cause for careful reflection in government circles about the nature of those responses.

A final point about the criticisms of the limited role of the Convention is to note that such criticisms are not uncommon. Robert Goodin, for one, does not see any particular problems with this. He readily admits that these conventions can appear "toothless". But, he continues, the very act of involving ordinary citizens "might afford otherwise powerless people some real power over the policy process and the outputs that eventually emerge from it".[31] They get to speak; those in power get to hear them speak and learn how they frame issues; and the real potential is there to influence outcomes.

4. Conclusion

Across the world's established democracies, the trend in recent years has been towards engaging with citizens, of increasing the scope for ordinary citizens to have a say. People's conventions can be seen as part of this "democratic transformation".[32] For Mark Warren, processes such as this form "a potential part of the ecology of democratic institutions".[33] They are a complement to other representative institutions. People's conventions like the Irish Constitutional Convention are not without their weaknesses, but what cannot be denied is that at their heart they represent a serious intent by our political elite to re-engage with society, and they are a step towards a form of democracy that seeks to place the citizen centre stage—a democracy, in Goodin's estimation, actually centred more on inputs than outputs.[34]

Obviously, it is too soon to know for sure about the full impact of people's conventions—and certainly it is far too early in the Irish case, given that its work is still ongoing—but we can at least speculate, as John Ferejohn does, about how the practice of deliberation could yet provide "a way to redeem, to some extent, the ancient promise of democracy as a form of popular government – in Lincoln's words, as government 'by' the people".[35]

---

30 *Resolution of the Houses of the Oireachtas of July, 2012* https://www.constitution.ie/Documents/Terms_of_Reference.pdf (last accessed 16 May 2013).

31 Robert Goodin, *Reflective Democracy* (Oxford University Press, 2003) 167.

32 Russell Dalton, Bruce Cain and Susan Scarrow, "Democratic Publics and Democratic Institutions" in *Democracy Transformed? Expanding Political Opportunities in Advanced Industrial Democracies* (Bruce Cain, Russell Dalton and Susan Scarrow ed, Oxford University Press, 2003).

33 Mark Warren, "Citizen Representatives" in *Designing Deliberative Democracy: The British Columbia Citizens' Assembly* (Mark Warren and Hilary Pearse ed, Cambridge University Press, 2008) 69.

34 Robert Goodin, *Reflective Democracy* (Oxford University Press, 2003).

35 John Ferejohn, "Conclusion: The Citizens' Assembly Model" in *Designing Deliberative*

It is too soon to know if such lofty ideals are to be visited upon Irish citizens. The early months of operation of the Irish Constitutional Convention bode well. Whether its recommendations ever see the light of day in referendums and, if they do, whether those referendums pass is a story for another day.

Democracy: The British Columbia Citizens' Assembly (Mark Warren and Hilary Pearse ed, Cambridge University Press, 2008) 213.

Chapter 12

Different Perspectives on 75 Years of Irish Constitutionalism: Constitutional and Administrative Law Explored Through Irish–Italian Dialogue

John O'Dowd[1]

1. Introduction

The current collection offers a fascinating juxtaposition of Italian and Irish perspectives on the development of both the main branches of Irish public law—constitutional and administrative[2]—over the last 75 years, with specific reference to the impact of Bunreacht na hÉireann in this area. What emerges is a series of contrasts and parallels between the insights into the development of Irish constitutional and administrative law that our Italian colleagues have generously brought to this dialogue, and the responses of their Irish counterparts to the stimulus they have provided.

Very recent, potentially very significant, developments in constitutional interpretation warrant a particularly close examination of the issues dealt with in the chapters contributed by Ms Pulice and Dr Carolan, but it is also appropriate for me, as one of the co-editors, to make some responses to the other excellent contributions to the symposium, without attempting to summarise or paraphrase them.

2. Ferrari

Professor Ferrari's overview of the manner in which Irish constitutional law defines and protects citizens' and human rights and the way in which the need to accommodate the relevant norms established by the European Convention on Human Rights and European Union law provides an excellent introduction to the other contributions to this volume. It is thus unnecessary to seek to paraphrase or summarise the overall content of his chapter and the reader is referred to it as a basis for understanding more fully the remaining chapters. However, Professor Ferrari makes many acute observations on several aspects of the development of Irish constitutional law; three of these are especially worth highlighting and exploring further here.

---

[1] Lecturer, UCD School of Law.

[2] The distinction between these two branches of law is, of course, both drawn and understood differently in various legal systems, the Irish and the Italian included, but a broad differentiation between the two is appropriate in the present context.

Firstly, Professor Ferrari notes one unusual feature of the Constitution of Ireland, that it terms as the rights of "citizens" many fundamental rights that are now more commonly described, in most modern constitutions and, above all, in international human rights instruments, as human rights, usually enjoyed by any person who finds himself or herself within the jurisdiction of a state. This anomaly is perhaps not unconnected with another somewhat opaque contrast between the "nation" and the "people" under the Constitution.

The Irish courts have not been blind to some of the conundrums posed by the way in which the Constitution specifies the fundamental rights as being those of citizens, rather than human beings generally. In *Re Article 26 and the Electoral (Amendment) Bill, 1983* the Supreme Court had, for example, to consider the argument that if the fundamental personal rights described by the Constitution as being those of citizens could be shared by non-citizens, then so too could the constitutional right to vote at a Dáil election, a presidential election or a referendum be extended at least to certain categories of non-citizens (in that case British citizens).

> The most powerful argument against this interpretation of Article 16 and, in particular, of Article 16, s. 1, sub-s. 2, and of the associated Articles [under which the right to vote may not be constitutionally extended to non-citizens] is the contention, strenuously submitted on behalf of the Attorney General, that various other rights such as the freedom of association, the freedom of conscience, inviolability of a dwelling and other similar rights are granted in the Constitution to citizens, and the Courts have interpreted those provisions as having the effect, at least in certain circumstances, of not excluding the existence or the granting of similar or identical rights to persons who are not citizens. It is the view of the Court that that argument fails by reason of the clear distinction between the provisions of Article 16, Article 12 and Article 47, which provide the mechanism by which the people may choose and control their rulers and their legislators, and Articles such as Article 40 and Article 44, which grant to individuals particular rights within society and in relation to the organs of State.[3]

This decision was given, in early 1984, at a point before the Irish courts had engaged in any substantial way with the many challenges that have been posed to the use of natural law reasoning in constitutional interpretation (which Professor Ferrari describes with great acuity in his chapter). It is interesting then that the Court avoided any mention of the possible natural law basis of these fundamental rights, when distinguishing them from the rights of political participation created by the Constitution. We can also find another, more recent, example of this approach to understanding how constitutional rights differ in the personal scope of their application, not by reference to the express identification of rights-holders contained in the Constitution, but by reference to a broader purposive or structural interpretation of the Constitution (without, however, invoking the natural law or any similar concept). In *Re Article 26 and sections 5 and 10 of the Illegal Immigrants Trafficking Bill, 1999* the Supreme Court dealt with the basis on which constitutional

3 [1984] IR 268, 276. For an outline of the case law on the extension of constitutional rights to non-citizens, see JM Kelly, *The Irish Constitution* (4th ed, Gerard W Hogan and Gerry Whyte ed, Lexis Nexis Butterworths, 2003) pp 1485-86.

rights of access to the courts and fair procedures could be ascribed to non-citizens. It gave an answer to this question in terms broadly similar to those which it had adopted in the earlier decision on the 1983 Bill.

> "It would be contrary to the very notion of a state founded on the rule of law, as this State is, and one in which, pursuant to Article 34 justice is administered in courts established by law, if all persons within this jurisdiction, including non-nationals, did not, in principle, have a constitutionally protected right of access to the courts to enforce their legal rights."[4]

The Court elaborated on this point in relation to the right to fair procedures.

> "Similar considerations arise with regard to a non-national's right to fair procedures and to the application of natural and constitutional justice where he or she has applied for asylum or refugee status. The Refugee Act, 1996 and the Immigration Act, 1999 confer and regulate the legal right of non-nationals to apply for asylum or refugee status. Persons charged with taking decisions pursuant to those Acts are engaged in the administration of the law of the State. As regards judicial review of those decisions the court adopts the following statement of the law by Barrington J. in *The State (McFadden) v Governor of Mountjoy Prison (No. 1)* [1981] ILRM 113 at p 117:
>
> > 'The substantive rights and liabilities of an alien may be different to those of a citizen. The alien, for instance, may not have the right to vote or may be liable to deportation. But when the Constitution prescribes basic fairness of procedures in the administration of the law it does so, not only because citizens have rights, but also because the courts in the administration of justice are expected to observe certain forms of due process enshrined in the Constitution. Once the courts have seisin of a dispute, it is difficult to see how the standards they should apply in investigating it should, in fairness, be any different in the case of an alien than those to be applied in the case of a citizen.'"[5]

This structural approach to whether constitutional rights may be ascribed to non-nationals, which eschews any reference to the natural law as a basis for doing so, may be seen as one element in the receding influence of that kind of reasoning in Irish constitutional law, a phenomenon also reflected in Professor Ferrari's chapter. Support for this review might also be found in the Supreme Court's 2011 decision in *Nottinghamshire County Council v B*, in which the Court held that the family rights provisions of the Constitution, despite the manner in which they describe the rights of the family, do not warrant an extension of constitutional protection beyond the proper territorial limits of the Constitution's own application, so as to create a kind of sanctuary in Ireland for those who are seeking to avoid the application of family law norms at variance with those contained in Irish law.[6]

Secondly, Professor Ferrari also highlights the unresolved ambiguity in the constitutional text between references to "the nation" and "the people". The decision

---

[4] [2000] 2 IR 260, 285.

[5] *ibid*, 285-86.

[6] [2011] IESC 48 (15 December 2011).

of the Supreme Court in *Re Article 26 and the Electoral (Amendment) Bill, 1983* may also cast some light on this conundrum. The conclusion that the Supreme Court reached in that case was that the Bill that had been referred under Article 26 of the Constitution was repugnant to the Constitution, in that the provisions conferring the right to vote in at a Dáil election, a presidential election or a referendum on "citizens" must be interpreted as doing so exclusively, so that the proposed extension of these rights to British citizens was unconstitutional. The Court considered that each of the constitutional provisions in question—Articles 16.1.2°, 12.2.2° and 47.3—had to be interpreted against the background of a broader constitutional scheme or design.

> Support for this view is to be found in other provisions and in the general scheme of the Constitution. Article 6 proclaims that all powers of government derive under God from the people and, further, that it is the people's right to designate the rulers of the State and, in final appeal, to decide all questions of national policy. There can be little doubt that "the people" here referred to are the people of Ireland by, and for, whom the Constitution was enacted. In short, this Article proclaims that it is the Irish people who are the rulers of Ireland and that from them, under God, all powers of government derive and that by them the rulers are designated and national policy decided. It is not possible to regard this Article as contemplating the sharing of such powers with persons who do not come within the constitutional concept of the Irish people in Article 6.[7]

The Court was even more specific a little later in its judgment—

> ... Article 12 and Article 47 ... refer to the people as being the decisive authority but, in relation to the right to vote, each of these Articles declares that right to be exercisable by "every citizen who has the right to vote at an election for members of Dáil Éireann." In these Articles, therefore, there is an equation for electoral and referendum purposes of "the people" with "citizens" who have the right to vote at an election for Dáil Éireann.[8]

There is thus at least one distinction between "the nation" and "the people" as far as the Constitution is concerned. The current Article 2 makes it clear that the Nation is composed of "all persons ... qualified in accordance with law to be citizens of Ireland.' As Professor Ferrari notes, the former "entitlement and birth-right of every person born in the island of Ireland" to Irish citizenship has now been substantially qualified by the Twenty-seventh Amendment of the Constitution Act 2004. "The people", by contrast, appears to consist only of those citizens who have the right to vote at an election for Dáil Éireann. In almost all cases, that right depends on ordinary residence within the State, which in turn implies that the distinction between 'the nation' and 'the people' relates to the long-standing controversy in relation to proposals for extending these voting rights for Irish citizens who are

---

7 [1984] IR 268, 275.

8 *ibid*, 276. The Constitution was amended shortly thereafter to allow the right to vote at a Dáil election to be conferred by law on persons in the State who are not Irish citizens, but no similar amendment was made in relation to the right to vote at a presidential election or a referendum: Ninth Amendment of the Constitution Act, 1984. As the law stands, only British citizens have benefitted from such enfranchisement, though the possibility exists of doing so in relation to the citizens of any other EU member state, on the basis of reciprocity: Electoral Act 1992 s 8.

resident in Northern Ireland, emigrants and other Irish citizens who are not residents of the State. While the distinction is therefore reasonably clear-cut as a matter of constitutional law, it remains a very fundamental issue of public debate in relation to future legislative or constitutional changes to extend the right to vote to citizens outside the State.[9]

Finally, Professor Ferrari makes the very insightful observation in relation to the initial enunciation of the unenumerated rights doctrine that one might wonder

> ... whether the protection of an individual from the fluoridation of public water (as a measure to reduce dental caries) could not be included in the defense of 'the person' required by Article 40.3.1° and whether it really needed such an ambitious foundation in a non-textual right to 'bodily integrity' ...[10]

This same thought has not escaped at least one member of the Irish judiciary—Hogan J of the High Court—who has over the last two years or so, in a series of cases begun to employ just such an interpretive technique as a means of avoiding the theoretical and practical problems of continuing to rely on the doctrine of unenumerated personal rights.[11] As Professor Ferrari points out, the same Gerard Hogan, as an academic, was one of the most acute and articulate critics of that doctrine as it had evolved over its first quarter century.

Hogan J's capacious account of what the constitutional protection of "the person" entails contrasts sharply with the previous almost total neglect of this phrase in constitutional jurisprudence and it is analysed at some length, in connection with Ms Pulice's and Dr Carolan's contributions, later in this conclusion.[12]

3. Passaglia

As a complement to Professor Ferrari's excellent comparative overview of the substantive content of constitutional rights in Ireland and of the interaction between Irish and European systems of rights-protection, Professor Passaglia provides an excellent analysis of the Irish system of constitutional judicial review, once again in a rigorous comparative perspective. As with the other chapters, it is not proposed here to attempt a summary of Professor Passaglia's examination of this topic, but instead to offer merely a few observations on some of the points that he raises.

Professor Passaglia highlights the intermediate position of the Irish system between the models of 'diffuse' and 'concentrated' judicial review of the constitutionality of legislation. On the one hand, that power is not reserved solely to a specialised

---

9 This topic was considered by the Constitutional Convention, in relation to voting at presidential elections specifically: Ciara Kenny 'Convention supports voting rights for Irish emigrants' *Irish Times,* 28 September 2013 http://www.irishtimes.com/news/politics/convention-supports-voting-rights-for-irish-emigrants-1.1542915 (Last accessed 13 October 2013).

10 Giuseppe Franco Ferrari "Fundamental Rights in Ireland" at p 6 of the current volume.

11 These cases include *Kinsella v Governor of Mountjoy Prison* [2011] IEHC 235 (12 June); *H (a minor) v HSE* [2011] IEHC 297 (18 July); *Fleming v Ireland* [2013] IEHC 2 (10 January); *Sullivan v Boylan (No 2)* [2013] IEHC 104 (12 March). See also *Fleming v Ireland* [2013] IESC 19 (29 April).

12 See below, pp 210-222.

constitutional court; on the other, only two courts—the High Court and the Supreme Court—have such a jurisdiction, although the new Court of Appeal, once it is established, will be added to that number. If we seek reasons as to why the Constitution did not follow the US approach in its pure form and give a constitutional review jurisdiction to all courts and not merely those near the apex of the judicial hierarchy, it may be useful to reflect on the character of the other courts concerned. The restriction of the power of review dates back to Article 65 of the Constitution of the Irish Free State, although the provisions for judicial review of the constitutionality of legislation under that Constitution remained very much a dead letter.[13] In 1922, it should be recalled, many judges of the courts at the lowest level of the judicial system were still lay magistrates, a fully professional judiciary only being introduced with the establishment of a new courts system in 1924. Over and above that, however, other than the High Court and the Court of Appeal, the courts in existence in 1922 in Ireland were of local and limited jurisdiction only; broadly speaking that remains the case today. Indeed, pending the establishment of the new Court of Criminal Appeal the only ordinary courts specifically envisaged by the Constitution must be ones of local and limited jurisdiction.[14]

One point that Professor Passaglia understandably does not address in his excellent survey is the somewhat technical one of the meaning of the phrase "the question of the validity of any law having regard to the provisions of this Constitution", as it is used in Article 34.3.2°, which gives the High Court exclusive original jurisdiction over such questions. The consistent interpretation of the Supreme Court has been that "the validity of any law" can refer only to the validity of laws enacted by the Oireachtas that was established by the present Constitution and that it does not include the question, to be determined under Article 50, of whether any law enacted prior to the coming into operation of the Constitution or a rule of the common law was "inconsistent" with the Constitution and to that extent not carried over in the law of the State on that date (29 December 1937).[15] This distinction has a number of consequences, one being, for example, that the "one-judgment" rule does not apply when the Supreme Court is considering whether such a law was inconsistent under Article 50 and therefore not continued as part of the law of the State in 1937. One other consequence might appear to follow from the distinction, namely that courts of local and limited jurisdiction (the District Court and the Circuit Court) should also be able to consider and determine that question of the consistency of a pre-Constitution law or of a rule of the common law with its provisions.

The Supreme Court has, however, decided otherwise, on the basis that such a jurisdiction is inconsistent with the merely "local and limited jurisdiction" that the Constitution envisages that these courts should exercise and specifically, it seems, with the "local" character of that jurisdiction.[16] While the Court refused to depart from previous decisions about the meaning of the phrase "the validity of any

[13] JM Kelly, *The Irish Constitution* (4th ed, Gerard W Hogan and Gerry Whyte ed, Lexis Nexis Butterworths, 2003) pp 2161-63.

[14] Constitution of Ireland, Art 34.3. I leave aside for this purpose the special criminal courts that may be established under Art 38.3 or the fact that other courts of appeal, not prescribed by the Constitution may be established by law: *The People (AG) v Conmey* [1975] IR 341 (SC).

[15] *The State (Sheerin) v Kennedy* [1966] IR 379 (SC); JM Kelly, *The Irish Constitution* (4th ed, Gerard W Hogan and Gerry Whyte ed, Lexis Nexis Butterworths, 2003) pp. 772-73.

[16] *The People (DPP) v S(M)* [2003] 1 IR 606.

law" (so that Article 34.3.2° was irrelevant to the issue that it had to determine), it considered that the context showed that determining whether or not a law enacted by a parliament under a previous constitutional regime remained in force could not be a jurisdiction to be exercised on a local basis.

> "I have no doubt that it was not intended by the framers of the Constitution that an issue as to the constitutionality of a law, whether it took the form of legislation or a rule of the common law, should be determined by a court of local and limited jurisdiction. The Constitution, viewed as a legal instrument, cannot, in my view, be equated to a statute of the Oireachtas or any form of secondary legislation, such as statutory instruments or byelaws, which may have a limited and even a purely local application and which may, appropriately, be construed by courts of local and limited jurisdiction, afforded such assistance as they may require by the High Court or this court, through the case stated machinery. The Constitution, as the fundamental law of the State, has a universal character and adjudications by courts of competent jurisdiction as to the legal efficacy of primary or secondary legislation, or rules of the common law, having regard to the provisions of the Constitution, are binding in their effect on all three organs of the State, not merely in the instant case, but in all cases to which the laws in question have application. To hold that District and Circuit Courts throughout the length and breadth of the State are entitled to adjudicate on those issues in any case where they arise, leading potentially to a multiplicity of conflicting decisions and serious uncertainty as to the state of the law, would be to attach wholly excessive weight to the undeniable fact that such issues are not expressly excluded from the jurisdiction of those courts."[17]

Whether or not Keane CJ was correct to ascribe such a specific intention to the framers of the Constitution, it seems that the rationale that he employed for denying such a constitutional jurisdiction to the District Court and the Circuit Court is one of the main reasons why Ireland has a quasi-concentrated rather than a diffuse system of judicial review of the constitutionality of legislation.

Professor Passaglia undertakes a useful review of the 'one-judgment' rule, the arguments made in relation to it and how it compares with the practice in other European countries. Although without very much public debate, the arguments against it have now prevailed, with the enactment of the Thirty-third Amendment of the Constitution Act 2013, which scheduled its repeal (outside the context of Article 26) in conjunction with the establishment in the course of 2014 of a Court of Appeal. The effects of Article 26, however, remain unaltered, both in relation to the "one-judgment" rule and in relation to the continuing prohibition in Article 34.3° on any court questioning the validity of a law, or any provision of a law, the Bill for which shall was referred under Article 26 of this Constitution, or the validity of a provision of a law where the corresponding provision in the Bill for such law was so

[17] *ibid* p 618. The Supreme Court left open the question of whether a court other than the High Court or Supreme Court that was not a court of 'local and limited jurisdiction' (ie, the Court of Criminal Appeal) could have been given the jurisdiction to decide upon the applicability of Art 50: *ibid,* p 619. With the impending establishment of a Court of Appeal with an explicit jurisdiction to review the validity of laws, as a replacement for the Court of Criminal Appeal, that point will lose any practical relevance.

referred. There have been several proposals over the years for the abolition of that rule, for the reasons that Professor Passaglia points out and it is to be hoped that this will be the subject of a further constitutional amendment over the next few years.[18]

On a more general level, Professor Passaglia makes a convincing argument that the slow pace at which the Irish High Court and Supreme Court explored and expanded the scope of the jurisdiction to review the validity of a law having regard to the provisions of the Constitution is by no means exceptional by international standards. He has identified here a topic that richly deserves further study, especially in view of the need to account for several decisions in the first few decades after the enactment of the Constitution, before the generally acknowledged period of judicial activism began in the early 1960s that nevertheless represented quite dramatic judicial incursions into issues of current political or social controversy, on a wholly or partly constitutional basis.[19]

4. Pulice and Carolan

Ms Pulice's chapter provides a meticulous and penetrating survey of the different interpretative techniques that Irish judges have used as the process of constitutional interpretation has unfolded over the last nine decades, concentrating on the literal, historical, purposive (or broad), harmonious, natural law methods.[20] It is in relation to the last three that we can most fruitfully draw comparisons with other contributions to the collection, most notably with Dr Carolan's and Dr Cahill's.

As Ms Pulice points out, at least in a broad sense, a purposive interpretation of the Constitution lies at the root of the development of the doctrine of unenumerated personal rights. The reference that Kenny J made to the Christian and democratic nature of the State, when first setting out the justification for this doctrine, surely appeals to a purposive interpretation of the constitutional text, even if this is tacit rather than explicit.[21] Insofar as the purposes of the Constitution are to be gathered from reading the document as a whole, a purposive interpretation cannot be divorced, in this context, for the adoption of a harmonious one.

As Ms Pulice and Dr Carolan's contributions make clear, especially in relation to the identification of unenumerated rights, these purposive or harmonious strands to the interpretation of Art 40 (and other provisions) were at one time tightly bound up with a reading of the Constitution through the lens of natural law, with all the problems that this has presented to the Irish courts in the last few decades. Even if the courts have largely sidelined natural law terminology and concepts in the last few decades, the challenge remains of finding a methodology of interpretation that

---

18 JM Kelly, *The Irish Constitution* (4th ed, Gerard W Hogan and Gerry Whyte ed, Lexis Nexis Butterworths, 2003) p. 915.

19 Examples include *Re Article 26 and the School Attendance Bill, 1942* [1943] IR 334; *National Union of Railwaymen v Sullivan* [1947] IR 77 (SC); *Buckley v Attorney General* [1950] IR 67 (SC); *Re Tilson, Infants* [1951] IR 1 (SC); *Educational Company of Ireland Ltd v Fitzpatrick (No 2)* [1961] IR 345 (SC).

20 Professor Rason and Dr Petrillo also touch on this issue in their chapter in the current volume: Nino Olivetti Rason and Pier Luigi Petrillo, "The Dialogue among Constitutional Judges, Parliaments and Executives" 138.

21 *Ryan v AG* [1965] IR 294 (HC) 313.

attributes to the Constitution a sufficiently determinate set of purposes and values so as to guide interpretation in a meaningful way, without putting in question the objectivity and transparency of this process of interpretation itself. Ms Pulice and Dr Carolan both set out clearly the process by which the Irish courts have disengaged themselves from an unselfconscious identification of the content of constitutional norms with a transcendent natural law. Ms Pulice sets out particularly clearly how the courts have tempered the invocation, such as it still exists, of natural law by reference to the need for interpretation of the Constitution that takes account of changes in prevailing social values and norms. Both authors set out how the decision in *Re Regulation of Information (Services outside the State for Termination of Pregnancies) Bill, 1995*[22] sets a clear limit to the role of natural law, by making it subordinate to the People's will, as expressed at a referendum. Both authors also describe how many judges have sought to give effect to their doubts about the fundamental legitimacy of the unenumerated personal rights doctrine by placing limits on its possible future extension.

However, the challenge already mentioned remains—of attributing to the Constitution a sufficiently determinate content to produce coherent interpretation of it, without leading to the appearance of "judicial oligarchy".[23] Are there any recent indications of how the courts, and especially the Supreme Court, may be attempting to meet this challenge?

As it happens, a recent decision of the Supreme Court provides an example of what may be a new methodological rigour in approaching these questions, drawing on the jurisprudential legacy of Henchy J.[24] As Dr Carolan outlines in his contribution to this volume, in a series of cases he attempted to develop a "human personality" approach to defining the parameters of the unenumerated personal rights doctrine—attempting to relate these to the

> "personal freedoms or immunities ... necessary to ensure [the citizen's] dignity and freedom as an individual in the type of society envisaged. The essence of those rights is that they inhere in the individual personality of the citizen in his capacity as a vital human component of the social, political and moral order posited by the Constitution."[25]

In the recent *Fleming* decision, the Supreme Court appears to endorse this as the correct method of approaching the interpretation of the guarantee of personal rights contained in Art 40.3, both in its enumerated and unenumerated aspects. In assessing the appellant's claim that the sweeping prohibition on assisted suicide[26] violated

> "her right to personal and bodily autonomy and self determination: specifically

---

22 [1995] 1 IR 1 (SC).

23 See the discussion of these issues in Desmond Clarke, "Ireland: A Republican Democracy, a Theocracy or a Judicial Oligarchy?" (2011) 29 *Irish Law Times* 81.

24 On which, generally, see Gerard Hogan, "Judicial Thought and Prose of Mr. Justice Seamus Henchy" (2011) 46 *Irish Jurist* 96.

25 *Norris v AG* [1984] IR 36 (SC) 71.

26 Criminal Law (Suicide) Act 1993, s 2(2).

> her right to make and carry out decisions about her own life including death; her right to privacy, her right to live (including her right to die)",[27]

the Court clearly saw its task as ultimately being to engage with "the values [the Constitution] protects in the rights it guarantees."[28] In this context, it was the appellant's own argument that relied on the passage from Henchy J's judgment in *Norris v AG*, part of which has already been quoted and which is discussed in greater detail in Dr Carolan's contribution.[29] However, the Court took Henchy J's postulates as the starting point for a very different kind of argument from the one that the appellant had urged on them:

> "These comments provide valuable guidance. Even so, as Henchy J recognised, the test for the identification of an unenumerated right, or the determination of the extent of an enumerated right, is a test necessarily lacking in precision, and there are irreducible areas of choice. It is all the more important therefore that the reasoning be as explicit as possible. The approach that any right inheres in a citizen by virtue of his or her personality and should be fundamental to the personal standing of the individual in the context of the social order envisaged by the Constitution provides a useful structure and focus for analysis."[30]

The reader is referred to the decision itself for the specific conclusions, adverse to the appellant's claims, that the Court drew from these premises.[31]

The crux of its reasoning was as follows:

> "At the level of abstract reasoning it is of course possible to argue that if a citizen has a right to life that must comprehend abandoning or terminating it. It is also possible to construct a libertarian argument that the State is not entitled to interfere with the decisions made by a person in respect of his or her own life up to and including a decision to terminate it. However, it is not possible to discern support for such a theory in the provisions of the Constitution, without imposing upon it a philosophy and values not detectable from it."[32]

It is notable, however, that—apart from referring to the express protection of life and of the person in Art 40.3.2°—the judgment is silent as to which specific features of the constitutional text contemplate a social order and reflect values that would be the "antithesis" of the right to terminate that life or have it terminated. Perhaps the Court considered that these features, apart from Art 40.3.2°, were so obvious that mention of them would be superfluous and one could speculate on what these might be, starting with the references in the Preamble to the ultimate accountability of the

---

27 *Fleming v Ireland* [2013] IESC 19 (29 April 2013) para 109, Denham CJ.

28 *ibid,* para 110.

29 The Court also referred to Henchy J's anticipation of his reasoning in *Norris* in the shorter passage from his judgment in *McGee v AG* [1974] IR 284, 325, where he refers to "what the Constitution, expressly or by necessary implication, deems to be fundamental to the personal standing of the individual in question in the context of the social order envisaged by the Constitution" as the yardstick for proper interpretation of Art 40.3.

30 *Fleming v Ireland* [2013] IESC 19 (29 April 2013) para 113.

31 *ibid.*

32 *ibid.*

individual to God, the dignity of the individual and "true social order". However, the laconic nature of the judgment does point to some problems with this new standard methodology, if that is what it proves to be, adopted from Henchy J's pioneering judgments in *McGee* and *Norris*.

First, it seems doubtful that the Court meets its own requirement (or perhaps its aspiration) that "the reasoning be as explicit as possible" when judges identify (or refuse to identify) an unenumerated personal right or determine the extent of an enumerated personal right. Secondly, the editors of JM Kelly's *The Irish Constitution* rightly observe that while the doctrine of harmonious interpretation (of which the approach taken in *Fleming* is a sub-type) "seems highly rational and useful" in certain specific contexts, its admission, "unless related to other parts of the express text of the Constitution, seems to open the door widely to judicial policy-making."[33] Furthermore, Dr Aileen Kavanagh has acutely analysed how Henchy J's judgment in *Norris* represents an inflection of the notion of "Christian and democratic" values in the direction of a preference for the dignity and freedom of the individual, as opposed to an acceptance of the religiously based attitudes that prevailed in 1937 as setting limits to the rights of sexual minorities.[34] It is useful to recall a passage that Dr Carolan partly cites in his chapter:

> "[B]y referring to the purposive Christian ethos of the State as set out in the Preamble, Henchy J was thereby emphasising the ultimate constitutional goal of respecting the dignity and freedom of the individual, rather than invoking Christian or Catholic teaching in order to assess the constitutionality of this particular law. Ultimately, the minority judgments in *Norris* were based on the dignitarian, democratic and liberty dimensions of the Constitution, rather than those aspects which seemed redolent of Christian beliefs. The majority judgment was based on the view that the Constitution recognised the supremacy of Christian values.
>
> What this line of case law shows is that there were various strands of judicial thought emerging on the Irish Supreme Court on the role of Christian values when interpreting the Constitution. One line … gave pride of place to the dignity and freedom of the individual in the context of a judicial decision which was informed by the values of prudence, justice and charity which could change over time. The other gave greater emphasis to Christian values and the Christian ethos of the Irish people when they enacted the Irish Constitution in 1937. Of course, these Christian and dignitarian strands are not necessarily mutually exclusive, since the value of the dignity of the individual is part of Christian ethics. Therefore, whether a judge pursued one strand or another would not necessarily lead him or her to different outcomes. Nor is it the case that reliance on Christian values would necessarily lead to a "conservative" outcome or one which would align with Catholic social teaching relating to sexuality. For example, even in the trenchant dissents in *Norris*, Henchy and McCarthy JJ drew on some of the Christian elements in the Constitution to support their position which came down in favour of the liberty and freedom of the individual. And although the decision in *McGee* went against the

---

33 JM Kelly, *The Irish Constitution* (4th ed, Gerard W Hogan and Gerry Whyte ed, Lexis Nexis Butterworths, 2003) 12.

34 Aileen Kavanagh, "The Irish Constitution at 75 years: Natural Law, Christian Values and The Ideal of Justice" (2012) 48 *Irish Jurist* 71.

> Catholic Church's position on contraception, it was justified in part in terms of the importance of marriage and the Christian value of charity.
>
> Be that as it may, the *Norris* case showed that sometimes these different strands could come apart and therefore the general question about the appropriate approach to constitutional adjudication really mattered."[35]

Restoring in this way the original context of the passage from Henchy J's dissent in *Norris* on which the Supreme Court places so much reliance in *Fleming* helps to make clear how the "explicit reasoning" employed in that case falls short of the standard set in that earlier case. There, at least, the differences of approach between majority and minority were reasonably plain see, as Dr Kavanagh explores. In *Fleming*, by contrast, any such argumentation about the values with which the Constitution is imbued is largely tacit, and much is left to the reader's powers of implication to reconstruct exactly how the Court gets from its broad premises to its actual conclusion. This opacity may be a result, of course, of the one-judgment rule (which Ms Pulice lucidly describes and which did not apply in *Norris*, since the case dealt with a pre-Constitution statute). Nevertheless, the clear contrasts between the different interpretations adopted in *Norris* are a reminder of the difficulties inherent in any methodology of constitutional interpretation, whether it chooses to bring them to the surface or not. As will be discussed presently, the contrast between the High Court and Supreme Court judgments in *Fleming* itself goes some way to confirming this.

Another feature of *Fleming*, which may ultimately be of more or less significance than the endorsement of Henchy J's methodology for the identification of unenumerated personal rights, is the possible endorsement that the Supreme Court gives to Hogan J' recent attempts, in effect, to substitute for a large part of the existing *corpus* of unenumerated personal rights a new and quite broad understanding of the enumerated personal right to protection of "the person" in Art 40.3.2°. Hogan J has been engaged in this project for the last several years, but this appears to have been the Supreme Court's first opportunity to pronounce on his success in persuading two of his High Court colleagues to adopt this approach in the judgment of the Divisional Court in *Fleming*.[36] Although none of these decisions fully clarify the relationship of the enumerated personal right to "similar and over-lapping rights such as the right to bodily integrity and personal privacy which have been judicially

35 *ibid,* 85–86.

36 *Fleming v Ireland* [2013] IEHC 2 (10 January 2013) para 49 (Kearns P, Carney and Hogan JJ). Some of the earlier cases (and one subsequent one) in which Hogan J pioneered this new approach are: *Kinsella v Governor of Mountjoy Prison* [2011] IEHC 235 (12 June 2011); *H (a minor) v HSE* [2011] IEHC 297 (18 July 2011); *Sullivan v Boylan (No 1)* [2012] IEHC 389 (4 October 2012) and *Sullivan v Boylan (No 2)* [2013] IEHC 104 (12 March 2013). Before his appointment as a judge of the High Court, Dr Hogan had put on record his scepticism about the unenumerated personal rights doctrine, partly inspired by the ur-critic of that development, the late Professor John M Kelly: Gerard Hogan, "Unenumerated Personal Rights: *Ryan*'s Case Re-evaluated" (1990–1992) 45–47 *Irish Jurist* 95 [*Liber Memorialis: John M Kelly*]. For more recent, and more far-reaching, critiques of the doctrine, see Gerard Casey, "The 'Logically Faultless' Argument for Unenumerated Rights in the Constitution" (2004) 22 *Irish Law Times* 246 and Desmond M Clarke, "Unenumerated Rights in Constitutional Law" (2011) 18(2) *Dublin University Law Journal* 101. For a proposal that the courts should, essentially, embrace the indeterminacy of the constitutional text and use it for progressive social purposes, see Lesley A Walter, "Law as Literature: Illuminating the Debate over Constitutional Consistency" [2004] *Cork Online Law Review* 10.

held to be protected as implied personal rights for the purposes of Article 40.3.1",[37] it seems likely that, should this wide interpretation of the protection of "the person" ultimately prevail, those particular unenumerated rights will become redundant. The connection with Henchy J's methodology is clear, as the High Court—in addressing how to determine the content of the protection of "the person"—went on to cite the same passage from *Norris* on "the citizen ... as a vital human component of the social, political and moral order posited by the Constitution" as the Supreme Court endorsed in the *Fleming* appeal.[38]

The Supreme Court's decision in relation to the applicability and scope of Art 40.3.2° was, of course, conditioned by the argument presented to it by counsel, on which—as Dr Carolan points out in his contribution, echoing an observation of Dr Donal Coffey[39]—a court in the Irish system largely depends:

> "The appellant has not sought to identify any unenumerated right other than such as flows from the respect for and protection of life and of the person within the terms of Article 40.3. Within that context however the appellant invokes constitutional values of autonomy, self-determination and dignity. It is undoubted that the Constitution recognises and respects these general values in the rights protected by it. It does not follow, and it is not claimed, however, that every law which impinges on the life of individuals is even prima facie inconsistent with the Constitution. Whether therefore values of autonomy, self-determination and dignity, as they find expression in the rights guaranteed by the Constitution, provide constitutional protection for the performance of specific acts depends on a concrete analysis of the impact of any law which is impugned in a particular case on the life of the individual, and a careful consideration of the provisions of the Constitution and the values its protects in the rights it guarantees."[40]

One immediate observation can be made from a comparison of the High Court and the Supreme Court decisions in *Fleming*. The High Court considered that the application of a general methodology of this kind led to the following conclusion:

> "Inasmuch, therefore, as the plaintiff advances a conscientious and considered decision to seek the assistance of others to take active steps to end her own life in the face of a terminal illness which has ravaged her body and rendered her life one of almost complete misery, we consider that such a decision is *in principle* engaged by the right to personal autonomy which lies at the core of the protection of the person by Article 40.3.2. In that respect, therefore, such a decision is not really properly to be regarded as either an implied constitutional right in its own right or a right derived from an implied constitutional right in the manner discussed (and rejected) by the US Supreme Court in *Washington v. Glucksberg* 521 US 207 (1997): it is rather a facet of that personal autonomy

37 *Fleming v Ireland* [2013] IEHC 2 (10 January 2013) para 49.

38 *ibid,* para 50; *Fleming v Ireland* [2013] IESC 19 (29 April 2013) para 111.

39 Eoin Carolan, "Evaluating the Judicial Role in Developing the Irish Constitution" (this volume) 65 citing Donal Coffey, "The Judiciary of the Irish Free State" (2011) 33 *Dublin University Law Journal* (ns) 61, 65.

40 *ibid*, para 110.

> which is necessarily protected by the express words of Article 40.3.2 with regard to the protection of the person."[41]

The High Court then rejected the applicant's claim on the basis that s 2(2) of the Criminal Law (Suicide) Act 1993 was a constitutional restriction of that right, applying the test of proportionality.[42]

The Supreme Court, which placed the right to life and its possible corollaries in the foreground, rather than the protection of the person, reached a diametrically opposite conclusion in relation to whether any constitutional right was engaged by the appellant's desire to end her own life in these circumstances.

> "113. … Can it be said that the right to life as so guaranteed, whether on its own or in conjunction with the guarantee of the protection of the person, necessarily implies as a corollary, the right of every citizen to terminate his or her life and to have assistance in so doing? … [I]t is not possible to discern support for such a theory in the provisions of the Constitution, without imposing upon it a philosophy and values not detectable from it. A right which extends to the termination of life must, as counsel for the appellant recognised in closing submissions, necessarily extend to a right to have life terminated by a third party in a case of total incapacity. The concept of autonomy which extends not just to an entitlement, but to a positive right to terminate life and to have assistance in so doing, would necessarily imply a very extensive area of decision in relation to activity which is put, at least prima facie, beyond regulation by the State. When it is considered that recognition of such a right implies correlative duties on the State and others to defend and vindicate that right (and which must necessarily restrict those parties' freedom of action), it is apparent that the right contended for by the appellant would sweep very far indeed. It cannot properly be said that such an extensive right or rights is fundamental to the personal standing of the individual in question in the context of the social order envisaged by the Constitution. The right to life which the State is obliged to vindicate, is a right which implies that a citizen is living as a vital human component in the social, political and moral order posited by the Constitution. … [T]he protection of the right to life cannot necessarily or logically entail a right, which the State must also respect and vindicate, to terminate that life or have it terminated. In the social order contemplated by the Constitution, and the values reflected in it, that would be the antithesis of the right rather than the logical consequence of it.
>
> 114. Thus, insofar as the Constitution, in the rights it guarantees, embodies the values of autonomy and dignity and more importantly the rights in which

[41] *Fleming v Ireland* [2013] IEHC 2 (10 January 2013) para 52. In this respect, the High Court's decision seems to be more in keeping than the Supreme Court's with an emerging trend in the European Court of Human Rights towards recognising "that an individual's right to decide the way in which and at which point his or her life should end, provided that he or she was in a position to freely form his or her own judgment and to act accordingly, [is] one of the aspects of the right to respect for private life within the meaning of Article 8 of the Convention" App No 67810/10, *Gross v Switzerland* (Second Section) judgment of 14 May 2013, para 59, citing *Pretty v UK* (2002) 35 EHRR 1 (Fourth Section, 29 April 2002) para 67; App No 31322/07, *Haas v Switzerland* (First Section) judgment of 20 January 2011, para 51 and *Koch v Germany* (2013) 56 EHRR 6 (Former Fifth Section, 20 July 2011) paras 51–52.

[42] *ibid*, paras 72 and 77.

> they find expression, do not extend to a right of assisted suicide. Accordingly the Court concludes that there is no constitutional right which the State, including the courts, must protect and vindicate, either to commit suicide, or to arrange for the termination of one's life at a time of one's choosing."[43]

The *Fleming* case is a reminder, therefore, that despite both courts' efforts that their "reasoning be as explicit as possible", the "irreducible areas of choice" in judicial interpretation of the Constitution acknowledged by the Supreme Court remain.[44] One thing one can say specifically of *Fleming* is that although the Supreme Court's *conclusion* that no right of the kind claimed by the appellant exists is stated clearly and emphatically, its implicit assertion that it was "as explicit as possible" in explaining the *reasons* why it came to this conclusion is questionable. While the conclusion and the structure of the argument that leads up to it are quite clear, it is left almost entirely to the reader to extrapolate for himself or herself why it is that "the personal standing of the individual in question in the context of the social order envisaged by the Constitution" is inconsistent with the claim being made by the appellant. In view of the significant differences in hermeneutic and ethical standpoints that Aileen Kavanagh has identified as the context for Henchy J's original introduction in *McGee* and *Norris* of the sort of methodology that found favour in *Fleming*, it is particularly regrettable that these aspects of the Court's reasoning remain to be inferred in this way.

On the issue of "transforming" some unenumerated personal rights into aspects of protection of "the person" under Art 40.3.2°, questions might also legitimately be posed about the actual effect this will have on the clarity or predictability of judicial reasoning. This process of judicial re-interpretation of the Constitution parallels, in part, a long-standing suggestion for an amendment of the Constitution in a similar sense.

> "One solution would be to amend the Constitution by incorporating in Article 40 an expanded recital of specific personal rights, laying down in each case the standards upon which the Oireachtas may delimit such rights. We would then be back to the simple principle of testing black-and-white constitutional norms."[45]

Gerard Hogan was an influential member of the Constitution Review Group, whose report, published in 1996, remains a starting point for many discussions of questions of constitutional reform. The Group's basic recommendation in this area was as follows:

> "On balance, the Review Group favours an amendment of Article 40.3.1° which would provide a comprehensive list of fundamental rights which could specifically encompass the personal rights which have been identified by the Irish courts to date, and which might also include those set out in the European Convention on Human Rights and the International Covenant on Civil and

---

43 *Fleming v Ireland* [2013] IESC 19 (29 April 2013) paras 113–114.

44 *ibid*, para 113.

45 JM Kelly, *Fundamental Rights in the Irish Law and Constitution* (2nd ed, Allen Figgis, 1967) cited by Gerard Hogan, "Unenumerated Personal Rights: *Ryan*'s Case Re-evaluated" (1990–1992) 45–47 *Irish Jurist* 95, 116.

Political Rights, so far as may be considered appropriate, and other personal rights which might be particularly appropriate in an Irish context, and which should confine further recognition of fundamental rights by the courts to those necessarily implicit in the rights expressly listed."[46]

The group specifically anticipated and discussed the problem of deciding at what level of generality these rights should be stated and how much should be left to judicial interpretation.

> "In any such comprehensive listing, the rights should be expressed with a sufficient level of generality to enable the courts to identify within them specific rights which would be necessarily implicit within the broadly described rights. …
>
> Generally speaking, it would seem desirable, in attempting to formulate a comprehensive list of rights, to state the rights in as broad a form as possible. If it is clear that one right is merely a particular instance of a more general right, it should be sufficient to state the general right."[47]

This approach to the recasting of personal rights guarantees has been the subject of some quite sharp criticism.

> "[W]hen it comes to putting meat on the bones of [their] proposals, the Review Group, ironically, having criticised the unenumerated rights doctrine for its lack of a coherent fundamental rights theory commits exactly the same error. Its approach is entirely ad hoc. …
>
> Nowhere does the Constitution Review Group tell us what common coherent theory of fundamental rights informs the current list of unenumerated constitutional rights. Nor does it attempt to undertake the same task in relation to the international instruments mentioned. … Thus, while the Review Group's recommendations may resolve the judicial legitimacy problem of unenumerated rights jurisprudence, it does not nothing to address the larger question of the legitimacy of rights protection, and which version of rights the Constitution should follow."[48]

The Supreme Court certainly made no objection in *Fleming* to subsuming a large number of the personal rights of the citizen, previously understood to be unenumerated in the sense of being protected by the general guarantee in Art 40.3.1°, under the heading of protection of "the person" in Art 40.3.2°. In the account that Hogan J and the Divisional Court in *Fleming* have so far given, that second guarantee includes protection of "not simply the integrity of the human body, but also the integrity of the human mind and personality",[49] "a holistic approach to the protection of [a minor]'s welfare and general best interests",[50] protection from "subjection by unlawful means … to what would objectively be regarded as acute

---

46 Constitution Review Group *Report* (Pn 2632) (Stationery Office, 1996) 258.

47 *ibid*, 258, 260.

48 Andrew Butler and Rory O'Connell, "A Critical Analysis of Ireland's Constitutional [*sic*] Review Group Report" (1998) 33 *Irish Jurist* 237, 250–251.

49 *Kinsella v Governor of Mountjoy Prison* [2011] IEHC 235 (12 June 2011) para 9.

50 *H (a minor) v HSE* [2011] IEHC 297 (18 July 2011) para 15.

mental distress"[51] and "the right to personal autonomy which lies at the core of the protection of the person".[52] In *Fleming*, the High Court also tells us that some unenumerated rights, such as rights to personal privacy, bodily integrity and dignity, are "similar and over-lapping rights" or "overlapping and ancillary" in relation to the protection of "the person" under Art 40.3.2°.[53]

We may take this process of reinterpretation as an analogue of the kind of constitutional amendment suggested by Kelly in 1967, Hogan in 1992 and the Constitution Review Group in 1996. How does it compare in terms of the goals that each of those proponents set? The new interpretation does avoid the embarrassment of having to rely on Kenny J's reasoning in *Ryan v Attorney General* and the lack of any alternative justification for reaching the conclusion he did, which can come under ever more searching scrutiny in recent years.[54] In this sense, it does resolve that aspect of the "judicial legitimacy problem" in the sense that Butler and O'Connell (cited above) have described. The "Henchy" methodology adopted in *Fleming* does make some attempt to counteract the objection that constitutional rights are identified (here, by implication rather than through cataloguing) in an ad hoc manner—though perhaps with limited success, as we have seen. Does referring some many different rights, albeit somewhat specific ones, to the protection of "the person" that stating "a general right" "in as broad a form as possible", as the Constitution Review Group envisaged? In relation to the specification of personal rights, in a new and comprehensive list, the Review Group, insofar as is relevant in present context, recommended the following should be included in the catalogue for Art 40:

> "3 1° revised general personal rights clause
> 2° i right to life and *person*
> ii no death penalty
> iii *right to bodily integrity (including the right not to be subjected to experimentation, not to be tortured or inhumanely treated and to have one's health protected)*
> iv right to one's good name
> v *right to privacy*
> 3° right to life of unborn…"[55]

If this is what the Review Group proposed by way of stating "general rights" "in as broad a form as possible", it seems questionable whether referring all of the rights referred to in the words italicised above to the protection simply of "the person" in Art 40.3.2° does much better than the existing unenumerated rights doctrine does in meeting the desiderata set out by Kelly, Hogan, the Review Group and others over the years. Judicial interpretation, of course, has to make the best of the

---

51 *Sullivan v Boylan (No 1)* [2012] IEHC 389 (4 October 2012) para 23.

52 *Fleming v Ireland* [2013] IEHC 2 (10 January 2013) para 52.

53 *ibid*, paras 49, 77.

54 See particularly the critiques of Casey and Clarke, cited at n90.

55 Constitution Review Group, *Report* (Pn 2632) (Stationery Office, 1996) 265. Emphasis supplied. Curiously, the Review Group recommended retaining the existing reference to the right to "the person" even though there was hardly any indication in 1996 as to what that provision meant: JM Kelly, *The Irish Constitution* (4th ed, Gerard W Hogan and Gerry Whyte ed, Lexis Nexis Butterworths, 2003) 1404–1402. A glimmer of the recent development in case law is visible in the passing comment here that "this word might have been plausibly made into the immediate root of some of the 'unspecified personal rights' derived from Article 40.3.1°"; *ibid*, 1403.

constitutional text as it finds it, a rigour from which the proposers of amendments can largely escape.

It is true that each of the "bundle of rights" that Hogan J has identified in the last two years, with their recent extension in *Fleming*, does have some plausible relationship to an accessible concept of human personality, so that the sub-rights associated with the protection of "the person" of every citizen do have an affinity or coherence that cannot be attributed to the wide and varied catalogue of unenumerated personal rights that have so far been identified. How far it can be expanded beyond that is as a yet unsettled. One can easily see how certain other unenumerated rights could also be subsumed under the protection of "the person", such as the right to know the identity of one's natural parents,[56] the right to marry,[57] or the right to procreate.[58] There could also be a foreseeable extension to embrace the right of access to the courts and the right to fair procedures,[59] a development that would certainly be supportable, at least in part, by reference to Art 16 of the International Covenant on Civil and Political Rights: "Everyone shall have the right to recognition everywhere as a person before the law."[60]

It seems doubtful that one could legitimately extend the scope of protection of "the person" to encompass fully all of the unenumerated personal rights that have thus far been recognised—such as the right to work and earn a livelihood,[61] the right to strike[62] or various socio-economic rights, whose existence is in any event increasingly doubtful.[63] Whether and how far other unenumerated rights, notably the

[56] *O'T v B* [1998] 3 IR 321 (SC).

[57] *O'Shea v Ireland* [2007] 2 IR 313 (HC).

[58] *Murray v Ireland* [1985] IR 352 (HC); [1991] ILRM 542 (SC).

[59] JM Kelly, *The Irish Constitution* (4th ed, Gerard W Hogan and Gerry Whyte ed, Lexis Nexis Butterworths, 2003) 640–661 and 1446–1466.

[60] UN General Assembly, *International Covenant on Civil and Political Rights*, 16 December 1966, UNTS vol 999, p 171. See UN Human Rights Committee (HRC), *General Comment No 17: Rights of the child (Art 24)*, 7 April 1989, paras 7 and 8; *General Comment No 28: Equality of rights between men and women (article 3)*, 29 March 2000, para 19. This concept has special significance for the rights of people with disabilities, in view of its reinforcement by Art 12(2) of the Convention on the Rights of Persons with Disabilities: UN General Assembly, *Convention on the Rights of People with Disabilities*, 13 December 2006, UNTS vol 2515, p 3, Art 12(2). See Amita Dhanda, "Universal Legal Capacity as a Universal Human Right" in *Mental Health and Human Rights: Vision, Praxis, and Courage* (Michael Dudley, Derrick Silove and Fran Gale ed, OUP, 2012) 177–188; Gábor Gombos, "Human rights-based capacity legislation long overdue" *Irish Times*, 23 May 2013, http://www.irishtimes.com/news/crime-and-law/human-rights-based-capacity-legislation-long-overdue-1.1374176 (last accessed 23 May 2013); Joint Committee on Justice, Defence and Equality, *Report on hearings in relation to the Scheme of the Mental Capacity Bill 2012,* http://www.oireachtas.ie/parliament/media/michelle/Mental-capacity-text-REPORT-300412.pdf (last accessed 23 May 2013). See also the opinion of Judge Vučinić in App No 26828/06 *Kurić v Slovenia* (2013) 56 EHRR 20 (Grand Chamber).

[61] JM Kelly, *The Irish Constitution* (4th ed, Gerard W Hogan and Gerry Whyte ed, Lexis Nexis Butterworths, 2003) 1425–1436.

[62] *ibid*, 1478–1481.

[63] *ibid*, 1481–1483. For two more recent judicial rejections of similar claims, see: *Magee v Farrell* [2009] 4 IR 703 (SC); *MEO v Minister for Justice, Equality and Law Reform* [2012] IEHC 394 (5 September 2012). In the latter case the basic issue of constitutional law concerned was certified by the High Court as being fit for appeal to the Supreme Court: [2012] IEHC 448 (2 November 2012).

right to travel[64] or the right to communicate[65] can be encompassed under the "new" constitutional protection of the person remains less clear. In the case of the latter right, there would seem to be a clear basis in the existing case law for reassigning it to Art 40.3.2° in that manner Hogan J proposes—

> "It appears to the Court that the right to communicate must be one of the most basic rights of man. Next to the right to nurture it is hard to imagine any right more important to man's survival. But in this context one is speaking of a right to convey one's needs and emotions by words or gestures as well as by rational discourse."[66]

This is confirmed by the Supreme Court's contrast between that right and "the public activities of the citizen in a democratic society", which are the subject of the enumerated rights to freedom of expression, freedom of assembly and freedom of association.[67]

As a general matter, one can say that the more one inflates the category of sub-rights protected by the reference to "the person" in Art 40.3.2°, the less clear it becomes that this new doctrine has satisfactorily answered any of the most substantial objections made to the existing unenumerated rights doctrine. It hardly seems more justifiable to attribute an overly inflated category of rights to the reference to "the person ... of every citizen" in Art 40.3.2° than it does to attach them to the reference to "personal rights of the citizen" in Art 40.3.1°, even if it does overcome some of the specific objections to the interpretation upon which the second approach rests.[68]

Perhaps one useful source of guidance might be the case law of the European Court of Human Rights on the meaning of the phrase "private life" in Art 8 of the Convention. That Court often has to explore where the outer limits of that broad concept lie and some of its case law on, for example, the extent to which restrictions on access to professions or occupations may involve an interference with respect for "private life", might prove helpful to the Irish courts, should they further pursue Hogan J's project of giving substantive content to the notion of protection of "the person".[69] While any such reference to the case law would have to take account of the different nature and structure of the two instruments and, specifically, of the differences in the complementary relationship between rights that are recognised by each, some support might be derived from the Strasbourg case law in trying to create an account of how some personal rights arise under Bunreacht na hÉireann that gains wide acceptance as being as more coherent and defensible than the unenumerated personal rights doctrine. It is, in any case, too early to make any definitive assessment

64 *ibid,* 1467–1468.

65 *ibid,* 1475–1477.

66 *Murphy v Independent Radio and Television Commission* [1999] 1 IR 12 (SC) 24.

67 *ibid.*

68 Gerard Casey, "The 'Logically Faultless' Argument for Unenumerated Rights in the Constitution" (2004) 22 *Irish Law Times* 246; Desmond M Clarke, "Unenumerated Rights in Constitutional Law" (2011) 18(2) *Dublin University Law Journal* 101.

69 See, for example, App Nos 55480/00 and 59330/00 *Sidabras and Džiautas v Lithuania* (2006) 42 EHRR 6 (Second Section) (exclusion from public employment and professions); App Nos 46133/99 and 48183/99 *Smirnova v Russia* (2004) 39 EHRR 22 (Third Section) (deprivation of identity card); App No 26828/06 *Kurić v Slovenia* (2013) 56 EHRR 20 (Grand Chamber) (denial of citizenship).

of whether this new doctrine of what one might call "semi-enumerated" personal rights will make a significant difference to Irish constitutional law and whether it can be categorised as an improvement to it, especially bearing in mind the standards by which the unenumerated personal rights doctrine has thus far been assessed.

5. Comba

Professor Comba's chapter is a penetrating and subtle examination of constitutional and other sources of legitimacy in Irish administrative law, making ample reference to the previously published work of another of our contributors, Dr Carolan.[70] Referring to Dr Carolan's work, Professor Comba outlines the problems with the "transmission belt" theory,

> "according to which the political legitimacy of the legislature is transferred to the administration in so far as the administration, being part of the executive power, limits itself to the execution of the will of the Parliament."[71]

He also outlines "other possible reasons for the legitimacy of the administration" such as "technical expertise … to justify the exercise of discretionary power by administrative bodies".[72] These remarks are particularly apposite in view of one particular recent decision of the Supreme Court holding to be constitutionally invalid the legislative provisions under which provisions of collective agreements ("registered employment agreements") could be made binding, under pain of criminal sanctions, on employers and employees who were not parties to the agreements when they were made.[73] To a great extent, the decision is an example of the courts applying the principle of the non-delegation of legislative power. In this respect, O'Donnell J, giving the judgment of the Court, takes some pains to distinguish the case before the Court from *Cityview Press v AnCO*[74] (and by implication, at least, to disagree with Professor Casey's characterisation of the implications of the decision in the earlier case[75]). In that regard, the decision will no doubt contribute to a continuation of a general discussion of the non-delegation doctrine and its merits.[76] However, one aspect of the Supreme Court's reasoning in *McGowan* is worth some more detailed attention:

> "What is unusual and possibly unique is that the law making power granted under the 1946 Act is granted over a broad area of human activity to private persons, themselves unidentified and unidentifiable at the time of the passage of the legislation. … [I]t is clear that this specific provision is being made, not by a subordinate public body governed by public law, but by participants in the industry who were empowered to make regulations for themselves and for all others within that industry who may be competitors and whose interests may not be aligned with the makers of the REA. This is not a grant of a power to

[70] Eoin Carolan, *The New Separation of Powers* (OUP, 2009).
[71] Mario Comba, "Legitimacy of Administration under the Evolving Influence of Constitutional Law" at p.84 of the current volume.
[72] *ibid* at p.85.
[73] *McGowan v Labour Court* [2013] IESC 21 (9 May 2013).
[74] [1980] IR 381 (SC).
[75] James P Casey, *Constitutional Law in Ireland* (3rd ed, Sweet & Maxwell, 2000) 223.
[76] Eoin Carolan, *The New Separation of Powers* (OUP, 2009) 62–63.

> make regulations over a limited area subject to explicit or implicit guidance and review. It is an unlimited grant of power in relation to employment terms, made to bodies unidentifiable at the time of the passage of the legislation and without intermediate review. On its surface therefore, this appears to be a facial breach of Article 15.2.1."[77]

In assessing the function of the Labour Court, which had to approve the registration of employment agreements in order for them to become binding on non-parties, the Court made a related point:

> "[T]he power of approval and registration is itself delegated to an intermediate body, in this case the Labour Court. The degree of autonomy and discretion afforded to that body and the lack of a mechanism for appeal or review on the merits, means that any control of the exercise of the regulation making power is necessarily attenuated."[78]

These aspects of the Supreme Court's reasoning in *McGowan* clearly show a strong attachment to some version of the "transmission belt" theory, but overlapping with a concern about the scope of judicial review of the making of norms that are imposed by law on those who do not consent to their making. In that respect, it might be more productive for the courts to re-examine the scope of the judicial review jurisdiction itself, rather than to force statute law—through compliance with the non-delegation—to adhere to a formal template that may have little correspondence to administrative, economic and social realities. This aspect of *McGowan* highlights the value of a nuanced view that Dr Carolan has elsewhere taken of the proper re-conceptualisation of "the administration" and of breaking the dependence of judicial review upon the *ultra vires* concept, so that judicial review becomes "an independent process of value-oriented review".[79] In particular, the nature of the judicial argumentation in *McGowan* suggests that Dr Carolan's proposal for a widening of the field of judicial review would be a more productive response to the situation the Court identifies, rather than a falling back on a formalistic account of the nature of delegated power—

> "[J]udicial review ought to be extended to encompass all aspects of administrative governance—including those third parties who are involved in the exercise of governmental power."[80]

It is also possible that *McGowan* was miscast as a case primarily concerning the delegation of legislative powers in the first place. The principle or policy that terms of employment across a particular sector of employment ought to be determined,

---

77 *McGowan v Labour Court* [2013] IESC 21 (9 May 2013) para 25. The Court also implicitly contrasted AnCO with the original parties to employment agreements, by describing the former as a "public law body exercising powers constrained by statute" (*ibid*, para 23). A finding of unconstitutionality could still have been avoided had the legislation provided for the Labour Court's powers of approval and registration in such a way that registered employment agreements merely gave effect to principles and policies that were contained in the Act itself, but this was not the case here: *ibid*, paras 26–30.

78 *ibid*, para 26.

79 Eoin Carolan, *The New Separation of Powers* (OUP, 2009) 224.

80 *ibid*, 192. See also Catherine Donnelly, *Delegation of Governmental Power to Private Parties: A Comparative Perspective* (OUP, 2007).

with the force of law, by collective bargaining by representative groups of employers and employees is arguably quite a clear one, without having to specify what the content of those agreements might be. It is also a principle of policy that, prima facie, seems generally consistent with the broad corporatist influence that is discernible in several parts of the Constitution.[81] A more productive and meaningful exercise might have been to analyse whether that policy or principle, as implemented in the legislation under review, was an unjustifiable interference with constitutional rights (whether those of employers or employees) such as property rights, freedom to run a business or earn a livelihood, or freedom of association.

In that regard, there are several prior decisions of the Supreme Court that are arguably more relevant than the delegation to a meaningful consideration of the constitutionality of the legislation at hand.[82] Apart from the fact that the courts generally have to decide cases on the basis of the arguments made to them, it is true that the same features of legislation may point both to a violation of the separation of powers and of the constitutional rights of those affected.[83] Nevertheless, to approach these cases from the point of view of the effect of the legislation on the constitutional rights of those affected, rather than in terms of a somewhat formalistic version of the separation of powers would, it is suggested, make the fundamental issues—relating to principles of social justice—more transparent and the courts more accountable for their decisions. This would be particularly the case if the courts were to act on Dr Carolan's laudable suggestion of significantly extending the scope of judicial review to encompass third parties—such as the employers and employees whose agreements were sought to be enforced across the sector—who are involved in the exercise of governmental power.

Professor Comba's chapter proceeds from an examination of the role of delegation theory in Irish administrative law to a consideration of the substantive values that Dr Carolan and others have suggested provide the basis for values-oriented judicial review: legitimate expectations, proportionality, procedural fairness and the duty to give reasons.[84] These closely parallel the three constitutional influences on Irish administrative law that Gerard Hogan has outlined: the constitutionalisation of the right to impartial administrative procedures; the right to damages for the breach of constitutional rights; and the principle of proportionality, under the perspective of the legitimate expectations doctrine.[85]

In the very valuable closing part of his contribution, Professor Comba examines the differing roles that the last-mentioned doctrine plays in Irish and Italian

---

[81] Consitution of Ireland, Arts 15.3, 18, 19 and 45. See Anthony Whelan, "Constitutional Democracy, Community and Corporatism" in *Irish Human Rights Yearbook* (Gerard Quinn ed, Round Hall, 1995) 97.

[82] For example, *National Union of Railwaymen v Sullivan* [1947] IR 77 (SC) and *Re Employment Equality Bill, 1996* [1997] 2 IR 321.

[83] As was the case in *John Grace Fried Chicken Ltd v Catering JLC* [2011] 3 IR 211 (HC).

[84] See *Mallak v Minister for Justice Equality and Law Reform* [2012] IESC 59 (6 December 2012) for an emphatic confirmation of the general character of the duty to give reasons in Irish administrative law.

[85] G Hogan, "Introduzione alla costituzione irlandese" in *Le Costituzioni dei Paesi dell'Unione europea* (E Palici di Suni, F Cassella and M Comba ed, Cedam, 2001) 435, cited by Mario Comba, "Legitimacy of Administration under the Evolving Influence of Constitutional Law" 84.

administrative law. The decisions of Clarke J in *Lett v Wexford Borough Council*[86] and *Atlantic Marine Supplies Ltd v Minister for Transport*[87] offer particularly clear and thoughtful analyses of that doctrine. In *Atlantic Marine Supplies*, he decided a point that he avoided in *Lett*,[88] by concluding that damages can be awarded for a breach of a legitimate expectation.[89] That conclusion was confirmed by the Supreme Court in the appeal in *Lett*, which held—in contrast to Clarke J's approach in the decision under appeal, which had avoided this issue—that damages may be awarded in this situation:

> "I recognise the reasons for caution in this regard not least because this is an issue which would benefit from more extensive argument in a future case but it seems to me in principle at least, and indeed by analogy with the position in estoppel in private law, that the issue for the Court is that once a legitimate expectation or estoppel has been identified, it is necessary to make good the equity so found, and that in such circumstances again in principle, the Court can make an order, whether characterised as damages or restitution, in order to make good the breach identified."[90]

In addition, Clarke J's recent judgments offer a nuanced and convincing account of the distinction between substantive and procedural legitimate expectations and the factors that are particularly relevant to each.

6. O'Neill

Dr O'Neill's chapter, although it concentrates on one specific topic (the right to fair procedures) in relation to one specific case (*Dellway v National Asset Management Agency*), ably demonstrates how this case illustrates some more general themes concerning the development of the unenumerated rights doctrine and of this specific right in particular. As such many facets of her chapter reflect elements found in other contributions to this volume, for example in relation to the philosophical underpinnings of unenumerated rights where her analysis overlaps with those of Professor Ferrari and Professor Passaglia, Dr Pulice and Dr Carolan. Her overall theme—the interface between constitutional principles and administrative law—also makes her chapter a natural companion for Professor Comba's.

One of the overall themes that emerges from the current collection is the multiplicity of different rationalisations that can be given for the unenumerated personal rights that have been recognised by the Irish courts over the last fifty years. In the last few years, as is discussed at greater length in relation to Dr Pulice's and Dr Carolan's contributions (and as Professor Ferrari's remarks anticipate),[91] the more specific issue has arisen as to how many of these previously unenumerated rights can be

---

86 [2007] IEHC 195 (23 May).

87 [2011] 2 ILRM 12 (HC). See also *Carbery Fishing Ltd v Minister for Agriculture, Fisheries and Food* [2011] IEHC 427 (15 November 2011) and *Kennedy v Minister for Agriculture* [2011] IEHC 187 (15 April 2011).

88 *Lett v Wexford Borough Council* [2007] IEHC 195 (23 May) para 4.15.

89 *Atlantic Marine Supplies Ltd v Minister for Transport* [2011] 2 ILRM 12 (HC) 35.

90 *Lett & Co Ltd v Wexford Borough Council* [2012] IESC 14 (2 February 2012) para 23 O'Donnell J.

91 Giuseppe Franco Ferrari, "Fundamental Rights in Ireland" at p 6 of the current volume.

reconceptualised as aspects of the explicit guarantee of protection of "the person" under Article 40.3.2°. The right to fair procedures would represent an interesting case study in both these respects. In terms of Dr Oran Doyle's categorisation of the sources of unenumerated rights, which Professor Ferrari endorses,[92] the right to fair procedures does not appear to be distinctively derived from any of them. The vagueness of the "Christian and democratic" of the State is thrown into relief when one considers whether it helps to specify in any way the content of the right. It is true that some support for the concept of constitutional justice does seem to have been derived from a broad natural law background, as in the case of the dicta of O'Higgins CJ in *G v An Bord Uchtála*, cited by Dr O'Neill,[93] but this seems to be hardly more than a rhetorical invocation. In relation to how the right to fair procedures might be related to the "human personality" rationalisation of unenumerated rights (or to the newly expanded reach of the guarantee of protection of "the person") Dr O'Neill's reference to "dignitarian" rationales for the observance of fair procedures ("the idea that as individuals, litigants are entitled to be treated fairly and that it is the process of this treatment–as opposed to any outcome of it–that is important")[94] does suggest a way in which that new emphasis under Article 40.3 need not in any way threaten established status of the right to fair procedures. The final method suggested by Dr Doyle for deriving unenumerated rights–as protections implied from other provisions of the Constitution–also seems to hold considerable promise in relation to the right to fair procedures. We have already seen, in relation to Professor Ferrari's reflections on the possible discrepancies between citizens' and human rights, how the Supreme Court in *Re Article 26 and sections 5 and 10 of the Illegal Immigrants Trafficking Bill, 1999* derived the enjoyment of several rights by citizens and non-citizens alike from "the very notion of a state founded on the rule of law" and that the right to fair procedures figured among these.[95]

A foreign, or even a domestic, observer might wonder why so much might be thought to turn on the issue–which Dr O'Neill discusses at length[96]—of whether the right to fair procedures is an autonomous constitutional right or whether it is engaged only when other constitutional rights are in some way being impinged upon. One reason why this could be an important decision may be as follows.

Dr O'Neill draws attention to the fact that Hardiman J was the judge who placed most emphasis on the free-standing character of the right to fair procedures in a case such as this one and the absence of any requirement that other constitutional rights should be shown to have been impinged upon in some way before the right to fair procedures arises. Although no reference is made in Dellway Investments to the earlier decision of the Supreme Court in *Meadows v Minister for Justice*[97] it may be instructive to engage in a brief comparison of the views that Hardiman J expressed there with his judgment in *Dellway Investments*. In brief, in that earlier

---

92 *ibid,* citing Oran Doyle, *Constitutional Law: Text, Cases and Materials* (Clarus Press, 2009) p 85.

93 *Garvey v Ireland* [1981] IR 75, 91 cited in Ailbhe O'Neill "Rights and Freedoms in the Domestic Context – Fair Procedures in difficult times" at pp 112-13 of the current volume.

94 *ibid* at p. 114.

95 [2000] 2 IR 260, 285-86.

96 Ailbhe O'Neill, "Rights and Freedoms in the Domestic Context – Fair Procedures in difficult times" at pp 112-15 of the current volume.

97 [2010] 2 IR 701 (SC); Hilary Biehler, "Curial Deference in the Context of Judicial Review of Administrative Action Post-*Meadows*" (2013) 49 *Irish Jurist* 29.

case, Hardiman J joined the other members of the Court in denying that judicial review in cases where constitutional rights (or other rights considered similarly important) requires "anxious scrutiny". However, Hardiman J (with whom Kearns P concurred) went further, in dissenting from the majority's conclusion (variously expressed) that, in cases where constitutional or other rights at stake, considerations of proportionality had a role to play in determining whether a decision had been shown to be so "unreasonable" or "irrational" as to be liable to be quashed. In his view to modify the general administrative law test by reference to considerations of proportionality was equivalent to the "anxious scrutiny" test that the court had rejected and opened the way to "a substantial transfer of power from the politically responsible organs of government to an unelected judiciary".[98] What is particularly relevant in the current context is one of the reasons he gave for rejecting the idea that the "new" standard of review would apply to some discrete class of cases in which judicial review of a decision was sought:

> "I believe that it must be acknowledged, on the basis of experience of judicial review applications, which are now among the major components of the case load in this court, that a great many such applications arise in areas where there can be little doubt that a constitutional right is implicated. A review of the disposition of a criminal matter by the District Court would almost certainly be in this category as would the great majority of, if not all, asylum cases. The great bulk of litigation arising from tribunals and commissions of inquiry also deals with constitutional rights to good name and otherwise which are said to be implicated and an enormous number of cases where the points made are fundamentally procedural involve the constitutional value of "fair procedures", a preoccupation of the courts since at least the decision of *In re Haughey* [1971] IR 217.
>
> Accordingly, it is predictable that if the criteria for application of judicial review is changed in cases involving constitutional rights, the remnant of cases which will not be subject to the change will indeed be a poor remnant, hard enough to define in theory in light of the wide range of constitutional (not to mention Convention) rights and, I should imagine, very rarely met with in practice."[99]

This, perhaps, is one element of Hardiman J's reluctance to characterise a case such as *Dellway Investments* as involving an entanglement of different constitutional rights. In the approach to judicial review that he adopts, the fact that the enjoyment of a constitutional right – such as in *Dellway Investments* the right to property, the right to earn a livelihood or the right to good name – is affected by an administrative decision does not, as such, alter the standard of reasonableness review to be applied (albeit in a "particularly careful and thorough" manner). By contrast, the free-standing right to fair procedures, which does not depend on any impingement on these other rights, does provide a legitimate basis for a court intervening to set aside an administrative decision not on the basis that the grounds for it were inadequate, but that the proper procedure was not followed.

[98] *ibid,* p 785.
[99] *ibid,* p 784.

7. Rinella

Professor Rinella seeks to place the preamble to the Constitution of Ireland in a comparative context and, in so doing, brings a number of valuable insights to bear on its significance and function.

Professor Rinella's outline of the categorisation of constitutional regimes in terms of the relationship of public power and religion reminds us of the need to place the constitutional text in the context of the social and cultural background, at both the time it was enacted and as it now falls to be interpreted. The importance of these contexts (especially the former) is something that the Supreme Court had recalled on several occasions. In *Quinn's Supermarket Ltd v Attorney General*, for example, the Court referred to the Preamble as an acknowledgement that "we are a Christian people", albeit that the Constitution as it was enacted did "not prefer one to the other and it does not confer any privilege or impose any disability or diminution of status upon any religious denomination, and it does not permit the State to do so."[100] In subsequent cases, the Court appears to have paid more attention to the historical background than to the Preamble itself in order to set the context for the interpretation of constitutional provisions relating, directly or indirectly, to the role of religion in public life. In *Crowley v Ireland*, for example, O'Higgins CJ invoked history as an explanation for the qualified nature of the constitutional right to free primary education—which the State is obliged to "provide for" but not itself to "provide"—

> "When one remembers the long and turbulent history of the church schools in Ireland, and the sustained struggle for the right to maintain such schools by the religious authorities of all denominations in all parts of Ireland, one can well understand the care with which the words used must have been selected."[101]

Kenny J made observations in the same vein in his judgment—

> "The history of Ireland in the 19th century shows how tenaciously the people resisted the idea of State schools. The Constitution must not be interpreted without reference to our history and to the conditions and intellectual climate of 1937 when almost all schools were under the control of a manager or of trustees who were not nominees of the State."[102]

A more sustained examination of the history of Church-State relations in Ireland (again in the field of education) and their bearing on the interpretation of relevant constitutional provisions, building on the dicta in *Crowley v Ireland*, was undertaken in *Campaign to Separate Church and State in Ireland Ltd v Minister for Education*.[103] As Professor Rinella himself notes, a similar regard for the prevailing attitudes of the main religious groups in the State in 1937 is shown by the majority in *Norris*

---

[100] [1972] IR 1, 23. The reference in the latter part of this quotation is to the portions of Art 44.1 that were subsequently deleted by the Fifth Amendment of the Constitution Act 1972 but that amendment merely reinforces Walsh J's point.

[101] [1980] IR 102, 122.

[102] *ibid*, 126.

[103] [1998] 3 IR 321 (SC) 348-55 (Barrington J); 362-66 (Keane J). Hamilton CJ, O'Flaherty and Denham JJ concurred with Barrington J's judgment and Hamilton CJ and O'Flaherty JJ with Keane J's.

v Attorney General, where this was held to preclude the recognition of a right to engage in sexual conduct which was then and, as the Court found, was still in 1983 condemned as gravely sinful by the main Christian denominations.[104] For this purpose, the majority judgment referred to the Preamble, as showing not merely "a deep religious conviction and faith" but also "an intention to adopt a Constitution consistent with that conviction and faith and with Christian beliefs".[105]

What one can gather from this is that the Supreme Court generally seems more inclined to look to historical background than to draw out general implications from the Preamble, when it comes to defining the constitutional parameters that govern the role of religion in public life in Ireland. As several authors in this volume have pointed out,[106] the Preamble has been relied upon in a more general sense, as a guide to the implication of unenumerated personal rights, for example. However, in this context, it increasingly tends to be the references to "the dignity and freedom of the individual" and "prudence, justice and charity" that are highlighted and not the specifically religious elements. This reflects the process of the removal in the 1990s of almost all the remaining Catholic influences specifically introduced in the 1930s, most notably by the Supreme Court's decision in 1995 in *Regulation of Information (Services outside the State for Termination of Pregnancies) Bill, 1995*,[107] which both Ms Pulice and Dr Carolan mention in their chapters. Both those chapters also discuss the challenge facing the Irish courts to articulate the values that underpin unenumerated rights and constitutional interpretation, in the absence of any easy assurance that a reference to Christian ethics could resolve these problems. On the other hand, Walsh J—speaking on his own behalf, it must be remembered and not for the Supreme Court—had anticipated some of the complexities of this interpretive task in *McGee v Attorney General*, albeit within the framework of a theistic concept of natural law.[108]

On the one hand, therefore, the Preamble does not appear to have had a significant independent influence on the constitutional parameters established by the Irish courts for Church-State relations. On the other, insofar as it has influenced the interpretation of the rights provisions of the Constitution more generally, it has increasingly been the parts of the Preamble that do not invoke specifically religious beliefs that have been most influential. Professor Rinella's chapter is therefore a timely reminder of the range of functions—symbolic as well as normative in the narrow sense—that a constitutional preamble may play some role in. It is in that context that we should assess, as Professor Rinella invites us to do, with his own verdict, the appropriateness of retaining the religious references in the current Preamble. The criteria for making that assessment are also suggested, both positively and negatively, by what Professor Rinella has to say on the subject. There is probably an agreement that goes wider than religious believers that it would be appropriate to recognise that, on some level,

104 [1984] IR 36, 64.

105 *ibid.*

106 Giuseppe Franco Ferrari, "Fundamental Rights in Ireland" at p 7 of the current volume; Paolo Passaglia "Irish Judicial Review of Legislation: A Comparative Perspective" at p 28 of the current volume; Elisabetta Pulice "Constitutional Iinterpretation in Ireland" at pp 44, 48-50, 54-57 of the current volume; Eoin Carolan "Evaluating the Judicial Role in Developing the Irish Constitution" at pp. 66, 68 of the current volume; Ailbhe O'Neill "Rights and Freedoms in the Domestic Context –Fair Procedures in difficult times" at pp 98, 106 of the current volume.

107 [1995] 1 IR 1 (SC).

108 [1974] IR 284, 318-19.

that "human laws, human authority and human rights are not without limitations and conditions" and that "the human being cannot be the measure of all things", as Professor Rinella puts it. However, even if "there is no doubt that the rights pertaining to the dignity of the human person cannot be adequately protected except in the context of a democratic order" recent bitter debates in Ireland (notably over the regulation of the termination of pregnancy) may have raised doubts in the minds of a significant proportion of the population about whether it is unreservedly true that "the rules of democracy, in fact, ensure full respect for human dignity".

8. Rason and Petrillo

Professor Rason and Dr Petrillo provide a fascinating and informative account of the dialogue among constitutional judges, parliaments and executives and, in particular, of the techniques that the first group has for issuing "admonitions" and other warnings to the second and third, drawing especially on detailed study of Italian practice in this regard.

Some traces of a similar practice have long been faintly discernible in Irish case law.[109] Recent years have, however, seen a determined effort by Hogan J to create a more nuanced form of judgment that would correspond more clearly with the Italian practice that Rason and Petrillo describe. Taking the form of the order made by the Supreme Court in *Carmody v Minister for Justice, Equality and Law Reform*[110] as his starting point, in cases where invalidation of the impugned legislation would confer no actual benefit on the applicant, he has sought instead to make a declaratory order protecting the applicant from the consequences of the legislature's omission.[111] In so doing, he has drawn specific parallels between this practice and the *Appellentscheidung* (admonitory decision) that is available to the German Federal Constitutional Court.[112] It has yet to be seen whether or not his fellow High Court judges and the Supreme Court will be receptive to the suggestion that *Carmody* should spawn such declaratory orders addressing legislative lacunae in such a wide range of situations.

As yet, however, there seems little indication of a natural complement to such a power—namely, the concomitant power to place a stay on the effect of a declaration of invalidity (or inconsistency with the Constitution) of a statutory provision or a rule of common law. While considerable refinement has been introduced in dealing with the temporal effects of a declaration of invalidity, it still appears to be the

---

109 For example, in *Blake v AG* [1981] IR 117 (SC) or in *McMenamin v Ireland* [1996] 3 IR 100 (SC). See the discussion of this point in JM Kelly, *The Irish Constitution* (4th ed, Gerard W Hogan and Gerry Whyte ed, Lexis Nexis Butterworths, 2003) 262–263. Something similar is at work in other cases where the court considers that a declaration of the Government's legal obligations is a sufficient remedy for an unconstitutional situation that has been identified in the court's decision. Good recent examples are *Doherty v Government of Ireland* [2011] 2 IR 222 (HC) 246–247 and *McCrystal v Minister for Children and Youth Affairs* [2012] IESC 53 (8 November 2012) para 9.

110 [2010] 1 IR 635 at 668–670.

111 *G(B) v Judge Murphy* [2011] 3 IR 748 (HC). He also contemplated, but did not find it necessary to make, such an order in *Efe v Minister for Justice Equality and Law Reform* [2011] 2 IR 798 (HC). He had previously, as a member of the Bar, urged such arguments on the courts, see *McBrearty v Morris* [2003] IEHC 154 (13 May 2003).

112 *G(B) v Judge Murphy* [2011] 3 IR 748 (HC) 771.

case that the courts' adherence to the notion that an invalid law is void *ab initio* precludes placing a stay on the effect of such a declaration for a specific period, so that the legislature may address the consequences of that declaration and may pass appropriate remedial legislation before that declaration comes into effect.[113] However, this is by no means a closed issue and, especially should the type of admonitory decision favoured by Hogan J gain wider currency, it is possible to envisage the Irish courts giving themselves such remedial flexibility as to the date of effect of the Court's order.[114]

Rason and Petrillo also note the general trend towards presidentialisation in parliamentary democracies,

> "characterised by a loss of power to influence the decision-making processes of the assemblies, a power that is being shifted on to the executive power and, even more, on the head of the executive. In other words, the recipients of the warnings of the constitutional courts are the parliaments, in their capacity as holders of the legislative power and as producers of the subject matter of the judicial review. However, nowadays, parliaments seem to have increasingly become stone guests, albeit with significant powers, in the democratic circuit, as they have lost their traditional activities and have not yet understood what is happening."[115]

At least one modest indication of such a trend, and its effect on the dialogue between the courts and the other branches of government, can be found in the decision of the High Court in *Doherty v Government of Ireland*.[116] In that case, the function of triggering the statutory procedure for a by-election to fill a casual vacancy in the membership of Dáil Éireann lay with the House itself by way of a direction given by the chamber to its presiding officer to in turn direct the Clerk of Dáil Éireann to issue the necessary writ.[117] The High Court decided that the Constitution required that this statutory provision be construed as incorporating a requirement that a by-election be held within reasonable time of the vacancy arising; in the circumstances of this case, a 16-month delay was not a reasonable one.[118] Specifically, the Court observed that

> "a constitutional approach necessarily means that section 39(2) of the Act of 1992 must be interpreted as being subject to a temporal requirement that a

---

113 *A v Governor of Arbour Hill Prison* [2006] 4 IR 88 (SC); JM Kelly, *The Irish Constitution* (4th ed, Gerard W Hogan and Gerry Whyte ed, Lexis Nexis Butterworths, 2003) 895–903. O'Donnell J also touched on this general issue in his judgment in *Minister for Justice, Equality and Law Reform v Tobin* [2012] IESC 37 (19 June 2012) para 55.

114 JM Kelly, *The Irish Constitution* (4th ed, Gerard W Hogan and Gerry Whyte ed, Lexis Nexis Butterworths, 2003) 904–6.

115 Nino Olivetti Rason and Pier Luigi Petrillo, "The Dialogue among Constitutional Judges, Parliaments and Executives" in the current work, 151.

116 [2011] 2 IR 222 (HC).

117 Electoral Act, 1992 s 39(2). Amending legislation followed the change of Government in 2011: Electoral Act, 1992 s 39(2A) (inserted by the Electoral (Amendment) Act 2011 s 2). This provides that, if no such direction is given by Dáil Éireann within a period of six months from the date on which the vacancy occurred, the writ for the by-election is to issue as soon as practicable after the end of that period.

118 *Doherty v Government of Ireland* [2011] 2 IR 222 (HC) 242.

> by-election motion be either moved by the Government or not resisted by it within a reasonable time of the vacancy arising."[119]

Lest there was any ambiguity about what this meant, the Court went on to refer to "obligation falling on the Government *to exercise its control of the Dáil* to move or not oppose a motion".[120] Thus, the Court made no effort to conceal the fact that, in practice, the Dáil's control over the Government—envisaged by several constitutional provisions—means the Government's control of the Dáil.[121] Although the Court did not make a declaration that specifically stated that the Government was "obliged to set down and support the motion for the issue of a writ or at least not impede or oppose such a motion", it assumed from the political realities of the situation that this would be the Government's response to its interpretation of the relevant sub-section and its declaration that there had been unreasonable delay in moving the writ for the by-election.[122] This was, in fact, the Government's response.

However, the Court did cite Geoghegan J's dicta in the earlier *Dudley* case, which implied that such a specific form of declaration could be issued if this seemed necessary and appropriate.[123] Geoghegan J considered that a declaration could not be made that the members of Dáil Éireann were obliged to vote in favour of any proposition, as there was no way of following up such a declaration with an enforceable order.

> "No enforceable order can be made by the courts against the Dáil as such. Dáil Éireann can only give the direction if the majority of members vote for the motion but the court cannot *mandamus* the body of members of the Dáil as such to vote in a particular way on a particular motion."[124]

However, although it was unnecessary at that juncture to decide whether such an order should be made, he considered that it was at least arguable that the Government had a constitutional obligation to set down and support motions for the issue of a writ for the holding of a by-election after a reasonable time has elapsed from the vacancy arising and that the Government could be judicially reviewed for a failure to discharge this obligation.[125] This approach can be criticised, of course, for its failure to distinguish the legal powers and duties of the Government and its component Ministers—whether constitutional or statutory in origin—which are clearly subject to judicial review and its role of political leadership over the majority in the Dáil. Since the Government's "control" over the Dáil is mediated through that political leadership role and the party whip system in particular, it is perhaps problematic to suggest that it can be subject to judicial review for making a political decision as to how its supporters in the Dáil should vote, any more than those individual TDs could be held accountable to the courts for their votes. When they are making

---

[119] *ibid,* 242.

[120] *ibid,* 244. Emphasis supplied.

[121] Constitution of Ireland, Arts 13.1, 13.2.2°, 28.4.1°, 17.1 and 28.10. The Constitution does, of course, acknowledge that the Government exercises some degree of control over the Dáil: Art 17.2.

[122] *Doherty v Government of Ireland* [2011] 2 IR 222 (HC) 247.

[123] *Dudley v An Taoiseach* [1994] 1 ILRM 321 (HC).

[124] *ibid,* 324.

[125] *ibid.*

such decisions, after all, the members of the Government are themselves acting essentially as TDs (or possibly Senators, in the case of no more than two of them) rather than as holders of any departmental office. An ultimately more satisfactory solution might have been to declare that s 39(2) was itself invalid because it placed the power to direct the holding of by-election in the hands of a body that was immune from judicial review.[126]

Whatever the proper approach to cases such as *Dudley* and *Doherty* ought to be, Geoghegan J developed his characterisation of the true relation between executive and legislature in the subsequent *Maguire v Ardagh* case.

> "[T]he U.S. Legislature functioning in a presidential system of government on the one hand and the Irish Legislature functioning in the context of a parliamentary democracy on the other hand [have wholly different practices and, indeed, cultures]. The Irish Parliament like the parliaments of all the European parliamentary democracies and respected non-European parliamentary democracies such as Australia, New Zealand, Canada, India etc carry on their parliamentary business for the most part in accordance with the plans and policies of the government of the day which in turn is formed out of the political parties. The idea that Dáil Éireann might in its independent existence contemplate the possibility of some form of legislation and seek to initiate a substantial fact finding inquiry aided by provisions regarding the compellability of witnesses etc. for that purpose is to a large extent a fantasy. It may well suit a government to procure that the Dáil would initiate inquiries of one kind or another to allay public worries and with a view to reporting on appropriate legislation but it would be the exception rather than the rule. For the most part, it is the Government and not the Oireachtas which proposes the legislation."[127]

Against that, one might set at least one fairly recent case in which the judge—Gerard Hogan, as it happens—unusually sent a copy of his decision directly to chairperson of each House of the Oireachtas (but also, it may be noted, to the relevant Minister) with a view to drawing their attention to a decision, on a point of statutory interpretation, which they might consider invited urgent remedial legislation:

> "The constitutional principle of the separation of powers is designed to serve a purpose and is not simply a technical formalism. While fully respecting the divisions which must necessarily exist between the legislative and judicial branches, a healthy dialogue between those two branches can only serve the public interest. This must be so where a court judgment has important policy implications and consequences which may not have been anticipated by the other branches of government. It is in that vein that I propose to transmit a copy of this decision to the Ceann Comhairle, the Cathaoirleach of the Seanad and

126 Some analogy could be drawn, in that event, with O'Hanlon J's decision in *State (Lynch) v Cooney* [1982] IR 337, 343 that s 31(1) of the Broadcasting Authority Act, 1960 was invalid because it authorised a restriction of freedom of expression by a ministerial order that was not subject to judicial review, on his reading of the relevant precedents. The Supreme Court overruled this decision, on the basis that the Minister's decision was subject to judicial review: *ibid*, 367.

127 *Maguire v Ardagh* [2002] 1 IR 385 (SC) 715.

> the Minister for Jobs, Enterprise and Innovation so that the Oireachtas may give consideration—should it think fit to do so—to the policy implications for the 2003 Act as manifested in this judgment."[128]

There are nevertheless good reasons to think that Irish judges are aware of, and influenced by, the fact that, in normal circumstances, any "constitutional dialogue" that takes place is between the judicial and executive branches, with only a marginal independent role for members of the legislature. If anything, this phenomenon is even more notable in Ireland than it is in Italy.

9. Cahill

Dr Cahill's chapter addresses a long-standing and fundamental issue in Irish constitutional law, posed by the nature of the "reception clause" for the law of the European Communities and, subsequently, of the European Union, present in the Constitution in more or less the same form since 1972. As she points out, the sweeping nature of this opening to EU law is hard to reconcile with some of the traditional postulates of the type of constitutionalism that is so evident elsewhere in the Constitution. This is true not only of the concept of national sovereignty but also, as she insists with some force, the very concept that national judges have the primary role of upholding the most basic norms of the national constitution. The tension between the supremacy of the constitution and its openness to European law is a widespread phenomenon and has attracted a great deal of scholarly attention.[129]

Dr Cahill takes the Irish constitutional guarantee of the right to life of the unborn as a paradigmatic case of the potential conflict between the claims of Bunreacht na hÉireann and European Union law. It is particularly striking, therefore, to recall Costello J's statement in *Attorney General v X*:

> "Our courts must enforce Community law; and if that law conflicts with Irish law, including Irish constitutional law, then Community law will prevail. It is submitted on the defendants' behalf that a light to travel abroad to obtain an abortion is conferred on the defendant by Community law and if this is so then, notwithstanding the provisions of the Constitution and the Eighth Amendment, the court cannot grant an injunction to stop her."[130]

In that case, of course, Costello J came to the conclusion that European Community law did not prevent such an injunction being granted and the Supreme Court did

[128] *Hussein v Labour Court* [2012] IEHC 364 (31 August 2012) para 24, Hogan J.

[129] For example, in various forms and from various points of view: Diarmuid Rossa Phelan, *Revolt or Revolution: The Constitutional Boundaries of the European Community* (Roundhall Sweet and Maxwell, 1997); Neil McCormick, *Questioning Sovereignty: Law, State, and Nation in the European Commonwealth* (Oxford University Press, 1999); Nick Barber *The Constitutional State* (Oxford University Press, 2010). See also William Phelan *Can Ireland Legislate Contrary to European Community Law?* Institute for International Integration Studies, IIIS Discussion Paper No.237/December 2007, http://www.tcd.ie/iiis/documents/discussion/pdfs/iiisdp237.pdf (last accessed 23 May 2013).

[130] [1992] 1 IR 1 (HC) 13–16.

not have to address the issue, since it held for the defendants on the basis of Irish constitutional law.[131]

The problem that Dr Cahill poses is, therefore, quite a stark one. As she points out, there is implicit in the Supreme Court's decision in *Crotty v An Taoiseach* an Irish constitutional law principle that filters the extent to which the obligations of membership of the European Union can be given effect in Irish law, despite the apparently unqualified terms of Art 29.4.6°. Thus far, in cases such as *Crotty v An Taoiseach*[132] itself and more recently in *Pringle v Government of Ireland*,[133] in which *Crotty* was reaffirmed and applied, the courts have had to consider only the question of whether the authorisations given by constitutional amendments since 1972 relating to Ireland's participation in the Union and the Communities are sufficient to allow the State to ratify further European Treaties, without a fresh amendment of this kind.

However, it seems plausible that Art 29.4.6° should be read as a provision that is consequential upon, and instrumental to, the authorisations given in Art 29.4.3° to join the European Community and in Art 29.4.5° to join the European Union. Therefore, the apparently unqualified language of Art 29.4.6° should probably be interpreted as not giving the effect prescribed there to "obligations of membership" of the Union that, in fact go beyond "the essential scope or objectives of the [Union]"[134] envisaged by the authorisations given in the earlier sub-sections. This would imply, in turn, that it is ultimately for the Supreme Court to decide whether even a decision of the European Court of Justice as to the nature of the State's obligations under the Treaties is at variance with the "essential scope and objectives" of the European Union, as determined by an interpretation of Art 29 of the Constitution of Ireland. If so, it would seem hard to see how that obligation, valid though it might be as a matter of international law, could be the basis for relying upon Art 29.4.6° to shield from invalidation on constitutional grounds (should they exist) any laws enacted, acts done or measures adopted by the State on foot of that obligation. To that extent, therefore, some kind of "solange" doctrine—at the very least—would be a conceptual requirement of the overall scheme of Art 29.4.3–10°.

It is another question entirely whether this means that the Irish constitution's treatment of the right to life of the unborn easily leads to the conclusion that there is a direct conflict between it and European Union law, to which the latter must therefore yield. Whatever approach the Irish courts take to Art 29.4.6° cannot plausibly take

[131] *ibid*, 59–62 Finlay CJ. The Opinion of Advocate General Van Gerven in Case C-159/90 *Society for the Protection of Unborn Children Ireland Ltd v Grogan* [1991] ECR I-4685, 4730 (para 38) could be read as implying that restriction of the movement of pregnant women out of the State for the purpose of obtaining a termination of their pregnancies in another Member State where that service was lawfully available was a violation of European Community law as it then stood, although his observations in relation to freedom of movement do associate it with "unsolicited examinations" of such women, which might distinguish the situation he had in mind from the facts of *AG v X*. Following the decision of the European Court of Human Rights in App No 25579/05 *A, B and C v Ireland* (2011) 53 EHRR 13 (Grand Chamber) it seems much less likely than in 1992 that an injunction such as the one granted by Costello J in *AG v X* could be regarded as compatible with Art 8 of the European Convention on Human Rights or with European Union law in relation to the freedom to travel to receive a service lawfully available in another Member State.

[132] [1987] IR 713 (SC).

[133] [2012] IESC 47 (19 October 2012).

[134] *Crotty v An Taoiseach* [1987] IR 713 (SC) 767.

the form of ignoring its provisions or simply carving out an exception from them in relation to any conflict between European Union law and the fundamental rights that are guaranteed by the Constitution of Ireland.

Ms Pulice discusses in her chapter the principle of harmonious interpretation of the Constitution;[135] that principle would hardly be compatible with a "nullifying" interpretation of Art 29.4.6°. Instead, the courts should seek a way of interpreting the fundamental rights guarantees and the obligations of membership in a harmonious fashion. One appropriate way of doing so might be to determine what the effect on fundamental rights of membership of the Union was reasonably understood to be at the time the authorisation to join it was given, making allowances for future developments within the Union's "essential scope and objectives" at that time. For example, given the nature of the law of the European Economic Community in 1973 it could have been foreseeable that the Court of Justice might, at some future point, disagree with the conclusion that Costello J reached in *Attorney General v X* on whether the free movement of persons would be violated by the type of injunction he granted,[136] whereas it might not have been foreseeable that the Court of Justice would decide that European law required the legalisation of abortions performed within the State—as has since been confirmed, of course, by Protocol No 17 to the Treaty on European Union, which seeks to exclude that possibility.[137]

In the context of "harmonious interpretation" it is interesting to review Walsh J's suggestion in *Society for the Protection of Unborn Children (Ireland) Ltd v Grogan*, a case central to Dr Cahill's argument:

> "It has been sought to be argued in the present case that the effect of the amendment of Article 29 of the Constitution, which was necessary to permit our adhesion to the treaties of the European Communities, is to qualify all rights including fundamental rights guaranteed by the Constitution. The 8th Amendment of the Constitution is subsequent in time, by several years, to the amendment of Article 29. That fact may give rise to the consideration of the question of whether or not the 8th Amendment itself qualifies the amendment to Article 29. Be that as it may any answer to the reference received from the Court of Justice of the European Communities will have to be considered in the light of our own constitutional provisions. In the last analysis only this Court can decide finally what are the effects of the interaction of the 8th Amendment of the Constitution and the 3rd Amendment of the Constitution."[138]

His final sentence here certainly contains a proposition with which one can readily agree. However, it seems questionable whether much weight should be given to the question of the temporal sequence of amendments that he raises. For one thing, it would seem inappropriate if the interaction of different constitutional provisions were to be largely on the basis of whether they were original to the version enacted in 1937 or, if not, of when they were added to the Constitution. If it were, then a constitutional

---

[135] Elisabetta Pulice, "Constitutional Interpretation in Ireland" at pp.47–48, 59–61 in the current volume.

[136] [1992] 1 IR 1 (HC)

[137] JM Kelly, *The Irish Constitution* (4th ed, Gerard W Hogan and Gerry Whyte ed, (Lexis Nexis Butterworths, 2003) 1501–1503, 1505–1507.

[138] [1989] IR 753 (SC) 768–769 Walsh J.

game of leap-frog might arise, with the Eighth Amendment being in turn "trumped" by, for example, the subsequent Eleventh Amendment of the Constitution Act 1992. In addition, harmonious interpretation requires us to look at all the constitutional provisions that are in play and seek an appropriate mutual adjustment of them. One could equally well argue that, when they enacted the Eighth Amendment, the People were aware of the provisions introduced by the Third Amendment and that the caveat "as far as practicable" in Art 40.3.3° is partly an acknowledgement of the legal, as well as factual, limitations on the defence and vindication of the right to life of the unborn. The issue of that kind of mutual adjustment of constitutional provisions is, in this context, probably best combined with a consideration of the requirement, already suggested, that Art 29.4.6° be confined within the limits of "the essential scope and objectives" of the Union, as they stood in 2009 when the last relevant constitutional authorisation was given.

Another point worth considering is that the Supreme Court's rejected in *Re Regulation of Information (Services outside the State for Termination of Pregnancies) Bill, 1995*[139] the suggestion that the right to life of the unborn, seen as a requirement of the natural law, could be invoked to invalidate a constitutional amendment that sought to limit the degree to which it was enforceable by the courts or other organs of the State as a matter of Irish constitutional law. For the reasons already given, if that is the case in relation to a provision subsequently added by way of a constitutional amendment (such as the second and third sentences of Art 40.3.3°) surely it is also true of any other provision of the Constitution (whenever it came into existence) whose effect a party seeks to nullify on the basis of some other, such as the first sentence of Art 40.3.3°. Instead, a harmonious interpretation has to be given to each provision in question which, in the case of Art 29.4.6°, will involve some concept of the appropriate division of competences between the State and the Union, in view of the latter's scope and objectives as matters stood in 2009.

However the Irish courts address, as one day they must, the conceptual issues that Dr Cahill's chapter subjects to such a searching and thoughtful analysis, her contribution, as also does Ms Pulice's,[140] highlights the extent to which these issues—and specifically the status of the right to life of the unborn—pose issues of constitutional identity, a topic that has recently been so comprehensively addressed by Professor Gary Jacobsohn, who takes the Irish abortion information cases as one of his case studies.[141]

10. Mezzetti

Professor Mezzetti's chapter provides a comprehensive and rigorous analysis of the concept of a semi-presidential regime and where, if anywhere, the Irish model fits within it. As he notes, any analysis of the office of President of Ireland has to take account of the fact that in both Ireland and Iceland:

> "the direct election of the president of the republic was proposed not to realise

---

139 [1995] 1 IR 1 (SC).

140 Elisabetta Pulice, "Constitutional Interpretation in Ireland" at pp.58–61, 119–132 in the current volume.

141 Gary Jacobsohn, *Constitutional Identity* (Harvard University Press, 2010) 195–201, 259–266.

> a dual executive but to confirm national independence from, respectively, Great Britain in 1937 and Denmark in 1944".

Further, he concludes as follows.

> In other words, from the constitutional scheme it emerges that the choice to found the presidential office on (and to equip it with) a direct popular legitimation was not dictated by the conviction determination of Irish framers to adopt a semi-presidential form of government as more fit to guarantee the stability and the effectiveness of the system, but by the need to definitely enact Irish independence, aiming to affirm and 'visually' to represent the wish will of the nation to decide its own national life autonomously."[142]

To that extent, the office of President of Ireland is another feature of Irish constitutional law and practice that serves to individuate the Irish state and polity, in the same way as do many constitutional provisions as to fundamental rights and their interpretation by the Irish courts, as emerges from Ms Pulice's examination of the latter topic in her chapter.

Professor Mezzetti's chapter convincingly demonstrates that at the heart of any meaningful characterisation of semi-presidential systems of government are the complex interactions between a prime minister, who heads a cabinet, a directly elected president, who has some degree of discretion in the selection of ministers, and the parliament, from which that prime minister and cabinet require continued confidence to continue in office. The nature of those interactions varies, both between semi-presidential systems and within each system over time. Nevertheless, we can surely agree with his conclusion that

> "it seems possible to describe the Irish constitutional order as a parliamentary regime corrected by the anomaly of the direct popular election of the President, rejecting the description of 'intermittent' semi-presidentialism … and preferring the definition of *merely apparent semi-presidentialism*."[143]

It is salutary to remember, however, that the opposition parties expressed real fears in 1937 that, despite the limitations that the constitutional text imposes on the office, the election of Eamon de Valera as President, if it were to occur, would rapidly lead to a concentration of executive power in his hands, as the effective political head of the governing party.[144] The depth of the antipathy and suspicion with which the

---

142 Luca Mezztti, "The Irish Form of Government: A Merely Apparent Semi-Presidentialism" at p.190 in the current volume.

143 *ibid.* Emphasis in the original.

144 See John Coakley, "An Ambiguous Office? The Position of the Head of State in the Irish Constitution" (2012) 48 *Irish Jurist* 43 at 52–54; *Bunreacht na hEireann (Dréacht)—Dara Céim (d'aththógaint)* (12 May 1937) 67 *Dáil Debates*, cols 229–234 (Professor John M O'Sullivan TD); cols 250–52 (James Dillon TD); cols 263–64 (Patrick Hogan TD); cols 268–76 (Dr T F O'Higgins TD); cols 299–304; *Bunreacht na hEireann (Dréacht)—Dara Céim (d'aththógaint)* (13 May 1937) 67 *Dáil Debates* cols 341–49 (James Fitzgerald-Kenny TD); cols 381–86 (Desmond Fitzgerald); cols 403–10 (Patrick McGilligan TD, a professor of constitutional law at UCD at the time of the debate and a future Minister for Finance and Attorney General). So current was this line of argument that de Valera had to devote a large part of his introductory speech on the Second Stage of the Draft Constitution to responding to it: *Bunreacht na hEireann*

opposition, and Fine Gael in particular, greeted the proposal can be gauged from the line of argument adopted by John A Costello (himself a former Attorney General at the time of the debate and a future Taoiseach):

> "[T]hese draft proposals are so framed by the framer of them that he is free to make up his mind whether he will be Prime Minister or President. If he is going to be Prime Minister, he has the whip hand and will put in somebody as President over whom he will have the whip hand. If he is President he will see that whoever is Prime Minister will be subordinate and subservient to him. That is the scheme embodied in the draft proposals which is to be submitted in this farcical way to a plebiscite of the people. We have heard speeches referring to the dangers inherent in this office of President. There is the graver danger that there are two men envisaged in this. It may be that you will have this clash of personalities and wills in years to come between the person who is President and the person who is Prime Minister; that you will have an equally serious situation if you have the position where the President is the dominant personality and the Prime Minister the 'yes' man; and an equally serious situation if you have the Prime Minister the dominant personality and the President the 'yes' man."[145]

The political experience of the Russian Federation over the last dozen years or so suggests that this scenario is not an inherently implausible one, in the relevant political context.

It is important to remember that the fears of the Constitution's political opponents were not realised, not only because of the provisions made in the constitutional text to confine the President's potential for executive leadership of any kind, but also because of consistent political practice from 1938 onwards, starting with the unopposed election of an indisputably apolitical, consensual candidate (Douglas Hyde) as the first holder of the office.[146]

One delayed consequence of the position of the President as a symbol of national sovereignty and national identity and of the expectations which his or her direct election creates has been the development, especially since the ground-breaking election of Mary Robinson in 1990, of a new role for the office: one of moral reflection and exhortation, within the limits that the avoidance of matters of partisan controversy imposes.[147] Although the President's disengagement from the process of forming or sustaining a government remains at a level where "merely apparent semi-presidentialism" remains an apt description, this hortatory or rhetorical role

(Dréacht)—Dara Céim (11 May 1937) 67 *Dáil Debates*, cols 38–54 and to return to it in closing the debate: *Bunreacht na hEireann (Dréacht)—Dara Céim (d'aththógaint)* (13 May 1937) 67 *Dáil Debates*, cols 421–45.

145 *Bunreacht na hEireann (Dréacht)—Dara Céim (d'aththógaint)* (12 May 1937) 67 *Dáil Debates*, cols 302–3 (John A Costello TD).

146 Patrick Maume, "Hyde, Douglas (de hÍde, Dubhghlas)" in *Dictionary of Irish Biography* (James McGuire and James Quinn ed, Cambridge University Press, 2009) http://dib.cambridge.org/viewReadPage.do?articleId=a4185 (last accessed 22 May 2013).

147 John Mee, "The Changing Nature of the Presidency: The President and the Government should be Friends" (1996) 14 *Irish Law Times* 2; David Gwynn Morgan, "Mary Robinson's Presidency: Relations with the Government" (1999) 34 *Irish Jurist* 256; James P Casey, *Constitutional Law in Ireland* (3rd ed, Sweet & Maxwell, 2000) 92–95.

of the office continues to develop, to the point where fresh controversy has arisen as to whether the current incumbent has overstepped the proper boundaries of the public statement he ought to make by entering into areas of controversy that may not put him directly at odds with the Government of Ireland, but that do address strongly disputed issues concerning, for example, European governance and economic policy.[148]

11. Farrell

It is perhaps too early to comment on how far some of the expectations about the Convention on the Constitution that Professor Farrell discusses in his chapter will be realised, since—at the time of writing—its work is ongoing and the Government has yet to respond to the body's first two reports (the first on the voting age and the presidential term and the second on men and women's place in family life and their participation in politics).[149] One can quickly and easily gather from Professor Farrell's contribution two of the cardinal features of the Convention on the Constitution: that its agenda is largely determined by the Government which established it and that its composition and working methods are designed to achieve the greatest level of "buy-in" by politicians (in the first instance, those participating and, more broadly, their colleagues and parties) that is consistent with genuine equality between the citizen members and the political ones.

---

[148] Notably the recent address by President Michael D. Higgins, "*Towards a European Union of the Citizens*", European Parliament, Strasbourg, 17 April 2013, http://www.president.ie/speeches/address-by-president-michael-d-higgins-towards-a-european-union-of-the-citizens-european-parliament-strasbourg-wednesday-17th-april-2013-2/ (last accessed 22 May 2013); Fiach Kelly, "President in 'unprecedented' critique of EU austerity policy", *Irish Independent*, 18 April 2013, http://www.independent.ie/irish-news/president-in-unprecedented-critique-of-eu-austerity-policy-29204661.html (last accessed 22 May 2013); John Waters, "The President has momentously said the unsayable about our economy" *Irish Times,* 19 April 2013, http://www.irishtimes.com/news/politics/the-president-has-momentously-said-the-unsayable-about-our-economy-1.1364716 (last accessed 22 May 2013); "President Higgins calls for 'radical rethink' on EU crisis" RTÉ News, 2 May 2013, http://www.rte.ie/news/2013/0502/389927-michael-d-higgins-european-union/ (last accessed 22 May 2013); Press Association, "President defends criticism of EU" *Irish Independent,* 3 May 2013, http://www.independent.ie/irish-news/president-defends-criticism-of-eu-29240126.html (last accessed 22 May 2013); Gerard Howlin, "Has President Higgins gone too far?" *Irish Examiner,* 3 May 2013, http://www.irishexaminer.com/analysis/has-president-higgins-gone-too-far-230179.html (last accessed 22 May 2013); Stephen Collins, "President's comments show a novel interpretation of his constitutional role" *The Irish Times,* 4 May 2013, http://www.irishtimes.com/news/politics/president-s-comments-show-a-novel-interpretation-of-his-constitutional-role-1.1382090 (last accessed 22 May 2013); Maura Adshead, "Column: We have a president with an opinion, what's the big deal?" *TheJournal.ie,* 15 May 2013, http://www.thejournal.ie/readme/president-higgins-opinion-speaking-out-907037-May2013/ (last accessed 22 May 2013). On some of President Higgins's other recent statements, see Kevin Myers, "President Higgins lost the right to speak on a wide range of issues once he entered the Aras" *Irish Independent*, 23 February 2013, http://www.independent.ie/opinion/columnists/kevin-myers/kevin-myers-president-higgins-lost-the-right-to-speak-on-a-wide-range-of-issues-once-he-entered-the-aras-26824849.html (last accessed 22 May 2013).

[149] *First Report of the Convention on the Constitution,* 26 March 2013 https://www.constitution.ie/AttachmentDownload.ashx?mid=e1f8e128-2496-e211-a5a0-005056a32ee4 (last accessed 22 May 2013); *Second Report of the Convention on the Constitution,* 8 May 2013, https://www.constitution.ie/AttachmentDownload.ashx?mid=268d9308-c9b7-e211-a5a0-005056a32ee4 (last accessed 22 May 2013).

Some of the developments that have occurred in other countries on whose experience the design of the Convention on the Constitution drew might tend to confirm the wisdom of those dispositions. For example, since the Convention on the Constitution began to operate in Ireland, the prospects of the work of its counterpart in Iceland (broadly speaking) resulting in a new constitution for that country appear to have receded considerably, larger as a result of a change of government at the recent general election.[150] It is also interesting to note that one of the reasons frequently given for the possible failure of the constitution-making process in Iceland is the lack of support for it shown by many lawyers.[151]

It is certainly interesting to note that the topics that the authors of the current volume have chosen to address are only tangentially amongst those that the Convention on the Constitution has been tasked with examining. The role of the President has been of some concern to the Convention, but only in the context—thus far—of whether the term of office of the President should be reduced from seven years to five. This is a potentially highly significant issue in a genuinely semi-presidential system—such as the French one—but the members of the Convention on the Constitution themselves struggled to see the need for any such change in the Irish system of "a parliamentary regime corrected by the anomaly of the direct popular election of the President", to use Professor Mezzetti's useful characterisation of it.[152] The Convention ultimately decided (by a margin of 57 to 43) to recommend that the term be left at its present duration. No doubt the expert presentation made to the Convention by Professor Robert Elgie[153] played some role in stimulating a wider discussion of the office, which led the Convention to recommend opening up the nomination process to more citizen participation and reducing the age of eligibility (currently 35), by votes of 94–6 and 50–47 respectively.[154] The Convention was evenly split (44–44) on the issue of whether the President should be confined to a non-renewable seven-year term.[155]

What is most significant in the current context is that the Convention was not asked by the Government to review whether the relationships of the President, Government and national parliament (the essential subject of Professor Mezzetti's comparative

[150] Thorvaldur Gylfason, "Putsch: Iceland's crowd-sourced constitution killed by parliament" *Verfassungsblog*, 30 March 2013, http://www.verfassungsblog.de/putsch-icelands-crowd sourced-constitution-killed-by-parliament (last accessed 16 May 2013); Giulia Dessi, "When politics strike back: the end of the Icelandic constitutional experiment?" *Open Democracy.net,* 26 April 2013, http://www.opendemocracy.net/giulia-dessi/when-politics-strike-back-end-of-icelandic-constitutional-experiment (last accessed 16 May 2013).

[151] Helgi Hrafn Gunnarsson of the Icelandic Pirate Party, quoted by Dessi (*ibid*).

[152] The main argument for making such a change is that it would enable presidential elections to be conducted in accordance with a fixed five-year schedule, simultaneously with European Parliament and local elections. This idea was emphatically rejected by the Convention: *First Report of the Convention on the Constitution,* 26 March 2013, https://www.constitution.ie/AttachmentDownload.ashx?mid=e1f8e128-2496-e211-a5a0-005056a32ee4 (last accessed 22 May 2013) 7.

[153] Robert Elgie, *Should the President's Term of Office be Reduced to Five Years? Briefing document for 25–26 January 2013*, 26 January 2013, https://www.constitution.ie/AttachmentDownload.ashx?mid=13e6a59a-ed67-e211-a5a0-005056a32ee4 (last accessed 22 May 2013).

[154] *First Report of the Convention on the Constitution,* 26 March 2013, https://www.constitution.ie/AttachmentDownload.ashx?mid=e1f8e128-2496-e211-a5a0-005056a32ee4 (last accessed 22 May 2013) 7.

[155] *ibid.*

survey) ought to remain the same, nor did it show any inclination to do so. It seems unlikely that they will embark on an examination of those issues when they come to examine, at a later stage, the issue of whether to give citizens resident outside the State the right to vote in presidential elections at Irish embassies, or otherwise. In this, the Convention appears to resemble the Constitution Review Group, which took it for granted, in reviewing the office that:

> "The President, freed from executive functions–and the divisiveness which political activity would necessarily entail–serves as a personification of the State. From the President the people seek a reflection of their highest values and aspirations. In return, the President takes precedence over all other persons in the State and is honoured in a style concordant with the republican character of the State and the social genius of its citizens.
>
> [I]n being elected by direct vote of the people, in taking precedence over other persons and, in effect, discharging the functions of a Head of State, the President, in performing official duties, does not and cannot represent any particular group or interest but must represent all the people. … [I]n providing that the President shall not be answerable to either House of the Oireachtas or to any court for the exercise and performance of the powers and functions of the office, the Constitution underlines the non-political, non-partisan nature of the office."[156]

Other topics addressed in the current volume have also arisen or will arise in the Convention's scheduled deliberations, but only in a similar tangential fashion. For example, issues of judicial interpretation of the fundamental rights guarantees contained in the Constitution are unavoidable when considering some of the issues that the Convention has already examined (such as the future of the provision on "woman's life within the home" or the issue of same-sex marriage) or is due to examine, according to its terms of reference (namely, removal of the offence of blasphemy from the Constitution).

However, although the Convention has yet to determine what other issues, of its own choosing, it will address at the one meeting (in December 2013) set aside for that purpose, it seems unlikely that these will include any wholesale review of the fundamental rights provisions of the Constitution or of the current role of the judiciary in seeking to uphold them. Perhaps the topic of Dr Cahill's chapter in the current volume—the constitutional regulation of Ireland's relationship with the European Union—or the related issue of how constitutional referenda are conducted may figure at that last meeting. As of the time of this writing, however, there is no indication of what additional topics of its own the Convention will choose to discuss, apart from its recent choice of additional sub-topics at its June 2013 meeting under the general heading of the Dáil electoral system: size of constituencies, the total number of deputies, direct democracy, non-parliamentary ministers and issues associated with the administration of elections (the last focusing on the possible role of an electoral commission).[157]

---

156 Constitution Review Group *Report* (Pn 2632) (Stationery Office, 1996) at p.25.

157 Convention on the Constitution, *Announcement of Results*, 19 May 2013, https://www.constitution.ie/ConventionVideos.aspx?cid=30 (last accessed 22 May 2013).

One decision that the Convention did reach at its May 2013 meeting was not to ask the Taoiseach to either: (a) alter its terms of reference so that it could consider whether Seanad Éireann ought to be reformed or abolished before a referendum on its abolition, due to take place in the autumn of 2013; or (b) postpone that referendum, so that the Convention could remain within its terms of reference, by considering that issue at its last scheduled meeting in December.[158] It seems from the contributions made to the debate on that proposal that the prime reason for rejecting it, especially in the minds of the citizen members of the Convention, was to preserve the body's perceived independence from any political alignment, interest group or lobby. While this decision may have been frustrating and even puzzling for many of those campaigning to retain the Seanad on a reformed basis, it could be seen as a healthy sign of the Convention's sense of the integrity of its own process and the limits of what it can usefully attempt within the framework set for it by government.

12. Conclusion

To sum up, this latest development in Irish constitutional law shows once again that it is a dynamic, evolving system but that, at the same time, it is never likely to escape from some of the perennial questions and challenges that the dialogue between Italian and Irish scholars on which this book is based has confronted so penetratingly and eruditely. We owe our Italian colleagues a great depth of gratitude for the initiative behind the symposium on which the book is based, and we look forward to further collaboration with them in years to come.

[158] Ruadhan Mac Cormaic, "Constitutional convention rejects motion on Seanad" *The Irish Times,* 18 May 2013, http://www.irishtimes.com/news/constitutional-convention-rejects-motion-on-seanad-1.1398972 (last accessed 22 May 2013) and "Vote against discussing Seanad abolition before referendum" *The Irish Times,* 20 May 2013, http://www.irishtimes.com/news/vote-against-discussing-seanad-abolition-before-referendum-1.1399516 (last accessed 20 May 2013).

INDEX